Biodiversity, Sustainability and Human Communities

Protecting beyond the Protected

Edited by

Tim O'Riordan

CSERGE, University of East Anglia

and

Susanne Stoll-Kleemann

Free University of Berlin, Germany

CAMBRIDGE
UNIVERSITY PRESS

PUBLISHED BY THE PRESS SYNDICATE OF THE UNIVERSITY OF CAMBRIDGE
The Pitt Building, Trumpington Street, Cambridge, United Kingdom

CAMBRIDGE UNIVERSITY PRESS
The Edinburgh Building, Cambridge CB2 2RU, UK
40 West 20th Street, New York, NY 10011-4211, USA
477 Williamstown Road, Port Melbourne, VIC 3207, Australia
Ruiz de Alarcón 13, 28014 Madrid, Spain
Dock House, The Waterfront, Cape Town 8001, South Africa

http://www.cambridge.org

First published 2002

Printed in the United Kingdom at the University Press, Cambridge

Typeface Plantin 10/12 pt   *System* LATEX 2_ε [TB]

A catalogue record for this book is available from the British Library

Library of Congress Cataloguing in Publication data

Biodiversity, sustainability and human communities: Protecting beyond the
protected / edited by Tim O'Riordan.
     p. cm.
Includes bibliographical references (p.).
ISBN 0 521 81365 4 – ISBN 0 521 89052 7 (pbk)
1. Biological diversity conservation.   2. Sustainable development. I. O'Riordan,
Timothy.

QH75.P798   2002
333.95′16′0973–dc21   2002023866

ISBN 0 521 81365 4 hardback
ISBN 0 521 89052 7 paperback

To Fay, who has made me love the future

Tim O'Riordan

Contents

Part IV Perspective

Figures

Tables

Contributors

DAVID ARDHIAN is affiliated to Yayasan Nastari Bogor, a Bogor-based NGO whose main concern is sustainable agriculture and rural democratisation.

DAMAYATI BUCHORI is Head of the Center for Integrated Pest Management in Bogor, Indonesia. She is affiliated to the Center for Environmental Research and Conservation at Columbia University and Wildlife Preservation Trust International – a non-profit organisation based in New York.

IONE EGLER is a Senior Administrator in the Ministry of Science and Technology, Government of Brazil.

JENNY FAIRBRASS is Senior Research Associate at the Centre for Social and Economic Research on the Global Environment at the University of East Anglia, Norwich, UK.

DANIELA HAMIDOVIĆ is an independent researcher in Zagreb, Croatia.

THOMAS E. LOVEJOY is Senior Advisor to the President of the United Nations Foundation and Chief Biodiversity Advisor at the World Bank. A biologist, he is also Research Associate at the Smithsonian Tropical Research Institute. He has worked in the Amazon on science and conservation since 1965.

NORMAN MYERS is an honorary visiting fellow of Green College, Oxford University. He has been recognised for his work on biodiversity through the Volvo Environment Prize, the United Nations Environment Prize and the Blue Planet Prize.

MARKUS A. NUDING has worked as a scientist for the German Technical Co-operation (GTZ) on wildlife management in the development context in eastern and southern Africa. He is based in Harare as an adviser for three German-funded projects on social forestry, indigenous

resource management and social science perspectives in natural resource management.

TIM O'RIORDAN is Professor of Environmental Sciences at the University of East Anglia, Norwich, UK and linked to interdisciplinary and
interactive research on sustainability issues.

JULES PRETTY is Professor of Environmental and Society at the University of Essex, UK, and Deputy-Chair on the UK government's Advisory Committee on Releases to the Environment. He was appointed
A D White Professor-at-Large by Cornell University from 2001.

WALTER V. REID is an ecologist and Director of the Millennium Eocsys-
tem Assessment. He is currently based at the Consultative Group on
International Agricultural Research in Penang, Malaysia. Until 1998,
he was Vice President for Program at the World Resources Institute.

MICHAEL STURM has worked as a National Park Manager for the
German Development Service in the Machalilla National Park,
Ecuador (January 1995–September 1997). Since 1998 he has worked
as a Project Manager of EXPO 2000 (a world exhibition project in
north Germany on Implementing Low Energy Concepts).

TODDI A. STEELMAN is Assistant Professor of Environmental and Natural Resource Policy at North Carolina State University's Department
of Forestry. Her work focuses on the role of public and community
involvement in environmental and natural resource governance.

SUSANNE STOLL-KLEEMANN is a Senior Researcher at the Free
University of Berlin in Germany. Her expertise is in the field of the
human dimensions of global environmental change, with an emphasis
on evaluating biodiversity and nature conservation strategies. A second research focus is on regional governance and climate change, including vulnerability analysis, public participation and social capital
formations.

MARTIN WELP is a Senior Researcher at the Potsdam Institute for
Climate Impact Research (PIK). His expertise and research interest
are in the field of public participation in environmental management
(including management of protected areas, coastal zones and river
basins).

AMANDA YOUNGE was Director of Planning in the City of Cape Town
1994–7, and co-ordinated the GEF-funded strategy to conserve biodiversity in the Cape Floral Kingdom, on behalf of WWF-South Africa.

Preface

The common theme for this text is that a resilient biodiversity is an indicator of a healthy planet and a sensitive human family that cares for its neighbours and its offspring. For this human family to be at peace with itself, it must also be at peace with biodiversity. Species mix is less important for future biodiversity than the connections between species, habitats and social, economic and political outlooks that care, anticipate and adapt. The diversity of species will be maintained only by a diversity of management styles and cultural outlooks that both protect the protected, and recreate biodiversity for a changing society and economy. To monitor, assess and evaluate the great variety of biodiversity management 'styles' will enable local action to become global trusteeship. In this spirit of enquiry and hope, the editors and authors will address four objectives.

1 To assess the current and future threat to biodiversity in terms of recorded losses, current dangers, and possible prognoses based on foreseeable developments in landuse change, alterations in climate futures, alien invasions of plants, animals and pathogens, pollution and toxification, all connected to global and regional agreements, and likely shifts in property rights and management regimes.

2 To develop the scope for combining ecological and social resilience by coupling the established management approaches of placing 'ecology' and 'people' first in the design and operation of safeguarding protected areas and recreating new biodiversity corridors and patches linked to such protected areas.

3 To examine, by means of illustrative case studies from across the globe, why it is proving so difficult to achieve this synthesis. In so doing, the authors will explore why the 'inclusionary' approach is so often avoided, or ignored, or introduced with too little attention to the feelings and outlooks of those whose co-operation is being sought.

4 To extend current theories within the social and ecological sciences to explain how it may become possible to combine ecological and social

adaptation in the cause of safeguarding and extending biodiversity. This task will be undertaken through lessons learnt from the case studies. The emphasis will lie on practical measures for widening the scope for effective and inclusive management rather than shaping theory for its own sake.

Part I

Setting the scene

1   Protecting beyond the protected

Tim O'Riordan

Biodiversity and the fraying web of life

This planet is unique, at least as far as we will probably ever know. It contains life, which is maintained through self-regulating flows of energy and chemical connections, the science of which is well described by Tim Lenton (1998). We also know that these webs of life are frayed (World Resources Institute 2000). We are by no means clear as to how much these life-maintaining flows and fluxes are damaged. An assessment by the World Resources Institute (2000: 9) entitled Pilot Analysis of Global Ecosystems (PAGE) indicates that there is still a fundamental ignorance of how this web joins, and of what it consists at any scale of analysis, or of human action. The Board on Sustainable Development of the US National Research Council (1999: 208, 220–1) points out that this ignorance is all the more worrying because of the complex multiple causes and consequences of this disruption. One of the major threats to ecosystem goods and services is our lack of understanding about how specific ecosystem functions may change with ecosystem transformations. Another cause for concern is our hesitation about deciding on options for coping with and ameliorating these fundamental changes. A third limitation is lack of knowledge about, or incorrect valuation of, the 'worth' of ecosystem functioning for social well-being and economic advantage.

A study attempting to calculate the 'worth' of ecosystem services (Costanza *et al.* 1997) came up with a range of estimates on the basis of heroic estimates and ingenious assumptions. These estimates all exceeded the current value of total economic activity for the globe, on an annual basis, by a factor of up to threefold. Frankly there is no way of knowing how accurate this calculation is. What is revealing is that a clever monetary estimate indicates our scale of dependency or 'free riding' on the web of interconnected life. More relevant, perhaps, is the danger of trying to place a market-equivalent value on a mystery for which we should be more in awe than in arithmetic.

3

The World Resources Institute study of global ecosystem services (World Resources Institute 2000: 12–15) summarises some of the vital, life-maintaining, roles of water, plants and soils.

1.7 billion people lack access to clean water, while $42 billion is spent world-wide on buying bottled water.

$52 million annually is spent on the kerosene that households in Jakarta must buy to boil water before use.

Thirteen national parks in Venezuela provide fresh water for urban water supplies that would otherwise cost some $200 million to cleanse.

Between 30 and 90 per cent of US soft fruit and horticulture production depends on pollination by honey bees. The total value of this service is estimated to be around $54 billion annually. Eighty-eight per cent of all the world's flowering plants rely on beetles for their pollination.

Extracts from plants and animals for medicinal drugs are worth $75–150 billion annually, while 76 per cent of the world's population uses traditional medicines for health care.

Some 60 per cent of the annual excess production of carbon is absorbed by oceans and vegetation. The long-term value of this role is incalculable.

We live in an unusually significant period in the interactive history of humanity and nature. The capability of humans to alter and to interfere with the life-maintaining processes of the globe has never been more comprehensive or interdependent. According to the World Resources Institute (2000: 6), 'the current rate of decline in the long term productive capacity of ecosystems could have devastating implications for human development and the welfare of our species'. Yet our ability to know the scale of what we are doing, and what fundamentally needs to be done to move us towards a sustainable outcome, has never been so well analysed. According to the Board on Sustainable Development of the US National Research Council:

a successful transition to sustainability is possible over the next two generations. This transition could be achieved without miraculous techniques or dramatic transformations of human societies. What will be required are significant advances in basic knowledge, in the social capacity and technological capabilities to utilise it, and in the political will to turn this knowledge and know-how into action. (US National Research Council 1999: 276)

We may not know the full picture, but we do know enough to change our ways and our moral framework. We have no excuse, except the comfort of looking the other way, or claiming that the mountains of reform and reconstruction are too steep to climb. To shelter behind the façade of indecision or inaction would be acts of reprehensible folly. Protecting beyond the protected is, therefore, the replacing of folly by conscious and co-operative transformation.

We cannot escape. According to an influential report by the UN Environment Programme, the US National Aeronautics and Space Administration and the World Bank (1998: xx), 'the Earth currently is approaching the point where its physical and biological systems may not be able to meet human demands for environmental goods and services, threatening the ability of nations to meet their populations' needs for adequate food and clean water, energy supplies, safe shelter and a healthy environment'. The PAGE report referred to above produced the most comprehensive account of this weakening of the capability of natural ecosystems to maintain life.

Half the world's wetlands have been lost in the past century.

Logging and conversion of woodland ecosystems have shrunk the world's forests by as much as half, and another quarter is being fragmented by roads, farms and residences.

About one in ten of all tree species is at risk of extinction.

Some 58 per cent of coral reefs are threatened by destructive fishing practices, tourism pressures and pollution.

Fishing fleets are 40 per cent larger than the ocean can sustain, with 75 per cent of global fish stocks either depleted or over-harvested and a further 44 per cent at the point of depletion.

Most freshwater and coastal ecosystems no longer have the capacity to maintain healthy water quality. The poor are especially exposed to declines in drinkable and reliable water. Poverty is an outcome of environmental degradation as well as a cause of it. Over-pumping for agriculture exceeds natural replenishment by over 160 million cubic metres annually.

Introduced species, transmission of pathogens and incurable damage to natural immune protection are leading to a chaotic reduction in species numbers and densities. The consequences for ecosystems, within which these species play a critical part, are unfathomable.

All of these outcomes breed on each other. Not only do ecosystems reach out across space. They also retain, up to a critical point, their capacity to absorb and respond to changed circumstances, and variations in species mix, through their flows of mutual support. The richness of populations and species interactions provides the basis for creative evolution. It is this evolutionary drive that in turn creates the capacity for resilience, or buffering against the unanticipated. But, as Tom Lovejoy reminds us in the next chapter, biological diversity is the ultimate integrator of environmental change. Losses of such diversity are clarion calls for humanity that their own well-being is in peril.

On biodiversity and resilience

Holling *et al.* (1998: 349) suggest that ecological resilience has two interpretations. One is based on the capacity to absorb or to repair ecosystem functions in the wake of a shock or damaging activity. This perspective assumes an in-built capacity to restore to the original condition. This is basically a rational, linear model of action and response. It finds its way in resource management into such concepts as sustainable intervention, sustained yield, allowable catches and various extractive quotas. As Berkes and Folke (1998a: 12) put it: 'discrete yield levels, such as maximum sustained yields of fish or timber, can be calculated, and perturbations (such as fire or pest outbreaks) can be controlled or excluded'.

This interpretation of ecological resilience is part of the cause of ecosystem fraying. Analysing 'allowability' in resource management does not take into account the critical interconnections between resources and ecosystems. Ecosystems are flows of support and nurture with assimilative buffers to cope with waste matter and unexpected perturbations. Resources mingle within ecosystems, so that removal is often disruptive and stressful, operating beyond these in-built absorptive capabilities. The very presumption of calculated removal is part of the cause of ecosystem disintegration.

A part-way position within this perspective is the practice of selective removal, through which individual trees, or other plants, are harvested by supposedly ecologically forensic measures. The aim is to extract on the basis of maturity, with minimal damage to surrounding vegetation and their ecological linkages, and to replant. This practice is recommended for the Forest Stewardship Council (FSC) qualifications. FSC is an international arrangement for ensuring the renewability of tree removal and abstraction as well as the well-being of forest inhabitants. Selective removal, coupled to non-extractive use of forest resources to benefit local economies, is becoming attractive as a 'half-way house' in ecological resilience. It is being promoted as a way forward in Brazil, as we shall see in chapter 10. It is necessary to include the 'people well-being dimension' before such an approach can be relied upon for maintaining sustainability. As for enhancing biodiversity, well, this is not always guaranteed. Yet what is biodiversity? If forest management can retain reliable species mix, ensure robust ecosystem functioning, and maintain local livelihoods, is this not a laudable objective? We shall see that as we reach out to protect beyond the protected, the concept of biodiversity will embrace a mosaic of objectives and management approaches.

The second notion of resilience is based on the proposition that ecosystems may evolve and respond chaotically, in a non-linear fashion, without clear trajectories of adjustment. The important test for resilience is the degree of disturbance that can be absorbed before an unpredictable and convulsive change in system functioning occurs. An example would be the removal of species diversity as 'islands' of biodiversity become more isolated. Ecosystems are seen as permeated by an unknown capacity for self-organisation, flows may be unpredictably discontinuous, and adaptive learning based on sensitive monitoring and 'environmental' knowledge may hold the keys to appropriate management action.

David Tilman (2000: 208–9) summarises the results of a vast range of ecological analysis as to the relationship between biological diversity and the efficiency and resilience (or stability) of ecosystem functioning. He reviews the growing body of ecological evidence that the richer and more heterogeneous the species mix, the more robust the ecosystem as a whole. The shifts towards more diverse ecosystems may be due to three main processes.

> Species are so varied that they respond very differently to changes in environmental circumstances. The more species that environmental change is averaged across, the less variable is the total species mix.
>
> Species in a similar trophic level tend to compete, so as one declines in abundance, another will increase. Overall, this 'negative covariance' tends to reduce variability.
>
> Community abundance tends to increase as species diversity grows, giving rise to greater total productivity and resilience.

Tilman concludes that 'resilient biodiversity' may well be the consequence of a variety of trade offs between competitiveness and co-operation leading to advantage and cohabitation. Society is simplifying species connections to the peril of the survival of ecological complexities. There is no evolution in ethics or management as scientific understanding progresses.

The loss of biodiversity will diminish the capacity of ecosystems to provide society with a stable and sustainable supply of essential goods and services. It seems likely that environmental policy that is optimal from societal perspective would be remarkably different now from that of 250 years ago. However, we still use environmental and landuse ethics codified in law that were articulated during an era when the human population, at one tenth of its present size, tamed wilderness with axe and ox. (Tilman 2000: 210)

Ecological resilience is enhanced by linkages across ecosystems in space and over time. To understand how humans can damage or repair, therefore, requires a profound knowledge of the interrelationships between ecosystems as ecosystems, and their combined interrelationships with society. In the absence of reliable observational evidence we may have to rely on what residents know through experience and social understanding.

Tilman (2000: 211) offers an even more profound insight as to the future of biodiversity. This is that any future for biodiversity will be the outcome of human choice, and, for the most part, intervention. In essence, our future biodiversity will be designed and created, as in tending a garden, rather than exclusively placed in 'hotspot' museums to be observed and recorded from afar. The phrase 'hotspot museums' applies to the strict protection of mega-diverse sites as identified by Myers and his colleagues and explained more fully in chapter 3. So the biodiversity of the future will depend on a science of intervention that is informed by creative scientific explorative analysis and ingenious experiments with resilience. This is why this chapter is entitled 'protecting beyond the protected'.

The earth will retain its most striking feature, its biodiversity, only if humans have the prescience to [establish an ethic as long lasting as a constitutional bill of rights or as religious commandments]. This will occur, it seems, only if we realise the extent to which we use biodiversity. (Tilman 2000: 211)

The Tilman message is given priority in this section on resilience because he suggests that biodiversity can be created as much as it is destroyed, by the application of co-operative science and management. He is not indicating that overall biodiversity can be regained. But he is commenting that co-ordinated and progressive management of sites and connecting zones of sympathetic human and ecological activity may achieve a more robust global biodiversity in the future. This is the message for Costa Rica, Namibia, South Africa and Europe in the chapters that follow. It is also the guiding theme for the title of the book.

Berkes and Folke (1998a: 12–20) point to the advantages of incorporating cultural traditions and norms into resource management so as to combine the learning practices of social and ecological sustenance. Not all customary practices act to sustain and restore. It is dangerous to presume that 'tradition' is somehow 'good' for ecosystem maintenance. Yet established practices are customary and valued by those who cherish them, partly because they bind and provide a sense of community identity. To ignore or degrade them without clearly creating communal acceptance of an alternative set of practices would be an act of folly (as identified above), a discourtesy, and profoundly unhelpful in achieving the kind of interactive management sought for ecosystems by integrative ecologists (Stoll-Kleemann 2001: 382). We shall see in chapters 5 and 13 that this notion of social resilience involves a more open use of scientific methodology, a mix of quantitative and qualitative techniques, awareness and empathy to feelings and instincts, and a wide range of monitoring and communicative skills and assessments. Such approaches not only are interactive with ecosystem resilience; they also require a form of management which regards society and nature as constantly revealing themselves through direct engagement and negotiation.

For example, we shall learn from the South African case (chapter 8) that the management of plant-rich 'fynbos', a particularly endemic mix of plants in a unique climatic and geological setting, will succeed when neighbouring human communities actually depend for their income on a restored and enhanced biodiversity, the establishment of which they actively contribute to. Effective biodiversity in South Africa can provide income through crafts and products, and services of eco-friendly tourism and local recreational pleasure. To make the whole relationship work, the social support services have to be responsive to the possibility of disruption and failure, as much as the natural resource management organisations are. Experience of wildlife management from Namibia (chapter 9) suggests that by bringing local people into partnerships of trophy, recreational and nutritional roles for wild animals, it is possible to devise agreed and communally protected schemes of game use that serve the needs of hunting, viewing and eating, all in the same ecological-economic zone. Yet the integrity of the ecosystem must always be given priority as this is the routeway to the integrity of local economies. The same lesson is painfully being learned via the accommodation to the Habitats Directive in the European Union (chapter 6). Protecting beyond the protected means ensuring that the capacity to absorb, to learn and to repair is incorporated into both the social and the natural worlds so as to create an adapting and self-organising unity, so long as the natural world remains essentially intact.

On the loss of biodiversity

Biological diversity, or biodiversity in its shorthand, means the variety of living organisms on earth, the range of species, the genetic variability within each species, and the varied characteristics of ecosystems. We shall see in the two chapters that follow that only about one tenth of all species are known, and that loss rates are possibly fifty to a hundred times greater than ever experienced in recorded history. Already the threat of extinction hangs over 10 per cent of known bird species, 20 per cent of known mammal species, 5 per cent of known fish species and 8 per cent of all recorded plant species (Chapin et al. 2000: 234). Yet genetic variability establishes the primary form of evolution, the adaptability of wild species to human-induced change, including cultivation and domestication, and the basis of special breeds of animals and plants that provide the fundamental basis for modern food production. This is part of natural protective functions that need to be protected.

Reducing biodiversity further will mean that additional alterations to ecosystems, especially in unpredictable combinations, could result in a much more devastating weakening of ecological absorptive capabilities.

Furthermore, well-meaning but limited attempts to restore ecosystems or reintroduce species will have less and less influence on the depleted restorative capacity of species and their habitats. Decreased biodiversity interferes with all manner of essential ecosystem functions such as pollination, the maintenance of soil health, water cleanliness, the assimilation of wastes, especially toxic wastes, and the cycling of carbon, nitrogen and sulphur. In short, biodiversity loss means, at the very least, contributing to undermining the capability of life to survive and reproduce itself with vigour and reliability.

Pimm and his colleagues (2001: 207) conclude, after extensive analysis, that the destruction of biodiversity has contributed, surprisingly and sadly, very little to overall human welfare. The humid tropical forest, once covering 14 per cent of the global land surface, yet housing 67 per cent of terrestrial species, is now cleared to about half of its original size. Much of this cleared land is unusable for agriculture. About a third of species-rich waterways are being diverted for irrigation that is almost always unsuitable for crop growing owing to desalination and toxification. Biodiversity loss is a double blow. Protecting beyond the protected means ensuring future well-being of life support to avoid senseless degradation of both human and ecological resilience.

To preserve biodiversity we choose to protect it. We cannot do this everywhere, so we protect in special places. The aim is to safeguard a sufficient range of species and habitats through protected areas management in order that the essence of biodiversity is preserved. Pimm and Raven (2000: 843) observe that many species found in a given habitat are found only in smaller areas within that habitat. So early phases of widening habitat alteration may not result in much noticeable species loss. Peak extinction rates may only occur decades later as habitat alteration continues. The rate of extinctions depends on how much of the habitat is altered, while the actual percentage of species removed is based on how much habitat is actually lost. Pimm and Raven (2000: 844) summarise research to show that, even if 5 per cent of tropical moist forest areas were safeguarded, 50 per cent of all species could remain. How long such an ephemeral state might continue to harbour those species without reservoirs of species nearby remains a matter for ecological speculation. Here is where Tilman's comments on biodiversity gardening become apposite.

As Norman Myers argues in chapter 3, species are particularly vulnerable to the damage to habitats in their range of survival. Because as much as 30–50 per cent of plant and animal species occur in 'hotspots' occupying only 1.4 per cent (but originally 12 per cent) of the land surface, what happens to these highly species-rich areas is vital to the totality of species availability. But random destruction of habitats outside of these areas, and especially linked to them, could create centres of extinction that match the hotspots (Pimm and Raven 2000: 844). We do not know enough about biodiversity to know what and where to protect. Even where we do protect, we may not be able to stop the continual reduction in survival capacity. Protecting does not necessarily mean protected. In any case, safeguarded zones need reservoirs of species and ecosystem functions beyond their artificial boundaries for their continuance as biological reserves. Tom Lovejoy in the chapter that follows reminds us that while restricting a habitat does not linearly remove species, fragmenting and disrupting habitats is much more likely to undermine species resilience.

Margules and Pressey (2000: 243) argue persuasively for the maintenance of safeguarding reserves as integral units of biodiversity. But the selection of reserves is often arbitrary, based on conflicting objectives or agency missions, or dependent on ownership. This means that most reserves are in economically marginal territory, while biodiversity as a whole is not protected. As a consequence, many species occurring in productive landscapes or landscapes with development potential are not protected, even though disturbance, transformation to intensive uses and fragmentation continue (Margules and Pressey 2000: 243). Box 1.1

BOX 1.1 STAGES IN SYSTEMATIC CONSERVATION PLANNING

Systematic conservation planning can be separated into six stages, with some examples of tasks and decisions.

1 **Compile data on the biodiversity of the planning region**

Review existing data and decide on which data sets are sufficiently consistent to serve as surrogates for biodiversity across the planning region.

If time allows, collect new data to augment or replace some existing data sets.

Collect information on the localities of species considered to be rare and/or threatened in the region (these are likely to be missed or underrepresented in conservation areas selected only on the basis of land classes such as vegetation types).

2 **Identify conservation goals for the planning region**

Set quantitative conservation targets for species, vegetation types or other features (for example, at least three occurrences of each species, 1,500 ha of each vegetation type, or specific targets tailored to the conservation needs of individual features). Despite inevitable subjectivity in their formulation, the value of such goals is their explicitness.

Set quantitative targets for minimum size, connectivity or other design criteria.

Identify qualitative targets or preferences (for example, as far as possible, new conservation areas should have minimal previous disturbance from grazing or logging).

3 Review existing conservation areas

Measure the extent to which quantitative targets for representation and design have been achieved by existing conservation areas.

Identify the imminence of threat to underrepresented features such as species or vegetation types, and the threats posed to areas that will be important in securing satisfactory design targets.

4 Select additional conservation areas

Regard established conservation areas as 'constraints' or focal points for the design of an expanded system.

Identify preliminary sets of new conservation areas for consideration as additions to established areas. Options for doing this include reserve selection algorithms or decision-support software to allow stakeholders to design expanded systems that achieve regional conservation goals subject to constraints such as existing reserves, acquisition budgets, or limits on feasible opportunity costs for other land uses.

5 Implement conservation actions

Decide on the most appropriate or feasible form of management to be applied to individual areas (some management approaches will be fallbacks from the preferred option).

If one or more selected areas proves to be unexpectedly degraded or difficult to protect, return to stage 4 and look for alternatives.

Decide on the relative timing of conservation management when resources are insufficient to implement the whole system in the short term (usually).

6 Maintain the required values of conservation areas

Set conservation goals at the level of individual conservation areas (for example, maintain several habitats for one or more species for which the area is important). Ideally, these goals will acknowledge the particular values of the area in the context of the whole system.

Implement management actions and zonings in and around each area to achieve the goals.

Monitor key indicators that will reflect the success of management actions or zonings in achieving goals. Modify management as required.

Source: Margules and Pressey 2000: 245.

summarises their views on co-ordinated conservation planning. Biodiversity cannot be maintained by protection alone: it requires the infusion of more comprehensive ecosystem management. For such a degree of management to be guaranteed, people living, working and playing either in reserves or in surrounding protected areas need to be enabled to be the sympathetic stewards of the ecological functions that maintain their health and well-being as much as the health of nature's species.

Margules and Pressey (2000: 249) show how ecological assessments of complexity and stability, represented as digitised maps of vulnerability (i.e., irreplaceability) and resilience (i.e., managed replaceability), can be used to assist landowners and other interested parties to negotiate biodiversity deals over future management. They also point out that resilience and vulnerability are dynamic concepts, constantly being re-evaluated as negotiations proceed and landuse decisions are taken. They argue for much greater adaptive and accommodative negotiations amongst all relevant parties, with each recognising the limits of knowledge and the sharing of a common perspective on ecological well-being.

The conservation of biodiversity is often regarded as less important than the short term economic or social interests of the sectors that influence it most heavily. A major requirement is to incorporate biodiversity concerns into other policy areas. (UN Environment Programme 1999: 41)

The future of biodiversity signifies the future of humankind. Its pathways to restoration or destruction are for humans to choose. By being cognisant, and by being morally alive, humanity can work to save its own body and soul. The planet is ultimately resilient and has absorbed ecological and geological shocks of enormous magnitude. Charles Darwin accepted that evolution was not gradual. Christopher Zeeman (1992: 101) shows how any process of natural selection galvanises species selection and evolution through punctuated equilibria, multiple species development at points of catastrophic change, abrupt frontiers in evolutionary progress, and invasions of territory. While it may be argued that evolution is gradual as well as convulsive, we shall see in the chapters by Tom Lovejoy and Norman Myers that current rates of extinction, and projected pathways of evolutionary disruption, lie well beyond catastrophic timescales. Processes of adaptation may be overwhelmed by unmanageable discontinuation arbitrarily imposed on the evolutionary process.

   John Tuxhill (1999: 97), surveying the record of species losses, believes we now live in a period of mass extinction. Well over 1,000 species per year may be disappearing, compared to only 1–4 species per year from the fossil record. He also points out that plants have generally weathered the previous mass extinctions well. They began to evolve as relatively recently as the end of the Cretaceous. Nowadays, the World Conservation Union (1997) estimates one in eight plants in the world is endangered or vulnerable to extinction. Purvis and Hector (2000: 216) suggest that the 'tree of life' on Earth can only 'afford' at most about three species extinctions per year without shrinking overall. The twentieth century saw the end of twenty mammalian species alone, a pruning that would take 'at least ten centuries to redress' (2000: 216). While species resilience could mean that 80 per cent of the life-tree could

BOX 1.2 THE ROOT CAUSES OF BIODIVERSITY LOSS

Wood and his colleagues (2000: 12–20) summarise the consensus over the fundamental causes of biodiversity losses. They point out that the five principal drivers are highly interconnected, and vary in the most diverse and unexpected ways at any point on the ground. It is the global to local and local to global interconnectedness that nowadays shapes biodiversity loss. Scale is not the framework any longer: it is a matter of perverse influences of economies, social selections, civil rights, property rights and political power, all played out through the panoply of culture, institutions and social psychology.

The proximate causes of biodiversity loss are:

climate change, with, as yet, unpredictable consequences for ecosystem in stability and vulnerability, especially as the other causes, noted below, add or remove stresses;

overharvesting, a function of inappropriate property rights, false price signals, rigged markets, unequal power relations, criminality and lack of 'intelligence' over the possible future 'tragedy' of losses;

habitat loss and alteration with all the attendant implications for species resilience and survival capabilities;

pollution and pathogenic incursion, again having huge potential consequences for resilience and vulnerability for species and habitats.

The socio-economic drivers of biodiversity loss include:

demographic change in the form of population growth and migration with implications for agricultural conversion and overharvesting, especially with the importance of new technologies and harvesting techniques that may destabilise cultures and ecosystems;

inequality and poverty driving people to overexploit marginal lands, and to break down traditional mechanisms for re-creating sharing and protecting resources; wealth accumulation drives the poor into more and more desperate measures and into ecological marginality;

public policies and markets usually acting against the protection of biodiversity, stimulating non-sustainable extraction and subsidising activities that undermine ecosystem and social stability;

trade and aid reinforcing the perversities of insensitive policies and markets;

social change and development often leading to outcomes that add to inequalities and vulnerabilities.

survive even if 95 per cent of species were lost, if the extinction is non-random, the ecosystem functioning could be impaired with relatively few removals.

Box 1.2 summarises the extensive literature on the principal causes of biodiversity loss. This analysis begs the question that 'biodiversity' is not fully understood, let alone agreed, as a concept and a guiding objective of planetary tenure. But it does provide the perspective of direct and indirect causes that are located in ecology, sociology and political relationships.

In chapter 12, Dami Buchori and David Ardhain point out that corruption and illegal practices can create serious damage to biodiversity, and undermine trust and faith in local stewardship practices. Arguably, the loss of honesty and integrity is a more damaging consequence than the immediate loss of habitat. Similarly in chapter 10, Ione Egler shows that well-intentioned partnerships with the private sector can be abused by weak surveillance and behind-the-scenes deals. Protecting the protected also means honesty and integrity in dealings with people and nature, and that begins with the inner soul and is led by interactive governance of the kind portrayed in chapter 5.

Setting the aims of the text

This co-operative partnership of nurture and responsiveness provides one of the frameworks for this text. The contributors consider the state of global biodiversity and the causes and consequences of its decline. They assess the quality of protection and the strength of management measures that are being devised to maintain or enhance that biodiversity. They also investigate how far people and the societies in which they live can be constructively and sensitively brought into the process of managing their health and the well-being of the ecosystems on which they depend. They assess the nature of the political and participatory methods that are being devised to facilitate this process of protecting beyond the protected. And they do all this by means of a series of case studies that illustrate the successes and obstacles of the challenges that lie before us if we are truly going to protect the protected. That phrase applies both to people and to ecosystems. Without the capacity to signal stress, to adjust and to adapt, and in so doing to retain the capacity to absorb and monitor change, then there can be no protection.

The contributors also recognise that there are no unique interpretations of any of the principal themes contained in this text – biodiversity, resilience, vulnerability, sustainability, participation and empathy. They deliberately take a broad view of these phrases, for they recognise that all contain varied scientific meanings, social interpretations and management opportunities. In some instances, species seem robust and remarkably resilient, surviving convulsive disturbance and reproducing against the apparent odds. This may be more common than is presently thought because we are only entering an era of genuine stress on the large scale. What we cannot know for sure is what happens when multiple stresses combine in many places. In other instances, people and species can co-exist and thrive, even though the species mix may be altered over time. Protected areas can enhance species directly, just as the act of protection may weaken ecological resilience owing to isolation. So there is no coherent solution to protecting beyond the protected, no template of management styles of universal application. What is evident is that stewarding biodiversity requires a culture change and a policy shift of huge proportions. We now know enough to be reasonably sure of what mix of transformational practices or outlooks and funding investments is required to protect the protected.

To achieve the combination of healthy societies in life-supporting ecosystems, and to do so fairly, tolerantly and inclusively, is one of the most fundamental requirements for the future of a sustainable society on this amazing planet. Our contributors are sure that this is a profoundly essential objective, by which to build upon success. There is no other road to travel to avoid certain failure.

The ultimate destiny of biodiversity may not lie in its annihilation. Its fabric could be so torn asunder as to cause wounds that heal only very slowly. If disruption of an unnatural kind continues, then surely that inherent capacity for creative renewal may be fundamentally impaired. As the UN Environment Programme study put it:

Our growing use of the environment is beginning to exceed the assimilative and regenerative capacities of the Earth's major biological and physical systems both regionally and globally. The Earth may be approaching a point where it may not be able to make the demand for environmental goods and services. These changes are beginning to have adverse consequences for human populations, especially the poorest segments of society. (UN Environment Programme 2000: 4)

The setting for this text is the belief that humanity knows enough, and cares sufficiently, about what it is doing to its planet. Indigenous knowing, namely how people everywhere come to respect their biodiversity, is more universal than is often supposed. Darrell Posey and his colleagues (2000) show the rich variety of 'ways of appreciating' biodiversity in many cultures. In chapter 4, Jules Pretty expands on these findings by describing imaginative efforts that are still ripe for experimentation.

The text also is shaped by the belief that merely protecting the protected is not sufficient for the creative survival of biodiversity. We shall have to manage whole ecosystems of which protected areas are crown jewels. To manage the wider protection will incorporate the livelihoods and the aspirations of many people – local landowners and a variety of human landusers, communities, diverse political cultures and international global regimes of regulation and support. This task may only be achieved by building confidence and enhancing capabilities in the range of cultures and economies involved. How to do this in the context of an outlook that is anxious not to lose the primacy of ecological protection is another critical theme of this text.

To widen the scope of ownership and responsibility for biodiversity, it will appear necessary to provide a fresh interpretation of human rights and nature rights through widened visions of property ownership and stewardship of the commons. The intellectual building blocks of such arrangements are steadily being put in place. For example, Elinor Ostrom (1990) has analysed six qualities of common property ownership to create management principles for shared ownership and responsibility. These centre on access and boundaries (i.e., regulations over use and monitoring of abuse), and institutions for decision making and arbitration, including conflict resolution and legal recognition. Dan Bromley (1992) has extended this work by gathering evidence of culturally appropriate and location-specific property rights regimes all over the world.

What is important for the scope of this text is the growing interest in some kind of global stewardship right in biodiversity that may extend over such local and long-held arrangements. Berkes and Folke (1998a: 6–8) edited a series of case studies that show how property rights and social learning for fairer allocation and compensation can work well, so long as there is a legitimate form of governing, there are no unexpected patterns of change due to shifts in technology or migration, and there is scope for financial and management partnerships across a range of governmental and private sectors. This is exemplified in Namibia (chapter 9) and shown to fail in Costa Rica (chapter 10) and Brazil (chapter 7). We are still struggling to define a joint property right to sustainable stewardship via private ownership. Efforts to bring in the private sector in Brazil, Costa Rica and Namibia all have their successes and failures. This is an important arena for sharing experiences of all kinds.

As is so often the case, what is regarded as constructive engagement between political will and action on the one hand, and social sensitivities and responsibilities on the other, is rarely judged in the same way by all those involved. In essence, it is now opportune to connect the *demos* (collectively identifying the interests of particular social groups) to the *polis* (the institutional design of governing to ensure the well-being of all). This means creating the scope for co-operative survival between people and nature so that both see their destiny as inescapably unified. This will encompass a moral outlook that will need articulation and cultural acclimatisation as the political responsiveness becomes confident of success. The difficulties involved in generating inclusionary biodiversity management are outlined in chapter 5.

As indicated in chapter 5, the model of governance that frames this book is one that is essentially shaped by elitist structures of power, at various scales from global to micro-local, but where there is a persistent and increasingly successful effort to be deliberative and inclusive in the struggle to share a little of this power. The key lies in social capital, as emphasised by Jules Pretty in chapter 4, and in the case studies of Namibia, the Monteverde Protected Zone in Costa Rica (chapter 11), and, to some extent, the emerging rural development–habitat management arrangements in Europe (chapter 6).

In practical terms, the immediate task is to incorporate the social interests with the natural setting, so that livelihoods and economies gain from improving the buffering capabilities of biodiverse ecosystems to replenish and maintain themselves. This in turn may involve creating socio-economic patterns of power, wealth creation and co-operative behaviour that provide resilience in the social and political spheres. This is by no means an accepted prescription. We are still some way from agreeing that natural resilience can be monitored and calculated, and that social resilience can stem from maintaining and recreating biodiversity. The fact that there is no scientific consensus over this relationship is enough to delay dramatic policy moves. More to the point, huge disputes in the political purposes of biodiversity protection and re-creation, revealed in the case studies that follow, mean that any policy for 'joint resilience' is not yet on the starting blocks.

Nevertheless, our contributors share the view that the ultimate aim of 'protecting beyond the protected' is to link the capacity for self-renewal of natural systems to a similar capacity for constructive well-being in social systems. Dudley and his colleagues (1999: 249–57) point out that threats to protected areas are almost universal to some degree, and that possibly as many as half are severely damaged. They propose a process of 'management reconstruction' to create effective re-creation of biodiversity with the help of communities and locally accepted monetary and evaluation techniques. In this way, ecological reconstruction becomes socially mediated through 'effective local partnerships'. So 'coupled resilience' becomes a social measure, shaped by synergies between managers, communities and global supportive funding.

In chapters 6 (Europe) and 12 (emerging democracies) there are good examples of how the transition to effective partnerships is still in progress. The European Union is beginning to recognise that the routeway to ecological integrity lies in rural economic and social inclusion with habitat protection. Similarly in Croatia and Estonia, both anxious to be part of the European Union for economic and security purposes, there is a recognition that bringing in people via livelihood gain is the best way to capture the excitement of a new democracy before local power-brokers destroy the scope for inclusion and ownership of beneficial biodiverse outcomes. These trackways will be strong and, at times, almost impassable. But the vision of ecological and social resilience is one that is strong in protective strategies in these nations undergoing creative metamorphosis.

Biodiversity holds the key to this connection. Biodiversity is the currency of co-operative survival of humans and nature. Protecting the protected means saving the souls of the planet and its human tenants.

BOX 1.3 THE FOUR PRINCIPAL AIMS OF THIS TEXT

The common theme for this text is that resilient biodiversity is an indicator of a healthy planet and a sensitive human family that cares for its neighbours and its offspring. For this human family to be at peace with itself, it must find peace with biodiversity. Species mix is less important than connections between species and habitats, and social and political outlooks that care, anticipate and adapt. The diversity of species will be maintained only by a diversity of management styles and cultural outlooks that both protect the protected, and re-create biodiversity in myriad ways for a changing society and economy. To monitor, assess and evaluate these experiments on the ground, as well as through global audit, will enable local action to become global trusteeship. In this spirit of enquiry and hope, the editors and authors address four objectives.

1 To assess the current and future threat to global biodiversity in terms of recorded losses, current dangers and possible prognoses based on foreseeable developments in landuse change, alterations in climate futures, alien invasions of plants, animals and pathogens, all connected to global and sub-global agreements, and likely shifts in property rights and management regimes.

2 To develop the scope for combining ecological and social resilience by coupling the established management measures of placing 'ecology first' and 'people first' in the design and operation for safeguarding protected areas and re-creating new biodiversity corridors and patches linked to protected sites.

3 To examine, by means of illustrative case analysis from across the globe, why it is proving so difficult to achieve this synthesis. In so doing, the text will explore why the 'inclusionary' approach is so often avoided, or ignored, or introduced with too little attention to the feelings and outlooks of those whose co-operation is being sought.

4 To extend theories within social and ecological science, to explain how it may become possible to combine ecological and social adaptation in the cause of safeguarding and extending biodiversity. This task will be attempted through lessons learnt from the case studies. The emphasis will lie on practical measures for widening the scope for effective and inclusive management rather than shaping theory for its own sake.

BOX 1.4 THE ROLE OF THE CASE STUDIES IN THIS TEXT

The justification of the case studies and the manner in which the research for each case study was conducted reflects the distinction between unmanaged biodiversity, protective and managed biodiversity and the complex relationship between local economic, social and political 'styles' in the inclusionary process. Special attention is given to the role of democratic reform in addressing the opportunity for inclusive participation in order to enhance sustainable local livelihoods.

The case studies are selected to represent three geographical scales for biodiversity management.

The first group covers regional constellations of sites, linked into some coherent plan, on policy context, and managed as a whole. The case for Brazil is particularly apposite as this country contains some of the most important 'hotspots'. It has also progressed from a period when local interests were often sacrificed in the name of commercial exploitation. Nowadays attention is being focused on winning economic gain for non-depletable management of biodiversity for the future of biotechnology, for pharmaceutical products and for food crops. This is potentially a very controversial issue, so it will be treated in the context of the current debate. South Africa is currently facing up to a major challenge to provide social and economic opportunities for disadvantaged peoples in the creative restoration and protection of its rich biomes. In addition South Africa has recently passed laws which, if implemented, could create the appropriate conditions for ecological and social resilience. West Africa forms the third example for this group. Here the management of game for local food supplies and tourist pleasure is being handled with great sensitivity.

The reports from Indonesia, Estonia, Croatia and Costa Rica exemplify interesting cases of incorporating local democracy and economies into biodiversity management through such cognate activities as preserving wild stocks, developing sustainable indicators and meeting the needs of ecotourism. These are often difficult objectives to juggle, especially in emerging democracies where poverty alleviation takes priority, though injustice often gets in the way.

The final case studies come from the national examples where the notion of inclusionary involvement is either ignored (Germany), attempted (the US) or managed (UK). Each national example provides a perspective on the relationship between informal and formal democracy, set in terms of the relevant political culture and statutes. Each also characterises the institutional political reasons why a more inclusionary approach is either shunned or welcomed.

The case study authors were asked to look at the following issues as far as space and emphasis allowed:
the state of biodiversity in the country concerned, in terms of safeguard, site damage and general ecological well-being;
the politics of biodiversity in the country concerned, with particular emphasis on the convention of biodiversity, the amount of public and private resources available for promoting biodiversity, the status of the main government and

private sectors involved in terms of their political clout, and the nature of the
involvement of non-government organisations and civil society generally;
the character of the national debate on single versus multi-site management
for biodiversity;
the policy stance *vis-à-vis* social justice and inclusionary procedures in the
designation and management of sites, taking especially into account the
political history of social and economic disadvantage;
examples of case histories dealing with participatory approaches to site selection and management, based on best practice and thoughtful critique of
poor practice;
suggestions based on this experience, as to how to improve the management
of biodiversity for sustainability in the countries concerned.

Biodiversity and ecosystem advocacy: some definitions and interpretations

Biodiversity is both an ecological and a social phenomenon. In a major
essay for *Nature*, Chapin *et al.* (2000: 239) comment that 'biodiversity
and its links to ecosystem properties have cultural, intellectual, aesthetic
and spiritual values that are important to society'. Species and habitats
may be measured by taxonomic methods. This gives a sense of diversity
and mix. Harper and Hawkesworth (1995) propose that biodiversity be
considered on three ascending levels. These are *genetic diversity*, at the
point of genetic change and adaptation; *organisational diversity* in terms
of organisms in place or in energy and chemical flows; and *ecological
diversity* in functioning ecosystems.

Tom Lovejoy (chapter 2) and Norman Myers (chapter 3) argue that
at the level of genetic diversity, one major threat to organisms is the incursion of pathogenic viruses and bacteria that lie beyond the tolerances
of internal genetic adaptation. An increasing number of these invasions
may cross species boundaries, so could be catastrophically eclipsing for
particular species. This introduced infection may be caused by breakdowns in immune patterns, or it could be due to species invasions, or
it may be a result of populations of species being forced to contract
into smaller physical space and higher densities. Various causal mechanisms may be involved, including stress and distress, endemic or chronic
fatigue, species transmission due to compulsive shifts in pathogenic
forms and genetic breakdowns, and reduction of tolerance to alien
invasions.

In a comprehensive review of invasive species, Mooney and Hobbs
(2000) conclude that climate change effects could swamp the efforts of
biotic transfer and migration in the more distant future, but that biological invasion is a more serious threat for the immediate prospect. The

BOX 1.5 POSSIBLE STRATEGIES FOR A GLOBAL INVASIVE
SPECIES PROGRAMME

background assessment	components	policy
• current ecological condition	• pathways of invasion	• integrating informal and formal monitoring
• predicted ecological change	• early warning monitoring	• creating toolkits for reporting and promoting community communication
• human disturbance	• preventative interventions	
• global change patterns	• rapid assessments of future states	• management training
	• comprehensive appraisals	• communications and reporting to a wider global audit
	• legal implications of action	
	• economic analysis of outcomes	

Designing a programme of scientific appraisal, informal and formal monitoring,
risk and support analysis, and communications and behaviour change should
assist in reducing the scope for species invasions.

Based on Mooney and Hobbs 2000: 430.

difference is that invasive species are not readily eradicable once they
have a hold. Global commerce, landuse alteration, tourism, intensification of agriculture, fire and genetic modification all play their part. Freshwater species are particularly susceptible to invasion, though alien trees
and bushes are causing huge devastation in the Cape Floral Kingdom in
South Africa, as Amanda Younge demonstrates in chapter 8. The Global
Invasion Species Programme, as summarised in Box 1.5, suggests that scientific programmes can be linked to strategies of prevention, monitoring,
awareness raising and local control in potentially highly effective ways. It
is even more imperative to conduct full assessments of any deliberate
introductions, and to ensure that the requisite funds for monitoring are
guaranteed over a long period of time. Monitoring as an early warning
device is also a vital function that can be employed by trained amateurs
and 'folk awareness' as much as by 'formal' scientific investigations. Integrating the two forms of monitored biodiversity change is the name of
the game.

Genetic pathology in biodiversity could become a critical variable in
the future management of healthy ecosystems. If protected reserves for

the survival of organismal and ecological diversity are the mainstay of biological diversity strategy, it is conceivable that pathogenic or species incursions could undermine this approach, even when the best measures of safeguard are in place. As yet, we simply do not know. Norman Myers (1996: 1,025–34, and in his chapter in this volume) suggests that the two greatest threats to the integrity of biodiversity may be the surprises of discontinuities and unanticipated interacting processes, not before encountered (synergisms).

Both discontinuities and synergisms constitute 'surprise' outcomes . . . with the capacity to be profoundly disruptive and to overwhelm anticipatory and preventative capacities. These phenomena are largely black holes of research and analysis. (Adapted from Myers 1996: 1,025)

Myers builds on the scope for cumulative disruption of both organismal and ecological diversity, but adds the capacity for pathogenic disorientation at the genetic level through his interpretation of synergisms. He notes that a biotic tolerance of one stress tends to be lower when other stresses are at work (1996: 1,028), and that a synergism-induced outcome may be a whole order of magnitude greater than the simple sum of component mechanisms. It is possible to envisage a synergistic onslaught at all these levels of biodiversity, operating at varying scales on the planet, creating outcomes that are initially unpredictable and unmanageable.

One, genuinely unknown, influence on biodiversity will be the consequence of climate change. Box 1.6 summarises the conclusions of the 'impacts' working group of the Intergovernmental Panel on Climate Change for the Third Assessment Report, published in 2001. This is an arena for 'unknown unknowns'. For one thing, there is no given future climate: there are only ranges of possible climate futures. Each will be dependent on patterns of atmospheric warming gases, landuse change and socio-political response to the unfolding climate change drama. To predict what climate change might do for species and ecosystems is only useful in that it provides some basis for 'telling stories' about future societies and emissions trajectories. Such predictions are valuable for learning, for guidance, for assessing possible economic strategies of mitigation and adaptation. They are not predictions. They are educative tools for increasing awareness and framing options. Nevertheless, there will be a biotic impact consequential on climate change, and possibly a cumulative onslaught beyond anything humans have done to species variability to date. We genuinely do not know, but we must be ready for 'doomsday vistas'.

BOX 1.6 BIODIVERSITY IMPACTS FOR CLIMATE CHANGE

The climate of the future will be human shaped, a combination of natural and anthropogenic influences in an inextricable embrace. The precise climates of the future, therefore, are very much what society will decree, either by its policies to reduce atmospheric warming emissions, or by its attempts to adapt to climate change. As a result, the possible consequences for biodiversity cannot be predicated: they can only be presented as scenarios. Each biodiversity 'story' depends on how societies evolve their economies, technologies, policies, political institutions and consumer cultures. There is no 'given' climate, only visualisations of climates as they may 'emerge' through our concern, or indifference, or engagement, or denial.

Nevertheless, the implications for biodiversity arising from climate change are potentially profound. The second working group report of the Intergovernmental Panel on Climate Change (2001: 9–10) suggests the following observations:

Migration of plants and animals will increase at rates faster than local adaptation.

Species sensitive to current temperature and precipitation patterns will become stressed, and more threatened. Extinctions will dramatically increase, including many of species not yet recorded.

Adaptation through gene banks, special reserves, transference corridors and zoos can offset such extinctions, but may prove costly and ecologically ephemeral.

Coastal ecosystems could be critically endangered owing to salt incursions as sea levels rise. Many of the most productive wetlands are at high risk. Coral bleaching and marine biological disease and invasions will be commonplace.

Insect pathogens and migration will influence human health in ways that are bound to impact more on the vulnerable, the diseased, the immunodeficient and those with least access to health care.

The 'natural resilience' of species to ecosystemic opportunities may be impaired, so that 'natural' mechanisms of response, adaptation, and migration and opportunism may be fundamentally impaired. What we may presume for ecological resilience today may not be so assumed for tomorrow.

Biodiversity disruption could undermine the kinds of agrodiversity prospects outlined in Box 13.3 (p. 305) that many regard as the mainstay of a future healthy agriculture. As a consequence, agrodiversity schemes will have to be even more culturally and ecologically adaptable.

Incorporating people for protecting biodiversity

The essence of chapter 5, and of the case studies that follow, lies in the need to incorporate people into biodiversity protection. The point has widely been made, even if it cannot be proven. To protect the protected means to manage beyond, as well as within, the biological 'hotspots'. Norman Myers and his colleagues (2000: 852), backed by Myers in chapter 3, believe that as many as 44 per cent of all species of vascular plants as well as 35 per cent of all species in four vertebrate groups are confined to twenty-five locations of supreme indigenous diversity. To protect these areas for all future, they make the case:

> In some areas outright protection is still the best option. In other areas this is not feasible because of human settlements and other activities long in place. These areas should receive a measure of protection as 'conservation units' that allows some degree of multiple use provided that species safeguards are always paramount. (Myers *et al.* 2000: 852)

The notion of 'species safeguard' taking precedence over day-to-day livelihoods has long been prominent in biodiversity management. These issues are developed by Jules Pretty in chapter 4. The early manifestation was attributed to a colonial era when 'fences and fines' were commonplace to remove people from reserves (Gbadegisin and Ayileka 2000: 89). The concerns over population increases, tourism needs and invasions of new harvesting techniques encourage many conservationists to retain a 'purist' approach to biodiversity management. Salafsky and Wallenburg (2000) suggest that core protected zones with no consumptive use of biological resources should still be central to protected areas management. Terborgh (1999) maintains that threats from immigration of desperate peoples and the attractiveness of the tourist dollar present grave dangers to high-profile sites. Wells and Brandon (1992) have shown persuasively that when conservation and economic development objectives are combined in integrated projects, sustainability objectives aimed at securing local livelihoods may fail to guarantee biodiversity.

The theme adopted in this text, and extensively reviewed by Lovejoy, Myers and Pretty in the chapters that follow, is that incorporating people into the practices of biodiversity can be achieved, and should be policy, so long as the primary objective remains the adaptive tolerances of ecosystem functioning. What the case studies reveal is that this is by no means an easy path to follow. For one thing, including people is not straightforward because we know as little about the workings of participatory democracy as we do about the functioning of ecosystems. Opening up management to societies of interest means establishing a creative mix of 'scientific' knowledge and 'cultural' knowing that is still basically untried. There is no blueprint, only experiments, trials and imaginative learning. This is the arena of sustainability science that is most open, most contested, most sensitive to success or failure, and most ideologically impregnated.

In chapter 5 Tim O'Riordan indicates that views on democracy are as advocatist and as argumentative as are emerging versions of ecology.

So ideologically promoted deliberative and inclusionary procedures rely on community connectedness and on patterns of governance that are still very rare. Such patterns need to be open, trusting, accommodating and sharing, yet effective and responsible. There are few good examples of management partnerships that can show off political history, power-framed property rights, civil injustices and the ambiguities of social and ecological co-operative adaptation. So we look to the case studies to give us guidance. They reveal all too clearly how biodiversity strategies reflect patterns of social and ecological history, arrangements of governance, structures and expectations of democracy and participation, and the changing rules of international regimes, business responsibility, internet advocacy by coalitions of pressure groups, and tricky evaluation techniques. The framing of management and the conduct of inclusive procedures carry more influence on biodiversity futures than the operations of the ecosystems themselves.

This introductory chapter lays out the arguments. Biodiversity is declining everywhere and there are still precious few signs of a change in direction. Despite the statistical finesse of Lomborg (2001), who is sincerely trying to portray a positive picture, all the signs, and the evidence, all the mainstream scientific reports, support this conclusion. Not to protect biodiversity means not to protect humanity from its communion with the planet. As we lose biodiversity, so we lose our individual and collective souls. To use biodiversity as a barometer for our ethos, and as waymarks for our pathways towards sustainability, is our best course. We can do this by a mosaic of means. We can strictly preserve where disturbance of any kind is undesirable, or where we do not know how to predict the consequences of disturbance. We can embrace non-extractive activities in renewable removal and in pleasure and wonder. We can create real income and genuine social well-being by sharing the biota with the economy through new forms of governance. And we can create whole new landscapes of biodiversity, designed for resilience against invasion and climate change, so that sustainable economies and societies can flourish in resplendently fresh habitats. There is no magic formula. All of these policies are possible, side by side, connected by corridors and social inclusion, and by the spirit of joy in sharing and redesigning the planet.

Postscript: a changing world order

This chapter is written in the unfolding aftermath of the terrorist attacks on the World Trade Centre in New York and the Pentagon in Washington. It is still impossible to forecast all of the consequences of those terrible events. Huge amounts of money will be diverted to a wide array of anti-terrorism activities, involving military, financial and diplomatic initiatives. In addition civil liberties will be affected, hopefully in such a way as to respect honest people and well-meaning associations of benign interests. It is possible that the sums of money involved in this necessary co-ordinated effort to bring peace and security to the daily lives of many millions will exceed all that could be directed into safeguarding and expanding biodiversity. Norman Myers offers some figures in chapter 3, and there are other estimates in this chapter; US$500 million could save the hotspots and some US$300 billion annually could safeguard all biodiversity world-wide. More figure are provided later in this chapter.

These are not 'either–or' matters. Safeguarding peace of mind throughout the globe is a desirable sustainability objective. Building and reinforcing social capital in every corner for humanity is also a desirable sustainability objective. Any global coalition against terrorism contains the scope for a companion coalition in favour of biodiversity for sustainability. The globalisation forces about which many feel uneasy will foster a demand for social distinctiveness and identity but within a sustaining whole. There is more scope for local economies in a world where mobility could usefully be curtailed to some extent.

It is far too early to tell what will be all of the consequences of the new world order. Hopefully the meeting of world leaders in Johannesburg in September 2002, the World Summit on Sustainable Development (www.worldsummit2002.org), will continue the global healing process so falteringly initiated in Rio de Janeiro a decade earlier. The Johannesburg 2002 event will focus on poverty, health, human rights (especially for women, children and indigenous peoples) and the safeguard of water and biodiversity. This text is aimed, in part, at this summit. It is possible that the coalitions of human security will metamorphose into partnerships for peace and mutual understanding. It is also possible that an effort to recognise cultural diversity and to infuse locality into globalisation processes will evolve out of the current moves to establish a world order against terrorism.

It is simplistic and naïve to suggest that bringing sustainability into that world order will help to eliminate terrorism and anger. This is a process that will take generations to carry out. All we can hope for is that world economic summits combine with world sustainability summits into the common wish for a healthy planet and healthy people that could be reached by protecting beyond the protected. If world political, religious and economic leaders combine the centrality of wealth, health, stability and security with sustainability, then there is a chance that the outcome of the unforgettable events of 11 September will generate a profoundly transformative legacy. This, at least, is the spirit in which this introductory chapter is written.

REFERENCES

Berkes, F. and Folke, C. 1998a. Linking social and ecological systems for resilience and sustainability. In F. Berkes and C. Folke (eds.), *Linking Social and Ecological Systems*, pp. 1–27. Cambridge: Cambridge University Press.

Berkes, F. and Folke, C. (eds.) 1998b. *Linking Social and Ecological Systems: Management Practices and Social Mechanisms for Building Resilience*. Cambridge: Cambridge University Press.

Bromley, D.W. (ed.) 1992. *Making the Commons Work: Theory Practice and Policy*. San Francisco: Institute for Contemporary Studies.

Chapin, F.S. *et al.* 2000. Global biodiversity scenarios for the year 2010. *Science* 287: 1,770–5.

Costanza, R. *et al.* 1997. The value of the world's ecosystem services and natural capital. *Nature* 387: 253–60.

Dudley, N. *et al.* 1999. Challenges for protected areas in the 21st century. In S. Stolton and N. Dudley (eds.), *Partnerships for Protection*, pp. 3–12. London: Earthscan.

Gaston, K.J. 2000. Global patterns in biodiversity. *Nature* 403: 220–7.

Gbadegesin, A. and Ayileka, O. 2000. Avoiding the mistakes of the past: towards a community oriented management strategy for the proposed National Park in Abuji-Nigeria. *Land Use Policy* 17: 89–100.

Harper, J.C. and Hawkesworth, D.L. 1995. Preface. In D.L. Hawkesworth (ed.), *Biodiversity Measurement and Estimation*, pp. 5–12. London: Chapman and Hall.

Holling, C.S., Berkes, F. and Folke, C. 1998. Science, sustainability and resource management. In F. Berkes and C. Folke (eds.), *Linking Social and Ecological Systems*, pp. 343–63. Cambridge: Cambridge University Press.

Holling, C.S., Schindler, D.W., Walker, B.U. and Roughgarden, J. 1995. Biodiversity in the functioning of ecosystems: an ecological synthesis. In C. Perrings, K.-G. Maler, C. Folke, C.S. Holling and B.-O. Jansson (eds.), *Biodiversity Loss: Economic and Ecological Issues*, pp. 48–83. Cambridge: Cambridge University Press.

Intergovernmental Panel on Climate Change 2001. *Third Assessment Report: Summary of Policy Makers*. Bonn: Climate Change Secretariat.

Lenton, T.M. 1998. Gaia and natural selection. *Nature* 394: 439–47.

Lomborg, B. 2002. *The Skeptical Environmentalist*. Cambridge: Cambridge University Press.

Mace, G.M. and Lande, R. 1991. Assessing extinction threats: toward a re-evaluation of IUCN threatened species categories. *Conservation Biology* 5: 148–57.

Margules, C.R. and Pressey, R.L. 2000. Systematic conservation planning. *Nature* 403: 243–53.

Mooney, H. and Hobbs, R.J. 2000. *Invasive Species in a Changing World*. Washington, DC: Island Press.

Myers, N. 1996. Two key challenges for biodiversity: discontinuities and synergisms. *Biodiversity and Conservation* 5: 1025–34.

Myers, N., Mittermeier, R.A., Mittermeier, C.G., da Fonesca, G.A.B. and Kent, J. 2000. Biodiversity hotspots for conservation priorities. *Nature* 403: 853–8.

O'Riordan, T. 2000. Environmental science on the move. In T. O'Riordan (ed.), *Environmental Science for Environmental Management*, 2nd edition, pp. 1–28. Harlow: Prentice Hall.

Ostrom, E. 1990. *Governing the Commons: The Evolution of Institutions for Collective Action*. Cambridge: Cambridge University Press.

Pimm, S.C. and Raven, P. 2000. Extinction by numbers. *Nature* 403: 843–5.

Pimm, S.C., and 32 others 2001. Can we defy nature's end? *Science* 293: 2,207–8.

Posey, D. *et al.* 2000. *Cultural Knowledge and Biodiversity*. Tokyo: UNU Press.

Purvis, A. and Hector, A. 2000. Getting the measure of biodiversity. *Nature* 403: 212–19.

Rosendahl, G.K. 2000. *The Convention on Biological Diversity and Developing Countries*. Dordrecht: Kluwer.

Sala, O. *et al.* 2000. Global biodiversity scenarios for the year 2100. *Science* 287: 1770–4.

Salafsky, N. and Wallenburg, E. 2000. Linking livelihoods and conservation: a conceptual framework and scale for assessing the integration of human-needs and biodiversity. *World Development* 28: 1431–8.

Stoll-Kleemann, S. 2001. Barriers to nature conservation in Germany: a model explaining apposition to protected areas. *Journal of Environmental Psychology* 21: 369–85.

Terborgh, J. 1999. *Requiem for Nature*. New York: Island Press.

Tilman, D. 2000. Causes, consequences and ethics of biodiversity. *Nature* 403: 208–11.

Tuxhill, J. 1999. Appreciating the benefits of plant biodiversity. In L.C. Brown and C. Flavin (eds.), *State of the World 1999*, pp. 96–114. London: Earthscan.

UN Environment Programme 2000. *Global Environment Outlook*. London: Earthscan.

UN Environment Programme, US National Aeronautics and Space Administration, World Bank 1998. *Protecting Our Planet, Securing Our Future*. Washington, DC: UN Environment Programme.

US National Research Council 1999. *Our Common Journey: A Transition Toward Sustainability*. Washington, DC: National Academy of Science.

Wells, M. and Brandon, K. 1992. *People and Parks: Linking Protected Area Management and Local Communities*. Washington, DC: IBRD and the World Bank.

White House Interagency Ecosystem Management Task Force 1995. *The Ecosystem Approach: Healthy Ecosystems and Sustainable Economics*. Washington, DC: The White House.

Wood, A., Stedman-Edwards, P. and Mang, J. (eds.) 2000. *The Root Causes of Biodiversity Loss*. London: Earthscan.

World Conservation Union (IUCN) 1997. *1997 IUCN Red List of Threatened Plants*. Gland: World Conservation Union.

World Resources Institute 2000. *People and Ecosystems: The Fraying Web of Life*. Washington, DC: World Resources Institute.

Zeeman, C. 1992. Evolution and catastrophe theory. In I. Bouriau (ed.), *Understanding Catastrophe*, pp. 83–102. Cambridge: Cambridge University Press.

Part II

Policy and management

2   Biodiversity: threats and challenges

Thomas E. Lovejoy

Introduction

Over the two decades since the term biological diversity came into existence (Lovejoy 1980a, 1980b; Norse and McManus 1980; Wilson, 1980) (later biodiversity – Wilson 1988), the tree of life has been transformed dramatically. Originally two stout trunks representing plants and animals with microorganisms near their base, today the tree of life is a low spreading bush of which two tiny twigs represent plants and animals (see Fig. 2.1) The remainder of the current 'tree' is mostly microorganisms, many with strange metabolisms probably dating to the early history of life on earth.

Current knowledge of biological diversity consists of roughly 1.5 million described species. The estimates of the total number of species – described and undescribed – vary considerably. The current consensus (Heywood, 1995) is about 10 million species, although estimates have run as high as 30 million to 100 million As major unexplored parts of the biosphere are investigated – tropical forest canopy, soil biodiversity and marine ecosystems for example – the estimate may well change. For example, an investigation of fungal endophytes (fungi which live in healthy plant tissues) of just two understorey tree species in Panama suggests an astonishingly rich flora of a group which is essentially unknown (Arnold *et al.* 2000). An All Species Inventory – 'ALL' – is being initiated to speed the exploration of the unknown and greater part of biological diversity (Kelly 2000). Yet despite these unknowns it is clear that there is a rapid decline in biological diversity (Heywood, 1995) and extinction rates are currently estimated to be 100 to 1,000 times normal.

Biological diversity is also a characteristic of each and every biological community. For example, a southern New England deciduous forest has ten to fifteen species of trees and a stretch of Amazon rain forest will have several hundred. So the number and kinds of species can be used as a characteristic.

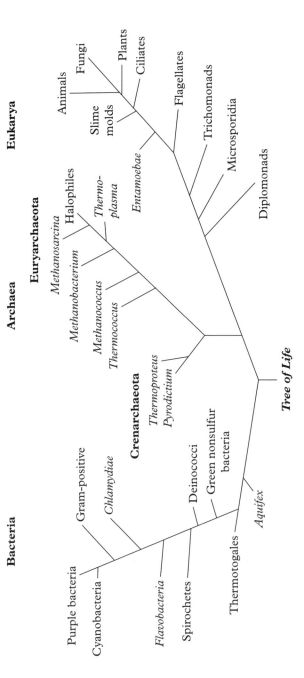

Fig. 2.1 The Tree of Life

In 1948 a line of research led by Ruth Patrick (1948, 1961) on freshwater communities in the United States (principally rivers) demonstrated that the number and variety of species reflected the natural physics and chemistry of a river *as well as* the stresses to which it was subject (e.g., pollution). This work, which deserves to be recognised as the Patrick Principle, can be generalized to all kinds of biological communities, i.e., marine and terrestrial as well as freshwater.

Put differently, environmental stresses are all defined as problems because they affect living systems (not just humans). So whether pollution, habitat destruction or climate change, they all impinge on biological diversity. Consequently biological diversity is the ultimate integrator of environmental change. When that change is sufficiently intensive and extensive it leads to species extinction. That, together with the scale and rate of the various kinds of environmental change, conspires to create the biological diversity crisis.

Humanity's first negative impact on biological diversity, and one which has endured for millennia, has been selective and directed at individual species, either for harvest of useful species or for elimination of unwanted ones. There is now abundant evidence from many islands in the Caribbean, the South Pacific and Hawaii that indigenous people eliminated numerous endemic species long before the arrival of European settlers. Loss of large and dangerous animal species – 'mega-fauna' – is believed to have been the work of early Amerindians in the New World, and of early Aborigines in Australia (Flannery 1990; Roberts *et al.* 2001). Although it is hard to prove on the basis of the limited evidence available, the losses of large flightless bird species – moas in New Zealand and the elephant bird (*Aepyornis*) in Madagascar – seem clear-cut cases of deliberate elimination.

On Easter Island, the impact of indigenous people went beyond selective elimination of particular species. The entire forest cover was removed along with all the constituent species, whatever they may have been (Diamond, 1995). Selective impacts (hunting and fishing) continue to be part of the picture, whether the loss of the passenger pigeon (once numbering in the billions but extinct by 1914 through hunting), the incidental catch of marine turtles in shrimp fisheries or of various species of albatrosses by long-line fisheries, or endangered fish stocks (freshwater and marine). These also include the pet trade (birds, aquarium fish) and dietary supplements (real such as ginseng and spurious such as rhinoceros horn). One of the more disturbing of these is the bushmeat trade which is most prominent in Africa (Wilkie and Godoy, 2000). What originally was subsistence hunting has become a trade supplying the tables of, among others, the wealthy in cities.

Habitat destruction is the current single greatest threat to biological diversity. While it is usually thought of as a threat to terrestrial ecosystems, it has its aquatic equivalents, whether the trawling of the sea floor (e.g., for scallops) or the conversion of a running (lotic) water habitat into still water through impoundment. Already, tropical forests are more than half gone and almost none of the great grasslands (prairies) of North America remains.

Destroying a habitat is like destroying a city: all the inhabitants (organisms in the first case and human organisms in the second place) are eliminated. There is not a linear relationship between amount of habitat destroyed and species lost; for example, destroying 2 per cent of a habitat does not lead to loss of 2 per cent of the species. Rather, it is a logarithmic relationship deriving from the well-known species–area relationship ($S = kA^z$ where S equals the number of species, k is a constant, A is the area of habitat, and z is a power constant often around 0.25) (Arrhenius, 1921; Hubbell, 2001). So at 10 per cent remaining habitat approximately 50 per cent of the species remain. This is, of course, a very general relationship and does not substitute for actual biological survey in such situations, but it does help to assess the general scale of biodiversity loss.

In many places, the process of habitat loss is extremely advanced. As Egler shows in chapter 10, the Atlantic coastal forest of Brazil is down to 9 per cent of its original extent. There are twenty-five relict areas of habitat around the world with concentrations of endemic species under great threat of further destruction. Termed 'biological hotspots' (Myers, 1988; Myers *et al.*, 2000), they are estimated to contain 30–50 per cent of all species – a quite imprecise but none the less important and large number – in about 2 per cent of the land surface of the earth. Originally they occupied 12 per cent.

Clearly hotspots represent critical conservation priorities, but they do not obviate the need (and were never so intended) to conserve biological diversity and to create biologically functional landscapes everywhere. New and additional hotspots would be created elsewhere if the habitats of more widespread biological formations were subjected to continuing destruction.

Fortunately, there are time lags involved, so a remnant habitat will initially hold more species than it will ultimately be able to hold if it remains isolated. While in one sense these species are the 'living dead' (Janzen, 1986, 2001; Wilson, 1992), they could in fact be salvaged from otherwise extinction if steps were taken to enlarge the remaining natural habitat and connect remnant fragments with corridors, using natural revegetation (using native species).

None the less, habitat fragmentation, the largely unrecognised hand-maiden of habitat destruction, generally makes the extinction problem even worse. Rarely if ever is remaining natural habitat of hotspots or other biological formations in a single block; rather it is fragmented. As a consequence, if 10 per cent of an ecosystem type remains in total, the constituent fragments will be able to support fewer than 50 per cent of all species. The lower percentage is a function of the extent of fragmentation (numbers of fragments of different size).

In addition, fragments develop edge-related changes, so the actual area (in a conservation sense, the effective area) of a fragment is smaller than the actual fragment itself. In the Amazon, for example, edge-related changes penetrate close to 100 m from the edge of forest fragments. There, some of the changes relate to wind throw occurring in unprotected forest edges; they can be so extensive in small forest fragments (1 to 10 ha) that up to 30 per cent of the biomass can be lost (Laurance et al. 1998).

An illustration of how and why species drop out of forest fragments involves the Australian honey possum, which depends on a series of plant species to provide a nectar supply throughout the twelve months of the year. Any fragment too small to have the full set of nectar sources will lose the honey possum.

Fragmented habitats have fragmented populations of the constituent species. This means each of these populations is subject to the problems which face small populations (Young and Clarke 2000). Low genetic diversity and inbreeding represent loss of biological diversity at the genetic level. The small populations themselves are subject to stochastic perils of various sorts, giving them low likelihood of persistence.

Another cause of extinction is the introduction of alien or exotic species to places where they do not occur naturally. In the United States this is considered the third most important factor affecting biological diversity (Office of Technology Assessment, 1993; Mooney and Hobbs 2000). In Hawaii and New Zealand, the number of introduced plant species exceeds that of surviving native species. Predation by introduced species (e.g., foxes, or rats which are nest predators) is a major problem in Australia, Hawaii and the Galapagos. On Guam, the Philippine brown tree snake has eliminated or decimated a number of endemic bird species, while in Lake Victoria, introduction of the Nile perch has led to a cascade of extinctions of endemic fish species. Feral domestic species are equally problematical, such as rabbits in Australia or goats in the Galapagos and the Caribbean Channel Islands, right down to the lighthouse keeper's cat which eliminated the Stephens Island wren. In the United States, the introduction and spread of the domestic honeybee is thought to have excluded the Carolina parakeet from its nesting holes and led to its extinction.

Invasive species are of equal importance in freshwater and marine systems, such as the zebra mussel in North America, or the lamprey which invaded the Great Lakes and ruined the lake trout fishery (Elton 1958). Sometimes the introductions are deliberate, as with sport fish species. They appear to represent one of the causal factors in the endangerment of frogs in the California Sierra. A comb jellyfish, *Mnemiopsis leidyi*, from the Atlantic coastal waters of the western hemisphere was transported in ballast water to the Black Sea in the early 1980s. Its population exploded so that its biomass is now equal to that of the $250 million/year anchovy fishery which it undercut by short-circuiting of the food chain (Carlton 1989).

An important class of introduced species is that of pathogens. A classic example is the introduction of chestnut blight to the United States, where it eliminated the American chestnut, a dominant tree species (and major wildlife food source) from the eastern forests (Elton 1958). In Western Australia, a fungal pathogen from Java, *Phytophora cinnamomi*, has essentially removed jarrah trees from the jarrah-marri forests. That pathogen has a broad spectrum capacity to eliminate many species of native flora (e.g., *Banksia* species) and is a major conservation problem.

The various forms of pollution represent yet another threat to biological diversity. The petrochemical industry of the coastal city of São Paulo generated such strong air pollution that at one point most of the trees in the neighbouring Atlantic forest had died, leading to landslides. The use of DDT and related chlorinated hydrocarbons in the United States led to the elimination of the peregrine falcon east of the Mississippi, as well as major declines in populations of birds at the end of long (therefore pollutant-concentrating) food chains, such as ospreys, bald eagles and brown pelicans.

A disturbing class of pollutant chemicals are those which mimic endocrine systems, the 'endocrine disruptors'. They tend to disrupt normal developmental and reproductive processes. While conclusive evidence has yet to be obtained on the effects of these chemicals on human beings, there are well-documented cases of effects on wildlife (Colborn *et al.* 1996; Krimsky 2001: 27).

Pollution has now become regional. Acid rain is still a serious problem in the United States and has in some instances been shown to leach essential cations from the soil, with forest growth consequently slowing or ceasing at least temporarily (Likens 1979; Driscoll *et al.* 2001). The runoff from industrial agriculture in the middle west of the United States now produces an annual anoxic 'dead zone' in the Gulf of Mexico

(Turner and Rabelais 1991). Inappropriate landuse in South America and in south-east Asia, combined with cyclical El Niño dry periods, has resulted in major fires and in one case a smoke cloud as large as Brazil. Respiratory illness and closure of airports because of lack of visibility have been immediate consequences. The implications of the above for biological diversity are clear even if the detail is still being worked out.

The scale of human impact is such that it can be seen affecting large systems and their natural processes. In Western Australia, a region which includes one of the twenty-five global hotspots, removal of the natural woody vegetation to create the 'wheat belt' has permitted groundwater to rise through saline deposits, causing a salinity problem for both agriculture and remaining natural habitat.

Two great South American systems are similarly vulnerable. In the Amazon basin a hydrological cycle is responsible for approximately half the rainfall (Salati and Vose, 1984). As air masses move in from the Atlantic and move westward towards the Andes, they drop rain. Much of the water is returned to the atmosphere as it evaporates off the complex surfaces of the forest or is transpired by the woody vegetation. This then becomes rain further to the west. This system depends on forest cover. At the moment little is understood about the implications of deforestation for the maintenance of the cycle, although clearly these will vary from place to place and with vegetation type. In the meantime deforestation proceeds incrementally, with no sense of what each increment means for the cycle.

The Pantanal represents a similar system. South America's greatest wetland is the product of the Parana – Paraguay drainage, with the Pantanal essentially acting as a giant sponge storing water during the rainy season which then both evaporates slowly and drains during the dry season. Various proposals to alter the drainage, including building levees to prevent rainy season flooding, all have the potential to affect the Pantanal's hydrology. The Centro de Conservacao do Pantanal is in the process of building a hydrological model through which such proposals could be tested for their potential biodiversity impacts before decisions are taken.

Finally there are the implications of human-induced climate change for biological diversity. The increase of greenhouse gases in the atmosphere as a consequence of the burning of fossil fuels, as well as biomass (especially forest) burning, could in fact be viewed as pollution on the global scale. Carbon dioxide levels are already 30 per cent higher than in the pre-industrial era. The Intergovernmental Panel on Climate Change has become quite firm in its view that human-caused climate change is already happening.

Climate change is, of course, nothing new in the history of life on earth. Certainly in the recent past there were major advances and retreats of glaciers in North America, in Europe and at high altitudes in the tropics. Plant and animal species seem to have succeeded quite well in tracking their requisite conditions during those times of climate change. Today, however, species are confronted very often with highly modified landscapes – essentially obstacle courses which will make it harder to disperse successfully. It is likely, therefore, that climate change will generate a huge number of extinctions. To avoid that, there must be a dramatic slowing of greenhouse gas accumulation and a major effort to put natural connections back into the landscape to enhance dispersal (Peters and Lovejoy 1992).

Biological diversity may in fact be the key to answering a critical question about climate change, namely what is the 'acceptable' level of greenhouse gases (see Hannah *et al.* 2002). Interestingly the Framework Convention on Climate Change contains a significant passage: 'within a time frame sufficient to allow ecosystems to adapt naturally'.The idea is that climate change should occur slowly enough so species can disperse successfully. Yet there are some ecosystems which cannot adapt, no matter how slow the rate of change. These are ecosystems on the tops of mountains or on low islands. It appears that the succulent karoo, a global hotspot in South Africa, will be largely eliminated under climate conditions influenced by a doubling of the pre-industrial amount of CO_2.

Through the application of the Patrick Principle, biological diversity provides the basis for defining the acceptable upper limit of greenhouse gas concentration. The implications for biological diversity are of course very great, so it is critically important that there be excellent research trying to define this level. Then the prudent policy approach would be to aim for something below that level, to avoid any unpleasant surprises.

There are many other challenges to be met in ensuring that as much biological diversity as possible passes successfully through the bottleneck of human population and economic growth. Food production for the additional billions of people is a major one. The 'Green Revolution' succeeded by intensifying agriculture but did so at the expense of a lot of fertilizers and pesticides and loss of cultivars. None the less the needed food production was achieved with far less land area than would otherwise have been the case, thus sparing much natural habitat.

Will it be possible to provide the food for the additional billions by intensification of agriculture in tropical areas and thus to minimise further conversion of natural areas? It is not clear at this point, but an approach is needed which balances the need to minimise conversion of natural areas with minimal use of artificial chemicals, yet also is less of a monoculture, and protects remaining cultivars and indigenous varieties while producing the necessary food. Given the mixed picture on genetically modified organisms (GMOs) (which in fact derive from natural biological diversity), it is not clear how much they will contribute. Used judiciously they do hold the potential to move agriculture more towards a low-input system.

Another important factor will be the extent to which population remains or becomes further urbanised. In countries like Brazil the ratio of population has moved from 70 per cent rural to 70 per cent urban. In the Brazilian Amazon the state of Amazonas has one of the lowest deforestation rates because of the concentration of population in the city of Manaus, an economic free zone. Those concerned with conservation of biological diversity have thus come to have a vested interest in the quality of life in and around cities. An important variant of this involves urban sprawl such as occurs in the United States. Interestingly, public transportation, which is an important element in this context, is also important for greenhouse gas reduction.

Another important challenge is taking a regional, ecosystem approach to conservation, landuse and sustainable development. An interesting example in progress in the United States involves the south Florida ecosystem. This ranges from the Kissimmee River and Lake Okeechobee down through the Everglades National Park, Florida Bay, the Florida Keys and the nearby coral reef. Over almost a century, a series of decisions about land and water – each seeming reasonable in its context and time – led to a situation where this ecosystem (which basically depends on a sheet flow of water) was releasing only 25–50 per cent of normal freshwater flows to Florida Bay. Indeed not a drop of water flows naturally in the system. Water birds are disappearing from the national park, the sea grass beds have vanished in Florida Bay, and hypersaline water is coming through the Keys to the already stressed reef. This is a classic example of how seemingly reasonable incremental decisions become cumulatively problematical.

There is now a major multi-billion-dollar effort to restore the natural plumbing of south Florida. Basically the environmental problems of south Florida and their effects on biological diversity can only be addressed by tackling the problem on the system scale.

A similar effort is addressing biological diversity conservation in the southern five counties of California. This area is home to the coastal sage scrub ecosystem and to some of the most expensive real estate and extensive urban sprawl in the nation. Some species, including the California gnatcatcher, were approaching endangered status. To avoid possible application of the Endangered Species Act, a combined effort of the federal, state and county governments, together with local non-governmental organizations and industry, designed a landuse plan which should ensure the future of the coastal sage scrub ecosystem. This could not have been achieved on a piecemeal basis.

One of the greatest challenges is to match the scale of conservation and sustainable development to the scale of the forces working in the destructive direction. One recent effort was sponsored by the Center for Applied Biodiversity Science of Conservation International. An assembled group of scientists and conservation practitioners attempted to estimate what it would take to address the threats to the twenty-five global hotspots and to conserve major portions of the remaining wilderness areas. A summary (Pimm *et al.* 2001) should not be considered the definitive conservation blueprint. Rather it is an important attempt to alter the scale at which we think and act. The WWF is making a similar attempt in moving to an ecoregional analysis and attempting to get 10 per cent increments of national territory into protected area status. This line of approach is followed by Amanda Younge in chapter 8. The WWF–World Bank Brazilian government project designed to increase to 10 per cent of protected areas to the Brazilian Amazon will mean that approximately 40 per cent will be under some form of protection. The evidence is covered by Ione Egler in chapter 10.

It should be remembered that the Earth Summit in Rio de Janeiro in 1992 was just such an attempt to change the scale for environment, biological diversity and sustainable development. The expectations of major increases in overseas development assistance have not materialised. One important product, which has been substantial but far smaller than planned, is the Global Environment Facility intended for incremental costs incurred by developing countries in implementing the Conventions on Biological Diversity and Climate Change (as well as the Montreal Protocol and topics relating to 'international waters'). To date there have been 395 projects and enabling activities in 123 countries, with an investment of about $1.2 billion and an expected $2 billion in co-financing. Contributions to GEF have fallen far short of the initial target of $8 billion.

In addition, the World Bank has been supporting other biodiversity projects through its more traditional lending instruments, including actual loans. Cumulative biodiversity investments (including GEF) for the World Bank 1988–99 totaled $2.63 billion. One of the significant projects is the Pilot Program to Conserve the Brazilian Rainforest, an initiative of the G7. This effort is critically viewed in chapter 10.

Recognising that there is an additional need for small-sized quick-disbursing loans, the World Bank, at the initiative of Conservation International, has established a Critical Ecosystem Partnership Fund (CEPF). It is directed at conservation projects in the biodiversity hotspots. The Bank and GEF have each matched Conservation International's $25 million, while the MacArthur Foundation has committed an additional $25 million. Two additional partners are being sought to make a total of $150 million.

In a sense one of the greatest of all challenges is truly to integrate environment and development so that all sectors of government work in concert and environment occupies its influential rightful place. In most governments environment is a relatively weak ministry and most decisions are taken by the ministry of finance, often without consultation. This leaves environment to be reactive rather than playing a central role. An interesting case is the Meso-American Biological Corridor project, an effort by the Central American countries and Mexico to stitch together remaining forest blocs so that – as it was once characterised – a jaguar could walk unimpeded for the entire length. The current 'Puebla to Panama' vision of the new president of Mexico, Vicente Fox, is a series of infrastructure projects. This vision and the corridor could easily conflict but also could be crafted together into a sustainable-development whole. Sectoral integration is obviously key to the future of biological diversity.

Yet how should sustainable development be measured? How can it be recognised? It is difficult to take it beyond the generalities of the basic definition. Yet, biological diversity provides us with a way to measure. Once again the Patrick Principle applies. If a large area of some ecological cohesion – like south Florida for example – maintains its basic biological diversity and ecological processes, then it is at least sustainable from an environmental point of view. That means the basic species list does not change much over time and processes like the sheet flow of water in the peninsula are maintained. The social and economic elements of sustainability may not seem apparent, and yet if they are not sustainable there will be an unmistakable imprint on the biological diversity. So nature provides an uncompromising yardstick for measuring our way.

REFERENCES

Arnold, A.E., Z. Maynard, G.S. Gilbert, P.D. Coley and T.A. Kursar 2000. Are tropical endophytes hyperdiverse? *Ecology letters* 3: 267–74.
Arrhenius, O. 1921. Species and area. *Journal of Ecology* 9: 95–9.
Carlton, J.T. 1989. Man's role in changing the face of the ocean: biological invasions and implications for conservation of near-shore environments. *Conservation Biology* 3: 265–73.
Colborn, Dumanoski, T.D. and Myers, J.P. 1996. *Our Stolen Future*. New York: Penguin Books.
Diamond, J. 1995. Easter's end. *Discover* (August): 62–9.

Driscoll, C.T., Lawrence, G.B., Bulger, A.J., Butler, T.J., Cronan, C.S., Eager, C., Lambert, K.F., Likens, G.E., Stoddard, J.L. and Weathers, K.C. 2001. Acidic deposition in the northeastern United states: sources and inputs, ecosystem effects, and management strategies. *BioScience* 51: 180–98.

Elton, C.S. 1958. *The Ecology of Invasions by Animals and Plants*. London: Methuen.

Flannery, T.F. 1990. Pleistocene faunal loss: implications of the aftershock for Australia's past and future. *Archaeology in Oceania* 25: 45–67.

Hannah, L., Midgley, G.F., Lovejoy, T., Bond, W.J., Bush, M., Lovett, J.C., Scott, D. and Woodward, F.I. 2002. Conservation of biodiversity in a changing climate. *Conservation Biology* 16: 264–8.

Heywood, V.H. 1995. *Global Biodiversity Assessment*. Cambridge: Cambridge University Press.

Hubbell, S.P. 2001. *The unified neutral theory of biodiversity and biogeography*. Princeton: Princeton University Press.

Janzen, D.H. 1986. The future of tropical ecology. *Ann. Rev. Ecol. Syst.* 17: 305–324.

2001. Latent extinctions – the living dead. In S.A. Levin (ed.), *Encyclopedia of Biodiversity* 3: 689–99.

Kelly, K. 2000. All species inventory: a call for the discovery of all life forms on Earth. *Whole Earth Catalogue* (Fall) 4.

Krimsky, S. 2001. Hormone disruptions: a clue to understanding causes of disease. *Environment* 43(5): 22–31.

Laurance, W. F., Laurance, S.F., Ferreira, L.V., Rankin-deMerona, J.M., Gascon, C. and T.E. Lovejoy 1998. Biomass collapse in Amazonian forest fragments. *Science* 278: 1117–18.

Likens, G.E. 1979. Acid rain. *Scientific American* 241: 43–51.

Lovejoy, T.E. 1980a. Foreword. In M.E. Soulé and B.A. Wilcox (eds.), *Conservation Biology: An evolutionary-ecological perspective*, pp. v–ix, Sunderland, MA: Sinauer Associates.

1980b. Changes in biological diversity. In G.O. Barney (ed.), *The Global 2000 Report to the President*, pp. 327–32. Harmondsworth: Penguin Books.

Mooney, H.A. and R.J. Hobbs, (eds.), 2000. *Invasive Species in a Changing World*. Washington, DC: Island Press.

Myers, N. 1988. Threatened biotas: 'hotspots' in tropical forests. *The Environmentalist* 8: 187–208.

Myers, N., Mittermeier, R.A., Mittermeier, C.G., da Fonseca, G.A.B. and J. Kent, 2000. Biodiversity hotspots for conservation priorities. *Nature* 403: 853–8.

Norse, E.A. and McManus, R.E. 1980. Ecology and living resources biological diversity. In *Environmental Quality 1980: The Eleventh Annual Report of the Council on Environmental Quality*, pp. 31–80. Washington, DC: Council on Environmental Quality.

Office of Technology Assessment 1993. *Harmful non-indigenous species in the U.S.* Washington, DC: US Government Printing Office.

Patrick, R. 1948. Factors affecting the distribution of diatoms. *Botanical Review* 14: 473–524.

1961. A study of the numbers and kinds of species found in rivers in eastern United States. *Proceedings of the Academy of Natural Sciences of Philadelphia* 113: 215–58.

Peters, R.L. and Lovejoy, T.E. (eds.) 1992. *Global Warming and Biological Diversity*. New Haven and London: Yale University Press.

Pimm, S.L., Ayres, M., Balmford, A., Branch, G., Brandon, K., Brooks, T., Bustamante, R., Costanza, R., Cowling, R., Curran, L.M., Dobson, A., Farber, S., da Fonseca, G.A.B, Gascon, G., Kitching, R., McNeely, J., Lovejoy, T., Mittermeier, R.A., Myers, N., Patz, J.A., Raffle, B., Rapport, D., Raven, P., Roberts, C., Rodriguez, J.P., Rylands, A.B., Tucker, C., Safina, C., Samper, C., Stiassny, M.L.J., Supriatna, J., Wall, D.H., and Wilcove D., 2001. Can we defy nature's end? *Science* 293: 2,207–8.

Roberts, R., Flannery, T., Ayliffe, L., Yoshida, H., Olley, J., Prideaux, G., Laslett, G., Smith, B., Jones, R. and Smith, M. 2001. Timing and possible triggers of gaint marsupial extinctions in Australia during the late Quaternary. *Science* 292: 1,888–92.

Salati, E. and Vose, P.B. 1984. The Amazon basin; a system in equilibrium. *Science* 225: 129–38.

Turner, R.E. and Rabelais, N.N. 1991. Changes in Mississippi River water quality this century: implications for coastal food webs. *BioScience* 41: 140–8.

Wilkie, D.S. and Godoy, R.A. 2000. Economics of Bushmeat. *Science* 287: 975–6.

Wilson, E.O. 1980. Species extinction. *Harvard Magazine* 82: 21.

1988. *Biodiversity*. Washington, DC: National Academy Press.

1992. *The Diversity of Life*. Cambridge, Mass: Belknap Press.

Young, A.G. and G.M. Clarke, (eds.) 2000. *Genetics, Demography and Viability of Fragmented Populations*. Cambridge: Cambridge University Press.

3 Biodiversity and biodepletion: the need for a paradigm shift

Norman Myers

Introduction and background

We are witnessing the start of a mass extinction of species that will, if allowed to run its course, leave a deeply depauperised biosphere for at least 5 million years – a period twenty times longer than humans have been humans (Myers and Knoll 2001). The phenomenon must rank as one of the most defining episodes in humanity's history. No other human-induced event has imposed a planet-wide impact for more than a few centuries at most. Yet we understand all too little about this phenomenon. We do not know, except in the roughest terms, how many species share the planet with us and how many we are eliminating each year. Will people in the year 2100, and people far further into the future, not look back with astonishment that we were so little concerned with an episode that could turn out to be the most exceptional of its kind since the dinosaurs' demise 65 million years ago?

Moreover the repercussions of what we do – or don't do – in the next couple of decades will affect people for the next several million years, i.e., the period that evolution will need to come up with replacement species. We are taking an implicit decision to the effect that all the future people during those several million years will make out well enough on a planet that will have lost perhaps half of its species – yet there is not a scrap of evidence to support that 'decision'. Indeed there is a stack of evidence that our descendants will be in severe trouble. For instance, how will our food crops fare if they are deprived of half of their wild pollinators (Myers 1999a)? Yet the situation is beset by a culture of apathy and denial as is outlined in the introductory and concluding chapters of this volume.

This chapter seeks to address this dimension of the biodiversity problem. Why, just why, are we failing so monumentally? Should we not admit that conservation efforts have been largely responding to symptoms of the problem, whereas we need to tackle sources of the problem? What are its root causes? Are they economic, legal, social, political, cultural, institutional, ethical (Wood *et al.* 2000)? We know all too little about how to address these questions.

Let us ready ourselves for another question that will surely be asked of us in the year 2020 when the extinction spasm will have become plain enough. The public will say to us, 'You were the experts in the year 2002. You knew what was going on; you were aware of what was at stake. Why did you not do more about it?' That is a question to which I do not have anything like a sufficient answer with respect to my own work.

Fortunately there is still time for us to get to better grips with the challenge. Along the way let us hearten ourselves by recalling the Janus-faced nature of our makeup. As noted in chapter 1, we are the only species with capacity consciously to drive a single species extinct. But we are also the only species with capacity consciously to save a single species from oblivion. Indeed we can still save species in their millions: no doubt about it. Not just a panda here or a tiger there or a blue whale somewhere else, but species in their many millions. This chapter examines some dimensions of that superb prospect.

Public support for biodiversity

To repeat the key factor: the crisis is being played out against a background of apparently wall-to-wall ignorance and indifference, if not apathy, on the part of the public at large and its leaders. Or could it be that the public is ahead of its leaders in terms of knowledge and understanding?

There is evidence that the public has grown sufficiently informed that it would be aghast if the mass extinction were allowed to run its course. Twenty years ago the British television guru Sir David Attenbrough showed that the only way to hold an audience was to focus on a single charismatic creature such as a tiger or a chimpanzee. Ten years ago he showed that viewers would accept a film on tropical forests without a tiger or a chimpanzee in sight: they could take on board an ecosystem, even though it was far more fuzzy (and far less furry) than an individual creature. Today he considers that people will watch a film on mass extinction – the very concept, no less. He put the idea to the test through a three-part series of one-hour specials on the theme in early 2001. The sheer size of the audiences drawn week after week by these prime-time programmes tells its own story. People are not merely interested in biodiversity in a natural history sense, they want to hear about the biotic holocaust underway, however disturbing that may be.

The individual's stance

When I first started out as an environmental scientist, I heard many of my conservation friends assert that the problem lay primarily with the public's shortcomings. Loss of species was due to people's ignorance (or ignore-ance), their general lack of caring. I checked my fellow citizens and I could not view them like that; indeed the opposite. In any case, they displayed lots of that key characteristic, biophilia, or an in-built affinity with nature (Wilson 1984). They mostly wanted to keep sharing the Earth with lions and whales and redwood trees. At the same time, they felt helpless to do much about it.

Why don't we get on with the challenge? As summarised in chapter 1, the costs of protective action need not be great relative to many other public outlays, yet the individual citizen may still feel that the price looms unduly large. He might ponder the costs of inaction. One of the biggest decisions any person can take is to have children. To bring up an offspring from cradle through college costs around one quarter of a million dollars. Having made an investment of that scale in the long-term future, would the parent not be willing to reinforce it by whatever further collective investment would ensure the offspring lived in a world not blighted by gross biological impoverishment, together with whatever broader socio-economic costs that would entail?

Leadership

So perhaps the question boils down to this: Where are the leaders? Answer: they are the politicians, the policy experts, the economic planners, the business chiefs, the media, the churches, and what is known as civic society writ large. Few of them show signs of knowing how to supply the crucial lead. They are generally acquainted with the nature and size of the challenge, yet they offer scarcely a cheep. In the recent national election campaigns in the United States and Britain, no candidate gave the merest mention to anything remotely resembling an extinction spasm.

We should be able to look for support from religions. After all, each species is a unique manifestation of creation, and the demise of dozens of species per day presumably constitutes an offence to the creator. One might expect the churches to be falling over each other to proclaim that mass extinction is a spiritual calamity (Hobson and Lubchenco 1997; Myers 1999b). Few religious leaders, however, speak up. The Alliance for Religions and Conservation, a UK-based body that embraces all the world's faiths, estimates there are 200,000 religious communities around the world involved in some form of environmental activity, many highlighting biodiversity (Mastny 2001). Regrettably the Alliance does not seem to do much to promote the biodiversity cause in the workaday arena. Pope John Paul II has affirmed that 'The ecological crisis is a moral issue', yet he suggests nothing on how to manifest this viewpoint to the Monday-morning world.

The Pope's colleagues in other faiths display a limited outlook of a different sort. They focus mainly on front-page issues such as global warming, with hardly a word on the grand-scale destruction of life's abundance and variety – a phenomenon surely of far more long-term impact than global warming. If they were to help to lead the biodiversity crusade, they could spread the message to an audience of 2 billion Christians, 1.4 billion Muslims, 750 million Hindus, 700 million Buddhists, and a lengthy list of smaller bodies, of whom at least 1 billion (every sixth person in the world) attends a place of weekly worship (Mastny 2001). What a captive audience, and what an opportunity missed.

Fortunately one religious leader has issued a specific admonition. Patriarch Bartholomew I, spiritual leader of the world's 250 million Orthodox Christians, has declared, 'For humans to cause species to become extinct and to destroy the biological diversity of God's creation, is a sin' (Hobson and Lubchenco 1997). Alas, the Patriarch's church has done little to show how these precepts can be put into practice.

As an alternative, the leader-seeking citizen might turn to the many non-governmental organisations (NGOs) involved in biodiversity. Whereas in 1956 the number of international NGOs devoted to environmental causes including biodiversity was less than 1,000, by 1996 it had topped 20,000 (Boli and Thomas 1997; Union of International Organisations 1997; Runyan 1999; Trzyna 2001). More than one American in twenty is a member of an environmental organisation – while in Denmark there are more memberships than Danes. This makes for formidable leverage in the political and policy arenas. Despite their many superb efforts over several decades to stem the biodiversity crisis, NGO members have not always exercised the full pressure available to them (Brulle 2000; Bryner 2001). They might note the activist muscle exhibited by the National Rifle Association in the United States. Whatever one's stance on guns, one must acknowledge that the Association's 2.5 million members are well enough organised to thwart the reiterated preferences of 85 per cent of Americans. Why don't the 15 million environmentalists do as much? Apparent answer, they do not display the disciplined organisation of the NRA, which can mobilise quarter of a million letters to Congress within days of a clarion call. Were each NGO member to send a letter to his or her Congressman, copied to the President, just once a month (a five-minute job?), that could knock a huge dent in the problem forthwith.

Institutional failures

Apart from the general public and its leaders, what else could be amiss? I set institutions in the dock, i.e., our ways of running our societies, our modes of organising our world, and our systems of governance generally. There are deficiencies if not failures in many of our institutions (Wood *et al.* 2000; Wolbarst 2001). These institutional roadblocks should not be surprising. Our institutions have been developed over centuries to meet the needs of a different world. From ancient times, there has been a premium on protecting private property as reflected through our structures of economics (notably the marketplace) and law (notably property rights). It is only very recently that common property such as water bodies, the atmosphere and the planetary spectrum of species have come under threat. Now that we need to devise urgent safeguards for these forms of common property, we have few established institutions to do the job (this has long been accepted; for pioneering appraisals, see Dales 1968; Dorfman and Dorfman 1972; Mishan 1972; O'Riordan and Turner 1983; Winpenny 1991). With respect to global biodiversity, everybody's heritage is treated as nobody's business. Of course this presents the situation in broad-brush terms, and there has been some progress in establishing markets for species and their habitats (Anderson and Leal 2001; Pearce *et al.* 1993), and in establishing legal mechanisms such as easements and covenants for biodiversity (Roodman 1998; Bliese 2001). But the essence of the problem remains. Common property is subject to uncommon difficulties (Anderson *et al.* 1995; Barnes 2001; Wolbarst 2001).

Here is not the place to go into the situation in detail. Suffice it to say that this is the big-picture context within which we should seek to protect the common property of biodiversity. It is a fundamental reason why we find it difficult to slow the mass extinction underway. It also epitomises the thought that if we are to succeed, we shall need to engage in fundamental reforms of our institutions (Andersson *et al.* 1995; Roodman 1998; Wood *et al.* 2000). It likewise indicates why the best efforts of individuals and NGOs, plus governments and international agencies, have thus far fallen sorely short of measuring up to the full challenge: it is like pushing an ever-larger rock up an ever-steeper hill. It further demonstrates that we should keep a critical eye on our traditional conservation responses. How can we make them more productive, more efficient, more tailored to the task overall? In short, we should envisage a basic shifting of the gears. Our efforts need to be not just 'more of the same, only more so and better so'. They must reach beyond that to become better adapted to the paradigm dictates that are the basic message of this chapter.

Let us examine some opportunities for a more expansive response to the challenge.

Perverse subsidies

A prime way to tackle sources of conservation problems lies with the economic institution of 'perverse' subsidies. These are subsidies that are harmful to both the economy and the environment (Myers and Kent 2001). A notable example lies with marine fisheries, which have left numerous fish species on the edge of commercial if not biological extinction. The fisheries catch – well above sustainable yield – costs roughly $100 billion a year to bring to dockside, whereupon it is sold for around $80 billion, the shortfall plus profits being made up with government subsidies. These subsidies persuade more fishermen to chase after fewer fish. The result is depletion of major fish stocks and endangerment of certain species, plus the bankruptcy of many fishing businesses and much unemployment.

Similarly subsidies are prominent in six leading sectors: agriculture, fossil fuels, road transportation, water, forestry and fisheries. Subsidies for agriculture foster overloading of croplands, leading to erosion of topsoil, pollution from synthetic fertilisers and pesticides, release of greenhouse gases, and grand-scale loss of biodiversity habitat. Subsidies for fossil fuels aggravate pollution effects such as acid rain, urban smog and global warming, with extensive impacts on wildlands. Subsidies for road transportation promote pollution at local, national and global levels, plus excessive road building with loss of landscapes. Subsidies for water encourage misuse and overuse of supplies that are increasingly scarce in many lands. Subsidies for forestry foster overlogging in Alaska and Amazonia alike. As noted, subsidies for fisheries foster overharvesting of depleted fish species. Not only do these environmental ills entrain economic costs in themselves, but the subsidies serve as direct drags on the efficient functioning of economies overall. All serve to degrade wildlands and thus to undermine species' habitats if not to threaten species directly (Myers 2001).

Perverse subsidies in these sectors are estimated to total almost $2 trillion per year (Myers and Kent 2001) (see Table 3.1). Were just some of these subsidies to be phased out, just some of the savings would offer vast funds to protect threatened species – and there would be far less habitat degradation and hence far fewer species becoming threatened in the first place. Of course there are sizeable political obstacles to eliminating the subsidies. In Washington DC the Congress is subject to special interests' lobbying to the extent of $100 million a month.

Table 3.1 *'Perverse' subsidies (billion $ per year).*
Perverse subsidies are those which are harmful to both the
environment and the economy.

Overproductive agriculture	510
Fossil fuels/nuclear energy	300
Road transportation	780
Misuse and overuse of water	230
Overharvesting of fisheries	25
Overlogging of forests	92
Total	1,950

By definition, these are funds going to support unsustainable
development. Contrast the Rio Earth Summit budget for sustainable
development, $600 billion per year.

Source: Myers and Kent 2001.

Fortunately a number of countries have demonstrated that the political
obstacles can be overcome. New Zealand, a nation more dependent on
agriculture than any other developed nation, has got rid of virtually all its
agri-subsidies. India has slashed its fossil fuel subsidies by 36 per cent,
Poland by 54 per cent and China by 60 per cent. South Africa and Mexico
are starting to charge the full cost of supplying water. Several other nations
have cut their subsidies in the other three sectors. But these efforts have
eliminated less than 5 per cent of all perverse subsidies. The cuts have
been due in major measure to citizen protest – as well might be the case. A
typical American taxpayer funds the subsidies with $2,000 per year, then
pays out another $1,000 through environmental repair costs and higher
prices for food and other goods (Myers and Kent 2001).

Efficient funding and biodiversity hotspots

Now for a strategy to foster more efficient conservation of biodiversity.
Despite the severe shortage of conservation funding, monies are often
spent with less than tight targeting. There is much scope to do a better job
through, for example, the 'hotspots' strategy, as mentioned in chapter 1.
In chapter 1, the contribution of 'hotspots' to global biodiversity was
given some prominence. Hotspots are vital as they contain the major
remnants of genetic stock for the planet as a whole. Their loss would impoverish the genetic heritage of the Earth in a truly catastrophic manner.
Hotspots are areas that (a) feature exceptional concentrations of endemic
species, and (b) face exceptional threat of habitat destruction (Myers
1988, 1990; Myers *et al.* 2000; see also Mittermeier *et al.* 1999). Some

twenty-five hotspots contain the sole remaining habitats of at least 44 per cent of all plant species and 35 per cent of four groups of vertebrate species (hence perhaps 40 per cent of all species) in a mere 1.4 per cent of Earth's land surface, these being areas that for the most part have already lost the bulk of their original vegetation.

The hotspots thesis has merited conservation priority to the extent that it has attracted $600 million during the past ten years, the largest amount ever assigned to a single conservation strategy. The sum is only a little over 1 per cent of the amount spent on biodiversity by governments and international NGOs during the same period, $50 billion (Myers *et al.* 2000), these monies being assigned mainly to across-the-board activities rather than the sharply focused efforts available through the hotspots approach. We could go far towards safeguarding the hotspots and thus a large proportion of all species at risk for just $500 million a year over the next five years, or eight times the annual average over the past ten years. This sum is to be compared with a recent estimate (James *et al.* 2001; see also Pimm *et al.* 2001) for a comprehensive conservation programme to safeguard all biodiversity world-wide, costing $300 billion annually. Much traditional conservation activity has sought to be many things to many threatened species and thus failed to be much to most such species. This approach should be complemented by a strategy with emphasis on the most cost-effective measures such as hotspots.

The hotspots approach could generate a handsome payoff in stemming the biotic crisis. It is often supposed that, were the global mass extinction to proceed virtually unchecked, as many as half of all species could be eliminated within the foreseeable future (Raven 1990; Wilson 1992; Pimm *et al.* 1995). The hotspots analysis indicates that at least one third of the overall problem could be countered through protection of hotspots covering an aggregate expanse of only a little over 2 million km^2. In short, the prospect of a mass extinction can be made far less daunting and much more manageable.

Protected areas: no longer the front-line strategy?

Many conservation efforts are reactive in character, as cited in chapter 1. They implicitly acknowledge that biodiversity habitats are being eroded away by the growth in human numbers and human demands; and they propose that a sound way to counter the erosive process is to build bulwarks against the rising tide of human impacts. 'Parks are the answer, we must have more parks.' True, there is massive reason to increase our networks of parks forthwith. Ecologists estimate we need at least twice as large an expanse, located more strategically and better protected.

Especially is this the case for tropical forests, plus coral reefs, wetlands and other tropical zones with ultra-rich assemblies of species (Myers 2001).

Alas, many present parks are 'paper parks'. One third of such areas in the tropics are already subject to encroachment by landless and impoverished peasants, sometimes known as 'shifted' (because displaced) cultivators. During the past few decades, some 200 million and conceivably as many as 500 million such peasants have found themselves squeezed out of traditional farmlands. Feeling they have no other option if they are to get supper on the table, they pick up machete and matchbox and head off towards the last unoccupied lands they know of, namely the tropical forests. Or they take their digging hoes to savannah grasslands, often desertifying them. This is the greatest landuse change in human history, precipitated by the greatest migration ever to occur in such a short space of time – yet it remains almost entirely undocumented in overall terms, even to the extent that we have next to no idea of how fast their numbers may build up in the foreseeable future (Myers 1996). In their desperation and poverty (cash incomes of less than $1 per day), these are marginal people driven into marginal environments. Too often, the marginal environments are parks and other protected areas.

There is further doubt whether protected areas can do an adequate job. First, even if current areas remain as wildlife habitat, some 30–50 per cent of species will still be lost, if only because the areas do not contain populations large enough to maintain the species in perpetuity (McNeely and Scherr 2001). Second, and more important, the twenty-five hotspots – in so far as they constitute the principal protection priority – contain more than 1.1 billion people or more than one fifth of the global population (Cincotta *et al.* 2000).

Third, and the most important, setting aside a park in the overcrowded world of the early twenty-first century is like building a sandcastle on the seashore at a time when the tide is coming in deeper, stronger and faster than ever. While building more and stronger sandcastles, we must also do more about the tide – to deflect it and reduce it. We must find ways to curb population growth, to relieve poverty, to cut back on environmentally harmful forms of consumption, to contain global warming, and lots of similar things besides – all things that we should be doing on plenty of other good grounds anyway.

All this must be undertaken within a context of the leading factors of modern economies, notably investment and other financial flows, markets, trade, pricing systems, accounting procedures and discounting methods – plus their deficiencies such as marketplace externalities and social inequities (for consideration of these further factors, see Cairncross

1995; MacGillivray and Zadek 1995; Prugh *et al.* 1995). Within the context of these potent forces, it is apparent that conservation policies are not primarily set by conservationists. Rather, and albeit by default, they are set by ministries of economic planning, agriculture, forestry, industry, energy, trade and human settlements, and also by investors and corporate leaders. It behoves conservationists to understand the principal determinants that shape the arenas within which they operate. There is not space here to do more than note these contextual factors; for a summary review, see Myers (1998), dealing with, amongst other issues, market restrictions, discount rates, pricing externalities, structural adjustments and international financial transfers of $1.5 trillion a day.

Alternatively stated, and in light of the growing pressures from these biodiversity-threatening factors, the time has come when we can save total biodiversity only by saving the total biosphere. This means pushing back the deserts, replanting the forests, restoring topsoil and stabilising the climate, plus a lengthy list of other measures – all of which we should be doing for all kinds of good reasons even if there were no biodiversity problem. It will make for a win–win outcome, with multiplier effects in both directions. Just as a rehabilitated biosphere would safeguard species, so a full panoply of species would supply environmental benefits (generation of further topsoil, safeguards for watersheds, barriers against desertification, et lengthy cetera) that would enhance the biosphere – all operating in mutually reinforcing fashion, and progressively so.

Consider a future envisaged by McNeely (1990), who proposed that in fifty years' time we may have no more protected areas, and for one of two reasons. First is that they will have been overtaken by landless peasants or global warming or other mega-threats. Or, second, we shall have found ways to manage all our landscapes in such rational fashion that we shall automatically make provision for species habitats.

Scientific uncertainty and public policy

A final roadblock lies with our lack of knowledge of biodiversity. As noted in chapter 1, we do not know within an order of magnitude the number of species that share the planet with us. Still less do we know, except in very rough-and-ready terms, how many species are becoming extinct per year, or how many have already been eliminated. Nor do we have much idea of how many species are threatened with extinction within the foreseeable future. In short, the entire species issue is subject to much scientific uncertainty.

We do not even have much insight into the scale of threats. Consider, for instance, the factor of 'shifted' cultivators in tropical forests. The forests are central to the entire save-species campaign on two grounds. They contain the great majority of all species; and they are being depleted faster than any other major biome. Hence they are far and away the number one locus of the mass extinction underway. The main agent of deforestation, accounting for fully two thirds of the annual loss, is the shifted cultivator. I mentioned earlier that we do not know how many shifted cultivators are already in tropical forests; our best estimates range from 200 million to 500 million (Myers 1996). It is surely a scandal of modern science that we have only a vague grasp of one of the principal determinants of the mass extinction. The fact that we remain so ignorant about the shifted cultivator numbers is also a measure of how far their impoverished plight is overlooked by politicians. Yet few governments or international agencies are attempting to get a firm handle on this vital factor.

There are many other forms of scientific ignorance, as pervasive as they are profound. Despite this, conservationists must work as best they can with such meagre knowledge as science offers. Not all factors and parameters can be quantified in comprehensive detail, nor can all analyses be supported with across-the-board documentation. This highlights the question of scientific uncertainty and how it should be addressed in the public arena when dealing with an issue of major import. The essential problem is: what is 'legitimate scientific caution' in the face of uncertainty – especially when uncertainty can cut both ways?

Some scientists consider that in the absence of conclusive evidence and assessment, it is better to stick with low estimates of species numbers and extinctions on the grounds that they are more 'responsible' (Lemons 1996; Lubchenco 1998). But note the asymmetry of evaluation at work. A low estimate, ostensibly 'safe' because it takes a conservative view of such limited evidence as is to hand in documented detail, may fail to reflect the real situation just as much as does an 'unduly' high estimate that is more of a best-judgement affair based on all available evidence with varying degrees of demonstrable validity. A minimalist calculation with apparently greater precision may in fact amount to spurious accuracy. In a situation of uncertainty where not all factors can be quantified to conventional satisfaction, let us not become preoccupied with what can be precisely counted if that is to the detriment of what ultimately counts.

Suppose a policy maker hears scientists stating they cannot legitimately offer final guidance about the biodiversity problem because they have not yet completed their research with conventionally conclusive analysis in all respects. Or suppose scientists simply refrain from going public about the problem because they consider, in accord with traditional canons of science, they cannot validly say anything much before they can 'say all'. In these circumstances, the policy maker may assume there is therefore little to worry about for the time being. All too unwittingly, the policy maker may assume that absence of evidence about a problem implies evidence of absence of a problem. By consequence, the policy maker may decide to follow the frequently preferred course of doing nothing – and to do nothing in a world of rapid change can be to do a great deal. In these circumstances, undue caution by scientists can become undue reckless-ness in terms of the policy fallout: their silence can send a resounding message, however unintentional. As in other situations beset with uncer-tainty, it will be better for us to find we have been roughly right than precisely wrong. Scientists should seek to describe the situation with as much precise imprecision as they can muster – however divergent that may be from mainstream science (Myers 1999c).

All this will not come readily to those biologists who are expert at flows of energy through ecosystems but are less acquainted with flows of influence through corridors of power. In addition, there is the risk of the cry-wolf syndrome, of losing that precious commodity, scientific credibility. But biologists might also reflect that in the upshot they could lose ultimate credibility if they refrain from asserting what they know, and describing what they do not know, about an issue of great moment. I endorse the arguments in chapter 1, namely the clarion call for an advocacy interdisciplinary science for sustainability.

Conclusion

I have postulated that while we are doing much to get on top of the prob-lem, the problem is getting on top of us faster than ever. It is certainly not defeatist to recognise that, even with redoubled conservation efforts of established sorts, we shall witness a mass extinction within the present century. Conservationists need to expand their policy purview, and ac-cept that they will achieve far greater success if they move beyond tackling problems to addressing sources of problems. These sources include mar-ketplace mechanisms, legal systems and various other institutions with their roadblocks.

In short, there is a premium on a paradigm shift in certain aspects of the ways our societies work (or do not work). As it is, conservation efforts fail to reflect the full scale of the public's ostensible interest in saving species. I am convinced that the public will go to considerable lengths to avoid being party to a mass extinction. Regrettably its wishes are not articulated by leaders (politicians, etc.) with sufficient vigour to induce a fundamental reform of our institutions. It is this factor, the institutional roadblocks (boring topic though it sounds), that lies at the heart of the conservation challenge, and receives only a modicum of attention from conservation scientists. It is a mode to move beyond tackling symptoms of problems and address sources of problems. That way we can cut the problems off at the pass.

REFERENCES

Anderson, T.L. and Leal, D.R. 2001. *Free Market Environmentalism* (revised edition). New York: St Martin's Press.
Andersson, T., Folke, C. and Nystromm, S. 1995. *Trading with the Environment: Ecology, Economics, Institutions and Policy*. London: Earthscan.
Barnes, P. 2001. *Who Owns the Sky? Our Common Assets and the Future of Capitalism*. Washington, DC: Island Press.
Bliese, J.R.E. 2001. *The Greening of Conservative America*. Boulder, CO: Westview Press.
Boli, J. and Thomas, G.M. 1997. World culture in the world polity: a century of international Non-Governmental Organizations. *American Sociological Review* 62(2): 171–90.
Brulle, R.J. 2000. *Agency, Democracy, and Nature: The US Environment Movement from a Critical Theory Perspective*. Cambridge, MA: MIT Press.
Bryner, G.C. 2001. *Gaia's Wager: Environmental Movements and the Challenge of Sustainability*. Lanham, MA: Rowman and Littlefield.
Cairncross, F. 1995. *Green Inc*. London: Earthscan.
Cincotta, R.P., Wisnewski, J. and Engelman, R. 2000. Human population in the biodiversity hotspots. *Nature* 404: 990–2.
Dales, J.H. 1968. *Pollution, Property and Prices*. Toronto: University of Toronto Press.
Dorfman, R. and Dorfman, N.S. (eds.) 1972. *Economics of the Environment*. New York: Norton.
Hobson, S. and Lubchenco, J. (eds.) 1997. *Revelation and the Environment AD 95–1995*. London: World Scientific Publishing Company.
James, A., Gaston, K.J. and Balmford, A. 2001. Can we afford to conserve biodiversity? *BioScience* 51: 43–52.
Lemons, J. (ed.) 1996. *Scientific Uncertainty and Environmental Problem Solving*. Oxford: Blackwell.
Lubchenco, J. 1998. Entering the century of the environment: a new social contract for science. *Science* 279: 491–7.
MacGillivray, A. and Zadek, S. 1995. *Accounting for Change: Indicators for Sustainable Development*. London: New Economics Foundation.
McNeely, J.A. 1990. The future of national parks. *Environment* 32(1): 16–20, 36–41.
McNeely, J.A. and Scherr, S.J. 2001. *Common Ground, Common Future: How Ecoagriculture Can Help Feed the World and Save Wild Biodiversity*. Gland: World Conservation Union.
Mastny, L. 2001. Religious environmentalism rises. In *Vital Signs 2001: The Trends That Are Shaping Our Future*, pp. 146–7. Worldwatch Institute, New York: Norton.

Mishan, E.J. 1972. *Cost-Benefit Analysis*. London: Unwin.

Mittermeier, R.A., Mittermeier, C. and Myers, N. 1999. *Biodiversity Hotspots*. Mexico City: CEMEX.

Myers, N. 1988. Threatened biotas: 'Hot Spots' in tropical forests. *The Environmentalist* 8: 187–208.

1990. The biodiversity challenge: expanded Hot Spots analysis. *The Environmentalist* 10: 243–56.

1996. The world's forests: problems and potentials. *Environmental Conservation* 23: 156–68.

1998. Emergent issues of environmental economics: what we should be analysing closely but haven't thought enough about. *International Journal of Social Economics* 25: 1271–8.

1999a. Population dynamics and food security. In A. E. el Obeid, S. R. Johnson, H.H. Jensen and L.C. Smith (eds.), *Food Security: New Solutions for the 21st Century*, pp. 176–208. Ames: Iowa State University Press.

1999b. Our environmental prospect: time of breakdown or breakthrough? In B. Thompson, *Report of Conference on Mission and Ministry in a Changing World: The Environmental Imperative*, pp. 86–94. St George's House, Windsor.

1999c. Environmental scientists: advocates as well? *Environmental Conservation* 26: 163–5.

2001. The biodiversity outlook: endangered species and endangered ideas. In J.F. Shogren and J. Tschirart (eds.), *Social Order and Endangered Species Preservation*, pp. xxv–xxvi. Cambridge: Cambridge University Press.

Myers, N. and Kent, J. 2001. *Perverse Subsidies: How Tax Dollars Can Undercut the Environment and the Economy*. Washington DC: Island Press.

Myers, N. and Knoll, A. 2001. The biotic crisis and the future of evolution. *Proceedings of US National Academy of Sciences* 98(10): 5389–92.

Myers, N., Mittermeier, R.A., Mittermeier, C.G., da Fonseca, G.A.B. and Kent, J. 2000. Biodiversity hotspots for conservation priorities. *Nature* 403: 853–8.

O'Riordan, T. and Turner, R.K. (eds.) 1983. *Progress in Resource Management and Environmental Planning*. Chichester: John Wiley and Sons.

Pearce, D.W., Brown, K., Swanson, T. and Perrings, C. 1993. *Economics and the Conservation of Global Biological Diversity*. Washington, DC: Global Environment Facility.

Pimm, S.L., Russell, G.J., Gittleman, G.L. and Brooks, T.M. 1995. The future of biodiversity. *Science* 269: 347–54.

Pimm, S.L., and 32 others. 2001. Can we defy nature's end? *Science* 293: 2,207–8.

Prugh, T., Costanza, R., Cumberland, J.H., Daly, H., Goodland, R. and Norgaard, R.N. 1995. *Natural Capital and Human Economic Survival*. Sunderland, MA: Sinauer Associates.

Raven, P.R. 1990. The politics of preserving biodiversity. *BioScience* 40: 769–74.

Roodman, D.M. 1998. *The Natural Wealth of Nations: Harnessing the Market for the Environment*. New York: Norton.

Runyan, C. 1999. NGOs proliferate worldwide. In L.R. Brown, M. Renner and B. Halweil (eds.), *Vital Signs 1999: The Trends That Are Shaping Our Future*: pp. 144–5. New York: Norton.

Trzyna, T. (ed.) 2001. *World Directory of Environmental Organizations* (6th edition). London: Earthscan.

Union of International Organizations 1997. *Yearbook of International Organizations 1996–1997*. Munich: K.G. Saur Verlag.

Wilson, E.O. 1984. *BioPhilia: The Human Bond with Other Species*. Cambridge, MA: Harvard University Press.

1992. *The Diversity of Life*. Cambridge, MA: Harvard University Press.

Winpenny, J.T. 1991. *Values for the Environment*. London: HMSO.

Wolbarst, A. (ed.) 2001. *Solutions for an Environment in Peril*. Baltimore, MD: Johns Hopkins University Press.

Wood, A., Stedman-Edwards, P. and Mang, J. 2000. *The Root Causes of Biodiversity Loss*. London: Earthscan.

4 People, livelihoods and collective action in biodiversity management

Jules Pretty

Saving nature in protected areas

The world's first formal protected area was established on 1 March 1872, when US President Ulysses Grant designated 800,000 ha of north-west Wyoming as the Yellowstone National Park. The next to appear was in 1885 when the State of New York set aside 290,000 ha of the Adirondacks as a Forest Preserve. In neither case was the conservation of nature and wilderness the primary reason. At Yellowstone, it was to stop private companies acquiring the geysers and hot springs, and New York's concern was to maintain its drinking water supply.

These were followed by the 1890 designation of Yosemite National Park, and the 1891 amendment revising land laws to permit the creation of more forest reserves. Following this, the then President, Benjamin Harrison, proclaimed fifteen reserves over more than 5.3 million ha (Nash 1973). Reversals followed designations, such as the 1897 Forest Management Act that allowed reserves to be cleared for timber extraction. In the African colonies, authorities gazetted the first protected areas in the early twentieth century. The leading conservationists were foresters from the Imperial Institute of Forestry at Oxford, who dissociated themselves from development responsibilities. Their management philosophy emphasised that 'the public good was best served through the protection of forests and water resources, even if this meant the displacement of local communities' (McCracken 1987: 190).

Since this time, parks and nature reserves have become the predominant way of preserving nature, both for wildlife and for whole landscapes. According to the 1997 United Nations List of Protected Areas (UNEP/WCMC 2001), there are 12,754 protected areas world-wide, covering an area of 13.2 million km^2. The World Conservation Monitoring Centre records an additional 17,600 protected areas on its database that are smaller than the UN's 1,000 ha minimum criterion, adding another 28,500 km^2 to the total. All 30,000 protected areas now account for 8.83 per cent of the world's land area. Of the 191 countries with protected

61

Table 4.1 *Number of protected area sites and designated area in strictly protected regimes (end of the 1990s)*

	Africa	Asia and Pacific	Latin America and Caribbean	Rest of world	Total
Number of sites					
Total	1,254	3,706	2,362	23,028	30,350
Number in categories 1–3 (nature reserves, wildernesses, national parks and monuments)	346	944	936	8,478	10,704
Number in categories 4–6 (managed resources)	908	2,762	1,426	14,550	19,646
Proportion in categories 1–3 (%)	28	25	40	37	35
Area (million km²)					
Total area	2.06	1.85	2.16	7.16	13.23
Area in categories 1–3 (strict protection)	1.21	0.72	1.37	3.82	7.12
Area in categories 4–6 (managed resources)	0.85	1.13	0.79	3.34	6.11
Proportion in categories 1–3 (%)	59	39	63	53	54

Source: Pretty 2002.

areas, thirty-six contain 10–20 per cent of their area as designated and a further twenty-four have more than 20 per cent.

A third of all UN listed protected areas (PAs), numbering 4,310, permit no local use of natural resources. Table 4.1 summarises data from all the 30,000 PAs contained on the UNEP-WCMC database. Of the 7,322 PAs in Africa, Asia and Latin America, where many local people are still likely to require wild resources for some or all of their livelihoods, about 30 per cent are strictly protected areas, with the proportion highest in Latin America (40 per cent). The area in these three categories, though, comprises 46 per cent of the 6.07 million km² designated – a very large area to which local people are not officially permitted any access for local resources.

The concept underlying the designation of protected areas is the conservation of a 'natural' state or wilderness untouched by people (Kothari *et al.* 1989; Manning 1989; Oelschlaeger 1991; West and Brechin 1992; Pretty and Pimbert 1995). These areas are explicitly seen as 'pristine environments similar to those that existed before human interference, delicately balanced ecosystems that need to be preserved for our enjoyment and use' (Gómez-Pompa and Kaus 1992: 271). They are presented as being useful to modern society because they are sites with high biodiversity or with unique or rare species.

This is not to say that strict protection of parks does not work. A recent study of ninety-three national parks of 5,000 ha or more in size in twenty-two tropical countries has shown the value of formal designations in safeguarding important biodiversity (Bruner et al. 2001). All the studied parks were subject to human pressure, with 70 per cent having people living within their boundaries. Half had residents who contested the government's ownership of some parts of the park. Yet more than 80 per cent of the parks had as much vegetation cover as when they were established (all were more than five years old). Parks suffered less degradation than the surrounding undesignated areas. Policing seems to pay – particularly in stopping illegal logging. The most effective parks were those with clearly marked boundaries and close relations between authorities and local communities, including making payments to local people.

The belief that humans are separate from nature is old and runs deep. It has led us to see 'natural' landscapes, ecosystems and wildernesses where actually they have been shaped by human interaction and management. Equally, though, we should not conclude that all nature is an emergent property of human–nature connections. Callicott et al. (2000) rightly suggest a middle way – these polarities are helpful metaphors and rhetorical devices to focus debate. Most people prefer to stand somewhere on a spectrum between these extremes. There are wildernesses, and there is a need for protection and controls. Most 'wild' nature is an emergent property of human interventions and, globally, most nature occurs in human-dominated ecosystems. This means that human decisions and visions matter, as they can make a difference by provoking all of us to think and act differently.

Wilderness ideas

The idea of the wilderness struck a chord in the mid-nineteenth century, with the influential writers Henry David Thoreau and John Muir setting out a new philosophy for our relations with nature. This centred on the core value of wildlands to people's well-being. Without them, we are nothing; with them, we have life. Thoreau said: 'in wildness is the preservation of the world'. And Muir in turn indicted that: 'wildness is a necessity; and mountain parks and reservations are useful not only as fountains of timber and irrigating rivers, but as fountains of life' (in Oelschlaeger 1991).

But as Nash (1973), Oelschlaeger (1991), Schama (1996) and others have pointed out, these concerns for wilderness represented much more than a defence of unencroached lands. They involved the construction of a deeper idea: an imagination of something that never really existed, but proved to be successful in reawakening in our consciences the fundamental value of nature. Debates have since raged over whether 'discovered' landscapes were virgin 'lands' or 'widowed' ones (left behind after the death of indigenous peoples). Did wildernesses exist, or did we create them? Worster (1993: 5) is right to point out for North America that 'neither adjective will quite do, for the continent was far too big and diverse to be so simply gendered and personalised'. In other words, just because we constructed this idea does not mean to say it was an error. None the less, we were wrong to indicate that the wildernesses in, say, Yosemite were untouched by human hand, as these landscapes and habitats were constructed by local Ahwahneechee native Americans and their management practices to enhance hunting and gathering of valued fauna and flora.

Wilderness is an idea, and it is a deep and appealing one. Some shaping of landscape can be so subtle that we would hardly notice. Many so-called traditional groups or tribes revere nature and rely upon it. Their touch is light. Today, our touch can be heavy, but the social meaning remains. Cooper (2000) asks how natural is a nature reserve, and identifies a range of places where nature resides in the British landscape, including biodiversity reserves, wilderness areas, historic countryside parks and companion places. In an almost entirely farmed landscape, where nature is as much a product of agriculture as it is an input, the efforts to recognise and conserve biodiversity and wildness are varied. All of these are treasured as much by the people who make them or experience them as by those who gaze upon the wildest forests, savannahs or mountains. These points will be explored further in chapter 6.

Modern dispossessions

Every continent has its own tragic histories of dispossessions of those who treat the land, or parts of it, as a common resource. The dark side of the Yellowstone history is that Crow and Shoshone native Americans were driven out of their area by the army, who then managed the park for forty-four years. Today, similar exclusions persist in many strictly protected areas – that is, permitting no human interference.

The assumption that conservation of natural resources is only possible through exclusion of local people is pervasive through history. Local mismanagement has been used as an excuse to exclude people – who in turn are often seen as different from ruling elites. They may be different tribes, or different because they move about rather than engage in settled farming. States have developed value-laden terms for some of these people, such as scheduled tribes in India, minority nationalities in China, cultural minorities in the Philippines, isolated and alien peoples of Indonesia, aboriginal tribes of Taiwan, natives of Borneo and aborigines of Peninsular Malaysia.

Many of these people, nomads, pastoralists, slash-and-burn hill tribes, hunter-gatherers, gypsies and itinerants, have been a thorn in the sides of states (Pretty and Pimbert 1995; Scott 1998). States have tried to settle them, or have moved settled peoples into their regions, such as the massive forced 'transmigrasi' of Javanese rice families to the outer regions of Indonesia during the 1980s. Excluded from their own rice cultures and landscapes, the Javanese were resettled in new areas that were without rice but with unfamiliar local people. Conflicts were inevitable, even though neither of the dispossessed groups wanted this to happen.

What does forced resettlement do to people? Kaichela Dipera (1999: 131–2), a Mukalahari from Botswana, says of the Bushmen of the Kalahari Game Reserve: 'The experience of moving away is so painful when you think of it because they are moving from a place where they have been living for a long time. They know what the plants are for; they know the source of water and food. When people are moved to a new place they are cut off entirely from their culture and are moved to a place where they must start a new culture.' In truth, such disconnections are more than painful. They take away from people the very meaning of life. And these social memories of painful dispossession last generations.

An inevitable result of these exclusions is that local people are forced to struggle for their lands, the rights to which are progressively denied. This has led to many open protests, rallies and acts of sabotage against national parks and protected areas themselves. In the early 1980s, more than a hundred clashes were reported from national parks and sanctuaries in India. Later, villagers set fire to large areas of the Kanha and Nagarhole national parks in the early 1990s, when denied access to the park for forest products. In remote areas, insurgents have taken advantage of local resentment to take over the Manas Tiger Reserve in Assam, to drive out forest guards, and to invade the Kutur Tiger and Buffalo Reserve in Madya Pradesh (Roy and Jackson 1993).

Enlightened professionals began to realise that this mode of conservation simply does not work. It is expensive: much of the budget for protected areas has to be spent on aircraft, radios, weapons, vehicles, salaries of armed guards, night goggles and other 'anti-poaching' equipment (Duffy 2000). Conservationists have also begun to realise that some of the biodiversity loss observed in protected areas stems from the very restrictions placed on the activities of local people. For example, the wildlife-rich savannah ecosystems of East Africa have emerged as a result of the connectedness and co-evolution of pastoralists, their cattle and local wildlife. Without one, the others suffer. With the expulsion of Maasai from their lands in Kenya, parks are increasingly taken over by scrub and woodland, leaving less grazing for antelopes (Adams and McShane 1992).

Knowledges of nature

The knowledge and practices of local communities are only just being acknowledged by conservationists. Here the word 'traditional' is problematic. To some, it implies a backward step, knowledge wrapped up in superstition or quaint old ways. Yet for many others, the notion of 'traditional' implies a link between different ways of knowing, not of a body of knowledge itself. Indigenous people, for example, observe the world carefully, share findings, conduct experiments and adjust conclusions on a continuing basis. Their knowledges are undergoing continuous revisions. Posey (1999: 4) quotes the Four Directions Council of Canada, which has one of the best definitions of traditional: 'what is "traditional" about traditional knowledge is not its antiquity, but the way it is acquired and used. In other words, the social process of learning and sharing knowledge ... Much of this knowledge is quite new, but it has a social meaning, and legal character, entirely unlike other knowledge.'

It is inevitable that such processes must lead to greater diversity – in cultures, languages and stories about the world. Close observation of specific local circumstances leads to divergence from those observing and responding to another set of conditions. The big challenge we face is to find effective ways of synthesising the best of traditional knowledges and the best that scientific analyses can bring. Neither tradition can tell us the whole story. And here we see critical elements of knowledge for sustainability – its local legitimacy, its creation and recreation, its adaptiveness, and its embeddedness in social processes. This knowledge ties people to the land, and to each other. So when landscape is lost, it is not just a habitat or feature. It is the meaning for some people's lives.

Such knowledges are often embedded in cultural and religious systems, which give them strong legitimacy. Sacred groves, for example are often protected as homes of ancestors, but also serve an ecological function for watershed, landscape and biodiversity protection (Kothari *et al.* 1998). And such knowledge and understanding takes time to build – though it is much more rapidly lost. Writing of American geographies, Lopez

(1998: 133) says, 'to come to a specific understanding...requires not only time but a kind of local expertise, an intimacy with a place few of us ever develop. There is no way round the former requirement: if you want to know you must take the time. It is not in books.'

As these connections are eroded, by modern farming that takes away the hedgerows or trees, or by sprawling suburban settlements, then this intimacy is also lost. People then stop caring, and the consequences are serious. Lopez (1998: 138) put it this way: 'If a society forgets or no longer cares where it lives, then anyone with the political power and the will to do so can manipulate the landscape to conform to certain social ideals or nostalgic visions. People may hardly notice that anything has happened.' When the intimates go, the landscape no longer has any defenders. Again, Lopez identifies the crucial issue: 'Oddly, or perhaps not oddly, while American society continues to value local knowledge, it continues to cut such people off from any political power. This is as true of small farmers and illiterate cowboys as it is for American Indians, Hawaiians and Eskimos.'

Cognition is the action of knowing and perceiving, so cognitive systems are learning systems – they take in information, process it, and change as a result. A cognitive system coheres – it sticks together different knowledges and still remains a single whole. It goes beyond the modernist single way, or even the post-modernist recognition of fractured and multiply different knowledges. It implies synthesis and capacity to change and adapt. The Santiago theory of cognition was developed by two Chilean biologists, Humberto Maturana and Francisco Varela (1982). Capra (1996: 261) summarises it thus: 'in the emerging theory of living systems, mind is not a thing, but a process. It is cognition, the process of knowing, and it is situated with the process of life itself.'

Maturana and Varela begin by posing the question, how do organisms perceive? They then indicate that all living organisms bring forth a world, because of the fundamental differences between the way internal neurological processes work and how these interact with the world. Thus we actively construct a world as we perceive it – we are, therefore, 'structurally coupled' with our environment and this creates knowledges. Such structural coupling describes the way a living system interacts with its environment, and these recurrent interactions trigger small changes, adaptations and revisions. Cognition is not a representation, but the continual act of bringing forth a world. The constant dance of cognitive learning systems, and continually shaping and adapting to the environment, currently describes the relationship between humans and nature.

Scott (1998: 311) uses the Greek term *mētis* to describe 'forms of knowledge embedded in local experience.' *Mētis* is typically translated as meaning 'cunning' or 'cunning intelligence', but Scott says this fails to do justice to a range of practical skills and acquired intelligence represented by the term. He contrasts such *mētis* with the 'more general, abstract knowledge displayed by the state and its technical agencies' by describing villagisation in Tanzania and Ethiopia, Soviet collectivisation, the emergence of high-modernist cities and the standardisation of agriculture. Ultimate failures come when we design out *mētis*, as the state never makes the kinds of necessary daily adjustments required for the effective working of systems. *Mētis* is 'plastic, local and divergent' (Scott 1998: 332). 'It is in fact the idiosyncrasies of *mētis*, its contextualities, and its fragmentation that make it so permeable, so open to new ideas.'

It would be wrong, therefore, to think of *mētis* as traditional knowledge – because this mistakenly gives the impression that such intimate local knowledge is unchanging, rigid and unable to adapt. Indeed, this is the pre-eminent view of the modernising state. Such knowledges are worthless, or old, and must be replaced by the shining and new. There is huge flexibility and plasticity in these local knowledges. They are always changing, with some elements being lost, and others gained. In this, our individual and cultural memories are vital, as they capture the value and so give meaning to us.

The idea of diverse, parochial conditions, with each place needing a differentiated approach, does not fit well with the standardising approach of modernist development. Modernism is efficient because it aims for simplification. The central assumption is that technological solutions are universal, and so are independent of social context. This is what makes it appealing – mass production for us all. But modernist thinking inevitably leads to arrogance about the social and natural world. It allows us to make grand plans without the distraction of consulting with people. It allows us to cut through the messy and complex realities of local circumstance, and so establish a new order: an order that brings freedom from the constraints of history, and the promise of liberty. Le Corbusier, the hugely influential modernist architect, coined the phrase 'by order, bring about freedom'. But simplified rules and technologies can never create properly functioning cities. There will always be something fundamentally missing.

Benton (1998: 29) indicates that: 'There is now quite widespread agreement that . . . the dualistic opposites between subject and object, meaning and cause, mind and matter, harm and animal, and above all, culture (or society) and nature have to be rejected and transcended. The really difficult problems only start here, however.' The key problem is that the dualistic modes of thought still go very deep. We have learned them well, and find it difficult to shake them off. Technological determinism is a dominant feature of modernist thought and action – science and technology are understood as having control over nature, with the solutions to nature's problems lying in cleverer and more sophisticated technologies. At the other end of the spectrum are those who suggest that nature itself is no more than a social construction, with no ecological absolutes or opportunities for technologies to provide any value. These themes were raised in the characterisation of ecological advocacy in chapter 1, and in the language of specialisms and expertise in the changing shape of power relations in the chapter that follows.

The answer lies somewhere in the middle. We are not separated from nature; we are a fundamental part of a larger whole; and we do have some technological and institutional fixes. But we still need clear thinking and theories to be sure that we do not imply that by joining hands with nature all will be well. A world faced by fundamental ecological challenges can be reshaped by collective cognitive action – mutuality, trust and common actions reconnect the world again, all for collective and personal benefit. This is very much the theme of the next chapter.

Social capital and collective action

There has been a rapid growth in interest in the term 'social capital' in recent years. The term captures the idea that social bonds and social norms are important for sustainable livelihoods. Its value was identified by Tönnies (1887) and Kropotkin (1902) in the nineteenth century, shaped by Jacobs (1961) and Bourdieu (1986), later given a novel theoretical framework by Coleman (1988, 1990), and brought to wide attention by Putnam (1993, 1995). Coleman describes it as 'the structure of relations between actors and among actors' that encourages productive activities. These aspects of social structure and organisation act as resources for individuals to use in order to realise their personal interests. Local institutions are effective because 'they permit us to carry on our daily lives with a minimum of repetition and costly negotiation' (Bromley 1993: 2).

As it lowers the costs of working together, social capital facilitates cooperation. People have the confidence to invest in collective activities, knowing that others will also do so. They are also less likely to engage in unfettered private actions that result in negative impacts, such as resource degradation. Four central aspects have been identified (Pretty and Ward 2001), namely (i) relations of trust; (ii) reciprocity and exchanges; (iii) common rules, norms and sanctions; (iv) connectedness, networks and groups.

Relations of trust

Trust lubricates co-operation. It reduces the transaction costs between people, and so liberates resources. Instead of having to invest in monitoring others, individuals are able to trust them to act as expected. This saves money and time. It can also create a social obligation – by trusting someone this engenders reciprocal trust. There are two types of trust: the trust we have in individuals whom we know; and the trust we have in those we do not know, but which arises because of our confidence in a known social structure. Trust takes time to build, but is easily broken (Gambetta 1988; Fukuyama 1995), and when a society is pervaded by distrust, co-operative arrangements are unlikely to emerge (Baland and Platteau 1998). Dispossession and dismissal of *mētis* can destroy pre-existing patterns of trust.

Reciprocity and exchanges

Reciprocity and exchanges also increase trust. There are two types of reciprocity (Coleman 1990; Putnam *et al.* 1993). Specific reciprocity refers to simultaneous exchanges of items of roughly equal value; and diffuse reciprocity refers to a continuing relationship of exchange that at any given time may not be met, but eventually is repaid and balanced. This contributes to the development of long-term obligations between people, which can be an important part of achieving positive environmental outcomes (Platteau 1997). Participatory biodiversity management thrives on such relationships.

Common rules, norms and sanctions

Common rules, norms and sanctions are the mutually agreed or handed-down norms of behaviour that place group interests above those of individuals. They give individuals the confidence to invest in collective or group activities, knowing that others will also do so. Individuals can take responsibility and ensure their rights are not infringed. Mutually agreed sanctions ensure that those who break the rules know they will be punished.

These are sometimes called the rules of the game (Taylor 1982), or the internal morality of a social system (Coleman 1990), the cement of society (Elster 1989), or the basic values that shape beliefs (Colins and Chippendale 1991). They reflect the degree to which individuals agree to mediate or control their own behaviour. Formal rules are those set out by authorities, such as laws and regulations, while informal ones are those individuals use to shape their own everyday behaviour. Norms are, by contrast, preferences and indicate how individuals should act;

rules are stipulations of behaviour with positive and/or negative sanctions. A high social capital implies high 'internal morality', with individuals balancing individual rights with collective responsibilities (Etzioni 1995). It is precisely this sense of interest bonding that can work to promote, or to antagonise, local communities. Hence the need to be highly sensitive in biodiversity management.

Connectedness, networks and groups

Connectedness, networks and groups and the nature of relationships are a vital aspect of social capital. There may be many different types of connection between groups (trading of goods, exchange of information, mutual help, provision of loans, common celebrations such as prayer, marriages, funerals). They may be one-way or two-way, and may be long established (and so not responsive to current conditions) or subject to regular update.

Connectedness is manifested in different types of groups at the local level – from guilds and mutual aid societies, to sports clubs and credit groups, to forest, fishery or pest management groups, and to literary societies and mother and toddler groups. It also implies connections to other groups in society, from micro to macro levels (Uphoff 1993; Flora 1998; Grootaert 1998; Ward 1998; Woolcock 1998; Rowley 1999; Pretty and Ward 2001). High social capital implies a likelihood of multiple membership of organisations and links between groups. It is possible to imagine a context with large numbers of organisations, but each protecting its own interests with little cross-contact. Organisational density may be high, but inter-group connectedness low (Cernea 1993). A better form of social capital implies high organisational density and cross-organisational links.

Connectedness, therefore, has five elements:

- *local connections* – strong connections between individuals and within local groups and communities;
- *local–local connections* – horizontal connections between groups within communities or between communities, which sometimes become platforms and new higher-level institutional structures;
- *local–external connections* – vertical connections between local groups and external agencies or organisations, being one-way (usually top-down) or two-way;
- *external–external connections* – horizontal connections between external agencies, leading to integrated approaches for collaborative partnerships;
- *external connections* – strong connections between individuals within external agencies.

Even though some management agencies may recognise the value of social capital, it is common to find that by no means all of these connections are being taken into consideration. For example, a government may stress the importance of integrated approaches between different sectors and/or disciplines, but may fail to encourage two-way vertical connections with local groups. Another management approach may emphasise formation of local associations without building their linkages upwards to other external agencies. In general, two-way relationships are better than one-way, and linkages subject to regular update are generally better than historically embedded ones. In Europe, as we shall see in chapter 6, the German and Finnish examples reveal the dangers of inadequate sensitivity to local connectedness. Now, the nature conservation agencies are learning to reach out, but many lack the experience and the understanding to enable participatory biodiversity to work. Benton (1998) was right: there is still a long way to go.

Social and human capital as prerequisites for improving biodiversity

To what extent, then, are new configurations of social and human capital prerequisites for long-term improvements in biodiversity? In chapter 1, we noted the ecological research that enables natural capital to be improved in the short term with no explicit attention to social and human capital. Regulations and economic incentives are commonly used to encourage change in behaviour. These include establishment of strictly protected areas, regulations for erosion control or adoption of conservation farming, economic incentives for habitat protection, and environmental taxes (Pretty *et al.* 2000). But though these may change practice, there is rarely a positive effect on attitudes: farmers commonly revert to old practices when the incentives end or regulations are no longer enforced (Dobbs and Pretty 2001).

The social and human capital necessary for sustainable and equitable solutions to natural resource management comprises a mix of existing patterns of resource usage and that which is externally introduced for some wider purpose. External agencies or individuals can act on or work with individuals to increase their knowledge and skills, their leadership capacity and their motivations to act. They can act on or work with communities to create the conditions for the emergence of new local associations with appropriate rules and norms for resource management. If these then lead to the desired ecological improvements, then this may work constructively for human relationships.

Although there is now emerging consensus for infusing social and human capital into resources usage (cf. Narayan and Pritchett 1996; Rowley 1999), there are surprisingly few studies that have been able to compare group with individual approaches in the same context. Most have observed changes over time, with changing performance of groups being compared with earlier performance of individual approaches. Many studies of rural development have shown that when people are well organised in groups, and their knowledge is sought, incorporated and built upon during planning and implementation, then they are more likely to sustain activities after project completion (Cernea 1991; Uphoff 1992; Pretty 1995a, 1998; Röling and Wagemakers 1997; Singh and Ballabh 1997; Uphoff *et al.* 1998).

There is a danger, of course, of appearing too optimistic about local groups and their capacity to deliver economic and environmental benefits. The following chapter summarises the divisions and differences within and between communities, and how conflicts can result in environmental damage. None the less, it is now clear that new thinking and practice are needed, particularly to develop and spread forms of social organisation that are structurally suited for natural resource management and protection at local level. This usually means more than just reviving old institutions and traditions; it commonly means new forms of organisation, association and platforms for common action. These are not the sole conditions for success, but are usually a necessary first condition.

For people to invest in these approaches, they must be convinced that the benefits derived from group, joint or collective approaches will be greater than those from individual ones. External management agencies, by contrast, must be convinced that the required investment of resources to help develop social and human capital, through participatory approaches or adult education, will produce sufficient benefits to exceed the often very considerable transitional costs (Grootaert 1998; Dasgupta and Serageldin 2000). Ostrom (1998: 18) puts it this way: 'participating in solving collective-action problems is a costly and time consuming process. Enhancing the capabilities of local, public entrepreneurs is an investment activity that needs to be carried out over a long-term period.' For initiatives to persist, the benefits must then exceed both these costs and the opportunism of individual 'chancers' (free-riders) in the group-based or collective systems.

Not all forms of social capital, however, are good for everyone in a given community. A society may be well organised, have strong institutions, have embedded reciprocal mechanisms, but be based not on trust but on fear and power, such as feudal, hierarchical, racist and unjust societies

(Knight 1992). Formal rules and norms can also trap people within harmful social arrangements. Again a system may appear to have high social capital, with strong families and religious groups, but contain some individuals with severely depleted human capital through abuse or conditions of slavery or other exploitation. Some associations can also act as obstacles to the emergence of sustainable livelihoods. They may encourage conformity, perpetuate adversity and inequity, and allow certain individuals to get others to act in ways that suit only themselves (Olson 1965; Taylor 1982). Thus social capital also has its 'dark side' (Portes and Landholt 1996). These characteristics can severely impede well-meaning attempts at participatory biodiversity as summarised in the following chapter.

It is important for natural resource management agencies to distinguish between social capital embodied in such groups as sports clubs, denominational churches, parent–school associations and even bowling leagues, and that in resource-orientated groups. It is also important to distinguish social capital in contexts with a large number of institutions (high density), but little cross-membership and high excludability, from that in contexts with fewer institutions but multiple, overlapping membership of many individuals. In the face of growing uncertainty (e.g., economies, climates, political processes), the capacity of people both to innovate and to adapt technologies and practices to suit new conditions becomes vital. An important question is whether forms of social capital can be accumulated to enhance such innovation (Boyte 1995; Hamilton 1995).

Participation and inclusive social learning

The term 'participation' is now part of the normal language of most development agencies. It is such a fashion that almost everyone says that it is part of their work. This has created many paradoxes. The term has been used to justify the extension of control of the state as well as to build local capacity and self-reliance; it has been used to justify external decisions as well as to devolve power and decision making away from external agencies (Pretty 1995b).

In conventional development, participation has commonly centred on encouraging local people to contribute their labour in return for food, cash or materials. Yet these material incentives distort perceptions, create dependencies, and give the misleading impression that local people are supportive of externally driven initiatives. When little effort is made to build local skills, interests and capacity, then local people have no stake in maintaining structures or practices once the flow of incentives stops. The dilemma for authorities is that they both need and fear people's participation. They need people's agreement and support, but they fear that such wider involvement is less controllable and less precise. If this fear permits only stage-managed forms of participation, distrust and greater alienation are the most likely outcomes. This makes it all the more crucial that judgements can be made on the type of participation in use.

'Participation' is one of those words that can be interpreted in many different ways – it can mean finding something out and proceeding as originally planned; it can mean developing processes of collective learning that change the way that people think and act. The many ways that organisations interpret and use the term participation can be resolved into distinct types. These range from passive participation, where people are told what is to happen and act out predetermined roles, to self-mobilisation, where people take initiatives largely independent of external institutions (Pretty 1995b).

It has become increasingly clear that social learning is a necessary, though not sole, part of the process of adjusting or improving natural resource management. The conventional model of understanding technology adoption as a simple matter of diffusion and cultural seepage, as if by osmosis, no longer stands. But the alternative is neither simple nor mechanistic. It is to do with building the capacity of communities to learn about the complex ecological and physical complexity in their fields, farms and ecosystems, and then to act in different ways. The process of learning, if it is socially embedded and jointly engaged upon, provokes changes in behaviour (Argyris and Schön 1978; Habermas 1987; Kenmore 1999) and can bring forth a new world (Maturana and Varela 1982).

The 1990s saw an increasing understanding of how to develop these operating systems through the transformation of both social and human capital. This is social learning – a process that fosters innovation and adaptation of technologies embedded in individual and social transformation. It is associated, when it works well, with participation, rapid exchange and transfer of information when trust is good, better understanding of key ecological relationships, and rural people working in groups.

The empirical evidence tells us several important things about the benefits. Social learning leads to greater innovation as well as increased likelihood that social processes producing new practices will persist. Recent years have seen an extraordinary expansion in collective management programmes throughout the world, described variously by such terms as community management, participatory management, joint management, decentralised management, indigenous management, user participation and co-management.

Lessons from inclusive social capital programmes with positive biodiversity outcomes

Advances in social capital creation have been centred on participatory and deliberative learning processes leading to local group formation in seven sectors: (i) watershed/catchment management; (ii) forest management; (iii) water management; (iv) integrated pest management; (v) wildlife management; (vi) farmers' research groups; and (vii) micro-finance delivery (Pretty and Ward 2001). Since 1990, some 408,000–478,000 new groups have arisen in these sectors – mostly in developing countries. Most have evolved to be of similar small rather than large size (as predicted by Olson (1982)), typically with 20–30 active members. This puts the total involvement at some 8.2–14.3 million people. Most groups show the collective effort and inclusive characteristics that Flora and Flora (1993) identify as vital for improving community well-being and leading to sustainable outcomes. In these groups, social capital is both operational and effective.

Table 4.2 summarises the biodiversity outcomes of these various collective action and group-forming programmes according to a hierarchy of target systems:

(i) effects on agro-biodiversity, especially crop varietal and animal breed diversity;

Table 4.2 *Biodiversity outcomes of collective action and group-forming programmes according to a hierarchy of target systems*

Collective action and socially inclusive programmes	Target systems for biodiversity improvements			
	Agro-biodiversity	Farm system diversity	Non-farm biodiversity on or near farms	Protected area biodiversity
(i) Catchment and watershed management groups	X	X	X	
(ii) Joint forest management groups			X	X
(iii) Water users' groups	X	X		
(iv) Integrated pest management groups	X	X	X	
(v) Wildlife management groups			X	X
(vi) Farmers' groups for farm and environmental improvements	X	X	X	

Note: Micro-credit programmes are not included in this table, as they do not necessarily have a specific impact on biodiversity at a particular level.

(ii) effects on farm system diversity, comprising increases in numbers of biodiversity components in the farm system (e.g., fish, trees, vegetables, animals);

(iii) effects on non-farm biodiversity on or near farms, including plants, animals and fish, in hedgerows, woodlands and forests, fishponds and gullies;

(iv) effects on protected area biodiversity, from which farming is excluded but in which collection and use of wild production may be permitted.

Actions are required at all these levels to achieve significant biodiversity improvements, though of course no single programme of action is able to do this alone. For example, watershed and catchment management programmes are usually targeted only on the first three system levels, while joint forest management addresses non-farm and protected biodiversity, but not agro-biodiversity and farm system diversity. The important conclusion is that a combination of these socially inclusive programmes will be required at any given location for there to be real improvements in biodiversity across whole ecosystems and landscapes. This is very rare.

Differing priorities, interests and concerns of implementing and policy agencies almost always mean that there are gaps. And these gaps may mean fatal flaws in desires to improve both welfare and biodiversity over large scales. A summary of selected programmes and initiatives from both industrialised and developing countries is shown in Table 4.3, with a focus on both features of success and the limitations for wider biodiversity improvements.

Conclusions for socially inclusive biodiversity protection

The fact that interactive groups have been established does not guarantee that resources will continue to be managed sustainably or equitably. What happens over time? How do these groups change, and which will survive or terminate? Some will become highly effective, growing and diversifying their activities, whilst others will struggle on in name only. Can we say anything about the conditions that are likely to promote resilience and persistence? There is surprisingly little empirical evidence about the differing performances of groups (though see Bunch and López (1996) for Honduras and Guatemala; Bagadion and Korten (1991) for Philippines; Uphoff et al. (1998) for Sri Lanka; Krishna and Uphoff (1999) for Rajasthan, India; Curtis et al. (1999) and Heisswolf (2001) for Australia). These variously show reasonably normal distributions from low-performing to mature high-performing groups, or very skewed distribution to either end.

Table 4.3 *Summary of programmes and initiatives with favourable biodiversity outcomes*

Programme or initiative	Features of success	Limitations for wider biodiversity improvements
Farm-level initiatives		
IPM Farmers' Field Schools in Indonesia	1 million farmers have adopted low-pesticide rice farming, with biodiversity now used as key functional input to farming	Focus is at farm level only
North Yorks Moors farm scheme, England	Farm scheme designed to protect nationally important upland landscape fashioned by farming	Incentive-led scheme, and farmers may revert if money stops
Water users' groups in Sri Lanka	33,000 irrigation groups, leading to more efficient use of water and less demand on vulnerable wetlands	Farm-level programme only
Cuban national sustainable agriculture policy	Increased diversity of farming, with improved productivity, using only local resources and biodiversity as functional input	Farm systems improved, but not linked to wild biodiversity
Fish, shrimp and low-pesticide rice farming in Mekong Delta, Vietnam	Fish and shrimp introduced into rice paddies after large reductions in pesticide use	On-farm biodiversity improvements only
Dehesa and *montado* agrosylvopastoral systems in Spain and Portugal	3.5 million ha of traditional systems with high farm and wild biodiversity, supported by national schemes	Programme too small to offset losses through continued intensification
Fair trade and organic coffee in Mexico	Socially inclusive co-operatives adopt organic methods and reinvest returns in local social and economic projects	Protected areas stay protected by default
Improved fallows in Kenya and Zambia	Two-year tree fallows introduced to farm systems to increase diversity and soil regeneration, with large increases in food production	Farm- and local-level biodiversity improvements only
Farm and local region schemes		
Catchment approach to soil conservation, Kenya	4,500 local groups formed by Ministry of Agriculture for whole catchment management, with large benefits for livelihoods and diversity of systems	Protected area diversity remains responsibility of other government departments

Table 4.3 (*cont.*)

Programme or initiative	Features of success	Limitations for wider biodiversity improvements
National Landcare Programme, Australia	4,500 landcare groups formed in a decade, with major changes in attitudes and practices	Programme tended to find it difficult to address protected biodiversity
Joint forest management in India and Nepal	35,000 groups formed for local forest management over 10 million ha, with both biodiversity and productivity improvements	Group-forming approach can lead to coercion by officials to meet new targets
Red kite project, Wales	Novel partnerships between farm, environmental and economic development agencies to encourage tourism, with visitor numbers up and farm incomes improved	Focus on one species only
Marais du Cotentin et du Bessin Park, France	Internationally important marsh habitats protected through local working groups involving all stakeholders	Voluntary programme, farmers responding to incentives
Microbacias programme, Santa Caterina, Brazil	Several thousand 'friends of the land' clubs formed for whole catchment management, and sustainable farming widely adopted	Very successful in farmed landscape, but less concerned with protected area biodiversity
La Albufera National Park, Spain	Traditional methods of rice farming reintroduced in 2,000 ha of wetland of international importance to prevent ecological damage	Voluntary programme based on subsidies, and so not all farmers sign up
Centro Maya project, northern Guatemala	Adoption of soil-improving sustainable agriculture discourages farmers from slash-and-burn of forests, and markets for minor forest products are increasing forest value	NGO-led programme spreading relatively slowly
Darby watershed, Ohio, USA	163,000 ha of diverse ecological and farm systems protected through novel partnerships, with many rare species protected	Only 30 per cent of farmers have adopted conservation plans

Table 4.3 (*cont.*)

Programme or initiative	Features of success	Limitations for wider biodiversity improvements
Protected area schemes		
Prespa National Park, Greece	Organic farming encouraged to prevent pesticide damage to wetland and bird habitats, with positive biodiversity and farm outcomes	Successful approach in park has not spread elsewhere
Willapa watershed, Oregon and Washington, USA	275,000 ha of forests and marine ecosystems protected through community action and value-adding, resulting in ecologically sound local economic development	Focus on non-farmed biodiversity only
Buffer zones around Royal Chitwin National Park, Nepal	93,000 ha for tiger and rhinoceros protection; but 275,000 people in villages near park suffered crop and life losses; now 30–50 per cent of park revenues returned to local people (~$US 200,000 per year)	Programme relies on progressive policies and attitudes of national policy makers, forest department officials and local people, plus continuing flow of tourists
Marine no-take reserves in Philippines	Marine management committees formed to close off no-take areas, leading to increased fish productivity and diversity in neighbouring areas	Government of Philippines has now devolved fisheries management to local authorities, but free-riders using destructive fishing methods still undermine improved systems
Ecotourism in Carpathians, Romania	Area of largest populations of wolves and bears in Europe, income from hunters and ecotourists invested in park and forest management	Protected area biodiversity only
Campfire programme, Zimbabwe	Community-based wildlife management, with increases in income to rural communities from wildlife hunting and tourism	Little change in farm practices
Tonda wildlife management area, PNG	590,000 ha protected for use of sixteen villages of mobile shifting agriculturalists and hunters	Success relies on local people's continued support and capacity to exclude others

Sources: Pretty 1998; Pretty and Hine 2001; McNeeley and Scher 2001.

There are five core components of biodiversity programmes that successfully promote social learning and sustainable natural resource management:

(i) a conceptualisation of sustainability as being an emergent property of systems high in social, human and natural capital;

(ii) the recognition that rural people can improve their agro-ecological understanding of the complexities of their farms and related ecosystems, and that this better access to information and practices can lead to improved agricultural outcomes;

(iii) that the increased understanding is also an emergent property, derived in particular from farmers engaging in their own experimentation supported by external professionals;

(iv) that if changes to individuals are embedded in social capital in the form of relations of trust, reciprocity and co-operation, then good ideas for improvements are more likely to spread from farmer to farmer, and from group to group;

(v) that social learning processes should become an important focus for all natural resource management programmes, and that professionals should make every effort to appreciate both the complementarity of such social processes with sustainable technology development and spread, and the subtlety and care required in their implementation.

What, then, can be done both to encourage the greater adoption of group-based programmes for environmental improvements, and to identify the necessary support for groups to evolve to maturity, and thence to spread and connect with others? It seems vital that international agencies, governments, banks and NGOs must invest more in social and human capital creation. The danger is in not going far enough – being satisfied with any degree of partial progress, with the result that, as Ostrom (1998: 8) puts it, 'creating dependent citizens rather than entrepreneurial citizens reduces the capacity of citizens to produce capital'. The costs of development assistance will also inevitably increase – it is not costless to build human capital and establish new organisations.

But although group-based approaches that help build social and human capital are necessary, they are alone not sufficient conditions for achieving biodiversity improvements. Policy reform, in the patterns of ownership, new incentives and protective regulations, plus the removal of destructive subsidies, is an additional condition for shaping the wider context, so as to make it more favourable to the emergence and sustenance of local groups. This has worked well in India for the spread of joint forest management, in Sri Lanka with the national policy for water users' groups taking charge of irrigation systems, in Nepal with buffer zone management, and in Brazil for micro-watershed programmes.

One way to ensure the stability of social capital is for groups to work together by federating to influence district, regional or even national bodies. This can open up economies of scale to bring greater economic and ecological benefits. The emergence of such federated groups with strong leadership also makes it easier for government and non-governmental organisations to develop direct links with poor and excluded groups, though if these groups were dominated by the wealthy, the opposite would be true. This could result in greater empowerment of poor households, as they better draw on public services. Such interconnectedness between groups is more likely to lead to improvements in natural resources than regulatory schemes alone (Röling and Wagemakers 1998; Baland and Platteau 1998).

But these policy issues raise further questions. What happens to state–community relations when social capital in the form of local associations and their federated bodies spreads to very large numbers of people? What are the wider outcomes of improved human capital, and will the state seek to colonise these new groups? What new broad-based forms of democratic governance could emerge to support a transition to wider and greater positive outcomes for natural resources? These matters are pursued in the final chapter of this volume.

Important questions also relate to the groups themselves. 'Successful' programmes may falter if individuals start to 'burn out' – feeling that investments in social capital are no longer paying. It is vitally important that policy makers and practitioners continue to seek ways to provide support for the processes that both help groups to form, and help them mature along the lines that local people desire and need, and from which natural environments will benefit.

There are, though, concerns that the establishment of new community institutions and users' groups may not always benefit the poor. There are signs that they can all too easily become a new rhetoric without fundamentally improving equity and natural resources. If, for example, joint forest management becomes the new order of the day for foresters, then there is a very real danger that some will coerce local people into externally run groups so as to meet targets and quotas.

This is an inevitable part of any transformation process. The old guard adopts the new language, implies they were doing it all the time, and nothing really changes. But this is not a reason for abandoning the new. Just because some groups are captured by the wealthy, or are run by government staff with little real local participation, does not mean that all are seriously flawed. What it does show clearly is that the critical frontiers are inside us. Transformations must occur in the way we all think if there are to be real transformations and improvements in biodiversity and the lives of people.

REFERENCES

Adams, J.S. and McShane, T.O. 1992. *The Myth of Wild Africa*. New York: W. W. Norton and Co.

Argyris, C. and Schön, D. 1978. *Organisational Learning*. Reading, MA: Addison-Wesley.

Bagadion, B.J. and Korten, F.F. 1991. Developing irrigators' associations: a learning process approach. In M.M. Cernea (ed.), *Putting People First*, pp. 73–112. Oxford: Oxford University Press.

Baland, J.-M. and Platteau, J.-P. 1998. Division of the commons: a partial assessment of the new institutional economics of land rights. *American Journal of Agricultural Economics* 80(3): 644–50.

Benton, T. 1994. Biology and social theory in the environmental debate. In M. Redclift and T. Benton (eds.), *Social Theory and the Global Environment*, pp. 28–50. London: Routledge.

  1998. Sustainable development and the accumulation of capital: reconciling the irreconcilable? In A. Dobson (ed.), *Fairness and Futurity*. Oxford: Oxford University Press.

Bourdieu, P. 1986. The forms of capital. In *Handbook of Theory and Research for the Sociology of Education*. Westport, CT: Greenwood Press.

Boyte, H. 1995. Beyond deliberation: citizenship as public work. Paper delivered at PEGS conference, 11–12 Feb. 1995. Civic Practices Network [URL at http://www.cpn.org].

Bromley, D. 1993. Common property as metaphor: systems of knowledge, resources and the decline of individualism. *The Common Property Digest* 27: 1–8. Hyderabad: Winrock and ICRISAT.

Bruner, A.G., Gullison, R.E., Rice, R.E. and de Fonseca, G.A.B. 2001. Effectiveness of parks in protecting tropical biodiversity. *Science* 291: 125–8.

Bunch, R. and López, G. 1996. *Soil Recuperation in Central America: Sustaining Innovation after Intervention*. Gatekeeper Series SA 55, London: Sustainable Agriculture Programme, International Institute for Environment and Development.

Callicott, J.B., Crowder, L.B. and Mumford, K. 2000. Normative concepts in conservation biology. Reply to Willers and Hunter. *Conservation Biology* 14(2): 575–8.

Capra, F. 1996. *The Web of Life*. London: HarperCollins.

Cernea, M.M. 1991. *Putting People First*, 2nd edition. Oxford: Oxford University Press.

  1993. The sociologist's approach to sustainable development. *Finance and Development*, Dec.: 11–13.

Coleman, J. 1988. Social capital and the creation of human capital. *American Journal of Sociology* 94, supplement S95–S120.

  1990. *Foundations of Social Theory*. Cambridge, MA: Harvard University Press.

Colins, C.J. and Chippendale, P.J. 1991. *New Wisdom: The Nature of Social Reality*. Sunnybank, Queensland: Acorn Publications.

Cooper, N.S. 2000. How natural is a nature reserve? An ideological study of British nature conservation landscapes. *Biodiversity and Conservation* 9: 1131–52.

Curtis, A., van Nouhays, M., Robinson, W. and MacKay, J. 1999. Exploring land-care effectiveness using organisational theory. Paper to International Symposium for Society and Natural Resources, Brisbane, University of Queensland.

Dasgupta, P. and Serageldin, I. (eds.) 2000. *Social Capital: A Multiperspective Approach.* Washington, DC: World Bank.

Dipera, K. 1999. Botswana – Kaichela Dipera – Mukalahari. In D. Posey (ed.), *Cultural and Spiritual Values of Biodiversity,* pp. 131–2. London: IT Publications and UNEP.

Dobbs, T.L. and Pretty, J. 2001. *The United Kingdom's Experience with Agri-Environmental Stewardship Schemes: Lessons and Issues for the United States and Europe.* Colchester: South Dakota State University Economics Staff Paper 2001-1 and University of Essex Centre for Environment and Society, Occasional Paper 2001-1.

Duffy, R. 2000. *Killing for Conservation: Wildlife Policy in Zimbabwe.* Oxford: James Currey.

Elster, J. 1989. *The Cement of Society: A Study of Social Order.* Oxford: James Currey.

Etzioni, A. 1995. *The Spirit of Community: Rights, Responsibilities and the Communitarian Agenda.* London: Fontana Press.

Flora, C.B. and Flora, J.L. 1993. Entrepreneurial social infrastructure: a necessary ingredient. *The Annals of the American Academy of Political and Social Science* 529: 48–55.

Flora, J.L. 1998. Social capital and communities of place. *Rural Sociology* 63(4): 481–506.

Fukuyama, F. 1995. *Trust: The Social Values and the Creation of Prosperity.* New York: Free Press.

Gambetta, D. (ed.) 1988. *Trust: Making and Breaking Cooperative Relations.* Oxford: Blackwell.

Gómez-Pompa, A. and Kaus, A. 1992. Taming the wilderness myth. *BioScience* 42(4): 271–9.

Grootaert, C. 1998. Social capital: the missing link. World Bank Social Capital Initiative Working Paper 5, Washington, DC: World Bank.

Habermas, J. 1987. *Theory of Communicative Action: Critique of Functionalist Reason,* vol. II. Cambridge: Polity Press.

Hamilton, N.A. 1995. Learning to learn with farmers. PhD thesis, Wageningen Agricultural University.

Heisswolf, S. 2001. Building social capital in horticulture: factors impacting on the establishment and sustainability of farmer groups. QM742 Extension dissertation, Rural Extension Centre, Gatton College, University of Queensland.

Jacobs, J. 1961. *The Life and Death of Great American Cities.* London: Random House.

Kenmore, P.E. 1999. IPM and farmer field schools in Asia. Paper for Conference on Sustainable Agriculture: New Paradigms and Old Practices?, Bellagio Conference Center, Italy.

Knight, J. 1992. *Institutions and Social Conflict.* Cambridge: Cambridge University Press.

Kothari, A., Pande, P., Singh, S. and Dilnavaz, R. 1989. *Management of National Parks and Sanctuaries in India.* New Delhi: Indian Institute of Public Administration.

Kothari, A., Pathak, N., Anuradha, R.V. and Taneja, B. 1998. *Communities and Conservation: Natural Resource Management in South and Central Asia.* New Delhi: Sage Publications.

Krishna, A. and Uphoff, N. 1999. *Operationalising Social Capital: Explaining and Measuring Mutually Beneficial Collective Action in Rajasthan, India.* Ithaca: Cornell University Press.

Kropotkin, P. 1902. *Mutual Aid.* Boston: Extending Horizon Books, Boston (1955 edition).

Lopez, B. 1998. *About This Life: Journeys on the Threshold of Memory.* London: Harvill.

McCracken, J. 1987. Conservation priorities and local communities. In D. Anderson and R. Grove (eds.), *Conservation in Africa: People, Politics and Practice,* pp. 000–00. Cambridge: Cambridge University Press.

Manning, R.E. 1989. The nature of America: visions and revisions of wilderness. *Natural Resources Journal* 29: 25–40.

Maturana, H.R. and Varela, F.J. 1982. *The Tree of Knowledge: The Biological Roots of Human Understanding.* Boston: Shabhala Publications.

Mills, T.M. 1967. *The Sociology of Small Groups.* Englewood Cliffs, NJ: Prentice Hall.

Muir, J. 1911. *My First Summer in the Sierra.* Boston: Houghton Mifflin (reprinted in 1988 by Canongate Classics, Edinburgh).

Narayan, D. and Pritchett, L. 1996. *Cents and Sociability: Household Income and Social Capital in Rural Tanzania.* Policy Research Working Paper 1,796, Washington, DC: World Bank.

Nash, R. 1973. *Wilderness and the American Mind.* New Haven, CT: Yale University Press.

Oelschlaeger, M. 1991. *The Idea of Wilderness.* New Haven, CT: Yale University Press.

Olson, M. 1965. *The Logic of Collective Action: Public Goods and the Theory of Groups.* Cambridge, MA: Harvard University Press.

    1982. *The Rise and Decline of Nations: Economic Growth, Stagflation and Social Rigidities.* New Haven, CT: Yale University Press.

Ostrom, E. 1998. *Social Capital: A Fad or Fundamental Concept?* Center for the Study of Institutions, Population and Environmental Change, Bloomington: Indiana University.

Platteau, J.-P. 1997. Mutual insurance as an elusive concept in traditional communities. *Journal of Development Studies* 33(6): 764–79.

Portes, A. and Landolt, P. 1996. The downside of social capital. *The American Prospect* 26: 18–21.

Posey, D. 1999. *Cultural and Spiritual Values of Biodiversity.* London: IT Publications and UNEP.

Pretty, J.N. 1995a. *Regenerating Agriculture: Policies and Practice for Sustainability and Self-Reliance.* London: Earthscan.

    1995b. Participatory learning for sustainable agriculture. *World Development* 23(8): 1247–63.

    1998. *The Living Land: Agriculture, Food and Community Regeneration in Rural Europe.* London: Earthscan.

    2002. *Agri-Culture: Reconnecting People, Land and Nature.* London: Earthscan.

Pretty, J.N., Brett, C., Gee, D., Hine, R., Mason, C.F., Morison, J.I.L., Raven, H., Rayment, M. and van der Bijl, G. 2000. An assessment of the total external costs of UK agriculture. *Agricultural Systems* 65(2): 113–36.

Pretty, J.N. and Pimbert, M. 1995. Beyond conservation ideology and the wilderness myth. *Natural Resources Forum* 19(1): 5–14.

Pretty, J.N. and Ward, H. 2001. Social capital and the environment. *World Development* 29(2): 209–27.

Putnam, R. 1995. Bowling alone: America's declining social capital. *Journal of Democracy* 6(1): 65–78.

Putnam, R.D. with Leonardi, R. and Nanetti, R.Y. 1993. *Making Democracy Work: Civic Traditions in Modern Italy.* Princeton, NJ: Princeton University Press.

Röling, N.R. and Wagemakers, M.A. (eds.) 1997. *Social Learning for Sustainable Agriculture.* Cambridge: Cambridge University Press.

Rowley, J. 1999. *Working with Social Capital.* London: Department for International Development.

Roy, S.D. and Jackson, P. 1993. Mayhem in Manas. The threats to India's wildlife reserves. In E. Kemf (ed.), *Indigenous Peoples and Protected Areas,* pp. 000–00. London: Earthscan.

Schama, S. 1996. *Landscape and Memory.* London: Fontana Press.

Scott, J.C. 1998. *Seeing Like a State.* New Haven, CT: Yale University Press.

Singh, K. and Ballabh, V. 1997. *Cooperative Management of Natural Resources.* New Delhi: Sage.

Taylor, M. 1982. *Community, Anarchy and Liberty.* Cambridge: Cambridge University Press.

Tönnies, F. 1887. *Gemeinschaft und Gessellschaft (Community and Association).* London: Routledge and Kegan Paul.

UNEP/WCMC 2001. UNEP World Conservation Monitoring Centre [at URL http://www.wcmc.org.uk/].

1993. Grassroots organisations and NGO in rural development: opportunity with diminishing stakes and expanding markets. *World Development* 21(4): 607–22.

1998. Understanding social capital: learning from the analysis and experience of participation. In P. Dasgupta and I. Serageldin (eds.), *Social Capital: A Multiperspective Approach,* pp. 000–00. Washington, DC: World Bank.

Uphoff, N. *et al.* 1992. *Learning from Gal Oya: Possibilities for Participatory Development and Post-Newtonian Science.* Ithaca: Cornell University Press.

Ward, H. 1998. State, association, and community in a sustainable democratic polity: towards a green associationalism. In F. Coenen, D. Huitema and L.J. O'Toole (eds.), *Participation and the Quality of Environmental Decision Making,* pp. 27–45. Dordrecht: Kluwer Academic Publishers.

West, P.C. and Brechin, S.R. 1992. *Resident People and National Parks.* Tuscon, AR: University of Tuscon Press.

Woolcock, M. 1998. Social capital and economic development: towards a theoretical synthesis and policy framework. *Theory and Society* 27: 151–208.

Worster, D. 1993. *The Wealth of Nature: Environmental History and the Ecological Imagination.* New York: Oxford University Press.

5   Deliberative democracy and participatory biodiversity

Tim O'Riordan and Susanne Stoll-Kleemann

It has always been a liberal ideal that 'the people' control their destiny. From Aristotle onwards, the notion of *kratos* (rule) by the *demos* (people) set the basis for a struggle over power and enlightenment. Needless to say, putting such concepts into practice is hugely problematic, since there is no agreement over how rules should be created or obeyed, let alone who constitutes 'the people'. What we learn from the troubled history of democracy is that any movement to inclusionary and deliberative practices is deeply embedded in institutions of power, social relationships and cultural expectations. It is possible there can be no deliberative democracy, only many quasi-deliberative democracies, each imperfect and only partially tested for equity and effectiveness. And, as we noted in chapter 1, there may only be a biodiversity that is the result of some form of participatory perspective, whether by agreement or by rule, or by a messy combination of science, politics and imperfect institutional design. There is apparently not a 'biodiversity' that is other than socially constructed, and managed by the exercise of power, authority and empathetic care.

The purpose of this chapter is to examine the drift towards a more inclusionary and deliberative politics in the modern age, to assess how far attempts to incorporate such approaches have worked in biodiversity management, and to take a cool, hard look at its prospects in an emerging world where enduring biodiversity may well have to be participatory.

On deliberative democracy

In today's complex and specialised politics, no one seriously believes that full-blooded participatory democracy can replace some form of accountable representative democracy. Political theorists such as Weber, Schumpeter and, more recently, Beetham and Fishkin have argued for some form of coupling of elitist democracies with professional bureaucracies, to create a more articulated deliberative democracy. This is a congested literature. For readers looking for a sense of perspective, read Fishkin (1991), Goodin (1992) and O'Neill (1993). For a richly referenced short overview, see Owens (2000). For a more measured political theory, see Birnbaum *et al.* (1978). At the heart of this relationship lies the concept of Congress of Opinions, introduced over 200 years ago by the political philosopher John Stuart Mill (1991: 116–18). Mill looked for a political process through which everyone who had an opinion could either articulate it, or allow others to do so on their behalf, knowing that such views would be listened to, respected, taken into account, and judged upon in open discourse.

For any effective deliberative democracy, three fundamental principles should apply.

1 People have a right to form an opinion, have the capacity to do so, and are free to articulate it, either in their own right, or through others whom they respect and in whom they place their confidence and trust.

2 The processes of opinion sharing, and opinion resolution, are fully understood, with no distortion or bias in the manner in which opinions are transformed into final decisions.

3 All this takes place in a political arrangement in which power is diffuse and shared, and where groups can form to create a combined opinion and articulate their biases persuasively and comprehensively.

Goodin (1992: 124–87) summarises the theoretical dilemmas in trying to achieve genuinely effective deliberative democracy.

> *Choice of the self.* Who are we trying to represent when we enter a deliberative participatory process? The drive may be personal and selfish; personal and more communal; or beyond self-interest and altruistic. More likely, the 'participating self' will be a confusing and contradictory mix of all of these motivations, and indeed many more. If there is limited sense of self-esteem, then the motivation may be even more difficult to discern. If the participant is not clear about the 'self' that is being advocated, then the political role may be unclear, and the nature of participation and knowledge unpredictable.

> *Choice for the self.* Self-determination presupposes a clear sense of purpose and engagement. It may be contradictory to discover that self-determination is essentially geared to matters of collective concern. At present, it is often the case that, for individuals and groups acting in a participatory process, the distinction between self-interest and common well-being depends on the nature of the process itself, the degree of shared 'community' amongst all the players, and a culturally innate sense of common destiny. These are not common attributes.

> *Choice by the self.* This assumes that the responsibility for any final choice is achieved only by oneself. What is decided, therefore,

is what the individual selects. In a very narrow sense of this interpretation, everyone would have a veto over any collectively determined outcome. Unless, of course, choice 'for the self' is construed as a matter of mutual self-interest.

From the point of view of participatory biodiversity, it would appear that successful inclusion requires that those involved in designation, management and incentives for livelihood improvement need to be aware of, and alive to, all interests involved, all relevant cultural perspectives, and how individuals relate to families, neighbours, social groupings generally and patterns of governance. The case studies that follow illustrate that these conditions rarely apply.

Underlying the notion of participatory deliberation, therefore, is a strong presumption that more open and collectively engaged decision making is likely to be 'better' than, 'fairer' than and 'morally superior' to those procedures that do not include and deliberate. We shall test these propositions throughout the text.

The interest in some form of greater participation is driven by a number of factors. First of all, the process of governing is becoming more complex, specialised and interdependent across many levels of geographical space and political authority, and increasingly centred on many nodes of activity and analysis. In short, it is impossible to govern effectively in the modern age without some degree of involvement of interests and social-political groupings. Second, the media, and especially the internet, have opened up a huge array of sources and communication of information to anyone who is 'online'. This means that decisions and outcomes are less easy to hide, or to distort, and that pressure can be brought to bear for a huge array of interests and actors. In addition, the very existence of the internet means that it is possible to consult and to respond with relative ease, so long as one has time, resources and commitment. In a way, consultation is encouraged if for no other reason than that it is relatively easy to set it up, even if it is difficult to make it effective and inclusive.

Third, the drive for consultation, namely on informing or providing analytical data, on deepening the methods of analysis, on canvassing possible policy options, or on incorporating the views of others, means that it is becoming more expected that interests will be contacted, on many issues, and over a broadening array of actors (covering minorities, specialised expertise and marginalised communities, for example).

Yet these notable shifts in the desire for and practice of consultation by no means guarantee either inclusivity (i.e., all relevant interests) or responsiveness (i.e., face-to-face negotiations to ensure awareness of each other's positions, and a genuine search for shared argument). It is this notion of *deliberation* (i.e., the degree of depth, comprehensiveness and broad understanding, as well as revealing to other participants how and why one's interests are relevant) and of *inclusion* (i.e., widening the net of interests, networks and individuals that should be involved) that lies at the centre of this analysis. Fishkin and Luskin (1999: 1–2) distinguish between deliberation for a genuine wish to understand and influence policy, and a more rational unwillingness to get involved in such immersion because the pay-off for any individual participation is so small. In more conventional political procedures, this distinction between quality of consultation and elitism of deliberation is normally characterised by a combination of discussion or informing via consultation, and deciding through specialised analysis and legislative debate. In essence, even where participation is sought, elite structures of dominant power may still hold.

This general point is examined by Goodin (1992: 124–32) and a number of others, summarised by Owens (2000: 1,146). Anything that might be characterised by the notion of civic politics has to assume an openness of governing structures, a willingness to share power, an adaptability of management, a responsiveness of action in the face of failure or incomplete outcomes, and a reflective mode of collective assessment of performance. As Owens (2000: 1,146) put it:

The nurturing of civic virtues presents a major challenge at a time when so many people have become practiced as consumers but alienated as citizens; why should they cast off the former identity and assume the latter simply by virtue of coming into some deliberative forum ... there is also a need for critical questioning of the institutional context in which people's preferences are formed.

In this context, deliberative democracy runs alongside representative democracy, each informing and legitimising the other. The idealised power relationship is a pluralist one, namely where political power is spread widely, though not evenly, throughout society. For such conditions to hold there has to be a free press, beyond commercial as well as political manipulation, a capacity for interests to recognise their stake and articulate it, and an ability to mobilise to gain attention and to exert pressure. Pluralism depends critically on the ability of popular causes to be informed and to be able to analyse and reveal their concerns or hopes, and an open and accommodative political system and bureaucracy.

Pluralism has always been a little problematic for political theorists. Andrew Cox and his colleagues (1985: 108–22) indicate the unease between those who tend to see structuralist power relations lurking in every dark political corner, and those who feel passionately that there is a civil culture of mobilisation and interest that becomes the political culture of pluralism.

Pluralism requires an open and non-manipulative use of information by both the governing and the governed, and a healthy mutual respect for what all parties can contribute to an outcome. It is also vital that all parties assume that the outcome of the process is going to be better (fuller, fairer, more legitimate, more enduring and tolerated) than if the process had not been pluralistic. We shall see in the next chapter that this is the drive for participatory biodiversity in the English case study.

Deliberative democracy, therefore, appears to require, for its legitimacy and potency, a degree of drift in political tides towards elitism and positional structures of organised power, a tendency that is noticed to the point of galvanising action. Deliberative democracy is not just a 'negative' drive for more inclusion, however. It is increasingly a feature of a widespread tendency towards seeking greater empowerment. This does not mean so much sharing power as gaining respect, ensuring the capacity to listen and to record, and the guarantee of some form of authenticity in the way in which views are analysed and taken into account. The path towards empowerment is part of a tradition for inclusion that marks 'modernist' forms of governance, a combination of tendencies that deserve greater theoretical attention.

Empowerment and shared governance

Pluralist power relations imply that all individuals are aware of their ability to recognise what is going on in their name, and that they have a capability to express their needs and reactions in such a manner as to be respectfully heard. Such conditions imply the capacity of empowerment. For Singh and Tiki (1995: 18–20) empowerment involves four minimum conditions:

> sovereignty, freedom and democracy through broad political participation;
>
> people's control over their own resources, and their access to relevant information;
>
> building a value system consistent with people's sense of their humanity and their links to the earth and its resources;
>
> mutual self-help amongst people working together for a common good.

Pluralism and empowerment set tough conditions for any representative democracy. In principle, the following conditions should apply:

> through *socio-economic empowerment*, communities obtain collective responsibility for their own future and become managers of their own development;
>
> through *political and educational empowerment*, people should have the capabilities to understand democracy and justice, to pursue their own thoughts and outlooks, and to feel that they are able to achieve their desired levels of well-being;

through *technological empowerment*, a combination of knowledge of nature and indigenous skills with technologies and management creates an innovative blend of styles of resource use that increases human well-being and reduces environmental burdens;

through *cultural and spiritual empowerment* the perceptions of the meaning of human existence and the connectedness and trust in communities and societies can be given purpose and meaning.

Such conditions symbolise the ideal. In practice, advocacy and pressure take over these libertarian dreams. Pluralism gives way to neo-elitism, where coalitions collude to determine what gets aired and how, and structuralism enables power to be mobilised and focused on behalf of the few with resources, skills and clout to get their way. Structuralists broadly believe that the state is partially independent of the capitalist basis of resource and production, but that it is still an institutional arena for conflict and coercion. This partial independence of the hegemonic forces of capitalism combines with the propensity for elites to enter into the state via networks of influence, ideas and specialised knowledge. These elites form communities of bias that shape the state (in part) and which may compete with the dominant mode of global market economies and developmentalist ideologies. For structuralists, therefore, there is an awkward analysis of a state that is both closed to genuine innovation and transformation, because of the dominance of conventional economic analysis, yet sufficiently open to entry by particular coalitions of interventionist ideas and perspectives that some variant of pluralist driven change and political accommodation can still take place. This position is broadly the basis of the analysis that follows.

This means that the political framework adopted here is that the dominant mode of political structures tends towards elitist patterns of power, relatively stable and self-generating policy communities of mutually protected interests, and networks for policy generation that maintain such arrangements. The theory of policy communities and advocacy coalitions is explained by Jordan and O'Riordan (2000: 82–5) and earlier by Marsh and Rhodes (1992) and by Sabatier and Jenkins-Smith (1993). Yet there is sufficient scope for accommodation, driven partly by the focus of inclusion, partly by the hostility generated by exclusion, and partly because of donor pressure to ensure openness and dialogue. Some variations of deliberation and inclusion are evolving in biodiversity management, and have been doing so for some time, yet they only partially meet the objectives of ecological and social resilience, and fairness of outcome.

Bureaucracies work, for the most part, to establish their positions and to change in directions which they feel they can control. In a world of rapid change in technology, globalised economies and cultural transformations, such directed shifts may be promoted more by advocacy coalitions of combined interests than by more managed incrementalism. In this more pragmatic model, elites may form out of partial pluralistic processes, to form various combinations of interests around patterns of change that suit their needs and expectations.

For such coalitions to form in a more deliberative format, issues have to be connected across policy realms, and regimes of governing need to be ordered in a reasonably predictable manner. The conditions for a more deliberative democracy thus become possible in a different form of policy space.

> Patterns of government become more interconnected via a combination of partial empowerment, and more open partnerships.
>
> Governance through processes of shared responsibility operate through networks of connected responsibilities rather than hierarchies of power and policy dominance.
>
> Advocacy emerges through organised combinations of pressure and interest articulation, assisted by a fairly open and responsive media, and greater freedom of civil rights.
>
> Procedures for respectful representation enable governing arrangements of common purpose and agreed rules of discourse and resolution to operate in an open and revealing manner, so that coalitions of interests are enabled to understand and appreciate each other.

On widening the basis of governance

The notion of 'governance, rather than government' implies a shared responsibility for devising policy, for preparing management plans, for assessing the likelihood of meeting targets, and for auditing performance. Governance means the networking of responsibility, proactive and 'smart' management, co-operative endeavour, joined-up budgets and combined sources of income and investment, and evaluations of performance and delivery based on citizen-created measures of support.

Political theorists like Gary Stoker (1998: 17) regard 'governance' as the emergence of new styles of governing in which the boundaries between international responsibility, national responsibility and local action become blurred, where the 'market' is both privately and socially regulated into a varied mix of incentives and prescriptions, and where formal government no longer controls all the levers of power and authority. Thus the 'steering' of public affairs becomes more and more a matter of joint responsibility amongst a variety of actors.

The term 'multi-level governance' is used to describe the rapidly changing scale relationships between global, multinational, nation state, regional and local (and, indeed, sub-local). It is possible, and in some uses desirable, to bypass formal governmental structures, and direct resources and responsibilities at the level of local communities and neighbourhoods. This is a perspective well developed by Roseneu and Czempiel (1992: 281–7). Rod Rhodes (1997: 15) visualises governance as a series of interorganisational and self-managing policy networks that complement market and regulatory structures. The result is a mix of governing arrangements from self-organising community action to various patterns of public–private 'partnerships', to more formal intergovernmental arrangements around international arrangements.

Throughout this book there is a 'model' of governance that assumes some form of international framing around the Convention on Biological Diversity, some form of public–private co-operation, and a number of means of local delivery involving people indirectly through consultation, and directly through participation. The functioning of these processes depends on shared experience, mutual trust and joint commitments to legitimacy.

Dirk Messner (1998: 171–4) summarises the underlying drivers for the new governance.

> The number of potential actors in organisations, parties, interests, coalitions and informed individuals is rising and becoming more articulate and communicative.
>
> Functional differentiation of economies and civil societies, based on varied conceptions of equity and justice, means that fragmentation of policy processes requires special measures of adaptive co-ordination.
>
> Mixes of private, public and civil actors require new forms of communication and conversing as well as fresh approaches sharing power and responsibility, otherwise the 'actor space' (gaining mutual understanding amongst more and more players) will become confused and crowded.
>
> Policy means are becoming increasingly complicated, overlapping and possibly contradictory, so some form of integration is necessary. That process requires very open and adaptable networks.
>
> Policy is being made by many actors over a huge variety of geographical spheres to link global to regional to local. There is

really no 'action space' nowadays that is not both global and local.

Many actors across many policy realms compete for attention and ideological bias. To overcome the changes of persistent conflict or institutionalised inaction, policy forums supported by patterns of existing networks of citizens' interests are necessary as a supportive guide.

Society is becoming active and critical, so it requires the benefit of shared knowledge and effective communication. Channels of accommodation are vital if the state is to retain its legitimacy.

Supernational institutions drive parts of the economy, and regulation of both consumer and economic interests and environmental safeguard. The role of the nation state is, in part, as a broker between the local and the global. At times the nation state may be bypassed by local outreach to international courts of justice, or through international lending and direct funding to derive its own resource base. When communities themselves have access to income and expertise, then power (and, possibly, responsibility) may become more diffuse.

All these forces of change towards shared governance suggest that the individual actor, and a policy space such as biodiversity management, is no longer controlled by a hierarchical order. Both are increasingly becoming a battleground between elitist retention of power and more dispersed redistribution of power and resources. Stability of political structures can only be guaranteed by regular assessments as to how actors relate to each other, and how far fragmented interests may become co-ordinated and unified in new frameworks of action.

We are still some distance from these outcomes. But there are glimpses of how governance for sustainability can emerge in a modern society and economy. Box 5.1 summarises the difference between problem solving governance and shared, systems thinking governance.

BOX 5.1 FROM PROGRAMMED GOVERNANCE TO SHARED GOVERNANCE

The diagram summarises much of the surrounding text. Patterns of governing increasingly require networks of knowledge, dispute resolution procedures, shared experience, trust building and agreed predictors for taking action. All of this requires advance intelligence, proactive thinking, precautionary management and regular assessments and corrections. It sounds messy, but it is probably inevitable. The case studies reveal various aspects of this in more detail.

The practical problem solving paradigm

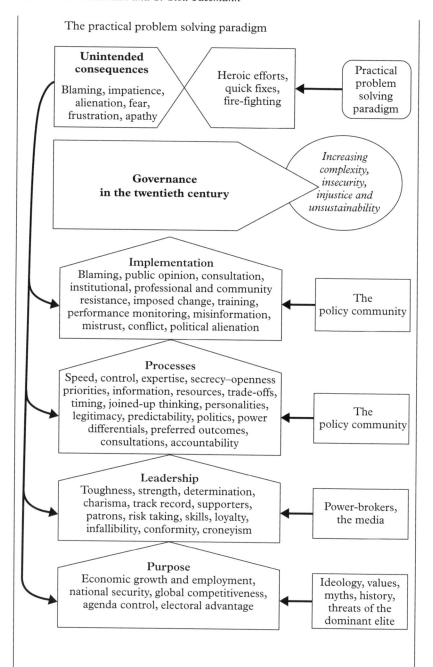

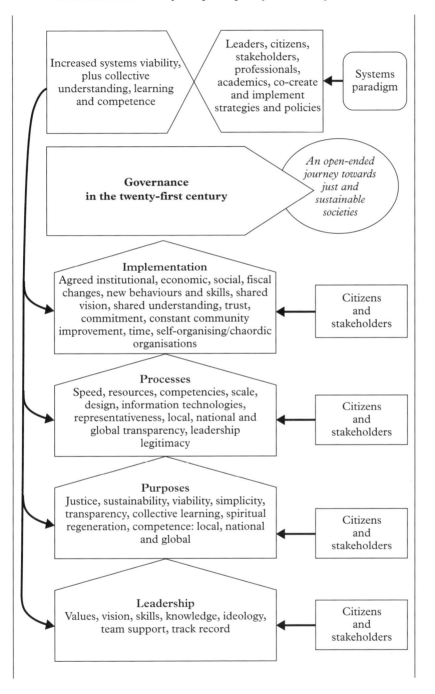

Within the systems thinking paradigm, processes for citizen and stakeholder participation play a crucial role, since it is they who, collectively, 'know' the whole system in its current state, and it is 'they who will' have to implement the new system that will achieve the purpose for justice and sustainability.

Based on Jopling 2000: 92–3.

The basis of shared governance is the concept of 'co-creation', the process of communities creating their own pathways to the future. For this to happen governance needs to combine the structures of neo-elitist power with community-based self-regulating patterns, a complex web of diverse social, economic and natural systems with resources to promote and implement their own creativity. This implies some degree of community identity and autonomy, patterns of responsibility and connectedness with a self-supported capacity to spread in terms of their own articulated needs. This suggests a process of community empowerment, an element of community income, and a network of community responsiveness to a representative democracy that is freed to create such deliberative democratic conditions.

Of course, much of this is an ideal. We have already pointed out that conceptions of democracy and polity are far from ideal in practice. Communities do not exist as collections of similar people with similar roles and expectations and demands. There are many 'communities' that form patterns of interest and association. The essence of 'community' lies in the fluidity of these networks, their scope for self-organisation and self-expression, the multiple roles that people play, and, crucially, that only a few are seriously active, but that many acknowledge their roles and responsibilities.

To bring people in may better be done by engaging them through their current activities and patterns of interests. A strategy for biodiversity may be built up from various component activities in agriculture, rural farming, entrepreneurship, forestry, leisure, wildlife conservation, as well as social justice. It is the essence of what makes associations work that must form the basis of people's inclusion. Through familiarity and identity, people can then learn to have confidence in the more coupled relationships and issues that full-hearted biodiversity management will inevitably throw up.

This suggests that the following conditions may be vital for participatory and deliberative processes to operate purposefully and progressively.

There is a vigorous community life that is broadly connected.

Action groupings and organisations may form the basis of early inclusion.

More people may be mobilised if they can be tapped on their interested enthusiasms but activated through local networks.

Participation can evolve through sequential action and increasing confidence and trust.

Actual delivery of specific strategies needs to be located where it is most effective.

This means that the patterns of delivering responsibility have to distinguish between what people are doing already, what they still want to do but cannot, and what they may be enabled to do given the resources and the capabilities to do so. This means shared, trusted and responsive governance across the board.

Dampening the enthusiasm

Deliberative democracy is an idea whose time is nigh, but which is not yet formally in place. The present structure of power and reason precludes pure empowerment and liberating capabilities. The German sociologist-philosopher Jürgen Habermas (1987) concluded that the emancipatory ideals of modernisation, articulated as the 'cultural spheres' of science, art and morals, are in danger of being subverted to the directed rationalities of commerce, expertise and private interests. Habermas believed that this take-over is being achieved by dictating the ways in which interests think and articulate their needs. This process of communicative distortion, he claimed, is a function of power, self-interest and deliberate misinformation to the point where interests cannot even realise, let alone articulate, their real needs and aspirations.

Subsequent analysts, summarised by Tewdyr-Jones and Allmendinger (1998: 1,975–6), have sought to clarify just how this deconstruction process works. They suggest three routeways.

Mobilising to meet desired ends whilst providing the respectability of listening and establishing 'fair' procedures, yet recognising pre-established patterns of power as the basis for effective decision making.

Creating structures of deliberation that enable particular rules to be shared based on pre-defined common values. By so doing, the frame of the discourse is established at the outset of any dialogue or conversation, and dominant values are undisturbed by the resulting 'conversations'.

The deliberate design of strategic behaviour through which the actor 'acts' rather than 'behaves'. By so doing, images of respectfulness, responsiveness and sharing are created that are designed to deceive and delude real objectives and desired outcomes.

These three mechanisms make it very difficult for the principles and practices of deliberative democracy to be fruitful. A critical condition for deliberative democracy is that of trust and legitimacy. Participants have to enter on the basis of trust in the processes in which they are operating, and in the spirit of reaching an outcome that is fairly and respectfully arrived at. This is the basis of political legitimacy, namely the shared acceptance of an outcome that may not be liked, but which is tolerated because it is arrived at by means that are trusted and understood. For this to occur, participants have to establish reflective means of process evaluation to be sure that in its execution the procedure has met the tests of fairness and legitimacy.

On a theoretical level, the Habermasian claim of undistorted dialogue, complete transparency of how decisions are reached, and freedom from any oppression or disempowerment, presupposes a political system that can effectively function by guaranteeing such conditions. In modern global market economies, even with a degree of social responsibility built in, and with the interest in shared power, such circumstances are remote. In any case, it is a moot point whether deliberative and participatory policies make either efficient or equitable decisions. According to David Held (1996: 281), 'it is at least questionable whether participation per se leads to consistent and desirable political outcomes; an array of possible tensions can exist between individual liberty, distributional questions of social justice, and democratic decisions'.

Consensus cannot be reached if there is a basic political schism between an individualistic and a more collectivist concept of individuals and societies. Disputes cannot be settled by discourse alone: some form of arbitration is necessary. Inevitably, any version of consensus shaping will involve a degree of inspiration through which various interests will be subjugated. As Tewdyr-Jones and Allmendinger (1998: 1,979) comment: 'the unifying assumptions and aims of communicative rationality are at odds with a desire for self-expression and difference'. To seek purity of expression in clarity of objective requires a concept of citizenship that may preclude individuality and distinctiveness. It also requires a fresh look at the dispersal of power. It is to these perspectives that we now turn.

The French philosopher Michel Foucault (see Flyvbjerg 1998 for a reliable interpretation) looked at the history of science to suggest that knowledge and the use of language were far from neutral. Indeed, power is both diffuse in society, and also concentrated in 'nodes' of discourse in ways that are shaped by expertise, specialist analysis and dominant structures of action. In chapter 1 we noted how ecologists are opening up a discourse of science into an advocacy of protection. In chapter 4, Jules Pretty suggests that participation itself influences the manner in which biodiversity is judged in terms of social practices and economic activities. Foucault's main contribution is to suggest that ways in which power is either concentrated or dispersed will be evident in the manner in which issues are raised, analysed and resolved.

In South Africa, for example, the Cape Action Plan for the Environment (CAPE) relies upon scientifically grounded, expert-driven botanical assessments of biodiversity potential as the basis for governmental and private donor involvement (legitimacy), as well as for prioritising management action and research investment in particular places (enablement). The day-to-day lives of local communities were not immediately associated with this specific approach to scientific assessment. The advocacy of biological protection was not primarily connected to the means of implementation, or indeed to the resulting implications of the daily living of local neighbourhoods, set in poverty and a general inability to obtain versatile and durable employment. Mark Botha (2001: 17), a South African conservationist, shows how the scientific narrowness of regulating plantations makes it impossible for biodiversity and local community enterprise to work hand in hand with the management of sterilised alien trees. Sterility protects biodiversity, but the trees cannot be incorporated in local conservation enterprises because they are 'alien'. Similarly, in Croatia, the long-eared bat became the vehicle for conservation action. The scientific discourse of threat and endangerment influenced the manner in which subsequent funds and management regimes were put in place.

According to Foucault, science has always been instrumental in the production of dominant knowledge, and this has helped to reinforce and shape power. He called this process of 'engraving' knowledge into outlooks and attitudes 'normalisation'. In this regard, Foucault is supported by planners such as Patsy Healey (1999) and Ortwin Renn and his colleagues (1995) who claim that the opening up of discourse through communication and awareness raising is a necessary precondition for deliberative democracy.

Owens (2000: 1,141) points out that efforts to involve stakeholder interests broadly operate on two models. One is the 'deficit' model of imperfect knowledge and non-expert 'governance', where the aim is to inform and enable understanding of preconditioned expertise. The other is the 'civic' model of deliberation and inclusion as comprehensively summarised by Holmes and Scoones (2000). This latter process is less to do with expertise, and more to do with other alternative explanations of both procedures and problem analysis. So the deliberative process aims to widen the basis of power by enabling participants to define problems from their perspectives and experiences, and to seek solutions which they regard as appropriate and suitable for their culture and aspirations. According to the Foucauldian model, the deliberative process relies on a genuine listening and accommodative mode of power dispersal and reconnection.

What is sought here is democratic engagement in the formation and articulation of values, and in policy formation and implementation – moving beyond prescribed responses to predefined problems and far removed from the quest for passive compliance with technological [or scientific] imperatives. (Owens 2000: 1,145)

This perspective of deliberative and inclusionary processes (DIPs) presupposes that there is a means of engagement and participation that will create fairer outcomes that are somehow more 'democratic'. This, in itself begs the question of whether any patterns of governance can be fair, and hence whether any particular form of DIP can be little other than the outcome of its own procedures and participatory views and adaptability. Renn and his colleagues (1995: 62) define procedural fairness as the equal opportunity for all to attend, to communicate authentically, to deliberate (i.e., accommodate to each other's position), and to decide. In practice, in any given deliberative and inclusionary process, such conditions should apply to the setting of the rules, to the procedures of deliberation, and to the willingness to share the outcome by those in power. As O'Riordan and Ward (1997) show with regard to shoreline management, these conditions do not apply, so there can be no sure mechanism for deliberation and inclusion unless citizens are assisted to become involved and helped to reach agreed outcomes, at times by changing the amount of money available and the policy envelope that frames the issue for deliberation in the first place. We shall see from the case studies that follow that this is a tough order.

The experience of participatory policy awareness

Holmes and Scoones (2000: 1) suggest that there are four ways in which civic 'knowledge' is brought to bear on policy.

> *Covert resistance.* Here individuals or groups operate in such a manner as to stop or thwart a given objective. This may be done by criminal means, or by informal means of protest, or by gossip or rumour. In a number of ways, Nuding demonstrates the resistance against a policy of preferring tourist-sought game over local food needs in Namibia, and the various ways in which the local populations are responding.
>
> *Social protest.* Here there is organised resistance by means of action by non-government bodies, or through articulated civic

disgruntlement. Some groups deliberately improve the capacity of local populations to become aware and to take opposing action. Stoll-Kleemann (2001a, 2001b) demonstrates this in the manner through which local landusing interests construct their outlooks and stereotypes to resist the designation and management of protected areas in Germany.

Formal political expression. Here the ballot box, referendum or some formal citizens' jury may be brought to bear. Biodiversity remains largely in the shadows of formal democracy, hence the claim in chapter 1 for a more advocacy but participatory science to bring out into the open the need to incorporate biodiversity into the modern political culture. In this context, Foucault is being proved right. Biodiversity is still a minority and, for the most part, a specialist and marginalised pursuit in modern political discourse. So long as this remains the case, no amount of sincerely meant deliberative and inclusionary procedures will work.

Inclusionary politics promoted by policy institutions. This forms the basis of the final analysis in this chapter. Here the attempt is specifically to identify and include as many interests as possible so that a more fully incorporated politics is brought into play. The chapter by Steelman illustrates the sincerity of attempts to incorporate community involvement into the process of conservation decision making.

Box 5.2 summarises the various purposes and 'styles' of deliberative and inclusionary processes. There are many purposes and many mechanism. So much depends on the political context and the conceptualisation of the issues under consideration. Holmes and Scoones see dangers in self-selection, as do many others (e.g., Chambers 1997; Guijt and Shah 1998),

---

BOX 5.2 CONCEPTIONS OF DEMOCRATIC DELIBERATION

Educative: This perspective views civic deliberation as a means of encouraging political learning about an issue or problem. The objectives range from simply providing individuals with more information and knowledge, to the greater expectation that as a result of such deliberation citizens can make collective political judgements and participate in decision making in the future.

Consensual: This approach stresses procedures by which participants can come to a common agreement on an issue, values or the direction of a future course of action. There is a desire to find 'common ground' through the expression of different points of view. Aware that complete consensus is unlikely, organisers following this orientation often ask citizens to use the

'I can live with it' rule to distinguish among proposals they can accept as reasonably close to their views and those they cannot accept.

Instrumental: This approach perceives direct political and legislative results as the purpose and end of democratic deliberation. Procedures are often organised around the communication of established political interests. Deliberative sessions can be judged by the standards of effectiveness, efficiency and influence. Instrumental results can include the development, improvement or blocking of a proposal.

Conflictual: This perspective emphasises giving the widest possible space to the expression and development of individual points of view without being constrained by other demands on public talk. This conception stresses conflict and difference over resolution and agreement. The results of such an orientation to deliberation may be educative and they may also serve as the basis for future decision making. But the primary focus is on unrestricted discourse.

FORMS OF DIPS USED FOR INSTRUMENTAL OBJECTIVES IN ENVIRONMENTAL POLICY MAKING

Information production: The production, through inclusive deliberation, of information/evidence needed for participants/stakeholders to examine the issues more fully.

Consultation: Policy makers bring stakeholders into the discussion about policy options, encouraging them to express their needs and views and to share their experiences. From the stakeholders' standpoint, consultation processes are best seen as an opportunity for expression. From the standpoint of policy makers, they present the chance to listen. Through consultation, policy makers can also figure out who is likely to support or oppose an initiative and how to increase support.

Monitoring and oversight: Task forces and standing committees can play an important role in oversight and in establishing broad directions for specific initiatives, while having no responsibilities for how actions are carried out. Such committees are legitimating mechanisms intended to increase support and reduce opposition among stakeholders, as well as to ensure that wide-ranging information and perspectives get incorporated into decision making and implementation.

Decision making and implementation: Delegation of planning and implementation to the non-state sector (community-based organisations (CBOs) and non-governmental organisations (NGOs)). Citizens' groups define problems, formulate solutions and action plans, and help implement activities.

Source: Holmes and Scones 2000: 5.

and recognise the inability of agencies searching out groups for inclusion as is often the case in participatory rural appraisal (see Jules Pretty in chapter 4). In many ways, such procedures can be helpful, if genuinely representative groups are incorporated. But Sanderson (1999: 303) is one of many analysts who criticise such approaches on the basis of 'ex-ante assumptions and prejudices' which may well result in no one being able to speak for the disempowered or marginalised. Unless there is not only a serious attempt at inclusivity, but also a genuine commitment on the part of those in power for the process to be aimed to work, then those involved will simply become professionalised (i.e., will do it because of their employment or interest group requirement) and alienated (i.e., they will pass through the process but with low expectations for genuine engagement).

Much of the literature reviewed by Holmes and Scoones reveals severe deficiencies in the creation and execution of deliberative and inclusionary processes. They summarise these as follows.

> Resource and time constraints usually inhibit the scale and depth of deliberation and analysis to those who can communicate effectively and speedily. This will show up in the US case study (chapter 7).

> Unwillingness to share power, especially when the outcomes are process dependent, means that many participants can rapidly become disillusioned and disengaged. This is evident in the Hickling case study, at least in its early stages (chapter 6), and also in Brazil (chapter 10).

> The demands of expertise and the capacity for adopting negotiative tactics make it difficult for those who are not expert, or accustomed to get involved. This could well be the case in the South African example (chapter 8).

> Inclusion may result in messy discourse as participants simply cannot find a common language for seeking a solution. This is evident in Namibia, despite strenuous efforts to overcome it (chapter 9).

> Bringing in a diversity of interests may 'dilute' the original objective of inclusion and result in a sub-optimal outcome. This is widely found in integrated resource development schemes as summarised by Jules Pretty in chapter 4, and by Wells and Brandon (1992) more generally.

On inclusionary participation and biodiversity management

Despite these findings, inclusion of stakeholders is widely regarded as of fundamental significance for the sustainable management of biodiversity (see West and Brechin 1991; Lucas 1992; Wells and Brandon 1992; McNeely 1995; Pretty and Pimbert 1995; Borrini-Feyerabend 1996; Batisse 1997; WBGU 2000; Brown 2001). The GEF (Global Environment Facility) (2000: 46) ties its support of National Biodiversity Strategies and Action Plans into such arrangements: 'All plans and guidelines for national biodiversity planning emphasise the importance of local participation and consultation, and these areas are allocated more than half of the budget norms of enabling activity projects.'

The following reasons are offered in favour of this participatory approach.

Democratic necessity. Bringing people into the management process recognises their self-worth, appreciates their vital role and respects their citizenship credentials. This approach also incorporates the role of local property rights (McNeely 1995; Pimbert and Pretty 1995; Barton *et al.* 1997).

Management legitimacy. Effective and efficient management requires the understanding and the support of those who have to live by the results. This is particularly evident in the Namibia case, as well as the Brazilian example (see chapter 10). Rigid management structures do not adjust easily to social, economic or ecological changes. Protected areas established authoritatively from above without prior consent may make them 'closed territories' with few links to the interrelated realms of hydrology, ecology and culture on which biodiversity so depends (Batisse 1997: 9). As McNeeley indicates, and also Nuding in the Namibian example in chapter 9, lack of serious involvement may also restrict opportunities for long-term cooperation over economic activities such as ecotourism (as advocated in Article 8 of the CBD) (e.g., McNeely 1995; Borrini-Feyerabend 1996).

Sharing knowledge and understanding is vital for the success of protected areas. All stakeholders have uniquely different perspectives as to what is a problem and what constitutes improvement. As many writers acknowledge, summarised by Holmes and Scoones (2000: 30), since human knowledge and understanding are socially constructed, what various stakeholders know and believe is a function of unique contexts and experiences. There is, therefore, no single 'correct' understanding. What is taken to be 'true' depends on the framework of knowledge and assumptions brought in by individuals and their social and occupational settings. It is essential to seek multiple perspectives on any 'problem assessment' by ensuring the wide involvement of different actors and groups (Pretty and Pimbert 1995: 10). Brown (2001) reminds us that local communities, often targeted for participatory processes, are rarely politically cohesive. They usually do not share a unified view and therefore do not always, or readily, see the need for peacefully linking multiple stakeholders and interests. Local politics, local power games, political histories, social memories and various customary biases all frame how a 'community' bonds or dissipates its energies, loyalties and trust. Rarely is a 'community' homogeneous. This is evident in the South African and Brazilian examples.

The GEF review of participation in National Biodiversity Strategy and Action Plans (NBSAPs) (GEF 2000: 40) accepts that participation is by no means easily attainable.

The broad participation of various stakeholders that started with the formation of multisectoral co-ordination committees or task forces has helped bring new information and ideas into the NBSAPs, thereby increasing their relevance and the prospects for support from various sectors. In many countries where broad participatory processes were implemented such as Argentina, Belize, Cuba, Mexico and Zimbabwe, a sense of ownership has developed. But it should be noted that the contribution of these participatory processes to sustainability depends on the extent and depth of participation by key stakeholders. Participation sometimes did not extend beyond the co-ordination committees and task forces. A significant number of countries, however, had difficulties in their participatory processes. Thus, the effect of participatory processes on sustainability also depends on continuing these processes and ensuring they complement other factors that would support full implementation of the NBSAP.

Despite its beguiling attractiveness, therefore, the 'people-inclusive' approach is by no means easy to achieve. Barton *et al.* (1997: 75–7) provide a list of impediments that should be taken into consideration when designing and implementing participatory approaches for biodiversity enhancement.

> Participation by certain disadvantaged groups may clash with local customs (e.g., the participation of women, the landless, ethnic minorities, etc.) and may be quite alien to a local democracy as culturally interpreted (see also GEF 2000: 47).

> Participatory processes require specific investments of time and resources. In particular, the process of participation may require specialised facilitation and clear objectives in order to avoid chaotic meetings and a general loss of direction. The lengthy time element, notably the apparently slow progress in early stages, can tax the patience of donors, managers, staff and local people alike. Furthermore, the particular 'culture' of stakeholders may pose difficulties. For example, Stoll-Kleemann (2001b: 38–40) found that officials of German nature conservation agencies deeply distrusted farmers and foresters on the grounds that they were 'unsound' in their

attitudes towards the need for wildlife protection and habitat safeguard. For different socio-psychological reasons, the landusers resented the officiousness of agency personnel, and bonded into solidarities of supportive biases and outlooks in order to resist and oppose nature conservation management proposals and measures.

Some compromises in conservation objectives may need to be made. For instance, a conservation initiative designed by outsiders may propose a total ban on local access to natural resources, but this may be simply unacceptable to local residents. Also, to get any kind of consensus may mean deleting conservationist objectives as shaped by advocacy ecology.

Wells and Brandon (1992: 564) describe some important 'design dilemmas' when incorporating local participation into Integrated Conservation Development Projects (ICDPs):

what the project defines as a problem (which may be the entire reason for the project's existence), e.g. decline in a species, may not be a concern of local communities ... Community participation may lead the community to define a set of needs which are not linked to the conservation objectives ... [W]hat would happen if local people decided, through participatory mechanisms, that they wanted to use the resources in an unsustainable way?

From his review and experience of wildlife management programmes in Africa, Songorwa (1999: 2,062–4) reinforces the observations of Barton *et al.* (1997: 75–7). These failures of participation include:

Failure to adopt a 'bottom-up' participatory approach with genuine local involvement and understanding. Much of this is due to an absence of empathy amongst the implementing agencies. Other factors include unclear or contested property rights, so management agreements are difficult to establish. We shall see how this occurs in Namibia and Brazil.

Empowerment is by no means a 'clean' concept (Brown 2001). We have noted the general unwillingness to share power. In any case, empowerment operates on many social dimensions, and may not be achieved by economic measures alone (see also Agawal and Gibson 1999; Cleaver 1999). This is evident in the South African example.

An inability to address basic community needs and to ensure the fair and anticipated distribution of benefits. In Tanzania, Songorwa found that wildlife protection scouts rarely received payment, and were often at odds with poachers who were their neighbours. From the Namibian example, in chapter 9, it is evident that a number of farmers rarely received the wildlife meat they were promised.

Lack of trust in the implementing agencies, failure to underwrite donor grants for poor people unable to raise their own funds, and unreliable income flows combine to create a feeling of dis-illusionment and loss of faith in the process. This undermines the unwillingness to co-ordinate and participate.

Corruption amongst local officials and community leaders may result in serious mismanagement of project funds and wildlife benefits. Consequently, requests for volunteer labour, so es-sential for the success of participatory management, may be ignored or wilfully disobeyed.

A different problem associated with implementing participatory biodi-versity strategies is described in the GEF assessment (2000: 48).

In contrast, there have been cases of 'participation fatigue' . . . where relatively small, heavily stretched organisations – both governmental and NGOs – are being exhausted by opportunities to contribute inputs to internationally driven planning projects. In other countries, there is growing sense of frustration, especially in the NGO sector, with discussing well understood issues yet again without any tangible commitments of political willpower or resources of effective action. It is a constant challenge to find the appropriate balance between the level and type of participation needed to achieve consensus and attract broad commitment on one side, with the urgent need for less talk and more action on the other hand.

Inclusionary participation is not easy in terms of theoretical analysis of modern democracies. It is also not easy in practical terms. Yet it cannot be ignored, despite the difficulties and impediments. This is why we address the notion of deliberative and inclusionary democracy in so many ways in the case studies that follow. We will draw wider conclusions in the final chapter.

Acknowledgement

Material in this chapter is drawn from an article entitled From Participa-tion to Partnership in Biodiversity Protection: Experience from Germany and South Africa, *Society and Natural Resources* Vol 15, 2. Copyright 2002 From *Society and Natural Resources*, 2002, Vol 15, 2. Reproduced by permission of Taylor and Francis, Inc., http://www.routledge-ny.com.

REFERENCES

Agawal, A. and Gibson, C.C. 1999. Enchantment and disenchantment: the role of community in natural resource conservation. *World Development* 27(4): 629–49.

Barton, T., Borrini-Feyerabend, G., de Sherbinin, A. and Warren, P. 1997. *Our People, Our Resources.* Gland and Cambridge: IUCN (The World Conservation Union).

Batisse, M. 1997. Biosphere reserves: a challenge for biodiversity conservation and regional planning. *Environment* 39: 7–33.

BNL (Der Beirat für Naturschutz und Landschaftspflege beim BMU) 1994. *Zur Akzeptanz und Durchsetzbarkeit des Naturschutzes.* Bonn: BMU (Bundesministerium für Umwelt, Natruschutz und Reaktorsicherheit).

Botha, M. 2001. Conservation first? *Elements* 4: 16–19.

Borrini-Feyerabend, G. 1996. *Collaborative Management of Protected Area: Tailoring the Approach to the Context.* Gland and Cambridge: IUCN.

Brandon, K. 1997. Policy and practical considerations in land-use strategies for biodiversity conservation. In R. Kramer, C. van Schaik and J. Johnson (eds.), *Last Stand: Protected Areas and the Defence of Tropical Biodiversity*, pp. 90–114. New York: Oxford University Press.

Birnbaum, P., Lively, J. and Parry, G. (eds.) 1978. *Democracy, Consensus and Social Contract.* London: Sage.

Brown, K. 2001. Beyond consensus and empowerment: sustainability in linking conservation and development. *Geographical Journal* (in press).

CAPE Project 2000. *Cape Action Plan for the Environment. Implementation Programme Report.* Stellenbosch: CSIR.

Chambers, R. 1997. *Whose Reality Counts? Putting the Last First.* London: Intermediate Technology Publications.

Cleaver, F. 1999. Paradoxes of participation: questioning participatory approaches to development. *Journal of International Development* 11(4): 597–612.

Cox, A., Furlong, P. and Page, E. 1985. *Power in Capitalist Society: Theory, Explanations and Cases.* Hemel Hempsted: Wheatsheaf Books.

Davey, A.G. 1998. *National System Planning for Protected Areas.* Gland and Cambridge: IUCN.

Fishkin, J.S. 1991. *Democracy and Deliberation.* New York: Yale University Press.

Fishkin, J.S. and Luskin, R.C. 1999. The quest for deliberative democracy. *The Good Society* 10(1): 1–10.

Flyvbjerg, B. 1998. *Rationality and Power.* Chicago: University of Chicago Press.

Gbadegesin, A. and Ayileka, O. 2000. Avoiding the mistakes of the past: towards a community oriented management strategy for the proposed National Park in Abuja-Nigeria. *Land Use Policy* 17: 89–100.

GEF (Global Environment Facility) 2000. *Interim Assessment of Biodiversity Enabling Activities: National Biodiversity Strategies and Action Plans.* New York: Global Environment Facility.

Goodin, R.E. 1992. *Green Political Theory.* Cambridge: Polity Press.

GTZ (Gesellschaft für Technische Zusammenarbeit) 1994. *Participatory and Self Help Approaches in Natural Resources Management.* Eschborn, Germany: GTZ.

Guijt, B. and Shah, M.K. (eds.) 1998. *The Myth of Community: Gender Issues in Participatory Development*. London: Intermediate Technology Publications.

Habermas, J. 1987. *The Philisophical Discourse of Modernity*. Cambridge: Polity Press.

Haynes, J.S. 1998. Involving communities in managing protected areas: contrasting approaches in Nepal and Britain. *Parks* 8(1): 54–61.

Healey, P. 1999. Reconstructing communicative planning theory. *Environment and Planning A* 31(6): 1,129–35.

Held, D. 1996. *Models of Democracy*. Cambridge: Polity Press.

Holmes, T. and Scoones, I. 2000. Participatory environmental policy processes: experiences from north and south. IDS Discussion Paper. Brighton: University of Sussex.

Jopling, J. (ed.) 2000. *London: Pathways to the Future by Thinking Differently*. London: Central Books.

Jordan, A. and O'Riordan, T. 2000. Environmental politics and policy processes. In T. O'Riordan (ed.) *Environmental Science for Environmental Management*, pp. 63–92. Harlow: Prentice Hall.

Lucas, P.H.C. 1992. *Protected Landscapes: A Guide for Policy-Makers and Planners*. London: Chapman and Hall.

McNeely, J.A. 1995. *Expanding Partnerships in Conservation*. Washington, DC: Island Press.

Marsh, D. and Rhodes, R. (eds.) 1992. *Policy Networks in Britain*. Oxford: Clarendon Press.

Messner, R. 1998. *Die Netzwerkgesellschaft*. Deutsches Institut für Entwicklungspolitik, Band 108. Cologne: Weltforum Verlag.

Mill, J.S. 1991. *Considerations of Representative Government*. New York: Prometheus Books.

O'Neill, J. 1993. *Ecology, Policy and Politics*. London: Routledge.

O'Riordan, T. and Ward, R. 1997. Building trust in shoreline management: creating participatory consultation in shoreline management plans. *Land Use Policy* 14(4): 257–76.

Owens, S.E. 2000. 'Engaging the public': information and deliberation in environmental policy. *Environment and Planning A*, 32(7): 1,141–8.

Pimbert, M.P. and Pretty, J.N. 1995. *Parks, People and Professionals: Putting Participation into Protected Area Management*. Geneva: United Nations Research Institute for Social Development.

Pretty, J.N. and Pimbert, M.P. 1995. Beyond conservation ideology and the wilderness myth. *Natural Resources Forum* 19: 5–14.

Renn, O., Webler, T. and Wiedemann, P. (eds.) 1995. *Fairness and Competence in Citizen Participation: Evaluating Models for Environmental Discourse*. Dordrecht: Kluwer.

Rhodes, R. 1997. *Understanding Governance*. Milton Keynes: Open University Press.

Roseneu, J.N. and Czempiel, E.-O. 1992. *Governance Without Government: Ordered Changes in a World of Politics*. Cambridge: Cambridge University Press.

Sabatier, P. and Jenkins-Smith, H.C. 1993. *Policy Change and Learning: An Advocacy Coalition Approach*. Boulder, CO: Westview Press.

Salafsky, N. and Wollenberg, E. 2000. Linking livelihoods and conservation: a conceptual framework and scale for assessing the integration of human needs and biodiversity. *World Development* 28(8): 1,431–8.

Sanderson, I. 1999. Participation and democratic renewal: from instrumental to communicative rationality? *Journal of Environmental Management* 54: 291–303.

Singh, N. and Tiki, V. (eds.) 1995. *Empowerment: Towards Sustainable Development*. London: Zed Books.

Songorwa, A.N. 1999. Community based wildlife management (CWM) in Tanzania: are the communities interested? *World Development* 27(12): 2,061–79.

SRU (Rat von Sachverständigen für Umweltfragen) 1996. *Sondergutachten Konzepte einer dauerhaft-umweltgerechten Nutzung ländlicher Räume*. Bonn: Bundestagsdrucksache 13/4109.

Stoker, G. 1998. Governance as theory. *International Social Science Journal* 155: 17–28.

Stoll, S. 1999. *Akzeptanzprobleme bei der Ausweisung von Grosschutzgebieten. Ursachenanalyse und Ansätze zu Handlungsstrategien*. Berlin: Lang.

Stoll-Kleemann, S. 2001a. Opposition to the designation of protected areas in Germany. *Journal of Environmental Planning and Management* 44(1): 111–30.

Stoll-Kleemann, S. 2001b. Reconciling opposition to protected areas management in Europe: the German experience. *Environment* 43(5): 32–44.

Tewdyr-Jones, M. and Allmendinger, P. 1998. Deconstructing communicative rationality: a critique of Habermasian communicative planning. *Environment and Planning A*, 30(7): 1,979–89.

van Schaik, C. and Kramer, R. 1997. Towards a new protection paradigm. In R. Kramer, C. van Schaik and J. Johnson (eds.), *Last Stand: Protected Areas and the Defence of Tropical Biodiversity*, pp. 212–30. New York: Oxford University Press.

Venter, A.K. and Breen, C.M. 1998. Partnership forum framework: participative framework for protected area outreach. *Environmental Management* 22: 803–15.

WBGU (Wissenschaftlicher Beirat der Bundesregierung Globale Umweltveränderungen) 2000. *Welt im Wandel: Erhaltung und nachhaltige Nutzung der Biosphäre*. Berlin and Heidelberg: Springer.

Wells, M. and Brandon, K. 1992. *People and Parks: Linking Protected Area Management with Local Communities*. Washington, DC: The International Bank of Reconstruction and Development/The World Bank.

West, P.C. and Brechin, S.R. 1991. *Resident People and National Parks: Social Dilemmas and Strategies in International Conservation*. Tucson: University of Arizona Press.

Part III

Case studies

6   The politics of biodiversity in Europe

*Tim O'Riordan, Jenny Fairbrass, Martin Welp
and Susanne Stoll-Kleemann*

The changing policy environment for biodiversity
in the European Union

Europe likes to keep its biodiversity on hold. After two millennia of expansion of human activity, few of the original habitats and species are
unaffected. For the most part what is still of conservation value is located
in designated sites with very varying degrees of protection. The 'jewel
in the crown' philosophy of safeguarding living museums of biodiversity
has, for a long time, been the preferred strategy in Europe. However,
the growing scientific evidence is that many species and habitats of value
for biodiversity lie outside the protected areas. There is therefore some
pressure to expand the protection regime to areas beyond the safeguarded
borders. This process of widening the policy base is spurred by successful
coalitions of wildlife and rural amenity groups, by the growing tourism
and leisure industry, by the political and economic insupportability of
the EU Common Agricultural and Fisheries Policies, and by the shift to
emphasising rural distinctiveness as part of the identity of locality that is
sweeping throughout Europe (see O'Riordan 2001).

This chapter will assess the history and prognosis for European biodiversity. It will particularly examine the response by EU member states to
the EU Habitats Directive (the Council Directive 92/43 on the conservation of natural habitats and of wild flora and fauna). This assessment
will look carefully at the legal and management aspects of protection of
the Natura 2000 series of specially designated sites under the Directive,
as well as the evolving EU policy for insisting on stakeholder agreements
over designation and management of these sites. The attempts to incorporate a wide range of interested parties, formerly in conflict, over the
future management of one such EU site in England, Hickling Broad and
the Upper Thurne fen, will be given prominence. So too will the emerging biodiversity politics in Germany and Finland, as part of a general
picture of how a more serious approach to inclusive integration of rural
economic change is emerging in Europe.

Possibly of the greatest significance for the future of biodiversity protection in Europe, at least for the fifteen member states of the EU and prospective accession countries, is the emergence of a sustainable development objective and an environmental incorporation mandate, in EU policies and spending programmes. Under Article 2 of the 1997 Amsterdam Treaty, the EU seeks to 'promote a harmonious, balanced and sustainable development of economic activities'. Part of this noble aspiration should operate through the 'policy integrationist' Article 3c of the same treaty: 'Environmental protection requirements must be integrated into the definition of Community policies and activities . . . in particular with a view to promoting sustainable development.'

For the 2001 Gothenburg Summit, the European Commission presented its strategy for sustainable development in the context of Article 3c (Commission of the European Communities 2001a). The Commission did not define sustainable development. We do so in Box 6.1. The crucial feature of this analysis lies in changing the nature of governance along the lines examined in the previous chapter. In addition, the bedrock of sustainability lies in maintaining the life support functions of the planet. Crucially, this covers limiting climate change, enhancing biodiversity, reducing toxic and persistent pollutants, and moving development towards empathy and integration with natural patterns of ecosystem functioning. These themes are introduced in chapter 1.

In essence, the European Commission is seeking to adopt the following principles and measures in order to achieve sustainable development (Commission of the European Communities 2001a: 5.8).

All EU policies must have sustainable development as their core concern, including agriculture, fisheries, transport and regional development.

All legislative proposals must be subject to a careful sustainability appraisal of the advantages and disadvantages of action or inaction on local economies and vulnerable social groupings.

Subsidies that encourage wasteful resource use will be removed, and price incentives will be in place for any sustaining practices. (In essence, this is political posturing. The Commission has no powers to set taxation, and many member states rely on subsidies for their own political reasons. For instance, most member states maintain agricultural subsidies in the teeth of damage to ecosystem processes. Germany still heavily subsidises its brown coal industry in face of purported commitments to CO_2 reduction. Norman Myers presses this point in Table 3.1.)

All relevant interested parties are to be included in the enactment of all policies. (This suggestion does not include any prospect

BOX 6.1 THE DOMAINS OF SUSTAINABILITY

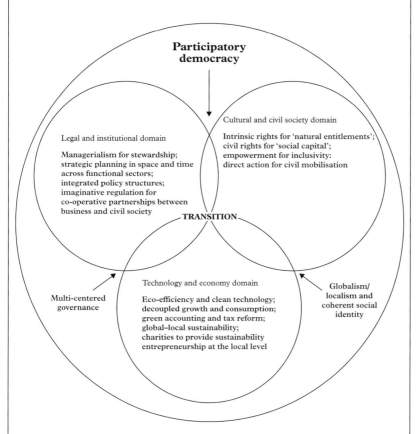

Sustainable development can mean almost anything, including the scope for fundamental contradiction. It is best to regard sustainable development as a constant process of transformation of a society and an economy towards acting as trustees for future generations of a planet who maintain and nurture life and habitability. Thus the aim is to protect and resolve material systems of re-plenishment and safeguard, to use natural functions as an economic and social asset, and to do so in such a manner that all people are enabled to appreci-ate, enjoy themselves and earn a living through maintaining neighbourliness and life support. In the diagram, this transition is approached through multi-centred and participatory governance, as described in the previous chapter, and by bringing the global to the local, and tying local actions to global con-nectedness. This is more easily claimed than achieved: hence the constant as-piration and attention. Biodiversity becomes part of natural and social rights, of appropriate pricing and incentives and of the vital link between local caring and global trusteeship. All these points were given an airing in chapter 1.

of operating through existing community networks in procedures that recognise the respect, dignity and needs of people
seeking to articulate their interests in their own ways, as outlined in chapter 5.)

Habitats and natural systems are to be protected and restored to
tackle the loss of biodiversity by 2010. Also the Commission
plans to establish a system of biodiversity indicators by 2003.

Putting these proposals into action will not prove easy for the EU. For
example, the European Commission does not have a strategic sustainability nerve centre in its pattern of policy making. There is no mechanism for bringing the strands of institutional reform in governing into
the various innovative interpretations needed of economic health, environmental integrity and social well-being. Moreover, given the character
of the EU polity, which is considered to be 'multi-level' by many EU
scholars (Jordan 2001), integrated policy making takes on the role of a
holy grail (i.e. is desirable but elusive). The essence of Jordan's careful
analysis of the EU studies literature suggests that policy integration, of
the kind that will be necessary to deliver the EU's biodiversity targets, will
not come through reforms in patterns of governance. It will probably only
succeed by establishing nationally based strategies of sustainable rural development, set in a broad framework of reforms to agriculture, fisheries,
regional development and social integration. This may be pragmatically
necessary as a 'first-move' strategy. But it will not create the degree or
type of protection that is advocated in this text. For the foreseeable future, it is likely that the European Commission will continue to cobble
together its policy initiatives and its inadequate audits in a makeshift manner, despite the aspirational rhetoric that has been forthcoming from EU
policy makers in recent years and months (see below). But the whole will
not be sustainable, because the processes of creating information and assessment will remain self-serving and detached. One particularly crucial
feature of the EU's failure of governance is its inability to incorporate
fiscal measures without unanimous support of the fifteen member states.
On the major themes of environmental taxation (see Gee 1997: 97–103)
the Commission is therefore impotent. In David Gee's analysis the losers
from any programme of ecological tax reform will be coal, lignite, oil, gas,
base chemicals, paper, cement and intensive agriculture. They are huge,
highly connected lobbies who hold the ear of the very finance ministers
who have to vote together to create the reforms that are so powerfully
opposed.

The application of biodiversity indicators proposed by the EU begs the
question of what the Commission believes biodiversity is for, and how it is
socially valued. For an ecologist microbial health may be a key indicator,

for an organic farmer it may lie in the 'feel and smell' of the soil, while for a farmer, tourist or Chamber of Commerce it may lie in a cherished species or a pretty panorama. Any indicators will need to have ecological sanity, social meaning and cultural value, and should emerge through the kinds of participatory processes outlined in the previous chapter. This is where the Hickling case study fits in. We shall see that when the science is ambivalent, or ignorant, the process of developing indicators for management plans is slow, costly and argumentative. However, before concentrating on a number of specific case studies in Germany, Finland and the UK we will review biodiversity policy at a general level in the EU, in terms of both past performance and developments in hand that are likely to impact on future strategy.

Fraying biodiversity in Europe

Europe's track record

According to a report by WWF Europe (2000: 8), more than two thirds of existing habitat types in the EU are considered endangered, and a high proportion of species are at risk of extinction. Sixty-four endemic plants have already disappeared, and 38 per cent of bird species are at high risk. Many causes have been identified. European settlement is expected to expand by 5–8 per cent over the period 1990–2010, with transport structures also swallowing up similar amounts of land surface. Some 200 habitat types listed as of European Community Importance are threatened by agricultural intensification and twenty-six such habitats are also threatened by the loss or neglect of agricultural practices that maintained their conservation status. The marine environment is especially in danger from excessive overfishing, pollution and fish farming practices, as well as tourism and general disturbance of littoral zones. None of the proposals made by the Commission for its projected sustainable development objectives is likely to overcome these root causes of biodiversity loss in the coming decade. The magnitude of the biodiversity issue in the EU is that the tides of losses, fragmentation and vulnerability by separation are continuing at a pace well beyond the repair strategies of protection of key sites and modest enhancement.

The EU has proceeded cautiously yet increasingly comprehensively towards biodiversity protection over the past twenty years. What is missing is the integrationist stand as opposed to the protectionist mission. The protection of biodiversity needs to meet certain ecological, moral and administrative purposes. Integration is altogether more difficult, and often not amenable to administrative mandates and bureaucratic grant aid. It requires a transformation in the very culture of a nation and its neighbour states. To understand better why this crisis of habitat and species loss is unlikely to be reversed or remedied in the foreseeable future, we look at the politics and implementation of the EU Habitats Directive.

The emergence and persistence of the EU Habitats Directive

Box 6.2 summarises the evolution of EU biodiversity policy. In the 1970s, there was much pressure from European citizens and interest groups over the loss of wild birds owing to shooting, pollution, drainage and inappropriate development. The migratory bird population is particularly symbolic of EU integration and co-responsibility by member states to play their part in maintaining habitats on flight paths. The result was the acceptance of the Birds Directive (70/409/EEC) in 1979. For many member states, this Directive merely reinforced existing national bird protection acts. But among the French, Spanish and Italians, the potential threat to their cherished cultural practice of shooting wild birds, especially song birds, led to much opposition and initial non-compliance.

The Birds Directive established sites known as Special Protection Areas (SPAs) as the basis for safeguard. But over the course of the first ten years, there was much foot dragging by member states in the face of the powerful agricultural and developmental lobbies. The designations of SPAs were long delayed and the sites were initially very ineffectively safeguarded. In the UK, for example, by 1992, only forty-eight SPAs had been designated, even though a larger number of internationally recognised Ramsar (wetland) sites had been proclaimed. According to the most recently available figures from the European Commission (Natura Barometer 2001), by the start of 2001 the UK had increased the number of designated sites to just over 200 SPAs. This equates to about 8,000 km^2 and accounts for about 3.5 per cent of the national UK territory. It represents a modest contribution to the overall EU site designation total of 2,920 SPAs (as at 31 January 2001) covering over 200,000 km^2.

The failure on the part of many EU member states either adequately to transpose EU biodiversity Directives or to implement fully or speedily enough has led to several crucial European court cases (see Fairbrass and Jordan 2001). European Court of Justice rulings in relation to the Birds Directive have defined some critical aspects of protected sites in the EU, and set the scene for the much broader, subsequent Habitats Directive.

These court rulings have clarified the intention of the EU to establish a sort of natural entitlement for the Natura 2000 sites. Here is a summary of the principal criteria for safeguards.

BOX 6.2 CHRONOLOGY: EU BIODIVERSITY

1979

Birds Directive 79/409/EEC

Bern Convention on the conservation of European wildlife and natural habitats was the basis of the EU Council of Ministers' Decision 82/72/EEC

Bonn Convention on the conservation of migratory wild animals was the basis of the EU Council of Ministers' Decision 82/461/EEC

1992

Habitats Directive (92/43/EEC)

Convention on Biological Diversity (CBD) signed by European Community and all of the member states at the UNCED in Rio de Janeiro

Regulation (EEC) No. 1973/92 established the LIFE financial instrument

1993

Council Decision 93/626/EEC (Oct. 1993) concerning the conclusion of the CBD

1998

Communication (COM (98) 42 final) from the Commission to the Council and the European Parliament (February 1998) on the European Community Biodiversity Strategy, based on CBD

Report on the Communication from the Commission on a European Community biodiversity strategy (COM (98) 42 and SEC (98) 348), by the Committee on the Environment, Public Health and Consumer Protection (Doc. EN\RR\362\362255 PE226.943/final)

1999

Communication from the Commission (COM (99) 543 final) entitled Europe's Environment: What directions for the future?

2000

February – Communication from the Commission (COM (2000) 154 final), Strategic Objectives 2000–2005, 'Shaping the New Europe'

March – Report from the Commission (COM (2000) 180 final) on the application of Directive 79/409/EEC on the conservation of wild birds

2001

January – Communication from the Commission (COM (2001) 31 final) on the sixth environment action programme of the European Community, 'Environment 2010: Our future, our choice'

March – Commission Communication (COM (2001) 162 final), Biodiversity Action Plan for the Conservation of Natural Resources (Volume II).

July – European Governance. A White Paper from the Commission (COM (2001) 428)

European Environment Agency publishes Europe's Environment: The Dobris Assessment

1 Economic considerations associated with development of a proposed site must not be used as an argument against designation so long as the scientific case for the integrity of the conservation status of the site is sufficiently robust. This means that a potentially significant development scheme can be thwarted by designation.

2 Where that scientific case cannot conclusively be proved, but where there is sufficient evidence that any proposed activity or development might prove a threat to the integrity of the conservation status of a site, then the precautionary principle must be applied and the development or activity amended, curtailed or prohibited in accord with the principle. This means that a biodiversity safety first policy is required, with any management scheme for a site being legally forced to place biodiversity first.

These two legal provisions are reinforced in the Habitats Directive of 1992. In one sense this appeared to be a response by the EU to the 1992 Convention on Biological Diversity. But in practice, the Directive was being promoted throughout the 1980s as part of the Environment Action Plans for the EU. It was essentially the result of particular lobbying by wildlife groups nationally and Europe-wide, together with their technical advice as to what species, and particularly habitats, provide the best protection for the range of wildlife regarded as vital for European biodiversity.

The Habitats Directive established a second category of site, the Special Area of Conservation (SAC), to complement the SPA. Together these two designations make up Sites of Community Importance (SCI), or Natura 2000, the platform for wildlife protection in the EU. In principle, all SCIs are supposed to be formally designated by 2004. At the time of writing, only about half of the proposed sites will be gazetteered. WWF Europe (2000: 35) suggests that about 35 per cent more 'shadow' sites should be designated if the aim of ensuring biodiversity is to be met. Many of these sites are located in areas where economic activity and local social values are incompatible with the objectives of the Directive. To bring them into the biodiversity fold will require much money and highly skilled participatory processes. These are not yet seriously being considered, let alone being prepared for.

Added to the SPA legal framework, summarised above, were two additional safeguards that now apply to all of Natura 2000 sites.

3 Plans and projects can only be pursued on a site when there is an imperative case of overriding national interest, and no feasible alternative exists for the proposed change. This places a straitjacket on almost all development proposals, though in practice this seemingly tough provision is often overridden by political imperatives.

4 In such circumstances compensatory measures must be secured by providing the equivalent conservation status adjacent to the existing site,

or elsewhere, according to agreed scientific advice, in order to maintain 'favourable conservation status'. So far, the scientific and participatory procedures for ensuring this are still to be assembled. So far, this will almost certainly involve many of the themes introduced in chapter 5. The crucial test of 'favourable conservation status' remains ambiguous. Essentially it means that the particular integrity, representativeness and interconnected functioning of ecosystems must remain intact, or be re-created, following any disturbance. In chapter 1 we noted that the science of biodiversity functioning has improved dramatically in recent years. In practice, however, such science depends on long periods of careful monitoring which lie well beyond the budget and staff power of competent conservation authorities and voluntary organisations. For the EU Directive to be fully effective, considerably more resources will need to be put into 'local conservation well-being' and scientific audits by coalitions of bodies, including the private sector, and a variety of local interests. Hence the issues raised in the previous chapter.

Beyond SCIs, the Directive obliges member states to improve the ecological coherence of the Natura 2000 network by ensuring that land management practices and planning procedures in linked areas, or corridors, or buffer zones, are compatible with the conservation management schemes which must be established for each site. This process has led to the formation of biodiversity action plans (BAPs) in a number of member states. These BAPs have proved to be very controversial in the UK for being too mechanistically dependent on science, insufficiently sensitive to cultural values and local customs, exclusive and formalistic in their preparation, and unable to cope with climate change, fragmentation and the continued erosion of species that remains the dominant biodiversity crisis (see Smart *et al.* 2001).

One crucial issue with BAPs, it seems, is that they fit into bureaucratic performance indicators and cover emblematic species (such as bittern and otter), so are susceptible to business sponsorship at the possible expense of the overall biodiversity value. Furthermore, they may beguile planners, developers and farmers into assuming that protection of biodiversity in managed sites is all that needs to be done. Yet as was explored in chapter 1, for biodiversity to progress, it must be regarded and promoted as a cultural and social value, locked into wealth securing activities and in tune with changing environmental circumstances and social outlooks. This is the vision that is still missing in Europe.

Monitoring performance

Since the adoption of the Birds Directive, the European Commission has itself conducted a number of progress reviews of implementation of the Birds Directive based on national reports. The most recent of these reports (European Commission 2000a) covers the years 1993 to 1995 inclusive and notes that there has been a continuing decline in bird species (almost 25 per cent over the past twenty years) owing to changes in landuse and management techniques. The report cites the intensification of agriculture as the main loss factor for 42 per cent of declining species (European Commission 2000a: 5). Subsequently, WWF Europe (2001: 12–27) has conducted a similar review of the performance of the fifteen member states in meeting the aspirations of the Habitats Directive. The main conclusions of this important review are as follows.

1 Nearly all member states have failed to transport the management and participatory features of the Directive into national legislation. This means that few SCIs are guaranteed participatory management plan preparation, and even fewer can be assured of adequate land management safeguards in their vicinity. (We shall see from the English example of Hickling Broad why this critical aspect of the Directive is proving so difficult to implement. The European Court has issued judgements against France for not incorporating management plans, and against Germany and Greece for not transposing the terms of the Directive.)

2 The timetable for proposing possible SCIs (by 1995), having these assessed for Europe-wide significance (by 1998) as candidate sites, and formally creating the network (by 2004) is slipping badly. Even by 2001, the review/assessment process had not been completed, representing a delay of three years. In addition, Germany, Greece, France, Portugal, Belgium, Italy and Ireland have all been reprimanded by the Commission for their failure to produce complete lists of proposed SCIs. All member states have yet to prove that their sites are coherently incorporated into a biodiversity strategy of habitat enhancement and linkage, rather than a collection of existing designated areas. Furthermore, most member states have been slow and evasive in their responses to 'reasoned opinions' (i.e., criticism and formal complaint) issued by the Commission. Marine sites are especially underrepresented, because they are particularly awkward to designate in the teeth of opposition by fishing, shoreline shell fishing, tourism, port and shoreline protection interests. The rule that economic bias should not influence designation is obviously being flouted.

3 No member state has yet financed adequately the management plan process, nor has adequate stakeholder participation been effective. In the UK, proposed marine sites are the subject of formal participatory procedures. Two test schemes are proving successful in ensuring

local trust and involvement. This process is only slowly beginning to reach out to terrestrial sites, as the Hickling case study indicates. In essence, the delivery of truly effective management plans for every European SCI will be at least a decade away, and even longer for the connected areas whose empathetic management will be vital for the integrity of conservation. Some successes are evident in France, which aims to establish *'documents d'objectif'* for all SCIs by 2004, and in the UK, where broad management plans are promised, also by 2004. Nevertheless these aims are still to be achieved. The objective of a 2010 stabilisation of biodiversity loss is unlikely to be met, unless there is a huge change in political will and financial and staff training resources.

4 Enforcement and monitoring the effectiveness of all these measures remains weak in all member states except Denmark, France, the Netherlands and Sweden. In similar vein, empathy and integration into planning, transport, agri-environment and development procedures are far from being added into coherent biodiversity strategies in almost all member states, despite sincere efforts in the UK, Belgium and the Netherlands.

5 Funds are available both nationally and Europe-wide for this vital integration process. In practice, not enough is being made of the Commission's offer to place elements of regional development (Structure and Cohesion Funds) and environmental protection (LIFE and Nature and agri-environmental schemes) into biodiversity enhancement. This is notably the case with regard to the linked arrangements in inhabited zones where a huge effort to incorporate and transform hostile local opinion will be vital (see Stoll-Kleemann 2001a, 2001b). To quote the WWF Europe study (2001: 22), the extent to which funding at the EU level is tapped has depended upon the efforts and success of individual NGOs and local organisations. Member states will have to look further into using budgets available under other policies such as the Common Agricultural and Fisheries Policies. The process of environmental integration should support this trend.

6 The incorporation of local interests and a broad range of values and outlooks has varied widely, with Germany and the UK making progress, and Italy, Ireland and especially Greece doing very little. The Commission is tying aid funds to the successful implementation of participatory approaches. This is proving especially effective in the case of Germany and France. This general policy of linking structural and regional development funds to comprehensive designation and management of SCIs is regarded by many as vital for the successful implementation of the Directive. In this way, biodiversity objectives should be seen as

an integral positive aspect of sustainable development, and not, as currently appears to be the case, as an impediment to economic and social progress.

Aspirations

It is clear from the review above that a good deal remains to be done to safeguard European flora and fauna fully. However, if recent EU policy statements and proposals are converted from 'aspirations' to 'reality', then a significant improvement in the track record of the EU on biodiversity protection might be on the horizon.

For example, the Commission's assessment (European Commission 1999: 8–9) of the EU's 5th Environmental Action Programme noted that with regard to nature protection and biodiversity some progress had been made in most member states. However, the report stressed that considerable efforts would still be required fully to implement the Natura 2000 network, and that priority would be given to integrating biodiversity protection into other policies. This report also argued that there should be 'full exploitation at national level of the opportunities created by the new CAP regime and Structural Funds'. Subsequently, in setting out strategic objectives for the period 2000 to 2005, the Commission (European Commission 2000b) acknowledged the degradation of the environment and called for a 'multiple Union response' in which 'a sustainable development strategy must reconcile environmental development, social progress and sustainable economic growth'.

In setting out the context for the 6th Environmental Action Programme, the Commission reflected (European Commission 2001c: 3) on the impact of the preceding one, noting that problems remained and the environment would continue to deteriorate unless:

> more progress were made with regard to implementation of environmental legislation in member states;
>
> integration of environment into economic and social policies driving the pressures in the environment was improved and deepened;
>
> stakeholders and citizens took more ownership of efforts to protect the environment;
>
> new impetus was given to measures aimed at addressing a number of serious and persistent environmental problems as well as a number of emerging concerns.

The programme document goes on to highlight four priority areas for action (European Commission 2001c: 4–5). These are: climate change, nature and biodiversity, environment and health, and sustainable use of natural resources and the management of waste. Each priority action area is assigned a specific objective. In the case of biodiversity, the programme calls for the protection and restoration of the functioning of natural systems and halting the loss of biodiversity in the EU and globally. It also demands protection against soil erosion and pollution.

It is possible that through action plans and associated target setting the EU may find the means of achieving the sort of policy integration that might assist with biodiversity protection. In a very recent Communication, the Commission describes (European Commission 2001d: 5) the action plans presented as part of that policy document as 'tools for integrating biodiversity considerations into policy-making and activities across a wide range of policy sectors'. The action plans list several objectives for the EU's biodiversity strategy and identify specific targets in each case. For example, in seeking 'fully' to implement the Habitats Directive as well as the Birds Directive, the Commission has set the target of 'full transposition' for both directives by all fifteen member states by 2002. To achieve that, the Commission will undertake to oversee member states' transposition, 'including if necessary initiating legal action, to ensure that directives are correctly incorporated into national legislation' (European Commission 2001d: 5–7).

At the broadest level, the EU has acknowledged its own failure of governance and has taken some steps that might begin to remedy identified weaknesses. To this end, in July 2001 the Commission published a White Paper (European Commission 2001b) on European Governance in combination with a consultative process (intended to continue until March 2002). The Commission openly acknowledges in the White Paper that there is a perceived inability on the part of the EU to act effectively, or where it does act effectively it does not get credit for its actions. In attempting to reform the governance of the EU, the European Commission's stated objectives include reforming policy making so that it becomes more inclusive and accountable. More effective enforcement of policy is also sought. In addition, there will be an attempt to 'refocus' the institutions so that policy becomes coherent and targeted at long-term objectives. It is possible that such reforms may create a framework in which biodiversity policy can be more potent.

In summary, the EU experience so far, with regard to biodiversity protection, is one of noble intent (reflected in the aspirational texts cited immediately above), spirited intervention on laggardly national and regional behaviour by the Commission and the Court, chronic underfunding and failure to integrate a rich interpretation of biodiversity into a wide array of policies. It remains to be seen whether these aspirations will become reality. Certainly, the difficulties of establishing and holding on to biodiversity indicators in a participatory age will also prove immense. To illustrate these challenges, we look at the current German and Finnish experience and the saga of the Upper Thurne Broads and Marshes in Norfolk.

The German experience

In Germany, the state of the environment is still a cause for concern and is far from being managed on a sustainable basis (SRU 2001): 69 per cent of the existing 500 biotope types in Germany are endangered, while one third of them face serious threats; 36 per cent of the fauna and 26.8 per cent of the flora are endangered while 90 per cent of these threatened plants and animals occur in remaining areas of natural biotopes or sites under extensive use (BfN 2000). The evidence suggests that the rate of loss of species and habitats has not slowed down significantly, and the aim to establish a national biotope network that would cover between 10 and 15 per cent is still far from being achieved (SRU 2001). It is clear that agricultural, forestry and tourism activities represent the most important environmental factors. This is influenced by a lack of funding for maintenance and monitoring, and weak legislation. As a consequence the proposal is to integrate nature conservation into the planning system and to establish management plans (Haarmann and Pretscher 1993; Eben 2001).

Nature conservationists anticipate much from the implementation of the Habitats Directive. The significance of the Natura 2000 network as a document created and ratified by all EU members is welcomed in Germany (Dieterich 1999; Ssymank *et al.* 1998; Müller-Motzfeld 2000).

The total sum of designated areas in Germany is 6.4 per cent under the Habitats Directive and 4.6 per cent under the Birds Directive. To put this into context, EU members Denmark and the Netherlands have proposed about 23.8 per cent and 17.0 per cent respectively of their national territory as SACs and 22.3 per cent or 24.1 per cent respectively as SPAs (European Commission 2001a). Nature conservation NGOs in Germany have criticised the proposed designations as being insufficient and not fully representative of the existing habitat types, and subsequently produced 'shadow lists' to complement gaps in the official lists (WWF 2000; Bund Naturschutz 1999).

The designation procedures of protected sites under Natura 2000 have not been met with wide acceptance amongst landusing and developmental interests. So there is a reluctance to implement by giving priority to economic interests. This has resulted in an incomplete list of proposed SCIs (WWF 2001).

This delay in SCI designation is a function of the German Constitution. The federal structure of Germany that divides the country into sixteen Bundesländer (federal states) means that the federal government in many cases only provides a framework legislation, while each of the Länder in turn is made responsible for implementing its own laws. This is the case for nature conservation (BfN 1997). The Länder arranged for individual timetables resulting in different schedules for implementation (BfN 1997). This has also happened with the Natura 2000 network (Stolpe and Korn 2000), where each of the Bundesländer is responsible for ratifying the Directive into its legislation (Dieterich 1999).

Differences in interpretations of the regulations between Bundesländer and ministries and government agencies within the Länder have led to a lack of co-operation and/or disagreement in how best to implement the Natura 2000 network. This is particularly true with regard to limited designation leaving out valuable sites, as well as the creation of management plans and provisions for monitoring. Inadequate financial provisions and lack of staff at both national and Länder level have also contributed to delays, as commented on by WWF (2001) and the Advisory Council of Experts on the Environment (SRU 2000). Moreover, data protection laws have made it difficult to contact landowners who do not always know how much of their property is being included in Natura 2000 designations.

Problems have also arisen from the management requirements (according to Art. 6(1), 43/92/EEC) for the management plans, found to be the most common weakness in all EU member states (WWF 2001). The management schemes are significant, because they will determine the success of the biodiversity strategy when it comes to establishing objectives for management schemes. This confusion is important for German biodiversity futures since Natura 2000 will require management plans to be implemented, so will only prove successful when such plans are reached in agreement with landusers or landowners (WWF 1999). The financial basis for these management agreements will play a crucial role in 'persuading' agriculture and forestry landowners to comply with nature conservation objectives.

Another factor in the delay in designation has been the difficulty for the state and federal nature conservation agencies to communicate in a faithful and non-threatening manner with local landusing interests. This particular aspect of stakeholder dialogue was examined in some depth in chapter 5. According to a detailed study by Stoll-Kleemann (2001a: 38–40), the nature protection agencies maintained an elite culture of scientifically driven 'ecological mission'. Capturing the analysis of the previous chapter, this professionalised management science maintained a Foucauldian power base of hierarchical superiority and dismissal of 'lay' opinion.

The science shapes the management risks that the conservation agencies apply by institutionalising the 'official culture' of land management...The science of habitat creation at management becomes a combination of practical necessities and established scientific principles, and when backed by legislative force and organisational requirement, takes on a moral niche. (Stoll-Kleemann 2001a: 39)

Because the agencies are politically weaker than their economic development brethren they tend to be more aggressive in their mission, are more strident over their moral crusade. Accordingly, they dislike the progressive practice of inclusion because many staff (less so the directors, interestingly) simply do not trust the farmers, foresters and hunters. For their part, the local landowners bond into socially supported tribes. These help to reinforce stereotypes of their self-proclaimed traditions and the conservationists' insensitivities, and lead to coalitions for effective resistance to designation and management plans (Stoll-Kleemann 2001b).

There is much political turmoil in Germany over the future of rural societies, environments and economies. This epitomises the politics of biodiversity laid down in chapters 1 and 5. Meanwhile the German biodiversity lobbies side with the conclusions of WWF Europe outlined earlier. There is still no coherence to the network, there is inadequate monitoring and funding, the pressures for development have not abated, landowners are by no means approached sympathetically. Such proposals of the Habitats Directive, and protected site management plans, could all too easily become creatures of local stakeholder deals rather than maintain biodiversity integrity. This is why supportive integrationist policies coupled to resources, training and championing leaders for participatory transformation will be vital if biodiversity is truly to be safeguarded.

The Finnish experience

Both the Convention on Biological Diversity and the Habitats Directive have given momentum to national efforts in the field of biodiversity protection in Finland. Even though Finland has long traditions in nature protection and has a comprehensive net of protected areas including national parks and strict nature reserves, these international efforts have extended the scope of biodiversity protection to include managed, non-protected areas. Also, the growing awareness of consumers of timber and paper products in Central Europe over the environmental impacts of intensive forestry has contributed to the adoption of forest management practices that are more in line with the objectives of biodiversity protection. Most notably, the implementation of the Habitats Directive brought the issue of biodiversity management onto the public agenda and into high-level political discourse at the national level.

The designation of Natura 2000 areas faced strong opposition, mainly from landowners. The protest was not new in the history of nature protection in Finland, but its intensity and media coverage reached unprecendented dimensions. Earlier conflicts had related to national conservation programmes, which were launched in order to select and designate special biotopes, like mires, old-growth forests, coasts or glacifluvial esker formations. Biodiversity also plays an important role in the use of forest resources, and forests hold the greatest number of threatened species (Rosenström and Palosaari 2000: 32). According to a recent study by Hellström (2001: 62–4) the intensity of environmental forest conflicts has been strong in comparison to many other European countries and is comparable to conflicts described by Toddi Steelman in the Pacific Northwest (chapter 7). Heated public discussions and direct action have taken place in conflicts between environmentalists and forest owners concerning the logging of old-growth forests (e.g., Kessi, Talaskangas, Kuusamo). Although the conservation of forests has been the major issue in the debate, the pressure to change forest management practices has also been very strong.

In Finland the designation of Natura 2000 areas was subject to intensive conflicts between landowners and the nature protection administration. Heated public debates took place in the mass media. Finland became a member state of the EU in 1995, three years after the EU had launched the Habitats Directive. Thus the selection of Natura 2000 areas had to start at a quick pace in order to keep up with the time schedule. Finland did not ask for a transitional period. Many other member states had started preparing a list of areas requiring special protection to maintain the favourable conservation status of habitats and plant and animal species defined in the EU Habitats Directive.

Almost no public involvement or informing took place in the early phases of the Natura 2000 process. Reasons for this were time constraints, limited resources (staff) and to some extent the predominant planning style in the nature protection administration. As in Germany, the latter did not consider public involvement as an important part of designation. There are diverging opinions about the extent to which the latter was a necessary outcome of the lack of resources. Some 40,000 landowners, some of them living in towns or abroad, would have had to be consulted. Only 400 nature protection professionals were involved in the selection of potential sites.

The strongest opposition towards Natura 2000 came from the rural population. The Central Union of Agricultural Producers and Forest

Owners (MTK) opposed the Natura 2000 process from the very beginning and caught the spirit of farmers and many other landowners characterised by opposition towards the EU and unpleasant experiences with earlier national conservation programmes. A political dimension was added to the process, since the Centre Party of Finland, at that time in opposition, was also able to channel the unrest of farmers and rural populations generally against joining the EU. Thus the strong opposition among the rural population mirrored the fear of an uncertain future caused by production quotas and numerous other regulations decided in Brussels. Typical forms of protest included letters to editors and demonstrations. Four farmers even started a hunger strike against Natura 2000. This and other events got unprecedented coverage in the public media. The conflict was especially intense in the years 1997–8. A letter addressed to the Ministry of the Environment illustrates one extreme position:

I will never accept any kind of protected area, not even to mention Natura 2000 areas, I own my land and water areas now and in future. I want to decide myself about my land I have inherited . . . and will bequeath to my children. I do not need any EU directives . . . Natura shall go back to Brussels.

The proposed sites were publicly announced and within two months 14,000 complaints were sent to the Regional Environmental Centres, which had selected the sites. Most of these complaints were sent by landowners, but other groups and individuals such as hunters also made complaints. In August 1988, the Finnish Government submitted the Natura 2000 proposals to the EU Commission. It included 1,457 sites that were compliant with the EU Habitats Directive or Bird Directive, with a total area of 47,700 km^2 – approximately 12 per cent of Finland's total surface area (Ympäristöministeriö 1999). The proposed sites were mainly existing protected areas, wilderness areas, and sites covered by national protection programmes. Parallel to this, complaints were brought into higher levels of the juridical system. The legal battle ended basically with a decision made by the Supreme Administrative Court in June 2000: almost all complaints were rejected. After that Finland worked on the selection of additional sites to complete the national Natura 2000 network proposals. The proposal, including 289 new sites or extensions to existing sites and with a total land area of 670 km^2, was approved by the Finnish Government in May 2002.

A direct dialogue between the nature protection authorities and various stakeholders did not take place in the Natura 2000 conflict. The discourse was characterised by accusations, rumours and political attacks in the public media. The outcome and the effects of the conflict were diverse.

On the one hand the conflict raised awareness concerning biodiversity protection. Natura 2000 is very well known among Finnish citizens. But on the other hand the conflict seriously endangered trust between nature protection administration and many landowners, forest owners and farmers. Nature protection professionals have criticised the fact that the Natura 2000 conflict too heavily dominated the public discourse. For example, the National Action Plan for Biodiversity in Finland, 1997–2000, sets out 124 specific measures, including for example required legislative reforms and the incorporation of biodiversity in the daily routine of administration, trade and industry (Ministry of the Environment 1997: 6–17). In comparison to the designation of Natura 2000 areas, the National Action Plan was very much a plan made within the public bureaucracy; it was not visible in the public media. Contrary to Natura 2000 the Plan has never entered the consciousness of the ordinary citizen.

The designation of Natura 2000 is an example of how too tightly scheduled top-down processes can negatively influence trust between users of natural resources and nature protection authorities. No effort was made to create a shared knowledge base for evaluation of potential Natura 2000 sites. In a recent publication, Saaristo (2000) asserts that the Natura 2000 process was too heavily based on expert knowledge. The selection of the sites was based on natural sciences criteria (Press release of the Ministry of the Environment 11.6.1997). Participatory assessment and the use of methods such as Integrated Assessment Focus Groups could have been used to involve ordinary citizens in the assessment of policy options (Kasemir et al. 2000). The scientific bias in discourse can be stultifying as much as persuading, as outlined in the previous chapter.

'Nature and its biodiversity, the environment and the national heritage are the responsibility of everyone', states Finland's new constitution, section 20 (2000). Thus people should be given an opportunity to participate in the selection and management of protected areas. The conflict and public debate have had a strong influence on later policy processes in the field of biodiversity protection. For example, in a recent policy effort to protect old-growth forests in southern Finland a broad-based committee has been established to find innovative and flexible mechanisms for biodiversity protection in privately and publicly owned forests.

The Hickling experience

Hickling Broad is the remnant of a man-made lake dating back to the mid-fourteenth century. Its 130 ha of open water are a key element in an area of internationally recognised wetland known as the Upper Thurne Broads and Marshes (see Box 6.3). The open-water habitat of the four broads

BOX 6.3 INTERNATIONALLY IMPORTANT ECOLOGICAL
FEATURES ASSOCIATED WITH THE UPPER THURNE
BROADS AND MARSHES (RAMSAR) SITE

Amalgamated interests associated with the open-water and marginal swamp
habitats include:

the open-water communities

rare species: holly-leafed naiad and the stoneworts *Nitellopsis obtusa, Chara
intermedia* and *Chara connivens*

outstanding numbers of wintering waterfowl, 3,000–4,000, including
notable populations of wigeon, gadwall, mallard (1,250), teal (1,250), shov-
eler (max. 700); other notable populations including mute swan and
pochard

marginal swamp providing breeding habitat for water rail, gadwall, garganey
and particularly significant numbers of pochard

marginal fen habitats with mixed fen vegetation

scarce species: cowbane, marsh sow thistle, milk parsley and greater water
parsnip

rare breeding birds: marsh harrier, bittern, bearded tit, Cetti's warbler and
Savi's warbler

notable for wintering hen harrier

rare or uncommon insect species including Swallowtail, Fenn's wainscot and
reed leopard

Broads features which are candidates for Special Area of Conservation	Upper Thurne Broads and Marshes	Hickling Broad and its margins	Comment on Hickling Broad and its margins
Fen with saw-sedge	YES	YES	Much of fen around the broad of European interest
Alder woodland	YES	YES	
Nutrient-rich water bodies with pondweed	YES	YES	Naturally nutrient-rich lakes with *Chara*/pondweed/ milfoil/yellow water lily community; Hickling Broad represents 43 per cent of Broads cSAC feature
Quaking mires Spring-fed fens Fen orchid	YES		
Desmoulin's snail	YES	YES	Records from marginal fen habitats

Broadland SPA features	Upper Thurne Broads and Marshes	Hickling Broad and its margins	Comment on Hickling Broad and its margins
Bittern	YES	YES	1912 re-established at Hickling, 1950s 15 boomers, 1980s 3 boomers, 1991 none recorded, 1999 2 boomers and one nest
Bewick's swan	YES		During the 1980s peak counts of 20–200 of recorded, up to a third of Broads population
Whooper swan	YES		Past decades average peak counts of about 20, representing about a fifth of the Broads population
Marsh harrier	YES		
Hen harrier	YES		
Ruff	YES		
Wigeon	YES	YES	1980s 200–700 roosted on the broad, 1990s reduced numbers; Broads population about 10,000
Gadwall	YES	YES	Up to 300 but 100 average, representing between a half and a quarter of the Broads population
Shoveler	YES	YES	1970s counts of 700 and 800; more recently fairly constant at about 100 birds; Broads mean population 675

Additional proposed cSAC features	Upper Thurne Broads and Marshes	Hickling Broad and its margins
Nutrient-poor water bodies with *Chara*	YES	YES Hickling Broad represents 76 per cent of Broads cSAC feature
Purple moor grass meadows	YES	
Otter	YES	YES

This table was compiled by English Nature, the competent nature conservation authority for the UK government. It reveals the potential for a fully biodiverse restorative programme through which sailing, fishing, boating and wildlife appreciation can work hand in hand. The essential ingredient, however, is the restoration of ecological integrity.

(lakes) contains species of community importance such as holly-leafed naiad, and five species of stonewort (*Chara* spp.), notably *C. intermedia*, *C. connivens* and *C. asperens*. A large number of resident and migratory birds occupy the site, all of which are of regional, national or international significance. The fen marshes include orchids, butterflies, dragonflies, and many birds, including pink-footed geese and 20,000 plus waterfowl (great crested grebe, cormorant, white-fronted goose, teal, pochard, tufted duck and coot).

The area is managed and owned by the Norfolk Wildlife Trust the National Trust and the Broads Authority. The first two are voluntary charities, the third a special statutory body with a remit to promote wildlife, enhance tourism and local livelihoods, and maintain navigation. Hickling Broad is also used for commercial holiday boating, for wind surfing and for dinghy and open-hulled yacht racing. Its culture of sailing is long established and deeply cherished. The local economy depends to a large extent on recreation (fishing, boating and sailing) and day-visitor spending in the nature reserves.

Since the 1950s Hickling Broad in particular has suffered from nutrient enrichment. This has primarily been caused by many thousands of roosting gulls, though local agricultural drainage and intensification has also been a contributory factor. Eutrophication has lowered plant density and encouraged algal growth and sedimentation. The broad is getting shallower, so sailing with deep-keeled boats is becoming confined to a specially dredged channel. In 1994 the Authority began a cutting programme of removal of two common plant species (not protected by the Directive), milfoil and pondweed. This took place over zones where sailing could continue, but the plants were also protected by buoys. This cutting programme was maintained at 60 cm height to protect the *Chara* and naiad.

The ecological science of the Upper Thurne Broads and Marshes is by no means well understood. The area experiences salt intrusion, but it is not clear whence such pulses emanate. The broad is tidal, and sea level rise plus lower water tables in dry summers could be influential. It is possible that if the whole upper catchment was 're-wetted' by removing the drainage, underlying salt water could be displaced into the broad. This degree of scientific uncertainty makes participatory management planning very awkward, yet exceedingly necessary, as a variety of 'knowledges' have to get involved.

Yet salt affects plant growth, as does bird grazing, and may increase outbreaks of *Prymnesium*, a blue-green alga that is toxic to freshwater fish. The surrounding farmlands are for the most part drained, and the drainage water contains nutrients and sediment. Again it is not known how these flows and fluxes affect the ecology of the broad. Ecologists are very unsure of precisely what might happen when the ecological clock is reversed. This level of ignorance breaches the precautionary principle, rendering the sensitive implementation of the Habitats Directive quite problematic. Scientific ignorance is especially disadvantageous for inclusive and consensus-based participatory processes, notably where ecological integrity is sought as the primary objective for future management. Following the points raised in the previous chapter, without the 'order' of scientific prognoses, or at least agreed principles of precaution, it is extremely difficult to share power through common understanding. It is this communicative uncertainty that is proving so troublesome to the Hickling process.

In early 1998 Hickling Broad became clear for the first time in several decades. *Chara intermedia* grew to 100 cm. Because this is a plant of European importance, cutting of the milfoil and pondweed was suspended. The plant became so dense as to impede boating in all but the dredged channel. The commercial and leisure boating interests were outraged that this plant could not be removed. The competent authority, English Nature, backed by the Wildlife Trust and the National Trust, refused the Broads Authority permission to continue cutting.

In August 1998 an experimental programme of trial cutting of *C. intermedia* was permitted by English Nature. This is a European protected species, so the experiments were designed to test the precautionary principle. To help set the ecological judgements, the Broads Authority established a scientific assessment team in 1999. This was designed to advise for the precautionary procedures suggested by the Directive and set in statute by the UK Conservation (Natural Habitats etc.) Regulations 1994. The team could not initially agree on a cutting programme, nor could it advise on what experimental schemes would be best. This delayed proceedings, reduced the navigation options for the summer of 1999 and introduced a further difficulty, namely the possible effects of cutting on populations of overwintering birds. Eventually a very modest programme of cutting was initiated with full monitoring, and little navigation.

Of interest here are six key issues for participatory biodiversity.

1 There was no serious attempt to bring the various parties together at an early stage. So attitudes and stereotypes of the kind examined by Stoll-Kleemann (2001a, 2001b) in Germany formed to reinforce prejudices, develop misunderstandings and misrepresentations, and increase a sense of bonded groupings of hostility and bias. There was no whiff of common understanding, and no trust in social networks, other than those of dispute and deceit.

2 There was no accredited management body with the competence or the capacity to mediate or to generate a management plan. There was no legal mechanism for such a plan, and so experience of participatory procedures of the kind outlined in the previous chapter was used to put the plan into effect.

3 Personalities got in the way of trust building and confidence. Within both the conservation and navigation camps there was no sense of unity or self-belief, no leadership, no mutual respect, and no serious attempt to reach consensus, even within self-interested networks. The economically important fishing interests lay in between and were effectively marginalised by the warring factions.

4 The scientific assessment panel could not agree on the depth of experimental cutting that should be tried out. In essence, the role of scientific authority, that helps to shape a participatory biodiversity process, was crucially missing. The fact that the assessment panel scrambled eventually to a set of recommendations, with limited evidence, but with experience on its side, illustrates the power of scientific appraisal, no matter how imperfect, as a guide to participatory processes.

To provide a dialogue for the parties, the Broads Authority established a Hickling Liaison Group. Originally this was meant to be inclusive of all interests. But such was the bad feeling that the conservation interests failed to attend meetings. In effect, this added to the sense of frustration and prejudice which had grown rife.

Eventually the Broads Authority, English Nature and the Wildlife Trust commissioned an interactive, trust-building analysis of all participants in the Hickling process. This effort took one year, involved intensive discussions face to face, built confidence amongst the groups, and enabled all participants to understand both the legal framework of the Directive, the crucial role of scientific assessment, and the cultures of sailing, navigation and angling on the broad. The result was a freshly fashioned Upper Thurne Working Group, fully inclusive of thirty-two stakeholder interests. This acts as an 'Upper Thurne parliament' for all preparations for the management planning for the whole region. It is likely that this concept will set the guidelines for participatory biodiversity in the Broads generally and possibly elsewhere.

The Hickling experience tells us a lot about the immense difficulties of triggering fully inclusive deliberative and participatory procedures for the pursuit of biodiversity. To create social cohesion and common outlooks takes time, patience, diplomacy and sound evidence. Confidence comes from a process of shared ownership, and, through that, a commitment to shared governance through the practice of co-responsibility. This is turn means a more formal pattern of collective responsibility between elected

local governments and informal, but fully participatory, procedures established by agencies which are not regarded as democratic. Only with deliberative democracy can this particular dilemma be solved. Throughout
this process, the ecological integrity of biodiversity must be paramount,
for this is the route to management, to commercially sound navigation,
to genuine boating and fishing pleasures, and to the local economy. In
any case, ecological integrity is the linchpin of the Habitats Directive. So
any claim to removal of plants for any economic or recreational purpose
can only be met within the precautionary principle, with enhancement
of biodiversity being the primary objective. It will take five years fully to
implement a management plan for the Upper Thurne. In so doing, all the
opportunities offered in the EU and being tested in Germany will have
to be pursued. Protecting beyond the protected is truly an integrationist
and culture transforming activity.

The Upper Thurne 'parliament' is now working systematically towards
a science plan, a scheme for inclusive communication and responsiveness
with local social networks, and the beginnings of a process of monitored
experimentation of water management and sympathetic landuse change
in the catchment. This arrangement involves many organisations and
landowners. It is dependent on precautionary science, a high degree of
acquired social capital (i.e., where groups learn to trust and to co-operate)
and the funds to relate environmental restoration with economic opportunity via fishing, tourism and educational projects.

REFERENCES

BfN (Bundesamt für Naturschutz) 1997. *Erhaltung der biologischen Vielfalt.
Wissenschaftliche Analyse deutscher Beiträge.* Bonn and Bad Godesberg: BfN.
2000. *Nature Data.* Bonn: BfN.
Bund Naturschutz 1999. *Netz des Lebens. Vorschläge des Bundes Naturschutz zum
europäischen Biotopverbund (FFH-Gebietsliste) in Bayern.* Bund Naturschutz
Forschung 3. Nuremberg: Bund Naturschutz.
Commission of the European Communities 1999. *Europe's Environment: What
Directions for the Future?*, COM(1999)543 final. Brussels: Commission of
the European Communities.
2000a. *Report from the Commission on the Application of Directive 79/409/EEC on
the Conservation of Wild Birds. Update for 1993–1995*, COM(2000)180 final.
Brussels: Commission of the European Communities.
2000b. *Strategic Objectives 2000–2005. 'Shaping the New Europe'*, COM (2000)
154 final. Brussels: Commission of the European Communities.
2001a. *A Sustainable Europe for a Better World.* Brussels: Commission of the
European Communities.
2001b. *European Governance*, COM(2001)428. Brussels, http://europa.eu.int/
comm/governance/

2001c. *Environment 2010: Our Future, Our Choice. The Sixth Environment Action Programme*, COM(2001)31 final. Brussels: Commission of the European Communities.

2001d. *Biodiversity Action Plan for the Conservation of Natural Resources. Volume II*, COM(2001)162 final. Brussels: Commission of the European Communities.

Dieterich, F. 1999. Ausweisung von Natura 2000-Gebieten in Deutschland und daraus folgende Konsequenzen. In *Natura 2000 : Eine Chance für den Naturschutz Europas*, pp. 14–25. Bundesministerium für Umwelt, Jugend und Familie. Tagungsband 14. Vienna: Schriftenreihe des BMUJF.

Eben, M. 2001. Nature conservation in Bavaria: can *Natura 2000* and a new agricultural & forestry policy make a contribution to safeguarding biodiversity? MSc thesis, University College London.

Fairbrass, J. and Jordan, A. 2001. Making European biodiversity policy: national barriers and European opportunities. *Journal of European Public Policy* 8(4): 499–518.

Gee, D. 1997. Economic task reform in Europe: opportunities and obstacles. In T. O'Riordan (ed.), *Ecotaxation*, pp. 81–106. London: Earthscan.

Gillies, D. 1999. *A Guide to EU Environmental Law.* London: Earthscan.

Haarmann, K. and Pretscher, P. 1993. *Zustand und Zukunft der Naturschutzgebiete in Deutschland: Die Situation im Süden und Ausblicke auf andere Landesteile.* Bonn and Bad Godesberg: Forschungsanstalt für Naturschutz und Landschaftsökologie.

Hellström, E. 2001. *Conflict Cultures – Qualitative Comparative Analysis of Environmental Conflicts in Forestry.* Silva Fennica Monographs 2. Helsinki: Finnish Society of Forest Sciences, Finnish Forest Research Institute.

Jordan, A. 2001. The European Union: an evolving system of multi-level governance ... or government? *Policy and Politics* 29(2): 193–208.

Kasemir, B., Dahinden, U., Swartling, A.G., Schüle, R., Tabara, D. and Jaeger, C.C. 2000. Citizens' perspectives on climate change and energy use. *Global Environmental Change* 10(3): 169–84.

Knightbridge, R. 2000. The UK BAP – five years on. *ECOS* 21(2): 2–8.

Ministry of the Environment. 1997. *National Action Plan for Biodiversity in Finland, 1997–2005.* Helsinki.

Müller-Motzfeld, G. 2000. Schützt die FFH-Richtlinie die, 'richtigen' Arten? Kriterien für eine Novellierung. In B. Petersen, U. Hauk and A. Ssymank (eds.), *Der Schutz von Tier- und Pflanzenarten bei der Umsetzung der FFH-Richtlinie*, pp. 43–55. Bonn and Bad Godesburg: BfN.

Natura Barometer. 2001. *Natura Barometer.* Copenhagen: European Environment Agency.

O'Riordan, T. (ed.) 2001. *Globalism, Localism and Identity: Fresh Perspectives on the Sustainability Transition in Europe.* London: Earthscan.

Rosenström, U. and Palosaari, M. 2000. *Signs of Sustainability: Finland's Indicators for Sustainable Development 2000.* Helsinki: Ministry of the Environment.

Saaristo, K. (2000). *Avoin asiantuntijuus. Ympäristökysymys ja monimuotoinen ekspertiisi.* Jyväskylä: Jyväskyliän Yliopiston Nykykulttuurin tutkimuskeskuksen julkaisuja 66.

Smart, J., Davis, R., Ducleworth, J. and Harper, M. 2001. Backlash against the BAR. *Ecos* 22(1): 13.

SRU (Der Rat von Sachverständigen für Umweltfragen) 2000. *Umweltgutachten 2000: Schritte ins nächste Jahrtausend.* Stuttgart: Metzler-Poeschel.

SRU 2001. *Stellungnahme zum Entwurf eines Gesetzes zur Neuregelung des Bundesnaturschutzgesetzes (Stand 2. Februar 2001).* Accessed at http://www.umweltrat.de/naturs.htm.

Ssymank, A., Hauke, U., Rückriem, C., Schröder, E. and Messer, D. 1998. *Das europäische Schutzgebietssystem* NATURA 2000. *BfN-Handbuch zur Umsetzung der Fauna–Flora–Habitat–Richtlinie und der Vogelschutzrichtlinie.* Bonn and Bad Godesberg: BfN.

Stoll-Kleemann, S. 2001a. Reconciling opposition to protected areas management in Europe: the German experience. *Environment* 43(5): 32–43.

20001b. Opposition to the designation of protected areas in Germany. *Journal of Environmental Management and Planning* 44(1): 109–28.

Stolpe, G. and Korn, H. 2000. Internationales Naturschutzrecht. In *Naturschutz in Entwicklungsländern*, pp. 49–58, (eds.) Gesellschaft für technische Zusammenarbeit and Bundesamt für Naturschutz. Heidelberg: Max Kasparek Verlag.

WWF Europe 2000. *A Shadow List of EU Habitats to Complement Official Designations.* Brussels: WWF European Policy Office.

2001. *A Race to Protect Europe's Natural Heritage: European Snapshot Report on the Status of Implementation of the European Habitats Directive.* Brussels: WWF European Policy Office.

Ympäristöministeriö 1999. *Natura 2000 – verkoston Suomen ehdotus.* Helsinki.

7 Community-based involvement in biodiversity protection in the United States

Toddi A. Steelman

Introduction

The United States possesses great diversity of ecosystems and species. The greatest threat to biodiversity loss in the US comes from the loss and/or degradation of existing habitat. The US has experienced limited success in habitat and species restoration, and more needs to be done to protect remaining special places and the plants and animals that inhabit them.

Federal efforts to protect ecosystems in the US have taken the form of establishing protected areas and enacting legislation, notably the 1973 Endangered Species Act (ESA), to safeguard species and their habitats. However, some question whether legislation and protected areas do enough to address the systemic causes connected to biodiversity loss. For example, Bean (1999) observes that the ESA has been built on insecure ecological foundations, that it does not provide reliable protection for ecosystems, that it has become politicised, so is more an arena for legal posturing than biodiversity management, and that it has not encouraged community involvement along the lines suggested by Jules Pretty in chapter 4. Against the backdrop of this debate about the adequacy of existing efforts to protect biodiversity, there has been a proliferation of community-based efforts since the mid-1980s to address environmental and natural resource problems, including biodiversity issues. Community-based efforts can be seen as a new and evolving response to the inadequacy of existing institutions to solve the pressing problems, including biodiversity loss, which individuals and communities face.

The strength of community-based efforts is that they can take into account the complexity of interests reflected in a community in a sincere attempt to reach a locally sustainable solution. If habitat and species protection are to be sustainable in the long run, then the interests of the local stewards of the land must be considered. Increasingly, however, there are mixed reactions to community-based efforts. Since such efforts tend to take into consideration a variety of values that affect local

interests, including cultural, economic, social and environmental concerns, among others, they fail to prioritise any single value. Consequently,
as noted in chapter 1, community-based efforts may compromise the
great gains made through environmental law over recent decades, and so
fail to achieve the biodiversity enhancement that is needed, especially in
the face of crisis.

The choices for biodiversity protection appear to rest on the horns of a
dilemma. If community-based solutions risk compromising environmental gains, then who can be trusted to develop appropriate and acceptable
solutions to biodiversity protection? Centralised, authoritative standards
and actions are perceived to be a better alternative in these situations.
The problem is that in the US these more authoritative efforts also have
failed. We need to understand better how national standards can coexist
with decentralised community discretion for the sake of better, and more
sustainable, biodiversity protection.

Biodiversity status and protection in the United States

The US supports more large-scale ecosystem types than any other nation
on earth. These diverse ecosystems are home to approximately 200,000
native species, which constitute 10 per cent of all species catalogued
by scientists thus far (Stein *et al.* 2000). The Chihuahuan Desert, the
California coastal sage scrub, the temperate broadleaf forests of the
Appalachian and Blue Ridge Mountains and the longleaf pine forests of
the south-eastern US are examples of globally significant, and threatened,
ecosystems within the US that contain diverse communities with aston-
ishing plant and animal richness and endemism (Ricketts *et al.* 1999).

Habitats within the US are threatened with destruction, degradation
and fragmentation; pollution; introduction of exotic species; and commercial exploitation. The single biggest threat to species survival in the US
is loss of habitat; almost 60 per cent of US landscapes have been altered in
major ways (Stein *et al.* 2000). For instance, only an estimated 5 per cent
of the original temperate forests of the United States remain, the rest having been logged heavily and/or converted to plantations (Ricketts *et al.*
1999). The most extensive grassland region in the world was originally
in the US, but the tall grass prairies have been reduced to 1 per cent of
their historical range (Noss and Peters 1995). An estimated one third of
US species are at risk of extinction and 500 species are estimated to be
extinct (Stein *et al.* 2000).

Efforts to understand the distribution, abundance and health of plants,
animals and ecosystems in the United States are incomplete. While no
standardised quantitative data on habitat loss exist over entire ecoregions

(Ricketts *et al.* 1999) the Association for Biodiversity Information and the Nature Conservancy have drawn together twenty-five years of natural heritage programmes in the various states to produce the most comprehensive audit yet of the nation's biota. The results are summarised by Bruce Stein (2001: 1–6). Most of the study in the US at the species level has focused on birds and mammals, and the trends are mixed, with some species declining, others increasing, while yet others are stable (LaRoe *et al.* 1995). Declining species, such as grassland species, shorebirds, ibises and red-cockaded woodpeckers, are associated closely with habitat loss. Increasing bird species include the American bald eagle, peregrine falcon, wild turkey and Canada goose. Among marine mammals, increases have been observed for grey whales, bowhead whales, harbor seals, California sea otters and California sea lions. Decreases have been noted in Stellar sea lion populations and several species of Pacific dolphin. White-tailed deer and North American elk have recovered from their declining trends, as have grizzly bears and grey wolves. Since 1978, amphibian and reptile species have increased from 454 to 507 species; none the less, many of these species also are experiencing habitat loss and degradation and there is no national programme to monitor populations (Lydeard 1996: 1,481). Habitat modification and degradation have imperilled native freshwater ecosystems, especially in the south-east, which possesses an abundance of rare freshwater fish and mussels. Very little information exists on the majority of invertebrate species. Stein (2001: 4) shows that the concentrations of imperilled endemic species are highest in Hawaii (124 species), south-western Virginia (27 species), the Southern Appalachians, and Florida.

To conserve biodiversity, the maximum diversity of habitats needs to be represented in protected area networks or other biodiversity protection efforts (Scott *et al.* 1993; Noss and Peters 1995; The Nature Conservancy 1996; Olson and Dinerstein 1998). How can this be done, given the hugely varying existing political, cultural, legal, economic and social contexts within which the United States operates?

Historically, the dominant means for protecting biodiversity at the federal level in the US has been in establishing protected areas on public lands in the form of national parks, national forests, national monuments, wilderness areas and wildlife refuges and through laws such as the Endangered Species Act.[1] The US currently has 3,063 protected

---

[1] The purpose of the ESA is to conserve 'the ecosystems upon which endangered and threatened species depend' and foster the recovery and protection of species that are 'listed' as 'endangered' or 'threatened' under the law. As defined, an endangered species currently is in danger of extinction throughout all or a large portion of its range, while a threatened species is likely to become in danger of extinction in the near future.

areas[2] that cover 123,120,000 ha, or 13.1 per cent of the US land area (World Resources Institute 2000). The ESA, passed in 1973 and amended in 1978, 1982 and 1988, is the major piece of federal legislation that provides a strong mandate to protect and manage threatened and endangered species and their habitats. The law is administered primarily by the US Fish and Wildlife Service (USFWS)[3] and the National Marine Fisheries Service (NMFS).[4] As of June 2001, 1,244 species[5] were listed as endangered or threatened and several hundred more were candidates for listing (USFWS 2001). While the ESA is the main federal statute for biodiversity protection, many states also have enacted species protection legislation. A recent study revealed that state threatened and endangered species laws generally are less comprehensive than the ESA (Goble *et al.* 1999).[6]

While the ESA and protected areas are two approaches for conserving biodiversity, there is growing concern that these tools are inadequate given the nature of the challenge (Brown 1997). The existing scale of many protected areas is too small to sustain species over a long time. The practice of managing species as individual units limits the ability to treat species as part of the greater ecosystems in which they thrive. While there is growing consensus that an integrated system of large nature reserves is needed to protect biological diversity at different biological levels and scales, it is unclear how this can be done within an American culture that places a premium on property rights, dislikes federal regulation, and increasingly seeks to manage its environmental and natural resources at decentralised levels of governance. These points were introduced in chapter 1: protection is rarely a function of ecological advice alone.

The division between public and private property is a major obstacle in the battle to sustain and restore biodiversity in the United States.

---

[2] Protected areas are defined as natural areas of at least 1,000 ha in five World Conservation Union (IUCN) management categories (strict nature reserve, wilderness area, national park, national monument, and habitat/species management area and protected landscape/seascape). IUCN defines a protected area as 'an area of land and/or sea especially dedicated to the protection and maintenance of biological diversity, and of natural and associated cultural resources, and managed through legal or other effective means.'

[3] The USFWS has responsibility for threatened and endangered terrestrial and freshwater organisms.

[4] The NMFS has responsibility for threatened and endangered marine species.

[5] This number includes both plants and animals. Listed as endangered are 379 animals and 593 plants, a total of 972. Listed as threatened are 128 animals and 144 plants, a total of 272 (USFWS 2001).

[6] Fifteen states have statutes that cover both plants and animals. Forty-three states have no provision authorising the designation of critical habitat and thirty-nine states have no protection against habitat destruction on either private or public lands. Only three states include any requirements that the wildlife management agency engage in recovery planning processes (Goble *et al.* 1999).

Threatened and endangered species fail to recognise arbitrary boundaries between publicly and privately owned lands. While federal agencies can mandate the protection of a *species* on public as well as private land, these efforts often fall short of securing *habitat* that may be appropriate for long-term protection.

Bruce Stein (2001: 45) also points to the dilemma between listing for endangerment as an ecological process, and listing for species protection via community concerns and political lobbying through conservation groups. Furthermore, he found that vertebrates are generally more quickly lost compared to invertebrates and plants, and that the ESA process tends to list endangered species much more readily than those species indicated by the Association of Biodiversity Initiatives as critically imperilled. In short, the ecological audit is a guide but not a driver of US biodiversity interpretation and action programmes.

The difficulties posed by biodiversity conservation, as well as other seemingly intractable environmental problems, have sparked in the last two decades a proliferation of new approaches to address a variety of environmental and natural resource problems that existing institutions have been unable to resolve. Among these new approaches are community-based efforts. These go by many names, among them community-based initiatives, community-based environmental management (Steelman 1999; Steelman and Carmin 2001), collaboratives (Wondolleck and Yaffee 2000; Brunner *et al.* 2002), grass-roots ecosystem management (Weber 2000), partnerships (Pelkey *et al.* 1999), community-based environmental protection (EPA 1997) and civic environmentalism (John 1994), to name a few. In most instances these efforts can be captured by Kenney and Lord's 1999 definition, 'ad hoc, voluntary and regionally-oriented partnerships that have organised in hopes of addressing and resolving resource and management problems that established institutions and organisations have failed to solve', and John and Mlay's 1998 definition, 'ad-hoc process[es] of custom designing answers to complex environmental problems in a specific location'.

Trends in community-based efforts

Community-based efforts developed in the US against a backdrop of changing societal perceptions of the environment, mounting frustration with traditional environmental regulatory approaches, and increasing political favour for decentralised policy solutions. One of the greatest strengths of community-based efforts is their potential to transcend narrow individual interests and form what have been called multiple-interest groups (Brunner *et al.* 2002). Pretty covers this distinction and transition in chapter 4. Community-based efforts can knit together and reintegrate the patchwork of interests and perspectives that are crucial to addressing multifaceted environmental and natural resource challenges. Perhaps because of this function, the number of community-based environmental initiatives is growing. While there is no comprehensive inventory of these efforts, different estimates range from several hundred to more than a thousand, depending on how they are defined[7] (Yaffee 1996; Carr et al. 1998; McGinnis 1999; Kenney et al. 2000).

Community-based efforts appear more frequently around watershed and forest issues, although they are not restricted to these areas. This may be for two reasons. First, communities tend to organise around a connection to place and especially local landscape (Kemmis 1990). People are drawn to their forests and bodies of water and so may be more closely connected to these places and thus more inclined to protect them. Second, waterways and forests provide habitat to some of the most threatened and endangered species in the United States. The greatest concentration of watershed initiatives is located in the Pacific Northwest, where salmon and spotted owl controversies have provided a strong incentive for new ways of approaching natural resource management (Kenney 1999a). In order to preserve local preferences instead of relinquishing control to state or federally mandated regulations, communities and agencies seek solutions that fit their diverse needs.

Community-based efforts, however, are not without their critics. First, some question whether community-based efforts offer a comparative advantage over traditional command and control regulatory efforts (Nickelsburg 1998). In this same vein, others criticise consensus decision making on the grounds that it is no more efficient or effective than traditional regulatory processes (Coglianese 1999), although this is challenged by others (Fairman 1999). Second, some question whether community-based efforts offer any palpable improvements in environmental quality (Kenney 1999b, 2000). Evaluating community-based efforts has been a challenge since they can contribute differentially to both social and ecological outcomes, thereby causing confusion about what constitutes success in these cases (Beirele 1999; Kenney 2000; Steelman and Carmin 2002). While on-the-ground environmental improvements are undoubtedly important, it is also clear that community-based efforts can stimulate

---

[7] Kenney et al. (2000) catalogue over 400 watershed initiatives in the West. McGinnis (1999) counts more than 200 watershed initiatives in California alone and has had discussions with others indicating that at least several hundred exist in the Northeast. Yaffee (1996) has identified a pool of 662 cases of ecosystem management. Carr et al. (1998) have conducted surveys with 113 employees on national forests engaged in collaborative efforts.

improvements in trust, build understanding and strengthen social ties in the communities most closely connected to the management of these resources (Beirele 1999). However, measuring these intangible benefits has proved difficult, if not elusive. The third category of critiques raises concerns that community- and consensus-based efforts undermine the national statutory framework through which many environmental gains have been made (McCloskey 1996; Coggins 1998). Some fear that collaborative decision making may provide federal regulatory agencies with an excuse to abdicate their power over environmental protection (Coggins 1998; Kenney 1999a). Others raise concerns about the ability and appropriateness of local representation in matters of national scope (McCloskey 1996; Coggins 1998).

The nature of these criticisms reflects the dual character of the United States' evolving environmental and natural resource regulatory structure outlined earlier in this chapter. There is a clash between the strong, centralised standard-setting system, while states and localities are attempting to encourage more pragmatic, community-based decision making structures that foster and take advantage of local cultures of stewardship (Brick 1998; John and Mlay 1998). The Endangered Species Act reflects this dilemma. It provides a strong standard against which future loss of species may be prevented. However, a top-down standard, regardless of how well intentioned, must still contend with communities that work, live and often share the habitat that is necessary for the survival of a species. This point also emerges in Europe, as the previous chapter demonstrated.

Perceived threats to national standards and interest groups may be real under some circumstances, but they are not present under *all* circumstances. The challenge is to identify the appropriate niches for community-based efforts and to cultivate them as they grow in hospitable places. The key, it seems, is to identify where community-based efforts have been used successfully, as well as unsuccessfully, and to understand what conditions promote these differential outcomes. Community-based approaches are probably not appropriate for all circumstances. The same can be said for using national regulatory standards. However, our collective understanding of when and how these approaches can be used is limited. Since community-based efforts are used or applied in different ways under varying contexts, it is important to provide an understanding of the institutional landscape that is central to this chapter.

People do not often change their behaviour unless they have good reason to do so. In most cases, people will respond to either positive or negative incentives. In the case of biodiversity protection, the Endangered Species Act provides a very powerful regulatory incentive for shifting behaviours for promoting biodiversity. Once species are placed on the federal endangered species list, they are provided with special protection. People are prohibited from 'taking a species', defined as acting to 'harass, harm, pursue, hunt, shoot, wound, kill, trap, capture, or collect, or attempt to engage in any such conduct' (ESA, Section 3 (19)). Those who violate this 'take' provision of the ESA face both criminal and civil penalties. The prohibitions protecting endangered species have been especially troubling for those who work or live in areas that provide habitat for these species. This is partly because the legal definition of 'harm' to a species includes habitat modification that impinges on day-to-day activities such as breeding and feeding.

The two cases discussed below deal with circumstances where community-based efforts were taken by a state agency in one instance, and by a community in the other, and then challenged by federal or national environmental interests. The two cases were chosen to highlight the opportunities, as well as obstacles, that arise when community-based efforts are used in the context of biodiversity protection. In the case of the Oregon Plan for Salmon and Watersheds, the state and watershed groups within Oregon acted to avoid the ESA listing of the coho salmon. In the case of the Quincy Library Group, a community acted to preserve several values that were important to it, including old-growth habitats for the California spotted owl, a species not listed as threatened or endangered, but none the less in peril. The following cases are not representative of all efforts throughout the United States, but are offered for the insight they provide about the tensions that exist between local and federal efforts to deal with biodiversity concerns.

The Oregon Plan for Salmon and Watersheds

Throughout the Pacific Northwest, salmon populations (*Oncorhynchus* spp.) are facing extinction. Given their anadromous lifecycle,[8] salmon are exposed to many threats. Consequently, multiple causes, such as agricultural impacts, dewatering from irrigation, timbering practices, fishing regulations, urban runoff and recreation have resulted in cumulative, detrimental impacts on salmon populations. Recognising the multiplicity of causes facing failing coho salmon populations, Oregon Governor John A. Kitzhaber sought a different approach to avoid a possible restrictive ESA listing that would place burdens on the politically influential timber

---

[8] Salmon begin their lives in freshwater streams, rivers and lakes. When the fish become fingerlings, they begin a long migration to the ocean. Once in the ocean, the salmon grow to adult size and then return to their freshwater origins to spawn. On account of this complex lifecycle, salmon pose some interesting challenges for those who wish to manage them.

and agricultural industries in his state, while also potentially hindering a more flexible response to recover the threatened species.

Oregon state agencies decided to pursue an alternative route to achieve the end goal inspired by the Endangered Species Act, namely the recovery of the species. What Kitzhaber realised was that listing a species under the ESA did not guarantee its restoration. For instance, Snake River chinook (*Oncorhynchus tshawytscha*) and sockeye salmon (*Oncorhynchus nerka*) had been listed for nearly a decade with no demonstrable improvements in their populations (Kitzhaber 1998). In Kitzhaber's opinion, the biggest problem with the ESA was its weak regulatory and enforcement provisions on private land. Over 65 per cent of coho salmon runs are on private land, and an approach was needed that could incorporate private landowners voluntarily into a recovery effort (Kitzhaber 1998). Thus the Oregon Plan was born.

The goal of the Oregon Plan is 'to restore Oregon's wild salmon and trout populations and fisheries to sustainable and productive levels' (Executive Order 1999). At the core of the Plan is recognition of the need to move beyond regulatory prohibitions and encourage informal efforts to improve the conditions for the survival of wild salmon and trout. Some of the innovations in the Plan include private and quasi-governmental efforts to restore and protect landscapes and provisions for local watershed councils (Executive Order 1999). Commercial and sport fishing, timber, agriculture and mining, urban areas and private citizens all have become involved in the salmon recovery effort. Important aspects of the plan included water quality and quantity improvements, fish management, fish passage, habitat protection and restoration, compliance and enforcement measures aimed at improving water quality, support for local efforts, community dialogue, educational and technical assistance, research, monitoring and assessment (Oregon Plan 2000).

Additional species of wild salmon and trout were added to the initial plan, as were different rivers and geographic locations. The umbrella term for all the initiatives is the Oregon Plan for Salmon and Watersheds. The total cost for the plan was estimated at $32 million. A voluntary contribution of $13 million from the timber industry, as well as money from anglers and the mining industry, partially financed the effort (Applegate 1997). Half of the funding was contingent on an ESA 'no list' decision from the National Marine Fisheries Service for the coho salmon.

In April 1997, the State of Oregon entered into a Memorandum of Agreement (MOA) with the National Marine Fisheries Service to initiate the plan. The NMFS accepted that the coho salmon did not warrant listing as a threatened or endangered species in May 1997 (Executive Order 1999). Commenting on his agency's interest in taking this route, NMFS spokesman Brian Gorm stated: 'It's a recognition that the federal government can't recover salmon alone. It has to be done with broad support from state, county and local governments and local property owners. Recovery won't be successful without strong local support' (Gentle, n.d.). However, state and national environmental groups challenged the MOA in court, stating that voluntary efforts were not sufficient and measures needed to be compelled by law.[9]

In June 1998, Magistrate Janice Stewart of the US Federal District Court for Oregon ordered the NMFS to reconsider its decision without taking into account any parts of the efforts made under the Oregon Plan, owing to their voluntary nature (Executive Order 1999). As directed, the NMFS reconsidered its decision and listed the Oregon Coast coho as threatened under the ESA in October 1998 (Executive Order 1999). At that time Oregon's eighty-one watershed councils and other groups had completed more than 1,200 stream improvement projects, including stream fencing, culvert replacement and road repairs to aid and encourage the protection and recovery of the salmon (Applegate 1998; Christensen 1998).

The ruling sent a message to those who had been working on the statewide task that their efforts were valued less since they were not compelled by law. Moreover, the ruling highlighted the contradiction inherent in the ESA. As Governor Kitzhaber noted, the ESA 'can *prevent* landowners from engaging in activities that "take" a listed species. The federal government cannot require individuals to restore watersheds', yet this is what is needed to provide an adequate ecosystem within which the salmon could be expected to thrive (Kitzhaber 1998). In spite of the ESA listing, Oregon continues to proceed with the full implementation of the Plan to demonstrate its effectiveness. 'The Oregon Plan has thousands of landowners working together to make changes in their management practices to improve habitat for salmon. It is those actions that count in species recovery,' proclaimed Kitzhaber (Applegate 1998).

To date, the benefits of the projects on the salmon population remain uncertain. Across the state a variety of projects are underway that entail assessment, monitoring, community dialogue, and land acquisition and restoration. These hundreds of projects will have a great variety of effects on the salmon, on the habitat and on future water quality. However, less than half of the projects undertaken as part of the Oregon Plan have engaged in any monitoring. These monitoring efforts focus less on the

---

[9] Oregon Natural Resources Council, Pacific Coast Federation of Fishermen's Associations, National Audubon Society, Sierra Club National, Native Fish Society and Coast Range Association were among the groups in opposition (Killam 2001).

biological and water quality conditions than on physical habitat changes and the structural integrity of projects, such as riparian tree growth, the pool to riffle ratio, culvert function and irrigation efficiency (Maleki and Riggers 2000). Though there is shortage of technical assistance and funding for watershed co-ordinators and organisational capacity, there has been a significant increase in both federal and state funding for watershed councils with $9 million in federal funds complemented by $32 million in state funds (Oregon Watershed Enhancement Board 2000).

Because the ecosystem conditions are so hugely varied and complex, it is imperative to gauge the ecological effectiveness of both regulatory and voluntary measures. This is the kind of social capital enhancement mentioned by Pretty in chapter 4. In the absence of careful biological and community-supported monitoring, the Oregon Plan has missed an opportunity to evaluate and track the ecological and social resilience that may accompany such community-based efforts.

It has taken 150 years for the salmon and its habitat to reach a critical state. It will take more than a few years to begin to see if the Oregon Plan, in conjunction with the ESA listing, will have beneficial impacts on salmon populations. Even then, a causal connection may never be established between changes in the salmon population and the efforts of the Oregon Plan. None the less, Oregon's experience to restore its salmon populations represents a new approach to biodiversity protection and enhancement that is worthy of continued attention. Instead of relying solely on the government to solve the problem, people are relying on a combination of public and private efforts that create an active stewardship of the land. In the words of Governor Kitzhaber: 'This whole thing is about how people in Oregon acquire a deeper level of understanding that how they live their lives affects the environment in which they live. It's about changing the culture' (Collete 2001: 149).

The Quincy Library Group

In the 1980s the timber wars that erupted among environmentalists in northern California's Sierra Nevada mountains gave way to a cautious truce and then stable peace in the 1990s in the form of the community-based Quincy Library Group. Made up of local environmentalists, the timber industry and local community residents, the QLG has faced many obstacles to implement its vision of creating resilience in both its ecosystems and social well-being.

The town of Quincy, population 5,000, is located in the geographic centre of the 1 million ha QLG management area that encompasses all of the Plumas National Forest, most of the Lassen National Forest and part of the Tahoe National Forest (Terhune and Terhune 1998). In the 1980s, timber wars pitted those who had environmental leanings and were concerned about old-growth forests and the California spotted owl, against others who depended on the timber industry for their livelihood. Several factors contributed to this tension. Timber harvesting in the National Forests began to fall in the late 1980s and early 1990s. As timber sales declined, so did county budgets for community-wide assets such as roads and schools. Local environmentalists blocked the remaining timber sales in efforts to protect the stands of old-growth and roadless areas in the surrounding forests. These formed the habitat for the California spotted owl (*Strix occidentalis occidentalis*), a species related to the endangered northern spotted owl (*Strix occidentalis caurina*).

Ironically, the tensions that had been the cause of escalating violence and animosity in the town of Quincy eventually provided the catalyst for co-operation. Recognising that the situation was untenable, Plumas County Supervisor Bill Coates and Sierra Pacific Industries forester Tom Nelson reached out to Michael Jackson, a local environmental lawyer and self-avowed 'environmental wacko', in 1992 (Marston 1997; Colburn 2002). No one, it seemed, was satisfied with forest management in Quincy. Moreover, the spectre of a catastrophic wildfire was perceived to be a real and dangerous threat to both human and owl populations throughout the forests. Federal fire policy over the past several decades and forest management that focused on larger merchantable trees had left large volumes of combustible biomass in the National Forests that posed great hazards (De Lasaux 2001). A truce was called and the three men decided to see if there was a way that they might work together to find a solution to the many problems facing the community.

In spring 1993, they held a meeting in the Quincy Library and thus became known as the Quincy Library Group. In the following months a town meeting was held and 250 residents attended. The founders described a vision that would protect riparian zones, roadless areas, riparian, aquatic and owl habitat and the remaining stands of old growth, while thinning the rest of the forest, focusing on small diameter trees. The goal was to find a balance between economics, fuel reduction and appropriate owl habitat. In the opinion of the three men, the group could proceed with trying to develop a plan that satisfied the diverse needs of their flagging community or they could maintain the current state of fruitless antagonism. In a vote estimated at 245 to 5, the town supported the QLG effort to find a better way (Marston 1997). In June 1993, QLG, now comprised of approximately forty core individuals, came up with a Community Stability Proposal that would manage the Plumas and Lassen

National Forests and Sierraville District of the Tahoe, over 1 million ha of public land.

While the QLG was crafting its plan, the Forest Service imposed regulations to protect the California spotted owl across the entire Sierra Nevada mountain range. The California spotted owl regulations (CASPO) meant that new restrictions were placed on the forests. No clear cuts were allowed, no even-aged management, no cutting of trees over 30 inches in diameter and no cuts that opened up too much of the forest canopy (Marston 1997). Moreover, it meant that the USFS had to conduct an Environmental Impact Statement (EIS) to evaluate the different options under the proposed CASPO regulations. Given their own concerns about the owl and old-growth forests, the QLG already had incorporated these restrictions into their plan.

The members of QLG were optimistic that the USFS would be receptive to their plan since it represented a joint effort that would avoid appeals and lawsuits, which often plague USFS planning processes, and had already taken into account many of the considerations necessary for the owl. The Group felt that the USFS could use their Community Stability Proposal as an interim plan during the five years the CASPO regulations were being prepared, decided, appealed and litigated (Colburn 2002). In this manner, the owl would be protected, jobs would be provided, and catastrophic fire potential would be mitigated. However, this was not to be the case. The Forest Supervisors from the three forests rejected the plan.

The QLG visited Washington, DC in early 1994 to inform their congressional representatives and others of their proposals. In the fall of 1994, USFS officials from Washington paid visits to the QLG and announced a $1 million budget allocation to implement projects compatible with the Community Stability Proposal. In 1995, Secretary of Agriculture Dan Glickman announced a $20 million appropriation for the local National Forests in the Quincy area, $4.7 million of which was to be for the implementation of QLG type projects.

At about the same time, the USFS was called upon by the Secretary of Agriculture and criticised for not taking into account the 'best available scientific data' for the CASPO process. The Sierra Nevada Ecosystem Project (SNEP), a concurrent process that was requested by Congress, was initiated in 1993 to evaluate the remaining old growth in the forests of the Sierra Nevada. Conducted by an independent panel of scientists, the SNEP was expected to be released in 1997. To take advantage of the best available scientific data, the USFS elected to redirect its CASPO efforts within the context of the larger SNEP, thereby putting on hold any decision about the QLG proposal for several more years (Colburn 2002).

After four years of perceived stalling from USFS officials, the QLG decided to go back to Washington to try to accomplish its goals. The trip ruffled many feathers, but QLG members felt they had little choice since it was their communities that were suffering the economic losses and potential fire risks posed by the inaction (Little 1998). At their request QLG's US Congressional Representative Wally Herger, sponsored the 'QLG Forest Recovery and Economic Stability Act' in the House of Representatives. In July 1997, the Quincy Act passed the House in a vote of 429 to 1. US Californian Senators Barbara Boxer and Diane Fienstein sponsored similar legislation in the Senate.

Following its passage in the House, the QLG Act became the target of fierce opposition from environmental groups. The Wilderness Society, the Natural Resources Defense Council, the Audubon Society and the Sierra Club, among others, all opposed the QLG legislation. This opposition rested on two dominant arguments. First, opponents stated that QLG failed to comply with existing environmental laws and procedures and urged QLG to be patient and wait for the USFS to make an administrative decision (Sease 1997; Sagoff 1999). Second, critics claimed that QLG followed a flawed decision making process that excluded affected interests and feared that the QLG proposal would set a precedent for local control over national forest management (Sease 1997; Sagoff 1999). However, QLG had attempted to have its voice heard in the decision making processes run by the USFS and their ideas were misrepresented and/or fell on deaf ears. Moreover, there was little room for groups like the Sierra Club to be involved in the QLG effort, since the Sierra Club had taken a 'zero logging' approach in the National Forests and opposed commercial cutting of dead timber even to establish fire breaks (Sagoff 1999). The Sierra Club was reluctant to attend QLG meetings, since being part of local processes undermined the larger objectives held by the national group. Therefore there was little room for compromise to find a sustainable solution for the communities most affected by job losses, failing ecosystems and catastrophic fire. Going to Congress was the only way to have their voice heard above the din of the USFS and national environmental community lobbyists.

The tension between the national environmental groups and the local community in the Quincy case is a microcosm of the larger debate about the role and validity of local versus national approaches to environmental management. On one hand, the local group was trying to create and implement a plan that served its diverse needs. On the other hand, national agencies and groups felt the need to support the legal processes, for which they had fought for many years, that had been established to protect environmental and natural resource values. The problem was that

Quincy and the other communities in the three forests were suffering the ecological and economic consequences as these national processes played out. The environmental assessment process and various scientific studies commandeered by Congress and the USFS prohibited any action from taking place. From their vantage point the community members were the ones seeing the jobs disappearing, the schools closing, the roads falling into disrepair, the fire risks growing more imminent, and their old-growth areas even more threatened.

Meanwhile, US Senator Barbara Boxer, under great pressure from environmental groups, withdrew her support and became an active opponent of the QLG legislation. Other Senators then sought to block the bill from making it out of committee, thereby preventing a vote on it. In spite of these political roadblocks, the QLG Forest Recovery Act passed the Senate in the fall of 1998 as part of a rider on the Omnibus Appropriations Bill and was signed into law on 21 October by President Bill Clinton (Terhune and Terhune 1998).

The Quincy Act stipulated that a five-year pilot project would be implemented on the Plumas and Lassen National Forests and the Sierraville District of the Tahoe National Forest. No special management powers were delegated to the QLG as part of the passage of the bill. However, the group and other interests were to be 'consulted' as part of the on-going process. Implementation of the plan rested with the Forest Service, yet little has taken place with regard to the implementation of the plan. While Congress has not provided funding so far, there were provisions in fiscal year 2001 for a full allocation of the funds requested, as part of continuing efforts by Senator Fienstein and Congressman Herger. The USFS has placed restrictions on the plan's implementation that effectively reduced the programme by 60 per cent and held the area to a higher standard than the rest of the Sierra Nevada for over eighteen months. The USFS also claimed that the fire hazard reduction restrictions proposed in the plan could harm habitat for the California spotted owl (De Lasaux 2001), even though the science behind these assertions remains uncertain (Lee 2001).

In the summers of 1999 and 2000, catastrophic wildfires swept throughout the western United States. The QLG proposal to use experimental firebreaks to help reduce the threat of wildfire was not in place and more than 40,000 ha burned throughout the QLG area. In one of the fires a roadless habitat area for the California spotted owl burned, demonstrating that inaction is just as risky as action in the case of fire protection in owl habitat (May 2000). In the meantime, timber representatives in the group are frustrated since they are not experiencing any of the jobs and small-diameter timber production that were part of the original agreement. A

newly retooled mill designed to process small-diameter logs from thinning has recently been closed permanently because of the lack of national
forest logs and depressed lumber prices. Over 150 mill workers have had
their lives and families disrupted. The population of California spotted
owls has continued to decline at a rate of 5–10 per cent per year while
this drama has played out (Verner 1999).

In the battle for biodiversity preservation, no one can afford to alienate potential allies. The QLG case study is illustrative of how difficult
it can be for a local group to work within the larger confines of a centralised system of legal standards and national actors. Both the USFS and
environmental groups have obstructed QLG's efforts to propose a solution to the multi-faceted problem facing their communities. In doing so,
both the USFS and the national environmental organisations have failed
to take advantage of the resources the QLG possesses to provide better
stewardship of the land. In the fight to maintain its authority over forest
resources, the USFS has alienated a potential ally in the QLG. Likewise,
national environmental groups have demonised the QLG, when these
community residents have demonstrated a commitment to the California
spotted owl that translates into day-to-day activities and actions that they
must oversee and implement.

Future directions for community-based biodiversity protection in the US

Community-based efforts often focus on managing for more than one
value. This leaves them open to criticism that they compromise biodiversity protection in favour of other values. The empirical evidence of exactly
how biodiversity has been compromised under recent community-based
efforts is sparse, as are examples of how biodiversity has been improved.
In most cases, simply not enough is known to point to precise causal factors in how specific actions relate to species loss or gain. We know habitat
is key, but whether habitat can best be protected and enhanced in the
long run through national laws or community efforts remains uncertain.
Given this uncertainty, it is unwise to alienate any potential ally in the
battle to preserve what remains of our biological heritage.

In both of the cases discussed here, community-based responses were
reactions to the perceived inadequacy of federal regulations and agencies to meet the needs of communities closer to the problems at hand.
These responses instigated counter-responses from the federal agencies
and national groups that also have vested interests in the protection of
resources they perceive to be of national significance. Consequently, the
lessons that flow from this chapter lead to a greater appreciation for how

community-based efforts can be integrated with existing national standards. These can be divided into lessons for communities, for environmental organisations and for state and federal agencies.

Lessons for local communities

Community-based efforts require hard work at the local level to make them a viable option. Individual members of the QLG have devoted countless hours over the past eight years to mastering the minutiae of fire ecology, owl habitat science and timbering techniques, among other topics, to devise realistic alternatives for managing the forests in which they live. Likewise, thousands of volunteers have devoted time, energy and effort to the many salmon improvement projects throughout Oregon. Without real commitment from communities, community-based efforts will fail to thrive. Thus, a limiting factor for community-based efforts in biodiversity is commitment from the community.

Communities must interact constructively with bureaucratic and organisational cultures unlike their own. Both agencies and national environmental organisations operate according to rules, norms and behaviours that may be foreign to local people. Communities need to recognise that their efforts fall within a broader framework of regulatory action. The understanding and support of public, private and non-profit actors at the local, state and federal level are important to protection efforts. Local communities, in most cases, will not operate in a regulatory vacuum. Consequently, communities need to demonstrate a willingness to learn and to appreciate the constraints within which agencies and organisations operate. If community members are not willing to understand the constraints affecting the professional agencies and organisations involved with the protection of a species, they will be ill prepared to communicate effectively with those that also have a vested interest in the management of the species or habitat.

Not all local interests are candidates for community-based approaches. One of the fears of the Sierra Club chairman Michael McCloskey is that, '[i]ndustry thinks its odds are better in local forums and it is ready to train experts to master the collaborative process. In communities where industry is strong, it can generate pressure in a way it cannot at the national level' (Duane 1997). Not all communities will have well-balanced interests or a predisposition to collaborate. None the less, in the last two decades, new environmental ethics have evolved, local and state watchdog non-profit environmental groups have sprung up and industry has taken on a greener veneer. While these ethics, groups and sentiments do not prevail in all places, in those places where sincere efforts to manage at the local level emerge, it makes sense to try to benefit from this nascent capacity for local governance and stewardship.

Lessons for environmental groups

National groups can play a more constructive role in facilitating local stewardship. The environmental movement is being devolved to more local levels. As a consequence, better ways are needed to integrate these newer, more localised efforts into the broader environmental institutional infrastructure that currently exists. National interest groups are resistant because community-based efforts threaten the hold on power that national interests have commanded for decades, as well as raising some provocative questions about the appropriate locus of decision making authority within environmental governance. It is not surprising that the Wilderness Society and the Sierra Club are threatened by groups such as QLG, but obstructing their efforts does little to take advantage of the interest and inventiveness of locals who ultimately must steward the resources in question. A more useful role for national groups would be to provide financial and technical support to community-based efforts and serve as a consultant or monitor practices on the ground.

Cultural differences exist between national and local groups. National groups work within a competitive interest group framework that thrives on conflict and a winner-takes-all culture. To be effective within this culture, they have adopted strategies and tactics that allow little compromise. In contrast to national groups, community-based efforts thrive in a collaborative culture and place a priority on finding common ground. Timber, agriculture and salmon all are important to the culture and economy of Oregon. While national groups see the focus on common interest as evidence of compromise and collaboration in their most derogatory connotations, local efforts like QLG and the Oregon plan are valued for their ability to co-operate and seek long-term, sustainable solutions. These cultures clash head on when attempts are made to integrate community-based efforts with broader national efforts to protect the environment. Greater appreciation for these cultural differences, and the functions they serve, is needed if local biodiversity protection experiments are to be integrated into national efforts. An awareness of the differences and a willingness to co-operate, where the appropriate conditions exist, would be a constructive first step.

National and local groups perform different roles. National groups like the Sierra Club and the Wilderness Society perform a different role from community groups. National groups have provided a national platform of very valuable environmental regulations that have served the United States well. At best, the national groups have provided a solid statutory framework that local groups can use to advance their own environmental agendas. At worst, this national response provides a uniform approach that leaves little room for innovation and creativity at the local level for achieving environmental, and community, sustainability. The strength of the community-based approach is its ability to integrate diverse values and craft responses that provide a better fit for the social, cultural and ecological conditions that are specific to their needs. Their greatest weakness is that they may be co-opted or captured by single interests and used inappropriately to undermine the progress made by federal agencies and national groups. Recognising the dual nature of environmental action, national groups need to reassess how their role at the local level is transforming. In those situations where national groups fear that community-based efforts could be co-opted by industry, a more constructive role for them could be in training and enhancing their local groups to provide better balance to these current imbalances rather than dismissing or undermining grass-roots activism.

Lessons for agencies

Agencies can play a more constructive role in facilitating community-based approaches. In those cases where communities wish to play an active role in the management of their resources, agencies should capitalise on this opportunity. However, many bureaucratic roadblocks can obstruct this, including the discretion in how agencies choose to work with communities. Some agencies invoke regulations to limit the scope of community involvement, while other agencies waive rules and regulations to facilitate community involvement. The USFS has played an obstructionist role in the case of QLG efforts to be more involved in the management of their national forests. Poor communication and turf battles have typified the interaction in the Quincy case and created an incentive for the QLG members to go around their local USFS supervisors to policy actors in Washington, DC. In contrast, state and federal agencies in Oregon have gone to great lengths to incorporate voluntary and community efforts in salmon recovery. Agency incentives and cultures will differ in different areas. Greater effort needs to be expended on understanding how agencies that work well with localities manage to do so. Likewise, in those cases where agencies are especially obstructionist, a greater understanding of the bureaucratic norms and incentives that prevent greater collaboration could shed light on how to create a culture that is more conducive to constructive agency–community interaction.

Individual commitment is a limiting factor in agency–community interaction. Working with communities is a time- and labour-intensive exercise for which there are few institutional rewards within agencies. The types of individuals who select themselves to work with groups are rare and easily exploited. Consequently, requiring agencies to participate in community-based efforts without altering the roles and training staff will make it difficult for agency personnel to participate in meaningful ways. The entire state of Oregon has marshalled its resources and authority to encourage salmon recovery, thereby creating a more comfortable environment for individual agency workers to work with local interests. This alignment of effort bodes well for the future of the salmon. In contrast, the USFS has given lip service to collaboration, but there are few rewards for individuals to engage in such enterprises, while there are many negative incentives. In those situations where individuals work constructively with communities, agencies need to do more to ensure that they provide greater flexibility in the work schedules to allow them to attend meetings, to reward them for their efforts, and not to ostracise them for exploring the limits of discretionary flexibility.

Agencies need more than the ESA to protect and restore biodiversity. If the end goal for agencies is to recover species and habitats, then the ESA is an incomplete approach. Mandates will be inadequate when large-scale collective action on public and private property is needed, as in the case of most biodiversity protection. The Oregon case demonstrates how voluntary efforts can work to supplement ESA efforts. The goal is not to replace the ESA, but to complement it with voluntary action where the mandate is weak or ineffective. Communities that believe in the management prescriptions and have a stake in them are necessary for state and federally mandated prescriptions to work. In Quincy, the USFS effort to protect existing California spotted owls and their habitat has alienated the community while also failing to protect the owl. None the less, the community remains committed to protecting old-growth habitats and the owl. In light of the great hardship faced by the residents in Quincy, their commitment to biodiversity preservation (among other values) should be seen as a *vital resource* in the overall fight for the preservation of the species and its habitat.

Agencies need to place greater priority on monitoring. Monitoring efforts have the greatest potential to provide data about what works and what does not. Given the uncertain science affiliated with habitat restoration and species recovery, agencies can play a constructive role in organising and overseeing comprehensive monitoring efforts. If agencies, environmental bodies and communities are to have faith in community-based efforts, then all parties need to take an active role in monitoring. This is vital to adapt management techniques as well as assess whether actions are appropriate or not. Given the scope of most monitoring efforts, more can be done to encourage the involvement of non-governmental groups at the local, state and national levels to participate in monitoring. In any case, the act of monitoring is a bonding as well as a learning experience.

Agencies need to engage in community-based approaches wisely. With all the zeal surrounding and celebrating community-based environmental management efforts, there exists a risk in their haphazard use. State and federal agencies should be wary of mandating community-based approaches without regard to the appropriate conditions for success. If these approaches are misused and their failures promoted widely, this promising tool will be discarded or at least devalued as a management and governance alternative. Community-based approaches are resource intensive in terms of time and money to facilitate their success. Agencies need to choose wisely which communities are most appropriate for collaboration.

Final observations

The trend towards community-based approaches will continue to grow as long as existing institutions and agencies fail to meet the diverse needs of communities that increasingly have the capacity to address their own problems. Federally mandated, institutionally implemented responses will continue to fit poorly the needs of diverse communities across America. As such, federal statutory approaches represent an imperfect solution for communities seeking feasible and realistic, from their standpoint, alternatives for environmental management problems. The lesson that flows from the two case studies in this chapter is that we are not faced with an either/or choice in many of these situations where national standards clash with community discretion. They can co-exist. Oregon demonstrates that in spite of the federal listing of the coho salmon on the ESA list, voluntary, community-based watershed-based efforts can continue. In the Quincy case, many obstacles remain, but so do many opportunities, if the advice of experience is attended to.

The larger lessons arising from this contemporary US experience are important for the objectives of this book. Biodiversity cannot be promoted and protected by centralised laws, national advocacy organisations or decentralised communities alone. They must all work together. The causes of biodiversity loss are complex, often arising from multi-faceted insults to habitat. Consequently the solutions, if they are to be effective, also must address this complexity. Government agencies, environmental advocacy groups and communities all hold pieces of the puzzle. Fitting these pieces together in the most beneficial way to serve threatened and endangered species is the trick. Local people have knowledge and a capacity for trust and reciprocity that, when guided through genuine dialogue, can enhance biodiversity and retain jobs and local cultural values. Agency personnel can be unduly buffeted by conservation cultures and lobbying, while policy communities of biodiversity promoters may fail to engage meaningful social capital at the local level. The result is less resilience in biodiversity and economy, with no experience of innovation and honest adaptation that biodiversity requires if protecting beyond the protected is to be honourably achieved.

Note

The author would like to thank Ron Brunner, Michael De Lasaux and Craig W. Thomas for their thoughtful comments on an earlier draft of this chapter.

REFERENCES

Applegate, R. 1997. Governor signs Oregon Salmon Plan legislation. Press release. Accessed at http://www.orgeon-plan.org/PR-03-25-97.html.
    1998. Governor releases State of Salmon Report. Press release. Accessed at http://www.oregon-plan.org/PR-05-20-98.html.
Bean, M. 1999 Endangered species, endangered Act? *Environment* 41(1): 12–18, 34–8.
Beirele, T.C. 1999. Using social goals to evaluate public participation in environmental decisions. *Policy Studies Review* 16(3): 75–103.
Brick, P. 1998. Of imposters, optimists, and kings: finding a political niche for collaborative conservation. *Chronicle of Community* 2: 34–8.
Brown, J.L. 1997. Preserving species: the endangered species act versus ecosystem management regime, ecological political considerations, and recommendations for reform. *Journal of Environmental Law and Litigation*, 12: 151–265.
Brunner, R., Colburn, C., Cromley, C., Klein, R. and Olsen, E. 2002. *Finding Common Ground: Governance and Natural Resources in the American West*. New Haven: Yale University Press.

Carr, D., Selin, S.W. and Schuett, M.A. 1998. Managing public forests: understanding the role of collaborative planning. *Environmental Management* 22(5): 767–76.

Christensen, J. 1998. Bringing the salmon back. *American Forests* 103(4): 16–20.

Coggins, G.C. 1998. Of Californicators, quislings and crazies: some perils of devolved collaboration. *Chronicle of Community* 2: 27–33.

Coglianese, C. 1999. The limits of consensus. *Environment* 42(6): 28–33.

Colburn, C. 2002. Forest policy and the Quincy Library Group. In R. Brunner, C. Colburn, C. Cromley, R. Klein and E. Olsen (eds.), *Finding Common Ground: Governance and Natural Resources in the American West*, pp. 205–261. New Haven: Yale University Press.

Collette, C. 2001. Oregon's plan for salmon and watersheds: the basics of building a recovery plan. In P. Brick, D. Snow and S. van de Wetering (eds.), *Across the Great Divide: Explorations in Collaborative Conservation and the American West*, pp. 140–9. Covelo, CA: Island Press.

De Lasaux, M. 2001. University of California Cooperative Extension, Natural Resources Advisor, Plumas and Sierra Counties. Personal communication. 24 February 2001.

Duane, T.P. 1997. Community participation ecosystem management. *Ecology Law Quarterly* 24: 771–800.

Environmental Protection Agency 1997. *Community-based Environmental Protection: A Resource Book for Protecting Ecosystems and Communities.* (EPA 230-B-96-003), Washington, DC: Environmental Protection Agency.

Executive Order 1999. Executive Order for Oregon Plan. Executive Order No. EO 99-01. Accessed at http://www.oregon-plan.org/Eo-99/htm.

Fairman, D. 1999. Evaluating consensus building efforts: according to whom? and based on what? Consensus Building Institute. http:// www.mediate. com/consensus/consensus/0199evaluation.htm.

Gentle, T. n.d. Oregon recovery plan tries to give everyone a role. Oregon State University Extension Service. http://eesc.orst.edu/salmon/restoration/roles.html.

Goble, D.D., George, S.M., Mazaika, K., Scott, J.M. and Karl, J. 1999. Local and national protection of endangered species: an assessment, *Environmental Science and Policy* 2: 43–59.

Hays, S. 1959. *Conservation and the Gospel of Efficiency: The Progressive Conservation Movement, 1890–1920.* New York: Atheneum.

John, D. 1994. *Civic Environmentalism: Alternatives to Regulation in States and Communities.* Washington, DC: Congressional Quarterly Press.

John, D. and Mlay, M. 1998. Community-based environmental protection: how federal and state agencies can encourage civic environmentalism. Working paper. Washington, DC: National Academy of Public Administration.

Kemmis, D. 1990. *Community and the Politics of Place.* Norman: University of Oklahoma Press.

Kenney, D.S. 1999a. Historical and sociopolitical context of the western watersheds movement. *Journal of the American Water Resources Association* 35(3): 493–503.

  1999b. Are community-based watershed groups really effective? *Chronicle of Community* Winter, 1999: 33–7.

2000. *Arguing about Consensus: Examining the Case against Western Watershed Initiatives and Other Collaborative Groups Active in Natural Resource Management.* Boulder, CO: University of Colorado School of Law, Natural Resources Law Center.

Kenney, D.S. and Lord, W.B. 1999. *Analysis of Institutional Innovation in the Natural Resources and Environmental Realm: The Emergence of Alternative Problem-Solving Strategies in the American West.* Research Report RR-21. Boulder, CO: University of Colorado School of Law, Natural Resources Law Center.

Kenney, D.S., McAllister, S.T., Caile, W.H. and Peckham, J.S. 2000. *The New Watershed Source Book: A Directory and Review of Watershed Initiatives in the Western United States.* Boulder, CO: University of Colorado School of Law Natural Resources Law Center.

Killam, G. 2001. Program Officer, River Network. Portland, OR. Personal communication, 23 Jan. 2001.

Kitzhaber, J.A. 1998. Governor's Statement on coastal Coho decision. Press release. Accessed at http://www.oregon-plan.org/PR-06-04-98.html.

LaRoe, E.T., Farris, G.S. Puckett, C.E., Doran, P.D. and Mac, M.J. (eds.) 1995. *Our Living Resources: A Report to the Nation on the Distribution, Abundance, and Health of U.S. Plants, Animals and Ecosystems.* Washington, DC: United States Department of the Interior National Biological Service. US Government Documents No. I 49.2:R 31-15.

Lee, D. 2001. Letter from Danny C. Lee, Research Ecologist at the USFS Pacific Southwest Research Station to Kent Connaughton and Peter Stine, Sierra Nevada Framework for Conservation and Collaboration. On file with author.

Little, J.B. 1998. Common ground: forest foes on northern California bury the hatchet but spark a new furor over three Sierra forests. *California Wild* Spring: 10–15.

Lydeard, C. 1996. U.S. Biodiversity Status Report. *Conservation Biology* 10(5): 1480–2.

McCloskey, M. 1996. The skeptic: collaboration has its limits. *High Country News* 28(9). Accessed at http://www.hcn.org/1996/may13/dir/Opinion_Theskipti.html.

McGinnis, M.V. 1999. Making the watershed connection. *Policy Studies Journal* 27(3): 497–501.

Maleki, S.M. and Riggers, B.L.K. 2000. *Watershed Restoration Inventory. Monitoring Program Report to the Oregon Plan for Salmon and Watersheds*, Governor's Natural Resources Office, Salem, Oregon.

Marston, E. 1997. The timber wars evolve into a divisive attempt at peace. *High Country News* 29(18): 1–13.

May, P. 2000. Innovative fire strategy takes root. *San Jose Mercury News* September 3, 2000.

Nicklesburg, S.M. 1998. Mere volunteers? The promise and limits of community-based environmental protection. *Virginia Law Review* 84: 1371–1409.

Noss, R.F. and Peters, R.L. 1995. *Endangered Ecosystems of the United States: A Status Report and Plan for Action.* Washington, DC: Defenders of Wildlife.

Olson, D.M. and Dinerstein, E. 1998. The Global 200: a representation approach to conserving the Earth's most biologically valuable ecoregions. *Conservation Biology* 3: 502–12.

Oregon Plan 2000. Overview of Oregon Plan. Accessed at http://www.oregon-plan.org/overview.html.

Oregon Watershed Enhancement Board 2000. Oregon Plan Quarterly Implementation Report. 1 July 2000 to 30 September 2000. Portland: OWEB.

Parker, V. 1995. Natural resources management by litigation. In R.L. Knight and S.F. Bates, (eds.), *A New Century for Natural Resources Management*, pp. 209–20. Washington, DC: Island Press.

Pelkey, N., Leach, W., Harrison, S., Cook, E., Zafonte, M. and Sabatier, P. 1999. The impacts of social and ecological conditions on the likelihood of stakeholder based resource management efforts. Paper presented at 1999 Annual Meeting of the Association of Public Policy Analysis and Management. Washington, DC.

Ricketts, T.H, Dinerstein, E., Olson, D.M., Loucks, C.J., Eichbaum, W., Della Sala, D., Kavanagh, K., Hedao, P., Hurley, P.T., Carney, K.M., Abell, R. and Walters, S. 1999. *Terrestrial Ecoregions of North America: A Conservation Assessment*. Washington, DC: Island Press.

Sagoff, M. 1999. The view from Quincy Library: civic engagement in environmental problem-solving. In R.K. Fullinwider (ed.), *Civil Society, Democracy and Civic Renewal*, pp. 151–83. Lanham, MD: Rowman & Littlefield.

Scott, J.M., Davis, F., Csuti, B., Noss, R., Butterfield, B., Groves, C., Anderson, J., Caicco, S., D'Erchia, F., Edwards, T.C., Ulliman, J. and Wright, R.G. 1993. Gap analysis: a geographic approach to protection of biological diversity, *Wildlife Monographs* 123: 1–41.

Sease, D. 1997. Sierra Club Legislative Director Testimony on Quincy Library Group Bill, Senate Subcommittee on Forests and Public Lands, Committee on Energy and Natural Resources, concerning S. 1028 and H.R. 858, 24 July 1977.

Steelman, T.A. 1999. Community-based environmental management: agency- and community-driven efforts. Presented at the 21st Annual Research Conference of the Association for Public Policy Analysis and Management. Washington, DC.

Steelman, T.A. and Carmin, J.A. 2002. Community-based watershed remediation: connecting organizational resources to social and substantive outcomes. In D. Rahm (ed.), *The Politics of Toxic Waste: 21st Century Challenges*, pp.145–78. Portland: McFarland Publishers.

Stein, B.A. 2001. A fragile cornucopia: assessing the status of US biodiversity. *Environment* 43(7): 1–8.

Stein, B.A., Kutner, L.S. and Adams, J.S. (eds.) 2000. *Precious Heritage: The Status of Biodiversity in the United States*. Oxford: Oxford University Press.

Terhune, P. and Terhune, G. 1998. Engaging, empowering, and negotiating community: strategies for conservation and development. Case Study of the Quincy Library Group. Presented at the Conservation and Development Forum. West Virginia University, 8–10 October 1998. Accessed at http://www.qlg.org/pub/miscdoc/overview.htm.

The Nature Conservancy 1996. *Priorities for Conservation: 1996 Annual Report Card for US Plant and Animal Species*. Arlington, VA: The Nature Conservancy.

US Fish and Wildlife Service 2001. Threatened and Endangered Species System (TESS). Accessed at http://ecos.fws.gov/tess/html/boxscore-dec-2000-print.html.

Verner, J. 1999. Review of A Preliminary Report on the Status of the California Spotted Owl in the Sierra Nevada. USDA Forest Service Pacific Southwest Research Station. 7 July 1999. Accessed at www.qulg.org/pub/miscdoc/vernerreview.htm.

Weber, E.P. 2000. A new vanguard for the environment: grass-roots ecosystem management as a new environmental movement. *Society and Natural Resources* 13(3): 237–59.

Wilson, E.O. (ed.) 1988. *Biodiversity*. Washington, DC: National Academy Press.

Wondolleck, J. and Yaffee, S. 2000. *Making Collaboration Work: Lessons from Innovation in Natural Resource Management*. Covelo, CA: Island Press.

World Resources Institute 2000. *World Resources 2000–2001 People and Ecosystems: The Fraying Web of Life*. Washington, DC: World Resources Institute.

Yaffee, S.L. 1996. Ecosystem management in practice: the importance of human institutions. *Ecological Applications* 6(3): 724–7.

Yaffee, S.L., Phillips, A.F., Frantz, I.C., Hardy, P.W., Maleki, S.M. and Thorpe, B. 1996. *Ecosystem Management in the United States: An Assessment of Current Experience*. Washington, DC: Island Press.

8 An ecoregional approach to biodiversity conservation in the Cape Floral Kingdom, South Africa

Amanda Younge

Introduction

At the outset of the new century, we face the prospect of global biodiversity loss and species extinction on a scale unprecedented in human history, largely at the hands of human society. Were such loss not occasioned by human activity, our response might be to let nature take its course. As it is, we are forced to take responsibility for our actions and derelictions. Although it is the cumulative effect of untold numbers of small actions that is driving the process, it is no longer adequate to hope that halting and reversing such loss can likewise be achieved by large numbers of small actions. It is increasingly evident that project-based approaches to conservation cannot hope meaningfully to engage the economic and social forces driving biodiversity loss at a global scale.

One response to this crisis on the part of some NGOs and government agencies has been to move towards conservation planning and action at a regional scale. The World Wildlife Fund (WWF) argues that, 'to halt the global extinction crisis that we now face, we must conduct conservation planning over larger spatial scales and longer time frames than ever before' (Dinerstein *et al.* 2000: 13). WWF has adopted what it terms the 'ecoregion' as the appropriate scale for conservation planning, and has identified over 200 ecoregions world-wide as priorities for action. WWF defines an ecoregion as:

A large area of land or water that contains a geographically distinct assemblage of natural communities that a) share a large majority of their species and ecological dynamics, b) share similar environmental conditions, and c) interact ecologically in ways that are critical for their long-term persistence. (Dinerstein *et al.* 2000: 241)

According to Gordon Orians, the move towards ecoregion-based conservation is based on several critical hypotheses:

First, conservation planning at scales higher than sites will more effectively conserve the full range of biodiversity and promote its persistence. Second, many significant threats to biodiversity operate at the scale of multiple sites . . . Third, co-ordinated regional effort can better achieve the goal of representation and avoid redundancy . . . Fourth, an ecoregional approach can more accurately define an area for restoration than approaches primarily based on connecting sites or tailoring plans to political boundaries or agendas. Finally, comprehensive ecoregion strategies will have a greater impact in leveraging political will and donor interest and support than initiatives focussed on sites. (Orians 1998: 1)

Taking an ecoregional approach to conservation offers a number of opportunities. It enables scientists to set targets for representation of biodiversity for the ecoregion as a whole, and offers opportunities to develop strategies to address threats to biodiversity in a holistic, integrated and systematic manner. It also enables a meaningful engagement with the social and economic forces driving biodiversity loss at a range of scales including regional and global. According to WWF, it enables conservation planning 'to better assess the proximate and root causes of biodiversity loss and to design policy and management interventions at appropriate levels, from international trade policies to site-specific park management or community development initiatives' (WWF 1998). Further, it permits the establishment of enabling frameworks of co-ordinated policy, laws and institutions to protect biodiversity. Ecoregional planning offers opportunities for an engagement with major stakeholders across political and administrative boundaries by developing a consensus on goals and strategic objectives and in creating a co-ordinated programme of action. As such it enables the development of powerful partnerships and the potential to mobilise significant resources to achieve its goals and strategic objectives. A further advantage of action at regional scale derives from the increased potential for raising public awareness of the economic and social consequences of biodiversity loss.

Most ecoregional planning initiatives are at a relatively early stage of development, exploring a variety of approaches both in terms of conservation science and in terms of the management of the strategic planning process and of stakeholder involvement. This chapter provides an overview of one such ecoregional planning initiative, the Cape Action Plan for the Environment (CAPE), which focuses on the Cape Floral Kingdom. A preliminary attempt is made to assess, on the basis of the CAPE experience, what it would take for ecoregional planning to achieve its objectives, and to identify lessons, issues and some concerns that could constrain the effectiveness of this and other ecoregional planning initiatives in the future.

Conservation of biodiversity in South Africa

South Africa is fortunate to be one of the biological 'megadiversity' countries in the world. This status is due in large part to the Cape Floral

Kingdom (CFK), the smallest of the world's six floral kingdoms and, for its size, the most diverse. This region is the only floral kingdom contained within one country.

South Africa is an emerging democracy, whose constitution contains amongst the strongest environmental protection in the world. The new government has shown its commitment to conservation by becoming party to the International Convention on Biodiversity, the RAMSAR Convention on Wetlands of International Importance, the Convention to Combat Desertification, the Convention on International Trade in Endangered Species of Wild Flora and Fauna, and the World Heritage Convention. It has strengthened the legal framework protecting the environment through a White Paper on Biodiversity (1997) and the National Environmental Management Act (1998) (O'Riordan *et al.* 2000) and is in the process of undertaking a National Biodiversity Strategy and Action Plan.

However, the country still suffers from extremes of poverty and inequitable resource distribution. Social injustice, environmental degradation, poverty and disease go hand in hand. The South African Environmental Justice Networking Forum has documented case after case of environmental danger due to toxicity, waste putrefaction, water pollution and insanitary and dangerous domestic environments (see Butler 1998 for comprehensive reviews). Democracy has of necessity brought about a switch of government funding towards economic development and socio-economic priorities in an attempt to rectify these problems. This has meant a shift in funding away from sectors such as conservation, with negative consequences for biodiversity. For example, in the Eastern Cape, South Africa's poorest province and where an important part of the remaining CFK is to be found, the majority of professional posts in the Department of Environmental Affairs lie vacant owing to the lack of public funds. In the Western Cape, staff costs in the Western Cape Nature Conservation Board (a prime player in the conservation of CFK) amount to 70 per cent of total budget, and at times there is insufficient funding for vehicle maintenance. It has rapidly become evident that in a country with such huge disparities, a successful conservation strategy needs also to address developmental issues, and that the development of public–private partnerships will be crucial to effective conservation (Stoll-Kleemann and O'Riordan 2002).

The country has in train a number of biodiversity conservation projects which are supported by or are seeking support from the Global Environment Facility (GEF). The most advanced of these is the Cape Action Plan for the Environment (CAPE), which has developed a strategy and action plan to conserve the Cape Floral Kingdom. CAPE's significance derives from a number of factors. First, it addresses the conservation of an entire floral kingdom, the CFK, which is one of the hottest global biodiversity hotspots. Second, it has developed innovative approaches to ecoregion-based conservation, along the lines of GIS-based integrated and adaptive ecosystem management of the kind introduced in chapter 1. Third, it demonstrates an approach to biodiversity conservation that integrates biological and socio-economic concerns (see Cowling *et al.* forthcoming, for a full account of this project).

Origins of the CAPE project

The Cape Floral Kingdom and adjoining marine areas have spectacularly high levels of plant and animal biodiversity (over 1,400 Red Data Book plant species), three marine provinces, important RAMSAR sites and many sites of scenic beauty. The CFK is extremely small, being only 90,000 km^2 in extent. At least 70 per cent of its 9,600 plant species are found nowhere else on Earth. Major threats include loss of habitat to agriculture, rapid and insensitive development, the overexploitation of marine resources and wild flowers, and the spread of alien species. Some important habitats have been reduced by over 90 per cent, and less than 5 per cent of land in the lowlands enjoys any form of conservation status. Underlying causes of biodiversity loss include lack of capacity and poor co-ordination between bodies responsible for management of natural resources, lack of awareness of the importance of biodiversity, and a short-term focus on meeting socio-economic and poverty alleviation needs (Younge and Ashwell 2000: 7).

In 1998, South Africa was granted US$12.3 million by the Global Environment Facility for the Cape Peninsula Biodiversity Conservation Project. While the bulk of this funding was directed at conservation of the Cape Peninsula, a small but highly significant part of the CFK, the need for a conservation strategy and action plan for the whole floral kingdom was also identified. US$1 million of the total grant was therefore dedicated to the development of the Cape Action Plan for the Environment (CAPE), a strategy and action plan to conserve the whole CFK. This project was undertaken over a two-year period from 1998 to 2000, and benefited from local in-kind counterpart funding of US$400,000. It was co-ordinated by the World Wide Fund for Nature South Africa (WWF-SA) in partnership with government, communities and the private sector. Its scope included biodiversity conservation in the terrestrial, marine and freshwater ecosystems of the Cape Floral Kingdom.

As a strategy-development process, CAPE forms the first phase of a long-term programme to conserve biodiversity in the CFK. The project was undertaken in three phases: situation assessment, strategy development and implementation programming, and was co-ordinated by

WWF-SA on behalf of government. The objectives of this initial strategy development phase were to:

> identify conservation priorities, based on assessments of bio-diversity and threats;
>
> develop a long-term strategy and vision for biodiversity conservation in the Cape Floral Kingdom;
>
> draft a five-year action plan and investment programme to address conservation priorities;
>
> identify potential sources of funding for these activities:

At the outset, CAPE faced a number of challenges. These derived primarily from the need to develop an approach to conserving terrestrial and aquatic biodiversity that would result in a single holistic integrated strategy and co-ordinate the activities of all actors in implementation. These challenges included the need to:

> develop a scientifically rigorous approach to the conservation of a representative sample of biodiversity patterns and ecological processes in the region;
>
> through a participatory process, formulate a strategy that meaningfully tackles the underlying causes of biodiversity loss, and mainstream implementation through the creation of buy-in by key government agencies;
>
> develop conservation approaches that deliver economic benefits to disadvantaged constituencies;
>
> ensure the sustainability of the implementation programme through supporting institutional development, developing partnerships between key players from relevant sectors (including government, the private sector and the conservation community) and creating opportunities for monitoring and review.

The approach adopted by CAPE to addressing these challenges is outlined below.

Biodiversity analysis

Conservation planning at ecoregional scale is a relatively new activity. As far as possible, it needs to be supported by scientific analysis that is able to address the objective of ensuring persistence of a representative sample of biodiversity patterns and ecological processes. A number of ecoregional planning processes have approached this challenge through the development of a 'clear biodiversity vision, set[ting] out the long term (e.g., 50-year) goals for conservation of the ecoregion's biodiversity, identifying key sites, populations and ecological processes . . . guiding the development of the Conservation Plan and also guiding strategic decisions as circumstances and opportunities change' (WWF 1998: 5). However, the terrestrial component of the CAPE project was instead based on a systematic series of steps in a planning protocol, analysing terrestrial biodiversity patterns and processes, setting targets and developing options to meet these targets (see Cowling *et al.* forthcoming) This approach, which utilises the GIS-based decision-support system known as C-Plan, offers the following benefits to ecoregional planning.

It enables a rigorous and systematic approach to setting defensible targets for both biodiversity pattern and ecological process across the whole region.

It offers the potential to develop a range of strategic options for the design of a co-ordinated reserve network, each of which can be evaluated in terms of effectiveness in meeting targets.

It is iterative, and makes underlying assumptions clear, supporting transparent, participative decision making.

It develops a decision-support system for the ecoregion that can be curated, maintained and updated, thus serving as a basis for ongoing evaluation of development proposals and conservation planning in the long term.

In addition, quantitative approaches such as this offer the potential to integrate biological and socio-economic concerns (WWF Central Africa Progam Office forthcoming) However, during the CAPE process, problems arose with regard to the integration of terrestrial and marine analyses in the ecoregion. Further refinement would be needed to ensure that such approaches are applicable to the conservation of marine ecoregions.

Analysis of key issues

CAPE's analysis of social and economic factors affecting biodiversity loss suffered initially from a lack of focus, a tendency that has become evident in a number of ecoregional planning exercises and which is currently the source of much debate. The problem appears to stem in part from poor communication between social scientists, economists and conservationists. There is also need for more innovative analytical approaches to the analysis of socio-economic aspects at regional scale. Much of this could be overcome by attending to accurate identification and understanding the underlying causes of biodiversity loss and the constraints to the successful implementation of conservation strategies. Within CAPE, the problem was addressed by identifying key issues and their underlying drivers. These included:

the spread of invasive alien species on both land and in the water; poor fire management;

poor and uncoordinated catchment management, with loss of
water availability, erosion and siltation;

inappropriate agricultural practices, leading to excessive water
use, invasions of alien vegetation, and nutrient/toxic chemical
pollution;

poor landuse planning controls, inadequate to address intensive
development pressures for both formal and informal landuses;

climate change and implications for water availability, erosion
and species stresses.

Underlying drivers of these threats to the integrity of the CFK were identified as being:

a failure to value the ecological services provided by intact ecosystems;

an inability to recognise the socio-economic opportunities linked
to conserving the biome, notably for alien removal, flower harvesting and nature-based tourism-related activities;

lack of general public awareness of the potential for economic
gain and social opportunity arising from conservation;

poverty and inequity of access to opportunities;

fragmented, uncoordinated and inappropriate laws, poor intergovernmental communication, lack of reliable funding for
long-term contracts, and contradictions in property rights law
over the global status of privately owned resources.

An important component of the situation assessment phase was an attempt to estimate the value of economic benefits of biodiversity in the
region. This analysis concluded that:

abalone catches are worth ZAR 78.4 million annually;

the commercial fishing industry is worth ZAR 1.6 billion annually;

the wild flower industry is valued at ZAR 150 million annually;

the deciduous fruit industry is worth ZAR 1.8 billion annually
and maintains 80,000 jobs;

tourism generally is worth 13 per cent of the regional economy
and supports 180,000 jobs;

the value of ecosystem services for the whole of the CFK is estimated at ZAR 300 million annually, while the purified surface
runoff for freshwater is regarded as worth R 3.6 billion per year
(Younge *et al.* 2000: 8).

Participative strategy development

A major objective of the strategy development process was to generate
a sense of ownership and commitment by executive agencies, primarily

government bodies, to implementation. It therefore needed to be as inclusive as possible, and to ensure that these agencies were an integral part of project planning and management. CAPE thus focused on building partnerships between executive agencies, non-governmental organisations, research institutes and the private sector and on creating legitimacy for the project process and support for its outcomes by all relevant stakeholders, including government at all levels, civil society, NGOs and the private sector.

In a region the size of the CFK, spanning two provinces and a small part of a third, with nearly 5 million inhabitants and a wide variety of organisations with an interest in biodiversity, stakeholder identification and involvement posed significant challenges. For example:

> while it was necessary to be as inclusive as possible, effective participation of local communities in the planning process posed an insurmountable logistical challenge in terms of time and resources;
>
> a concern at the outset was that political differences between the two major provincial governments could have led to lack of co-ordinated leadership and social inclusion;
>
> the abstract nature of strategic planning on a large scale could have reduced effective stakeholder participation.

Public participation was undertaken during each phase of the process. In order to ensure inclusiveness, stakeholders were identified on the basis of a number of criteria, including their impact on biodiversity (positive or negative), the potential role they could play in supporting or undermining conservation, and the economic or other interest they had in biodiversity conservation or its destruction.

To address the concern for effective involvement of large numbers of players, participation in the CAPE process was structured to allow different degrees and levels of involvement by different groups, depending both on their preference and on the roles that they would play in implementation. It was felt appropriate to ensure close engagement with regional organisations and bodies, involving them both in the governance of the project and in developing the analysis, strategy and action plan, while local organisations and individuals were kept informed and consulted on key decisions in the process. Fortunately for the project, political differences did not become an impediment to the process: on the contrary, there was a high level of inter-provincial co-operation. A public relations strategy was developed, ensuring that the abstract nature of the strategic planning process was downplayed, while the key issues were presented in the form of stories that were more meaningful to the public.

Addressing obstacles to inclusiveness

Ideally, a strategic planning process such as CAPE should be inclusive and achieve consensus on goals and a way forward, as outlined in chapter 5. However, there were certain stakeholders who were not sufficiently concerned or who lacked the requisite capacity to participate in the process meaningfully, and to commit to the consensus that was being developed. Two examples of this are agriculture and marine harvesting, both sectors where there tend to be significant short-term gains from exploiting the natural resource base unsustainably.

An engagement with key actors in the agricultural sector began during the CAPE strategic planning process. This engagement, however, remained to a large extent at the level of regional organisations and a limited number of concerned individuals. Within this sector, which has been responsible for the greater part of terrestrial biodiversity losses in the region, there was support for the programme from the relevant national and provincial government departments, as well as from organised agriculture. However, these groups lacked capacity to undertake programmes in support of CAPE's objectives without additional resources. Specific projects were therefore identified in the implementation programme to address these concerns, including a project to establish incentives favouring biodiversity, and a project to co-ordinate and enhance agricultural extension and soil conservation services in support of biodiversity. In addition, research is concurrently being undertaken by the National Botanical Institute to assess and publicise the benefits of conservation-friendly farming.

A particularly intractable problem arose in regard to marine conservation. Overexploitation was found to be the most serious problem facing marine biodiversity in the region: abalone, rock lobster and linefish are particularly threatened. Stocks of eight of the ten most important linefish species have collapsed, and the populations of some are now as low as 5 per cent of pre-harvesting levels. Although legislation has been developed in recent years to protect marine and coastal environments, poor enforcement has compromised its effectiveness. There is also increasing concern over the effects of pollution, harmful algal blooms, coastal development and the introduction of foreign species. Poaching of abalone stocks is at crisis level. The issue is highly contested and government efforts to achieve sustainable levels of harvesting in the past had met with only limited success, owing partly to the activities of international abalone poaching and smuggling rings, and the poverty of coastal fishing communities. The coastal zone has always proved the most difficult for inclusive and participatory involvement, and the South African experience is no exception. Marine sites are always difficult to manage, to police and to provide with guarantees for ensuring good practice. It proved impossible to involve all players in this industry in the CAPE strategic planning process, nor would such involvement have been able to address the specific problems faced by the industry. CAPE's implementation programme therefore included proposals to support and extend the work of the government agency responsible for marine conservation, in the hope that this would provide more effective management and enforcement capability, and more meaningful opportunities for participation.

A further constituency in particular that proved difficult to engage but whose involvement would be crucial to implementation, not as despoilers but as potential beneficiaries, was the rural poor. This was the result of these very diverse and essentially underrepresented groups being relatively poorly organised and difficult to access, and having low levels of awareness and severe resource and mobility constraints. More meaningful involvement of such groupings can, fortunately, be expected in the process of implementing local projects identified in the strategy, many of which have the potential to deliver economic benefits to local communities.

While CAPE was able to identify many of the benefits of biodiversity conservation to such sectors, it was beyond the resources and capacity of the project to undertake a wholesale targeted awareness programme to win over such constituencies, within the two-year strategic planning phase. This task was identified as a priority for the implementation programme, where it properly belongs.

Strategy development

The overall objective of the CAPE strategy was defined as securing the conservation of the biodiversity of the Cape Floral Kingdom, and through this, delivering economic benefits. The strategic planning process identified the following overall goal of the strategy:

By the year 2020, the natural environment and biodiversity of the Cape Floral Kingdom will be effectively conserved, restored wherever appropriate, and will deliver significant benefits to the people of the region in a way that is embraced by local communities, endorsed by government and recognised internationally.

The strategy directed itself to actions supporting both conservation and sustainable use, too often treated elsewhere as independent entities. In

BOX 8.1 ELEMENTS OF THE CAPE STRATEGY

Programme themes	Strategic components
Conserving biodiversity in priority areas	Strengthening on- and off-reserve conservation
	Supporting bioregional planning
Using resources sustainably	Ensuring that catchment management embraces a concern for biodiversity
	Improving the sustainability of harvesting
	Promoting sustainable nature-based tourism
Strengthening institutions and governance	Strengthening institutions
	Enhancing co-operative governance
	Promoting community involvement

addition, a range of cross-cutting supportive and enabling actions was identified, focusing on institutional strengthening and governance. Each of these programmatic themes comprises a number of strategic components, addressing the key issues identified in the situation assessment (see Box 8.1).

The themes and strategic components complement and reinforce one another: to ensure effective conservation inside protected areas, action is necessary beyond these areas, in the form of buffer areas and corridors. Conservation-friendly farming, sustainable use practices, and sustainable nature-based tourism also support effective protected areas. Conserving the fragments of rare habitat in commercial farming districts requires that landuse planning be based on sound biological information and meaningful off-reserve conservation strategies, again supported by conservation-friendly farming. It also calls for appropriate policies, creating incentives for the right kinds of investment and practice. Sustainable marine harvesting requires effective marine protected areas for restocking. Being able to show positive impacts on watershed management increases incentives to remove alien vegetation, because water supply is an important issue in this relatively dry region.

The third programme theme, strengthening institutions and governance, is a cross-cutting theme that supports the other themes and components. In order to implement these effectively, institutional strengthening is required, as is awareness creation, improved co-operative governance, effective community involvement in implementation, and further research (see Box 8.2). These actions are required both at the programme level and at the level of individual components and projects.

BOX 8.2 STRENGTHENING INSTITUTIONS AND GOVERNANCE: BRINGING THE PEOPLE ON BOARD

Three major areas of focus were identified to ensure long-term sustainability:
strengthening institutions
enhancing co-operative governance
promoting community involvement

Strategic goals

Strengthening institutions. The collective capacity and will of implementers is sufficient to sustain innovative and adaptive management in the Cape Floral Kingdom.

Enhancing co-operative governance. Role players are aligned and mobilised towards a common vision, policy and purpose for the conservation of the Cape Floral Kingdom.

Promoting community involvement. Well-motivated and capable local communities and resource users act to promote and conserve the Cape Floral Kingdom.

What is needed?

Biodiversity conservation is promoted in a number of policies and laws, but for these to be effective, South Africa needs a cohesive legal and policy framework that draws together and focuses biodiversity conservation policies from different sectors.

Legislation that is not enforced is useless. Conservation agencies urgently need to enhance their law enforcement capabilities in order to protect the biodiversity of the Cape Floral Kingdom.

Conservation agencies need to be strengthened to enable them to manage more effectively.

Better co-ordination between conservation agencies is needed in a number of fields, including research, training and capacity building, as well as in implementing the activities arising from the CAPE Project.

Co-operative governance and community participation need to be supported and enhanced in the implementation of CAPE.

Ongoing research into conservation is essential if the biodiversity is to be conserved in the long-term.

Local communities need to be aware of and actively participate in the conservation of the region.

Priorities for action

Designing an effective legal and policy framework for biodiversity conservation in the Cape Floral Kingdom.

Strengthening protected area management in the Eastern Cape.

A five-year research programme to support effective conservation management.

Developing programmes to raise awareness and promote the sustainable use of natural resources and conservation.

Source: Younge *et al.* 2000: 40.

BOX 8.3 THE WORKING FOR WATER PROGRAMME IN
SOUTH AFRICA

The Working for Water Programme was launched in 1995 by the Department
of Water Affairs and Forestry. Its aims are:

to recover water presently being lost to invading alien plants and to restrict
further losses;

to create jobs, empower individuals and build communities;

to conserve biological diversity, ecological integrity and catchment stability.

Working for Water is an integral part of the National Water Conservation
Campaign, and a vital component of the Reconstruction and Development
Programme and the macro-economic policy under equal employment opportunities and redistribution. Of 750 introduced tree species in South Africa,
some 161 are invasive. Some estimates suggest that they could expand to consume up to 35 per cent of the nation's water resources by 2020 (Davis and
Day 1998: 219). Eighteen million South Africans do not have access to clean
water, the runoff deficit in relation to need is 25 per cent, and 7 per cent of
South Africans still consume 70 per cent of all available water.

The Programme is nation-wide, but catchment specific. By 2000, some
25,000 people were employed to remove vegetation and treat the infected
areas. Of these, 54 per cent were women, 16 per cent were youths, 1 per cent
were disabled. About 125,000 ha had been cleared (some 15 per cent of the
whole infected area).

The main achievements have been the mobilisation of very poor people, the
responsibility of contractual relationships, local hiring and employee management, and the co-ordination of health, enterprise and welfare programmes.
The difficulties are associated with elements of corruption and mismanagement, conflicts over hiring, the attraction of migrants and how they are as-
similated, and the reallocation of the fresh water created by the Programme.
In addition, the sympathetic management by private landowners has been
facilitated by changes in the law that require clearance and subsequent land
management. The major cause for concern is the uncertain budget. Maintaining income is vital for the essential follow-up work. For the most part money
has finally arrived, but not before the workforce has been disbanded in some
cases. Reliability of public and private funding is considered utterly necessary
if this imaginative programme is to restore biodiversity, generate income from
new water resources, and create lasting opportunities for destitute people.

Source: Working for Water Programme Annual Reports, 1996–2000. Pretoria:
Department of Water Affairs and Forestry.

Biodiversity and socio-economic development

South Africa suffers from high levels of poverty, particularly in rural areas.
Unlike many other parts of Africa, the rural areas of the CFK contain
no communal farming areas of any significance, comprising primarily

commercial agriculture, much of which is orientated towards export markets. However, many commercial farms are becoming marginal and provide extremely limited incomes for farm workers. Recent legislation to protect farm workers has in many instances had the reverse effect, resulting in their being forced off the land. It can be argued that, in a number of ways, agriculture has failed the rural poor, and that conservation holds out perhaps the last hope for economic opportunities for this group. A current example of the potential benefit of conservation for the poor is the highly innovative 'Working for Water' programme initiated in 1996. This has demonstrated clearly that biodiversity conservation through removal of invasive alien vegetation can provide both socio-economic benefits and improved supplies of water, a scarce resource (see Box 8.3).

The CAPE strategy directed itself in part to achieving similar objectives. The test of whether CAPE is able to deliver meaningful benefits to the poor will come in the implementation phase. However, already a number of projects (in addition to Working for Water) have been recently initiated which point to a way forward. The areas of the strategy where most opportunities present themselves are:

    the development of three new 'mega-reserves' and the associated
    tourism activities;
    the development of lowland (off-reserve) conservation-related
    tourism;
    the sustainable harvesting of natural resources, such as wild
    flowers.

Tourism in the CFK is almost entirely landscape-based, and is a significant contributor to the regional economy. The creation of three mega-reserves, one of which will be in the desperately poor Eastern Cape province, would add significantly to the current tourism destinations in the region, in the form of malaria-free wildlife and wilderness areas. This is likely to have important economic impacts, particularly on rural incomes in the vicinity of these reserves.

Private nature-based tourism initiatives also present opportunities for economic development. An example of this is a small private nature reserve in the Agulhas Plain region, known as Grootbos, which, since its inception less than a decade ago, has created over forty new jobs and is making a meaningful contribution to conservation on its own property and in the surrounding district, through its support for conservancy activities by local farmers. The Grootbos Reserve (www.fynbosconservancy. co.za) has won an international award for its innovation as a private initiative which brings together the key elements of the CAPE action plan in microcosm: the scientific analysis of conservation potential and threat, land acquisition and management agreements, and local socio-economic involvement. Grootbos is funded in part by a tourist lodge, and has reached out to local people so as to involve them in training, conservancy management, gardening and tourism services.

A project focusing on the development of a model for sustainable harvesting of wild flowers in the region also offers important economic opportunities for rural communities. Implemented by Fauna and Flora International and Flower Valley Conservation Trust, it entails research on current harvesting practices, identification and implementation of sustainable harvesting levels, designing and establishing a biodiversity monitoring programme, support for the establishment of a certification system, identification and implementation of biodiversity-friendly micro-enterprises using fynbos products for the local communities in the project area, and development of a replication strategy for export to other areas in the CFK.

The Flower Valley enterprise employs fifty-five workers with 165 dependants. The network of farms that provide flowers employs 200 pickers with 500 dependants. The scheme trains six gardeners and ten alien-clearance contractors annually and provides education in nutrition, in wildlife conservation and in pre-school environmental awareness. Soaps, honey and perfume are produced, as well as greeting cards from the discarded pressed plant material. Future projects entail support for an alien-clearing programme on sand dunes in conjunction with local tourism development. It is a creative mix of biodiversity enhancement, public–private partnerships, and local community social and economic involvement, and holds prospects for larger-term financing from fees, incentives and international donors that are the hallmark of the CAPEbreak programme.

Implementation programming

As in any planning process, the effectiveness of ecoregional conservation will be measured in terms of the extent to which plans are implemented. A number of factors will play a role here, the most evident being the development of a coherent implementation programme, the commitment of government agencies to implementation, access to adequate funds and skills to undertake the programme, good management and co-ordination of the implementation programme, and participatory processes of decision making.

The CAPE implementation programme is built around the interrelated themes outlined above. These themes and their components provide the framework within which the individual projects fit to make a coherent whole, and comprise the first phase of the twenty-year conservation programme. Each theme will be taken forward through a 'cluster' of projects, many of which relate to more than one of the themes. Thirty-seven priority projects were identified at the outset, but more could emerge over time. The overall programme would be phased, with benchmarks for moving from one phase to the next.

Implementation of such a programme requires high levels of support from government agencies at national and provincial level. This has been demonstrated by the signing of the CAPE Memorandum of Understanding in September 2001. A further indication of the extent to which the CAPE project has been successfully mainstreamed is that, of the total funds required to implement the five-year programme, estimated at ZAR812 million (US$80 million), ZAR325 million will derive from local sources. Donor support is envisaged as being concentrated in the first five to ten years of the programme, diminishing thereafter.

The strategy seeks to mobilise funding from a range of traditional and non-traditional sources as indicated below:

> the budgets of government agencies at national, provincial and local levels, by realigning their activities (to the extent that this is possible) so that they support the strategy;
>
> Poverty Relief funding, for projects that directly support socioeconomic development amongst the poor;
>
> the private sector, by way of investment in viable businesses that support the strategy primarily in tourism, sponsorship as a marketing activity, and corporate social responsibility activities;
>
> internally generated funds, as a result of the activities of implementing agents as in admission fees, etc.;
>
> resource utilisation levies for water, fishing or other harvesting, and tourism;
>
> donor funding, focusing primarily on the first five years of the programme.

One important source of funding is the Table Mountain Fund (TMF), a trust supported by local contributions and endowed by the GEF in 1998 as part of the Cape Peninsula Biodiversity Project, to fund projects in the Cape Floral Kingdom. Its work centres on funding initiatives which offer the potential to play a role as pilot projects, testing out new participative approaches, or projects which can potentially catalyse action in support of the objectives of CAPE. In addition, while the greater part of the CAPE implementation programme focuses on work undertaken by major government agencies and associated non-governmental organisations, the TMF will play a complementary role in supporting smaller projects, especially off-reserve projects requiring community partnerships.

Co-ordination of implementation

The implementation of the programme is being undertaken by a number of agencies, thus requiring effective co-ordination and management. To strengthen the institutional framework for implementation, the government favoured the establishment of a single body to co-ordinate implementation and biodiversity conservation in the CFK in the long term. This decision was supported by an institutional best-practice study undertaken by CAPE (CSIR 1999). The preferred option was an authority to be established in terms of the World Heritage Convention Act, since the CFK was the subject of a current application for inscription on the list of the world's natural heritage in terms of the UNESCO Convention. In the interim, it was agreed that the responsibility for co-ordination should fall under the National Botanical Institute (a government-funded scientific organisation).

The functions of the co-ordinating mechanism will include ensuring programme coherence and co-ordinated implementation, planning, monitoring and evaluation, dissemination of results to support adaptive management; fundraising; overall financial management and accounting at programme level, stakeholder communication and public relations.

Lessons from CAPE

Scarcity of skills

Although it is too early as yet to evaluate the impact of ecoregional planning in stemming the loss of biodiversity, a number of conclusions can be drawn from the above account. It is clear, for instance, that ecoregional planning is an ambitious and enormously complex process to manage, requiring a range of skills including project management, co-ordination of complex processes, public involvement, public relations and strategic planning. Given that each ecoregion is unique in biological, social, political and economic terms, it is difficult to provide guidance for process management beyond the very general. In the words of WWF, 'We are inventing the science of [ecoregion-based conservation] as we go' (Dinerstein *et al.* 2000: 7). A concern is that the relative scarcity in appropriate skills in this sector may compromise attempts to develop strategic plans for all of the priority ecoregions globally.

Raising awareness and creating commitment

A crucial component of creating the political and economic consensus is creating awareness of the value of biodiversity and the consequences of biodiversity loss, in terms that are meaningful for political and economic roleplayers. One could almost say that the most important objective of ecoregional planning is to create this awareness, and that a failure to prioritise this issue may mean reduced commitment by policy makers to implementation, and less effective lobbying in support of implementation, by conservation groups.

Managing public involvement

It is enormously difficult to manage public involvement meaningfully at a regional scale, to get the right people to be part of the decision-making process at the right time and to manage a process of creating consensus amongst very disparate groups. A huge challenge is to get the buy-in of important stakeholder groups, particularly implementing agencies, key economic sectors, NGOs, community-based organisations and local communities into what is essentially an abstract strategic planning process, bearing little direct relation to their day-to-day concerns. Ecoregional planning has to identify constituencies and actors whose actions need to be harmonised with the goals of the programme, and whose participation and support is crucial to its success. It needs to make a sustained effort to create partnerships around co-ordinated implementation of the action plan, and to develop an effective institutional framework to manage and fundraise for implementation. Partnerships thus developed can be extremely powerful in leveraging funding, both at regional level and at local level. However, as demonstrated in the CAPE case study, it is sometimes extremely difficult to win over such constituencies, and failure to do so may significantly compromise implementation.

Engaging the drivers of biodiversity loss

Effective implementation may be inhibited in the future through a failure by ecoregional conservation to engage effectively with the economic forces driving biodiversity loss. The CAPE strategy was formulated on the assumption that several objectives needed to be achieved before biodiversity losses would be significantly curtailed: first, awareness of the long-term implications of biodiversity loss needed to be made evident to users; second, the costs of unsustainable resource-use needed to be borne by the user wherever possible; third, the benefits of sustainable use needed to be understood; fourth, poor communities needed to benefit directly and significantly from conservation-related activities, and finally perverse incentives needed to be removed and substituted with positive incentives. While the implementation programme was designed in part to address each of these concerns, it remains to be seen whether this will be effective.

Scientific approaches

A further issue relates to the viability of the approaches taken by researchers. For instance, while CAPE's terrestrial analysis was undertaken with a methodology which offers huge opportunities for a systematic analysis, for the integration of biological and socio-economic analysis, and for an interactive, transparent decision-making process, it proved difficult to integrate the terrestrial and aquatic analyses, particularly the marine analyses, using this approach. At the same time, as with many ecoregional planning initiatives, CAPE's analysis of social and economic factors affecting biodiversity loss lacked focus in the initial stages, although this was rectified in time. If adequate methods are not adopted in ecoregional planning processes, this can compromise sustainability.

Financing implementation

Another area of concern is that the strategic planning process needs to be rapid in order to respond to the rate of biodiversity loss, and as such it consumes significant resources: the CAPE project cost US$1 million over two years in donor funds, with about half as much again in counterpart funding in kind. Implementation of the five-year action plan has been estimated as costing US$80 million, of which one third would be provided in counterpart funds. Although this is relatively small change in the bigger scheme of things, it is important to note that failure to mobilise funding at this scale could result in implementation being stymied. In spite of the severe crisis facing biodiversity globally, and the efforts of a number of organisations to embark on ecoregional planning initiatives, funding for conservation at ecoregional scale is not yet easy to raise. A potential weakness of CAPE, as with other ecoregional conservation planning, is its dependence on international donor agencies for a significant portion of implementation funding, particularly in the initial phase. In spite of relatively high levels of capacity in local organisations and the commitment of a significant proportion of local resources to implementation, local action alone would be insufficient to counter the threats to biodiversity in the region. Donor funding, however necessary to the programme, brings with it potential delays and uncertainty. Partly with this in mind, the GEF has recently adopted what it terms a 'programmatic approach' to funding conservation planning at this scale. While this represents a positive response to the challenge, the process of raising such funding is still mired in bureaucracy, making it a lengthy, expert-driven process often dependent on mediation by expatriate skills.

Absorptive capacity

A related concern is that effective implementation needs a fairly significant amount of what is often called 'absorptive capacity': the ability of a country or countries to use donor funding effectively to achieve objectives. While the greater part of the CAPE programme will be implemented in the Western Cape Province by an agency with significant absorptive capacity, the Western Cape Nature Conservation Board, the same cannot be said for those components in the programme which fall into the Eastern Cape. The lesson in this is that it is essential for ecoregional planning to ensure that it develops plans and programmes that are grounded in the political, economic, social and institutional realities of the affected regions, in order to have greater chance of being mainstreamed by being integrated into the work programmes of government agencies responsible for conservation.

Conclusion

In a number of ways, the Cape Action Plan for the Environment represents an important milestone in ecoregion-based conservation, integrating terrestrial, aquatic and socio-economic concerns in a coherent conservation strategy and implementation programme. CAPE was able to gain the support of key stakeholders, to create commitment to implementation by executing agencies, and to demonstrate significant levels of financial support from local agencies as well as from the international donor community. It established clear targets for conserving a representative sample of biodiversity patterns and ecological processes, and developed mechanisms to enable effective monitoring and review of achievements. As such it can serve as a model for ecoregional planning elsewhere. At the same time, the CAPE process has raised a number of concerns and issues regarding this approach to conservation, and in the future will provide useful opportunities to evaluate the effectiveness of the ecoregional approach in addressing biodiversity loss.

REFERENCES

Butler, M. 1998. *Environment and Poverty*. Braamfontein: Environmental Justice Networking Forum.
Council for Scientific and Industrial Research (CSIR) 1999. *Cape Action Plan for the Environment: An Assessment and Review of the Current Policy, Legal, Institutional, Socio-economic and Financial Situation Affecting the Conservation of Biodiversity in the Cape Floristic Kingdom. Parts 1 and 2.* CSIR Report No.: ENV-S-C 99130 A. Prepared for WWF-SA.

Cowling, R. and Pressey, R.C. (eds.) (forthcoming). Systematic conservation planning for the Cape Floral Kingdom. *Biological Conservation.*

Davis, B. and Day, J. 1998. *Vanishing Waters.* Cape Town: University of Cape Town Press.

Dinerstein, E., Powell, G., Olson, D., Wikramanayake, E., Abell, R., Loucks, C., Underwood, E., Allnutt, T., Wittengel, W., Ricketts, T., Strand, H., O'Connor, S., Burgess, N. 2000. *A Workbook for Conducting Biological Assessments and Developing Biodiversity Visions for Ecoregion-Based Conservation. Part 1: Terrestrial Ecoregions.* Washington, DC: Conservation Science Program, WWF-USA.

Orians, G. 1998. The biological foundations. In *Proceedings: Ecoregion-Based Conservation Workshop.* Washington, DC. World Wildlife Fund.

O'Riordan, T., Hamann, R., Preston-Whyte, R. and Mangele, M. 2000. The transition to sustainability: a South African perspective. *South African Geographical Journal* 82(2): 1–10.

Pressey, G., Botha, M. and Turpie, J.K. 2001. Finding the optimal combination of on-and-off-reserve conservation strategies for the Agulhas Plain, South Africa. *Biological Conservation* (forthcoming).

Stoll-Kleemann, S. and O'Riordan, T. 2002. From participation to partnership in biodiversity protection: experience for Germany and South Africa. *Society and Natural Resources* 15(2): 157–73.

World Wildlife Fund 1998. *Proceedings: Ecoregion-Based Conservation Workshop.* Washington, DC.

World Wildlife Fund Central Africa Program Office (forthcoming). *Biological Priorities for Conservation in the Guinean-Congolian Forest and Freshwater Region.*

Younge, A. and Ashwell, A. 2000. *Cape Action Plan for the Environment: A Biodiversity Action Plan for the Cape Floral Kingdom.* Stellenbosch: WWF-SA.

9   Wildlife management in Namibia: the conservancy approach

Markus A. Nuding

> For wildlife and protected areas to survive on a significant scale, they must be socio-politically acceptable, economically viable and ecologically sustainable.
>
> Graham Child 1955

An African introductory scene

Think of Africa, more precisely of a semi-desert landscape between Etosha National Park and the famous Skeleton Coast in Namibia. Think of the silent and golden moments just before sunset. Then suddenly a sharp crack of branches as a herd of elephant feed on the banks of a small and now dry river in front of Palmwag Lodge. They are not concerned about the load of respectful tourists training cameras and binoculars on them. After a while the tourists return to their sundowners and comfortable chairs, awaiting the next wild offering of this evening. Later that night the herd moves out of Palmwag Concession Area and enters the small fields of neigbouring Grootberg Communal Land.

The next morning the Palmwag kitchen is offering a splendid breakfast of fresh fruit, cereals and yogurt, bacon and sausages, eggs and coffee and juices. The villagers of Humor, one of the settlements near the concessions boundary, are inspecting the trail of destruction caused that night. In just a few hours the herd has eaten or crushed more than half of a millet field which was to have made a major contribution to rural families' subsistence economy.

The elephants have damaged not only these few, precious grain crops. In the so-called Kunene Region the world-famous Kaokoveld elephants frequently break water installations, fences, fruit trees and small irrigated gardens around homesteads, or simply drink large quantities of the stock-farmers' precious water. Although the windmills and piping damaged by the elephants are repaired at government cost, the disrupted water supply – sometimes out of service for weeks before the repair team visits a farm – can cause major problems, including financial losses, for stock-owners in this arid region.

Another undoubtedly big attraction for tourists visiting Namibia's na-tional parks is lions. From the safety of a safari vehicle they can be viewed from close up in all their awesome splendour. But lions do not stay always inside protected areas. In particular, young males are driven away from the pride when they reach maturity. Then they have to seek safety outside the territories of their own and other prides. This often means crossing the boundaries of the wildlife sanctuary onto neighbouring farmland. Whole prides may periodically make forays into communal lands to add relatively easily caught donkeys, horses, sheep, goats and cattle to their natural prey. To give examples of this ongoing difficulty of co-existence between wildlife and people, every year a high number of predators are killed (e.g., in 1991 in Otjiwarongo alone thirty-six leopards, fifty-five chee-tahs, twenty-one cape hunting dogs, four lions and two spotted hyaenas, and on farms adjoining Etosha, fourteen lions). But all these animals are now endangered in most other parts of the world and they actually represent a highly valuable tourism resource.

This scenario reflects the reality of ecotourism in Namibia. On the one hand tourism is essential to the national economy by being the second-largest generator of foreign exchange in the country. On the other hand, the ordinary poor rural Namibian is being forced to bear the costs of living with the wildlife on which the multi-million dollar tourism industry depends. Not only do rural area dwellers receive no additional benefits for bearing the burden of the problems caused by wildlife. They are also often the people who, because they live in remoter corners of Namibia far from centres of development, receive the least infrastructural and financial assistance from government and the private sector.

Paying compensation to farmers for wildlife damage to address the issue of displaced animals is not realistic in Namibia, with its wide range of problem-causing wildlife and the enormous losses incurred annu-ally throughout the country. If the precedent is set to pay for elephant damage, for example, compensation would also be demanded for other problem animals which often cause greater economic losses. The cost to the state would be considerable, but more importantly, how would the system be implemented and monitored? Who would economically quantify each case of crop damage and livestock loss? Who would go to the scene and verify that a goat its owner claimed had been killed by a jackal had not died of disease or drought or been eaten by the herdsman himself?

The most promising solution to the problem is the integration of wild animals back into the country's economy so that financial losses are balanced by direct benefits. This has already been very successfully done on privately owned farmland in Namibia, and it has stimulated the growth of a booming, complementary industry based on trophy and photographic safaris, game harvesting and live game sales. Between 1972 and 1992 the number of species on privately owned land increased by 49 per cent and the quantity of wildlife on the same land has grown by a huge 80 per cent, i.e., nearly doubled.

In communal areas, the first step must be to redress the inequities and discrimination of the past. The existing nature conservation legislation must be amended to grant communal-land farmers conditional rights to use and market their wildlife resources similar to those that are given to private landowners. When the communal farmers get direct economic benefits through trophy fees and tourism enterprises – from the elephants that raid their crops – it will go a long way towards changing their attitudes to these and other national wildlife assets. From the income they receive, they as a community will be in a position to verify, evaluate and pay individual owners of damaged fields, if they so choose.

Some tourist enterprises are already attempting to share their profits with local people, for example Palmwag and Hobatere Concession Lodges which are collecting bed-night levies to be paid annually to their neighbouring communities.

However, economic benefits will not alone balance the high costs of wildlife. Rural communities must also be given a role in the management of the wild animals that share their land and affect their daily lives. Only when they are empowered to see themselves as genuine partners in the custodianship of the wildlife resources in their areas can we expect them to act responsibly towards them. This is the rationale behind the community game guard systems in the Kunene and Caprivi regions. Nongovernmental organisation (NGO) sponsored rhino-monitoring teams, drawn from local communities, are another aspect of this approach.

In the communal areas, where natural resources are common property, the long-term success of this new policy will hinge on the creation of appropriate, representative, local community structures for sharing responsibility, with the conservation authorities, for the management of wildlife outside of parks and reserves, and also for the equitable distribution of economic benefits accruing to the local people from its consumptive and non-consumptive use.

Let us have a closer look at Namibia's policy framework for biological diversity, at wildlife-based tourism, at trophy hunting and at endangered species treaties to understand the unique Namibian so-called conservancy approach and its contribution effectively to resolve the conflicts between wildlife and human needs – one of the greatest challenges facing all concerned with the long-term future of Namibia's rich and priceless biological diversity.

The modern policy framework

The fundamental policy regarding the utilisation of wildlife resources in Namibia appears in Article 95 of the Constitution, where 'the State shall actively promote and maintain the welfare of the people by adopting . . . policies aimed at . . . the maintenance of ecosystems, essential ecological processes and biological diversity of Namibia and utilization of living natural resources on a sustainable basis for the benefit of all Namibians, both present and future'. This policy not only enshrines the rights of citizens to use and benefit from wildlife resources, but also identifies the need for measures to ensure that such utilisation is sustainable and will not have a detrimental impact on ecosystems, ecological processes or biodiversity. Providing and enforcing such measures are a core responsibility of the Ministry of Environment and Tourism.

Its constitution, which came into effect at the country's independence in 1990, explicitly refers to biodiversity, providing that in the interests of the welfare of the people, the state shall adopt policies aimed at maintaining ecosystems, ecological processes and biodiversity for the benefit of present and future generations. More specifically, Namibia has launched a project to review and revise its environmental legislation, incorporating the Convention on Biological Diversity (CBD). Namibia's National Biodiversity Programme demonstrates its commitment to biodiversity conservation.

Namibia signed the Convention on Biological Diversity on 12 June 1992 in Rio de Janeiro, at the United Nations Conference on Environment and Development, and ratified it on 18 March 1997. Looking at the species and endemism richness of Namibia this step is already of great importance.

The overall root causes of diversity loss, recognised globally in chapter 1, also apply to Namibia:

> population growth and increasing resource consumption;
> ignorance about the roles of species and ecosystems;
> poorly conceived policies;
> effects of global trading systems;
> inequal resource distribution;
> failure to account for the value of biodiversity.

It is evident from this that human actions, economies and policies are the cause of most biodiversity loss. Legal efforts to address this loss must

BOX 9.1 NAMIBIA AT A GLANCE

Land area	824,000 km^2
Population	1.7 million (1998)
Population growth	3.0 per cent per year (1990–98)
Population density	2.0 persons per km^2
Population urban	39 per cent (1998)
Life expectancy	61 years
Gross domestic product	US$3,092 million (1998)
Economic growth	3.5 per cent (1990–98)
Climate	Hyper-arid (west) to dry subhumid (east)
Biomes	Desert, savannah, broadleaf woodland

Conservation ratios
people per cow	1
people per elephant	210
people per km^2 of protected area	14

Table 9.1 *Species and endemism richness of some indigenous Namibian taxa*

Taxa	Endemics[a]	All species	% Endemism[b]
Plants	686	4,138	17
Myriapods	13	45	29
Insects	1,541	6,331	24
Frogs	6	50	13
Fish	5	115	4
Reptiles	59	250	24
Birds	14	658	2
Mammals	14	200	7

[a] Endemism is defined as 100 per cent of global range occuring in Namibia for all taxa except birds (90%), amphibians, reptiles and mammals (all 75%).
[b] Figures in some case represent less than 20 per cent of the expected total. Data are therefore minimum estimates. For example, there are thought to be 35,000 insect species in Namibia.
Source: Ministry of Environment and Tourism 1998.

urgently consider these and other factors, and not only focus on the species and habitats which require direct priority action. Namibia's newly elaborated conservancy policy is trying to meet the overall objectives of the Convention in a very effective way.

Non-governmental organisations

Many solutions to biodiversity loss can be found at national and local levels. At these levels, it is important for contracting states to incorporate the expertise of non-governmental organisations. Because of their place in society, NGOs can bridge the gap between citizens and policy makers. They can also act as watchdogs to monitor biodiversity conservation at local, national and global levels. Meanwhile, Namibia does have many active environmental NGOs with a particularly strong lobby in the process of creating a proper framework for conservancies. It is to Namibia's advantage to strengthen these NGOs and involve them fully in the implementation of the Convention on Biological Diversity. This should be part of any future biodiversity assistance programme.

Wildlife-based tourism

The National Tourism Development Study applied a 32 per cent across-the-board increase in the 1990 figures to provide an estimate of 280,000 international tourist arrivals in 1992, spending a total of US$85 million in foreign exchange. Of this, about 65 per cent represented holiday expenditures largely on wildlife-based tourism. Using these national figures, it was estimated that wildlife-based tourism contributed N$200 million value added to Gross Domestic Product in 1992. The potential was also steadily growing. Tourist numbers were expected to increase at an average rate of 9 per cent per annum between 1992 and 2002. This means a doubling of tourist numbers by 2002 from about 300,000 per annum to over 600,000, with high-spending European tourists increasing fivefold. In 1998 already 560,000 tourist arrivals were counted, with an overall spending of US$288 million.

Trophy hunting activities

Compared with other wildlife tourism activities, trophy hunting is highly profitable to the economy. It makes very efficient use of the few animals in the population which are of trophy quality. For this reason game ranching and community-based wildlife projects are commonly dependent on trophy hunting activities for their financial viability.

Game has a high and rapidly realisable value. The fee for the hunting of one single elephant alone can earn more money than thirty households could generate from agriculture or livestock in one year. Added to that are licences for hunting concessions, and the meat of the hunted animals which is left for the communities in the communal areas. Game

Table 9.2 *Numbers of trophy animals hunted in Namibia per year*

Animals	1991	1996	1997	1998	1999
Black faced impala (*Aepyceros melampus petersi*)	1	8	29	16	21
Black wildebeest (*Connochaetes gnou*)	148	123	187	226	265
Blesbok (*Damaliscus dorcas phillipsi*)	367	265	503	505	538
Blue wildebeest (*Connochaetes taurinus*)	130	128	265	323	333
Buffalo (*Syncerus caffer*)	1	1	40	12	12
Cheetah (*Acinonyx jubatus*)	–	11	29	59	60
Dik dik (*Madoqua kirkii*)	2	5	13	19	29
Duiker (*Sylvicapra grimmia*)	42	47	105	188	166
Eland (*Taurotragus oryx*)	152	134	212	247	325
Elephant (*Loxodonta africana*)	14	1	20	35	39
Giraffe (*Giraffa camelopardalis*)	3	11	18	27	24
Hartebeest (*Alcelaphus buselaphus*)	663	471	1,156	1,195	1,111
Impala (*Aepyceros melampus melampus*)	116	91	173	252	251
Klipspringer (*Oreotragus oreotragus*)	4	5	22	64	33
Kudu (*Tragelaphus strepsiceros*)	847	692	1,584	2,230	2,152
Leopard (*Panthera pardus*)	11	15	38	36	52
Lion (*Panthera leo*)	–	2	4	3	10
Mountain zebra (*Equus zebra hartmannae*)	176	200	346	398	543
Nyala (*Tragelaphus angasii*)	–	2	–	2	4
Oryx (*Oryx gazella*)	1,206	1,414	2,339	2,626	2,626
Plains zebra (*Equus burchelli*)	65	63	126	155	143
Roan (*Hippotragus equinus*)	4	3	14	15	10
Sable (*Hippotragus niger*)	1	6	2	18	14
Springbok (*Antidorcas marsupialis*)	2,301	611	1,254	1,443	1,629
Steenbok (*Raphicerus campestris*)	193	24	502	655	680
Warthog (*Phacochoerus africanus*)	2,598	917	1,368	1,823	1,816
Waterbuck (*Kobus ellipsiprymnus*)	6	25	57	71	64

Source: Ministry of Environment and Tourism 2000.

is a rapidly regenerating resource which can be harvested frequently, as opposed to a forest that needs 100 years to regenerate to a usable state. This kind of exploitation of wildlife also requires little infrastructure. All that has to be done is to find a safari entrepreneur who is interested in a hunting concession in the communal areas, and can offer to sport hunters the animal species which have been released for hunting (Table 9.2).

In 1998 a total of about 13,000 trophies were taken in Namibia. The total number per annum of large mammals hunted as trophies, for meat (biltong or own use) and as animals exported live is roughly 110,000. This is a quite a low number compared to countries in Europe. In Germany for example 1,035,000 roe deer (*Capreolus capreolus*), 665,000 fox (*Vulpes vulpes*), 250,000 wild boar (*Sus scrofa*), 50,000 red deer (*Cervus elaphus*) and 40,000 fallow deer (*Cervus dama*) were hunted in 1998, just to name the more prominent species. Also in Germany, about 160,000 roe deer are killed through road accidents yearly.

Probably the most important influence on present safari hunting practices will be developments in Namibia's communal lands. The concession areas are mostly situated there, and there will be an empowerment of resident communities with rights over wildlife in their areas. Essentially, communities will take over much of the control of investment, management and use of wildlife on their land. The communities will be increasingly empowered with territorial use rights over their wildlife. They will collect the rent for concessions, which presently accrues to the state. Giving rural communities a stake in the process will contribute to their development as well as promote wildlife conservation.

Endangered species convention

The Convention on International Trade in Endangered Species of Wild Flora and Fauna (CITES) has been the world's premier conservation treaty since 1973. It provides the basis for international co-operation in preventing the unsustainable exploitation of wild animals and plants through international trade. Namibia became a party to CITES in 1991. It is represented by officials from the Ministry of Environment and Tourism, as the agency reponsible for the implementation of CITES in Namibia.

CITES international trade controls form only a relatively small part of the conservation and management requirements for ensuring the survival of wild fauna and flora. International trade in wild species has an insignificant effect on most fauna and flora from southern Africa compared to the threats from changed landuse and the loss of habitat. Prohibiting international trade in a species may even accelerate its disappearance. Such species usually lose economic value and may no longer be regarded as a resource. Namibia and southern Africa as a whole generally attempt to maintain or increase the economic value of wild species as an incentive for their conservation as part of the renewable resource base.

Fundamental to CITES are the infamous appendices, especially Appendix I. This is the world's list of ultimate conservation failures, which, paradoxically, may also be seen as the ultimate form of protection for species. Parties to CITES have been listing their own and other countries' species in the CITES appendices with abandon, as a way to protect species even when the primary threat was not from international trade. Deterrent and regulatory effects of trade control measures built into the Convention have accordingly been subverted by the sheer numbers of species listed as threatened and endangered. This has made it unworkable and impossible to enforce objectively and consistently. Many industrial countries run substantial CITES technical bureaucracies, while CITES administration in the developing world is, by contrast, often in the hands of an inappropriate institution and inadequately trained staff.

BOX 9.2 CITES AND NAMIBIA

In 1973, in Washington, eighty countries signed the then most important international treaty for the protection of flora and fauna: the CITES convention, also known as the Washington species protection agreement.

As the name Convention on International Trade in Endangered Species of Wild Flora and Fauna indicates, CITES is a trade agreement, which regulates the commercial transport across borders of animals and plants, or their parts (to date roughly 4,000 animal and 40,000 plant species are included). The kind and extent of the trade restrictions are decided during the regular conferences, with the participation of politicians, scientists and lobbyists and the currently 151 treaty countries.

There are three categories of trade restriction, the so-called 'annexes'. Annex I covers species which are *immediately threatened with extinction*. Trade in these animals, or in their parts, is fundamentally prohibited. Annex II concerns the species *whose survival is endangered*. Trade in these is allowed when a scientific authority of the country of origin certifies that the species will not be endangered through the export. Finally, Annex III protects species which are *declared endangered*, when a country itself declares that within its territory these are in need of protection. The classification must be ratified with a two thirds majority vote. Member countries that are not in agreement with the resulting vote can announce a reservation, and trade with countries which likewise voiced a definite reservation.

Namibia provides *in situ* species protection in the Nature Conservation Ordinance. The Ordinance provides that import and export of raw skins and raw meat are allowed only by permit, but needs updating to make reference to CITES, to which Namibia acceded in 1991. The Wildlife and Parks Management Bill will replace the Ordinance and will incorporate Namibia's obligations under CITES.

At the CITES conference in 2000 in Nairobi, Namibia, together with Botswana, South Africa and Zimbabwe, succeeded in winning acceptance of the principle that trade in ivory is an option for the future. The four southern African nations will be allowed to trade in elephant hides and meat – a business which can produce good revenues but which is not seen as a factor in the poaching of elephants. At the same time they agreed to hold off from any ivory sales at least until the next CITES conference in 2002 or 2003.

CITES has also become the principal tool of foreign organisations agitating against any trade and any form of consumptive use of wild species, reflecting their urban constituencies and currently fashionable western moral orientation. These organisations usually stem from societies based on non-sustainable economies and disproportionately high consumption rates of imported non-renewable resources, in environments marked by the worst degrees of transformation and loss of biodiversity. Conservation philosophies emerging from such conditions have to be treated with scepticism.

Producer countries like Namibia are increasingly sensitive that their sovereign responsibilities to determine the level of resource exploitation should be acknowledged. If this is not done, legitimate enterprises such as the lucrative sport hunting industry in southern Africa will remain vulnerable to external pressure.

Namibian elephants and CITES

The best illustration of the way that altered sovereignty affects wildlife is, of course, the African elephant. Conflicts between people increased sharply after Namibia's independence from South Africa in 1990. At the end of the war people settled in formerly unused lands, which formed a large part of the elephant range in communal areas. A national campaign to increase and diversify food production in the communal areas resulted in greater aspirations and greater intolerance of crop damage by elephants. With the short crop-growing season in Namibia, only one crop can be harvested per year. The gap between perceptions of elephants internationally and locally was increasing. Ever more rural people regard the revered animals of western fantasy and wonder as irredeemable agricultural pests and obstacles to their development. People in some marginal agricultural areas have nevertheless agreed to tolerate elephants as long as they can derive some form of compensation for damages caused by them. The challenge remains to generate sufficient revenue from elephants, given the international ban on the legal trade in ivory.

In some parts of Namibia elephants are or may become the single most valuable renewable resource for people, in view of the limiting effects of an arid climate and nutrient-deficient Kalahari sands on agricultural potential. Elephants – especially migratory or nomadic elephants – can survive on communal lands only if people who have to live with the animals can benefit more from them than they lose to them. Acceptable economic incentives to retain elephants are compromised by the continued listing of Namibian elephants by CITES. If legal ivory trading is not possible,

Table 9.3 *Economic significance of hunting in southern Africa*

	Species examples	Trophy fee incl. licences (US$)	Hunting fee per day/ per hunter (US$)	Days, minimum to be booked	Costs per animal shot (US$)	Alteration compared to 1996/97
Botswana	baboon	131				+ 5 %
	elephant	14,600	1,110	14	30,140	
Namibia	jackal	free				+ 6 %
	leopard	2,290	230	7	3,900	
South Africa	jackal	30				+ 4 %
	rhino	all-inclusive:			22,900	
Zimbabwe	birds	free	300	7		+ 7 %
	elephant	10,000	1,200	21	35,200	

Source: Nuding 1999.

the gradual displacement and ultimate loss of elephants as a resource are a major threat to biological diversity.

In 1989, CITES placed the African elephant on Appendix I, introducing a ban on commercial trade in elephant products. This was agreed, over the objections of Namibia and other nations in the region. What happened in practical terms as a result of the CITES decision is quite clear. Namibia had the elephants and remained both responsible and accountable for their future – but its options for elephant management were severely restricted. Namibia could manage elephants through sport hunting, but it could not trade in ivory, hide or meat. It could, at least in theory, undertake the reduction of elephant herds through culling, but in practice the high cost of culling precluded its adoption in the absence of any revenue from the marketing of by-products such as ivory.

Unlike modern international instruments like the Convention on Biological Diversity, which is a framework convention put together specifically to assist the resource-rich developing world in its efforts to manage, use and conserve its biodiversity, CITES was created more than twenty years ago as an old-fashioned 'command and control' and 'fines and fences' mechanism when our understanding of the threats to wildlife were much less complete.

Namibia's new conservancy policy

A significant development in wildlife management and use in Namibia is the concept of conservancies. Individual farmers have realised that it would be advantageous to pool natural and financial resources to form a larger unit of land in which to carry out integrated wildlife management practices.

A conservancy consists of a group of commercial farms or areas of communal land in which neighbouring landowners or members have put together their natural resources for the purpose of conserving and using wildlife in an ecologically and economically sustainable manner. Members practise normal farming activities and operations in combination with wildlife use on a sustainable basis. The main objective is the conservation of wildlife on combined land. Conservancies are operated and managed by members through a committee.

About 75 per cent of Namibia's wildlife is found outside formally protected areas. This includes elephant and endangered black rhinoceros, which roam communal land. On commercial farmland, especially in the northern regions, farmers are experiencing problems with migrating game populations. Migratory species like oryx, springbok, warthog, hartebeest, eland and kudu are not restricted by ordinary stockproof fencing. This results in over- and under-utilisation, causing friction between farmers about the ownership, use and financial benefits from game. These problems can often be overcome with a combined wildlife management and utilisation strategy.

Since 1967, commercial farmers have enjoyed the right to use and benefit from wildlife on their farms. This was based on the landowner meeting certain conditions imposed by the state. These included the type of fencing. Extending these rights to commercial farmers has improved conservation of wildlife on commercial farms because landowners realised that they could benefit from the game. Most evident was the development of a multi-million dollar game-farming, tourist and hunting industry. While contributing to the economic viability of individual farms and to the national economy, game-farming requires very little financial and technological support from the state.

In the communal areas, state control of wildlife resources has alienated people from that resource. This has resulted in a severe decline in game numbers in many areas, mostly as a result of increased poaching, and pressure for land proclaimed as game reserves to be returned to the people for grazing, water and other uses. No mechanisms existed for rural communities to participate in, or benefit from, wildlife management. All revenue from consumptive or non-consumptive use of wildlife went to the private sector or the central revenue fund.

The conservancy system enables people on communal land to enjoy similar rights to manage and use wildlife as those granted to commercial farmers. As people share the responsibility of wildlife management and

Table 9.4 *Wildlife and livestock utilisation enterprises on communal land in Caprivi, 1993*

Fiancial return (US$ per annum)	Livestock	Wildlife
Net revenue	2,753,486	3,568,545
Net revenue per hectare	1.41	1.83
Net revenue per kg	0.10	0.41
Net revenue per household	384	498
Net revenue exclusive of subsidies	556,369	3,111,795

Note: Comparative estimated livestock returns from slaughter for meat sale, and hiring of draught power. Comparative estimated wildlife returns from a combination of photo-tourism, trophy hunting, cropping and live sale. Based on 1.9 million ha in western and eastern Caprivi. Subsidies include government provision of water points and veterinary services received by the sector, but not specific to individual farmers.
Source: Ashley, Barnes and Healy 1994.

income from wildlife, it serves as an incentive to protect and conserve wildlife in their areas. This fosters wildlife-based rural development and improves the conservation status of wildlife as residents develop a vested economic interest.

The Ministry of Environment and Tourism (MET) has adopted a policy document on conservancies in Namibia. This makes no distinction between conservancies on commercial or communal land. The overall objectives are the same for both, namely to pool natural and economic resources and collectively to manage and utilise them on a sustainable basis.

Conservancies should have a properly drawn up constitution and set of rules, in line with the regulations laid down by the Ministry of Environment and Tourism. The constitution outlines the goals and objectives, while the rules spell out management and utilisation actions. The latter include determining quotas for hunting and other uses, and monitoring and recording aspects such as rainfall and vegetation. Wildlife numbers, sex ratios, mortalities and births have to be recorded as well. Monitoring wildlife populations on conservancies is vital for detecting trends and implementing effective management.

The ministry assists and guides conservancies on wildlife management and related matters during the formative years of the conservancy. Training will play a major role in the management, monitoring and determining of quotas, especially on communal conservancies. In communal areas the conditions for fencing for migratory game species cannot be applied as a criterion for the granting of wildlife utilisation rights. This would be impractical and undesirable given the migration patterns of large mammals such as elephants, besides being contrary to current government policy.

Any system for communal lands must balance the need of the people to have secure access to natural resources and the right to use and benefit from these resources, even if the land is owned by the state. The ministry believes the conservancy concept is the most appropriate way to address this.

Conservancies in communal areas would have the right to use and benefit from wildlife. Once a quota has been set for each species, the committee may allow hunting by members of the conservancy, culling of game for meat, sale of animals for trophy hunting or the sale of live game. The conservancy could enter into business contracts with private companies for some of these activities. It would have the right to build tourist facilities or to engage in commercial arrangements with a registered tourism operator to act on its behalf.

To obtain these rights, the communal conservancy must satisfy the Ministry of its capacity to manage wildlife resources. It must be legally constituted, with clearly defined boundaries. The members of the conservancy would be defined by the individuals in the conservancy. It could consist of all adults living within its boundaries. The members must be sufficiently representative of the community served by the conservancy.

Rights are:

> to use, manage and benefit from wildlife on communal land in accordance with the conservancy policy;
>
> to propose recommendations for quotas for wildlife utilisation and, in consultation with MET, decide on the form of utilisation;
>
> to enter into agreements with private companies and establish tourism facilities within the conservancy boundaries;
>
> to have ownership over huntable game (like game birds, bushpig, buffalo, oryx, kudu, springbok and warthog) on conservancies;
>
> to apply for permits to use protected and specially protected game (like elephant);
>
> to conduct trophy hunting and to buy and sell game.

Responsibilities are:

> to be legally constituted;
>
> to have clearly defined physical boundaries that are accepted by neighbouring communities and conservancies;
>
> to consist of members defined by the comunity within the conservancy (e.g., all adults living within its boundaries);

to have a conservancy committee which will be the executive body of the conservancy; it should consist of elected or appointed representatives of the community; the members must be sufficiently representative of the community served by the committee; members of the conservancy choose the conservancy committee, but it is suggested that people with leadership and communication skills are included;

to have a sound accounting system and effective secretariat; the conservancy committee must undertake to keep all members of the conservancy fully informed regarding decisions taken, income and expenditure;

to satisfy the MET that it is able to set its own sustainable yield quotas for use of natural resources;

all conservancy members to benefit, as it is believed that benefits provide incentives for people to manage the wildlife for the future; equitable shares are important so everyone has an incentive to manage resources.

Conservancies should have a properly drawn up constitution and set of rules or management plan. The constitution outlines the goals and objectives, while the rules spell out management and utilisation actions. This includes:

determining quotas for hunting and other uses;

monitoring and recording aspects such as rainfall, vegetation and status of natural resources;

recording wildlife numbers and impacts of management and utilisation;

defining areas for different landuses such as core wildlife areas, tourism concessions, multiple-use areas, etc.

The Ministry of Environment and Tourism and NGOs operating in an area can be called upon to assist with and advise on the drawing up of a constitution or agreements with the private sector.

The main functions and duties of a conservancy management committee will be:

to represent the interests of the conservancy members in matters related to natural resource and wildlife management and use within the conservancy;

to oversee the management of conservancy income and expenditure;

to represent the conservancy in negotiations with business ventures;

to discuss policy issues with the MET;

to arrange annual meetings of the conservancy;

to keep conservancy members informed and consulted on critical issues such as the distribution of money and use of resources;

to apply to the MET regional head for quotas for the use of wildlife;

to determine how game will be used once quotas are set;

to determine what technical assistance is needed from MET and other organisations;

to determine training needs of the conservancy;

to initiate projects for improved wildlife management within the conservancy;

to establish a practical problem-animal management programme;

to develop tourism initiatives within the conservancy;

to manage, if necessary, a community/conservancy game guard system.

To date on each about 40,000 km^2 of commercial and communal land are under conservancy status, thus making conservancies the major tool for the achievement of the conservation of biodiversity, the sustainable use of its components and above all the fair sharing of benefits which are the overall objectives of the Convention on Biological Diversity.

The Grootberg Conservancy

In the Grootberg area, members of the community established Namibia's fourth communal area conservancy under legislation amended in 1996 (Fig. 9.1). This gave communities the right to manage and use their natural resources and wildlife sustainably. Meaning 'elephant corner', the #Khoadi//Hoas Conservancy of Grootberg is committed to the protection of the Kaokoveld elephants, which it now regards as its property. The area also hosts a number of endangered black rhino amongst many other species.

For the approximately 3,500 people of #Khoadi//Hoas, the Conservancy will bring an extra income through tourism in an area with little employment and immense poverty. A management and utilisation plan has been developed for the area of approximately 356,000 ha. It will be zoned for different uses, such as trophy hunting, tourism, settlement, livestock and multiple purposes.

Wildlife is a collective property in the #Khoadi//Hoas Conservancy. Everybody, even the poorest farmers who do not own cattle or goats, profits from the communally organised utilisation of game. Poachers turn into thieves of common property; farmers with a lot of livestock are seen as wasting land which could be utilised better through wildlife management. In this respect it is important that the direct connection between

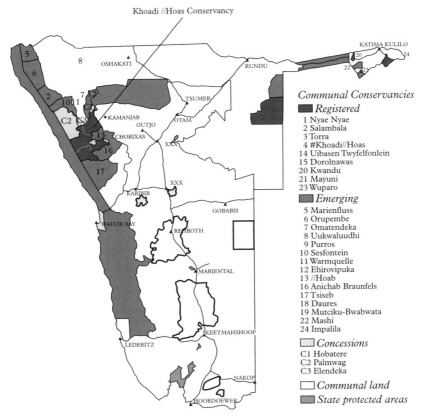

Fig. 9.1 Communal conservancies and location of #Khoadi//Hoas Conservancy

the protection of game from exploitation and the profits from wildlife management is seen.

Because of the necessity to have communal responsibility for the sustainable utilisation of game, the redistribution of profits from wildlife utilisation and the joint decision making about the use of those profits, democratic institutional structures have been created by the #Khoadi//Hoas Conservancy (Fig. 9.2). In future all other resources besides game will be utilised in a sustainable manner as sanctioned via the conservancy committee. Wildlife utilisation therefore becomes only a first and easily applied step in a whole chain of improvements and development possibilities to reach social acceptance and to become an economically viable and ecologically sustainable enterprise. Meanwhile more than 2,000 registered members are part of the Conservancy, the entire adult population of the Grootberg area.

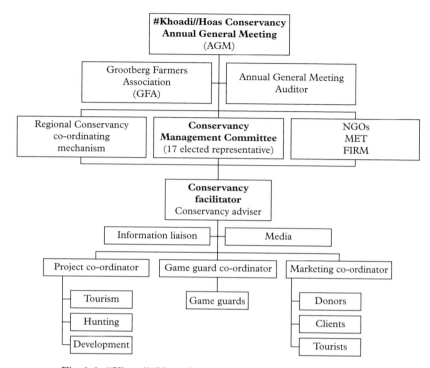

Fig. 9.2 #Khoadi//Hoas Conservancy structure

Greater conservation was achieved when the community divided the area into eight regions and employed environmental game guards (so-called environmental shepherds) to discourage poaching and stock theft. The game guards also inform the conservancy committee of problems experienced by the community, and monitor vegetation and rainfall. They will form an important contingent in the implementation of the Conservancy's elephant damage fund, established to compensate people for damages wreaked by elephants. This will be the first fund of its kind in Namibia and is aimed at increasing the tolerance of local people towards elephants.

Wildlife utilisation quotas are set according to counts and estimates by the environmental shepherds, with the Ministry of Environment and Tourism auditing the numbers and releasing the new quotas for every year (Table 9.5).

For the year 1999 the Conservancy generated N$135,000 with a similar quota for 2000, by leasing out the animals to a safari operator. Trophy animals are only hunted in a so-called exclusive wildlife management area in the south-west of the Conservancy. For every hunter there is one

Table 9.5 *Wildlife utilisation quota for #Khoadi//Hoas Conservancy 2000*

Species	Trophy animal	Own utilisation	Total
Baboon (*Papio ursinus*)	20	–	20
Black-backed jackal (*Canis mesomelas*)	10	–	10
Duiker (*Sylvicapra grimma*)	2	–	2
Elephant (*Loxodonta africana*)	1	–	1
Giraffe (*Giraffa camelopardalis*)	2	–	2
Helmeted guineafowl (*Numida meleagris*)	–	–	50
Klipspringer (*Oreotragus oreotragus*)	1	–	1
Kudu (*Tragelaphus strepsiceros*)	4	2	6
Leopard (*Panthera pardus*)	1	–	1
Mountain zebra (*Equus zebra hartmannae*)	4	–	4
Namaqua sandgrouse (*Pterocles namaqua*)	–	–	150
Oryx (*Oryx gazella*)	5	4	9
Ostrich (*Struthio camelus*)	2	6	8
Spotted hyaena (*Crocuta crocuta*)	1	–	1
Springbok (*Antidorcas marsupialis*)	10	40	50
Steenbok (*Raphicerus campestris*)	5	–	5

Source: MET, Directorate of Resource Management 2000.

observer from the Ministry of Environment and Tourism and one from the conservancy committee.

The #Khoadi//Hoas Conservancy area encloses the Grootberg plateau and in the north borders on the Hobatere Tourism Concession area (which again is adjacent to Etosha National Park). The community is currently negotiating with government to incorporate the Hobatere Concession area of 32,000 ha into the Conservancy. Again negotiations are already underway with the Hobatere Concession itself to sign a new contract with the Conservancy. The new lease fee will be N$74,000 per year, with 20 per cent as reinvestment into the concession area. This still leaves the sum of N$59,000 per year for the Conservancy.

Since the involvement of the Conservancy significant income has been derived from wildlife management in the Grootberg area, thereby giving wild animals an important value. On the other hand, poaching has reduced dramatically and for the years 1999 and 2000 not a single incident of poaching was reported.

Wildlife management in Namibia: the conservancy approach

Wildlife constitutes an important renewable and exploitable natural resource in Namibia and almost the entire tourism industry of the country is based on this asset. About 75 per cent of Namibia's wildlife is found outside formally protected areas. This is especially true for a substantial number of the country's elephant and endangered black rhino populations. Therefore, in discussing wildlife management models, resource utilisation and conservation of biological diversity are key issues. Namibia has developed a unique way to meet the requirements of two seemingly opposite approaches, people-orientated and wildlife-orientated, in its so-called conservancy policy. A conservancy consists of a group of commercial farms or areas of communal land on which neighbouring landowners or members have pooled resources for the purpose of conserving and using wildlife sustainably outside protected areas. Members practise normal farming activities in combination with wildlife use. They seek to increase local responsibility and ownership over wildlife and they benefit financially from wildlife and tourism through a range of activities. These include harvesting quotas, trophy hunting, sale of live game, tourism concessions and own non-consumptive tourism enterprises. Since the consumptive utilisation of wildlife (e.g., through hunting) generates a very emotional and controversial debate, wildlife management is especially hard hit by the confusion about how to conserve nature.

Some lessons learned

Among the proponents of wildlife management, a general confusion exists because of the polarisation of two seemingly opposite principles, the people-orientated approach and the wildlife-orientated approach. Since the consumptive utilisation of wildlife (e.g., through trophy hunting) generates a very emotional and controversial debate, wildlife management is especially hard hit by the confusion about how to conserve nature and about the goals of biodiversity in general.

Animal protection philosophies play a large role in the implementation of wildlife management projects as part of rural development. The reason is that animal protection and animal rights movements can generate intense pressure among the public as well as in politics and thereby prevent any kind of wildlife utilisation.

The two opposed approaches to nature conservation lie very far apart. The people-centred approach aims at income generation and maximisation of profits which can result in overutilisation of wildlife resources. The animal-centred approach, on the other hand, demands rights for each individual animal, a principle which will not advance the goal of nature conservation.

Wildlife management as a tool to safeguard biological diversity, however, can only follow utilitarian principles, which means that the well-being of each individual animal is important, but only of secondary importance compared to the overall conservation of species, populations, entire ecosystems and, above all, the legitimate interests of the participating people in their own development and improvement. Utilitarianism also means that utilisation, value and conservation are not only inseparable aspects of one and the same philosophy about nature conservation. They also support the sustainability of the basic premise of usefulness. Nature and species conservation can only succeed through the self-interest in conservation of the participating people, which is based on consumptive and non-consumptive utilisation of wildlife resources.

Parting reflections

No policy or philosophy will ever enjoy universal support, and especially not when it involves such subjective and emotionally charged notions as cruelty, animal rights and the best course of action in any particular set of circumstances. Sustainable use will always have its detractors, but none of them can offer an alternative that remotely challenges its potential to protect this planet's precious biodiversity and promote human development and well-being for generations to come.

REFERENCES

Ashley, C., Barnes, J. and Healy, T. (1994). *Profits, Equity, Growth and Sustainability: The Potential Role of Wildlife Enterprises in Caprivi and Other Communal Areas of Namibia.* DEA (Directorate of Environmental Affairs) Research Discussion Paper 2, Windhoek, Namibia.
Child, G. 1995. Wildlife and People: The Zimbabwean Success. Harare and New York: Wisdom Foundation.
Förster, H. (forthcoming). *Conservancies in Namibia.* Windhoek: Ministry of Environment and Tourism.
Ministry of Environment and Tourism Namibia. 1994. *Question and Answers about Communal Area Conservancies in Namibia.* Windhoek.
1998. *Interpretative Guide to the Legislation and Regulations Which Make Provision for Communal Area Conservancies and Wildlife Councils.* Windhoek.
2000. *Communal Area Conservancies in Namibia. A Simple Guide.* Windhoek.
Nuding, M. (2000). *The Potential of Wildlife Management for Development Cooperation.* Eschborn: German Development Corporation.

10   Brazil: selling biodiversity with local livelihoods

Ione Egler

The state of biodiversity in Brazil

Brazil is one of the richest countries in the world in terms of biodiversity. In its 8.51 million km^2 lies one third of the remnant tropical forest of the earth, the biggest wetland complex of the planet (the Pantanal), the biologically richest savannah (the Cerrado), more marsh area than any other country, and the biggest water reserve of the globe. Such wide territory and diversity of biomes renders Brazil in the first rank among megadiversity countries, sheltering an estimated 10 to 20 per cent of all the world's species (Mittermeier *et al.* 1997).

The data of Mittermeier and his colleagues and Dias (1996) show that over 55,000 species of Brazilian plants have been classified, representing 22 per cent of the recorded flora of the planet. In the animal kingdom, Brazil contains 10 per cent of the world's 4,629 described mammal species; 17 per cent of the 9,702 recorded species of birds; 9 per cent of the 5,460 classified species of reptiles; 10 per cent of the world's 5,020 identified amphibian species; and about 12 per cent of the 24,618 identified species of fish. Besides the diversity of species, Brazilian biodiversity is also important for the number of its endemic species, which, according to Mittermeier *et al.*, is only surpassed by Indonesia.

Recent estimates show that over 2 million species of plants, animals and micro-organisms may be found in Brazil. However, the precise number may never become known as biodiversity loss in the tropics seems to be faster than the ability of scientists to identify and describe new species, let alone study their potential uses and assess their genetic diversity (Raven 1988). Over seventy mammal species and 103 birds species are currently threatened by habitat loss (Brazil 1999).

Though biodiversity losses began with colonisation, the most recent changes have been brought about by large-scale land clearance and rapid urbanisation. In the period 1950–90, 70 per cent of Brazil's population turned from rural to urban. This process was promoted by rapid industrialisation and modernisation of the agricultural sector which intensively exploited natural resources.

Huge governmental programmes from the mid-1960s to the 1980s were designed to promote regional development of north-east, mid-west and north regions as well as to alleviate land tenure tensions caused by intensive agricultural conservation in the south and south-east. Those programmes supported mining, industrial logging, building and peasant settlement projects. These encouraged the migration of non-indigenous people to the north, where the population has leapt from 2 million to 20 million since the 1960s, causing a forest destruction rate averaging nearly 2 million ha per year (Laurence *et al.* 2001).

The Atlantic Forest – one of the most biologically diverse forests of the planet that 500 years ago stretched for about 1 million km^2 along the coastline – has been cut down to less than 9 per cent of its original size. The Brazilian savannah and steppe biomes, Cerrado and Caatinga, have been curtailed to 40 per cent and 50 per cent respectively, while the Amazon biome, the remotest part of the country and therefore considered the last frontier, has had around 15 per cent of its forests cleared, two thirds of it in the last thirty years (see Figs. 10.1 and 10.2).

Deforestation figures are likely to increase in consequence of the National Axes of Development that represent a priority scheme of public and private investments in Brazil, since the country resumed its macro-planning with the elaboration and approval of the Pluriannual Plan 1996–99 (PPA) (Law 9.276, 9 May 1996). The preparation of PPA by the Brazilian government and its approval by the Congress is a constitutional duty (article 165) that was made possible with the stabilisation that the Brazilian economy experienced from 1994.

The two decades of high inflation rates contributed to the dangers environmentalists see in the PPA. Although the plan of the government at that time – Mãos à Obra Brasil – had stressed that the new model for development to be pursued would be informed by three dimensions (economic sustainability, social sustainability and environmental sustainability), the social dimension and especially the environmental dimension were evidently curtailed. An example is the lack of any adequate environmental assessment of the proposed west–south axis that cuts one of the most important and fragile flooded biomes in the world – the Pantanal (Egler 1998).

A new version of the PPA was prepared for the period 2000–2003 (PPA 2000) (Law 9.989, 21 July 2000). This time the elaboration of the plan followed some regional public consultation at the end of the preparation process. That consultation process has been deemed important by potential foreign investors, by local and state governments and

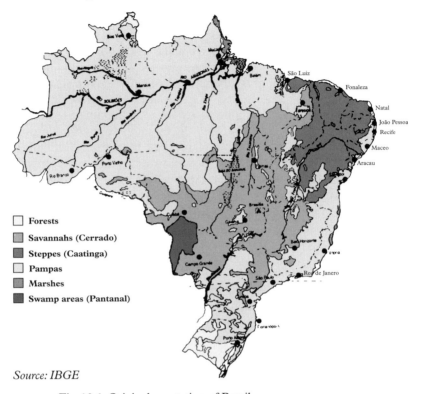

Source: IBGE

Fig. 10.1 Original vegetation of Brazil

by NGOs. Some adjustments were made with respect to the preparation process of PPA 1996–9. However, the need to approve the national
budget for 2000 as part of the plan (PPA 2000) jeopardised the effectiveness of the deliberation process as well as advice such as the results of
a regional workshop held in September 1999 by the project Amazonian
Biodiversity: Assessment and Identification of Priority Areas for Conservation, Sustainable Use and Benefits Distribution of Brazilian Amazonian
Biodiversity, implemented by Instituto Socioambiental (ISA) – a Brazilian
environmental NGO, under the support and co-ordination of the Ministry
of Environment.

A modelling attempt to assess the environmental impacts of economic
activities associated with the Development Axes in Amazonian Region
has recently shown that important conservation efforts in the Brazilian
Amazon are likely to be overwhelmed by transport schemes and their
related economic projects (Laurence *et al.* 2001). Figures 10.3 and 10.4
show the existing conflicts of two governmental projects, the Development

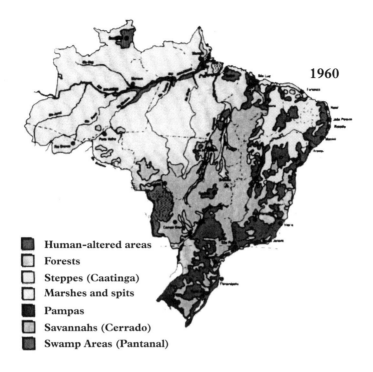

Human-altered areas
Forests
Steppes (Caatinga)
Marshes and spits
Pampas
Savannahs (Cerrado)
Swamp Areas (Pantanal)

Source: IBGE

Fig. 10.2 Land conversion in Brazil

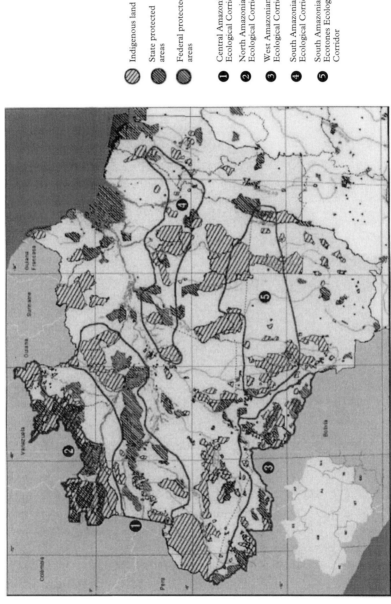

Indigenous land

State protected areas

Federal protected areas

1 Central Amazonian Ecological Corridor

2 North Amazonian Ecological Corridor

3 West Amazonian Ecological Corridor

4 South Amazonian Ecological Corridor

5 South Amazonian Ecotones Ecological Corridor

Fig. 10.3 Ecological Corridors proposed in 1998 under the Pilot Programme for the Protection of Brazilian Tropical Forests (PPG7) (*Source:* Brazil 1998)

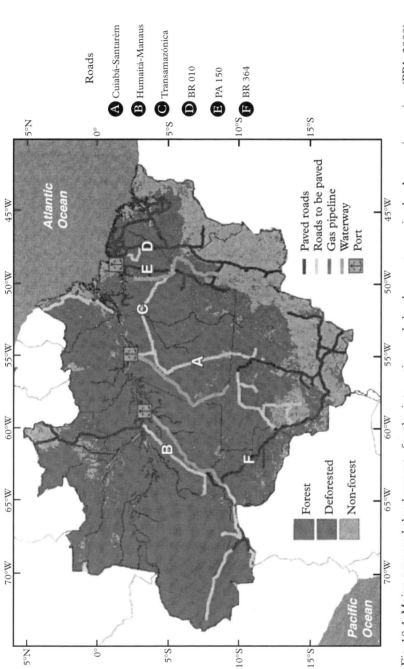

Fig. 10.4 Major proposed developments for the integration and development axes in the Amazonian region (PPA 2000) (*Source:* www.bsrsi.msu.edu/trfic/index.html)

Axis proposed by the governmental planning agencies, and the Ecological Corridor for Amazon Regions, funded by the G7 countries under the ambit of the Pilot Programme for the Protection of Brazilian Tropical Forests (PPG7).

The Amazonian Ecological Corridors project attempts to link thirty-eight protected areas and forty-four Indigenous Lands covering 17 million ha. This proposal represents an extensive scheme for bioregional planning since a considerable part of these corridors is constituted by lands which should follow special regimes of use, besides the protected areas it encompasses. Schubart (2000) argues that Brazilian Amazon regions share global economic development patterns with traditional indigenous practices. But the account of biodiversity value, in many or most of its dimensions, together with assessment of the global importance of the regional ecological processes such as the hydrological cycles, the energy balance and the carbon cycles, must have precedence in the planning process of the Amazonian region.

The first evidence of the environmental flaws of PPA 2000 forced the federal government to slow down activities in the Amazonian region and reassess the plan. In August 2001 the Ministry of Planning, Budget and Management proposed a comprehensive assessment of potential environmental, social and economic impacts derived from investment opportunities on Amazon Axes Madeira-Amazonas and Arco Norte as well as on West Axis (Brasil 2001). The proposal is to elaborate a strategic environmental assessment of these three axes, which seems too ambitious a programme for a single consortium.

Ideally, complex proposals such as this should involve sophisticated analysis of the economic, social and environmental implications, taken as an integrated totality. Such a review should be undertaken by a representative commission, composed of governmental and non-governmental representatives, such as the Commission for Sustainable Development Policies, created by the Ministry of the Environment in 1997. This, in turn, should ensure that the planning ministries take their recommendations fully into account.

I have suggested (Egler 1999) that this is an adaptive experience in which developing countries must strive to reach a clear national strategy to meet the legitimate global needs of economic development, yet improve social vitality and environmental quality.

Brazilian protected areas

The early stirrings of the conservation movement in Brazil emerged in 1963 with the formation of the Brazilian Institute for Forestry

Development (IBDF), with one aim to safeguard key sections of remaining forest from human invasion. Following the 1972 UN Conference on the Human Environment, the special Secretariat for Environmental Affairs (SEMA) was created in 1973. Though primarily designed to control pollution, SEMA's first director, Paulo Neto, was very instrumental in protecting biodiversity. Inspired by the notions that science should be closely related to the management of protected sites and that human presence was inevitable in many areas deserving a special protection status, Neto created three new categories of protected areas: Ecological Stations, Areas of Relevant Ecological Interest and Areas for Environmental Protection. These approximated exclusive biologically rich areas, areas of scientific ecological value, and sites suitable for protection of land and water from uncontrolled development.

Although SEMA and IBDF sought to manage protected sites from different perspectives for nearly two decades, both institutions were inspired by biological notions of conservation, such as the creation of a national system of protected areas in order to preserve *in situ* species populations and genetic variability, as well as examples of important ecosystems. Social and cultural components were barely studied or taken into account when determining the selection of protected sites. If anything, human actions were regarded by both SEMA and IBDF as obstacles to biodiversity conservation, and not as potential contributors to its improvement. In this important sense, Brazilian early biodiversity protection followed the scientific exclusive route, introduced by Pretty in chapter 4 and developed further in chapter 5.

Conservation strategies in Brazil started to change at the beginning of the 1990s, with the evidence from ethnoscientists about the importance of traditional communities for biodiversity maintenance and improvement (Anderson and Posey 1985; Posey 1984a, 1984b, 1985, 1987, 1998; Diegues 1988). There are many mythological characters in Brazilian folklore that express the connectedness between non-urban traditions and forests, rivers, lakes and biodiversity conservation. Mãe da Mata, Boitatá and Curupira punish those who destroy forests, Anhangá penalises people who treat animals badly, Tapiora rebukes everyone who kills animals in their reproductive season, and Mãe d'Água capsises canoes of overzealous fishermen who fish more than their needs (Cascudo 1972).

The rise of the sustainable development ideal, the recovery of democratic structures in the nation and more integrative institutional changes are other relevant factors in the promotion of social linkages into biodiversity strategies in Brazil in recent years. Many of the issues surrounding *mētis*, or learned knowledges, outlined by Pretty in chapter 4, are relevant to the change of heart in Brazilian biodiversity policy. An important institutional change was the creation, in 1989, of the Brazilian Institute for the Environment and Renewable Natural Resources (IBAMA), through the merger of SEMA, IBDF and two other governmental agencies. IBAMA is currently responsible for the maintenance of federal protected sites and other biodiversity management activities.

The creation of protected areas as a biodiversity strategy is well documented in this book. The actions of IBDF and SEMA put aside special protected sites in Brazil from the 1970s. However, this top-down model was too excluding. First, it barely observed the compatibility of protected sites in respect of other governmental development policies and programmes; second, it rarely made any sort of arrangement with lower administrative levels (states and municipalities) in order to promote a better acceptance of protected sites; and finally, it rarely included any public consultation with local residents.

These hierarchical procedures led to a number of administrative and political troubles with land tenure disputes and with well-documented conflicts over the rights of local communities to use natural resources. These conflicts became unbearable with the new democracy that the country experienced from the mid-1980s. This led to a massive decrease in the establishment of new reserves in the 1990s because the implementation of these reserves demanded the removal of inhabitants from within the boundaries of these sites, as well as a costly administrative effort in ensuring full regulation of poaching and other illegal activities in the reserves (see Table 10.1).

Economic recession and growing public debts at the end of the 1980s also caused reduction of public investments, which affected the successful implementation and management of newly protected sites. The federal government slowed down its efforts to create new reserves that demanded financial compensation to tenants, infrastructure investments, and expenditure with managers and staff wages, so essential for the implementation of sites establishment for integrated protection.

The lower costs for creating protected sites that allow for human usage, plus the sustainable development principle pushed by the government, are encouraging the creation and implementation of more sustainable publicly funded reserves such as National Forests and Extractive Reserves, as well as support for private reserves (see Tables 10.1 and 10.2).

Two new types of reserve were introduced in 1990: Extractive Reserves (RESEX) and Private Natural Heritage Reserves (RPPN). Extractive Reserves are defined as territorial spaces in which the local communities can sustainably exploit renewable natural resources (Decree 98,897/1990). This designation was in response to requests from various international groups, together with lobbies from traditional populations whose

Table 10.1 *Areas of Brazilian territory designated as federal protected sites in different periods (ha)*

Integral protection group	1934–69	1970–79	1980–89	1990–2000	Total
National Park – **PARNA**	1,131,933	4,307,723	4,614,279	1,278,526	11,332,461
Biological Reserve – **REBIO**	–	694,399	1,768,663	581,922	3,044,984
Ecological Station – **ESEC**	–	–	2,847,201	8,450	2,855,651
Private Natural Heritage Reserve – **RPPN**	–	–	–	421,455	421,55
Subtotal area	**1,131,933**	**5,002,122**	**14,232,265**	**2,290,353**	**17,654,551**
Sustainable development group	1934–69	1970–79	1980–89	1990–2000	Total
Area of Relevant Ecological Interest – **ARIE**	–	–	63,454	4,765	68,219
Area for Environmental Protection – **APA**	–	–	1,383,908	6,840,592	8,224,500
Extractive Reserve – **RESEX**	–	–	–	3,488,830	3,488,830
National Forest – **FLONA**	77,757	600,000	8,197,924	6,178,092	15,053,773
Subtotal area	**77,757**	**600,000**	**11,514,184**	**16,512,479**	**26,835,322**
Total area					

Sources: Modified from Rocha (1986); Bruck *et al.* (1995); Barreto Filho (1996) and www.ibama.gov.br

Table 10.2 *Federal, state and private protected reserves in Brazil*

		Integral protection	Sustainable use	Total
Federal	Area (ha)	17,233,096	26,857,084	44,090,180
	Number	94	109	203
	% Country	2.03	3.16	5.19
State	Area (ha)	5,969,143	23,796,189	29,765,332
	Number	267	184	451
	% Country	0.70	2.80	3.50
Private (RPPN)	Area (ha)	421,455		421,445
	Number	232		232
	% Country	0.05		0.05
Total	Area (ha)	22,714,694	50,653,273	74,276,957
	Number	593	293	886
	% Country	2.78	5.96	8.74

Source: Modified from Brazil 1999.

BOX 10.1 CHARACTERISTICS OF SOME RESERVE
CATEGORIES RECENTLY INSTITUTED BY THE
NATIONAL SYSTEM OF PROTECTED SITES

National Parks (PARNA). Protected sites in public areas by means of public
consultation aiming at the preservation of natural ecosystems of considerable ecological relevance and scenic beauty. Scientific research, environmental education and ecotourism are allowed, when not involving capture
and extraction of natural resources.

Biological Reserves (REBIO). Protected sites in public areas aiming at the
integral preservation with no human interference of the whole biota and
other natural attributes. Public visiting is not allowed and ecosystem recovery action is the only possible activity. The creation of REBIOs does not
require public consultation.

Ecological Stations (ESEC). Protected sites in public areas with the objective
of nature preservation and scientific research development. Public visiting
is not allowed. The crestion of ESECs does not require public consultation.

Private Natural Heritage Reserves (RPPN). Protected sites in private lands
legally instituted for perpetual preservation, in accordance with the demands of the owner and certified by environmental authority. Scientific
research, and visiting with tourist, leisure and educational objectives are
allowed.

Areas of Relevant Ecological Interest (ARIE). Protected sites instituted in
private or public lands of small extent, with extraordinary natural characteristics, sheltering rare species and with few or no human residents. The
main objetive of ARIEs is the maintenance of natural ecosystems of local
or regional importance promoting special means, measures and activities
towards environmental conservation.

Areas for Environmental Protection (APA). Protected sites created by means
of public consultation in public and private lands of considerable extent,
with relevant natural, aesthetic and cultural attributes that are important for
the quality of life of their inhabitants and surrounding populations. The
main objective is the conservation of biological diversity, and landuse regulation in order to ensure the sustainable use of natural resources. APAs
are managed by a council headed by the environmental authority and with
local and civil society representatives.

Extractive Reserves (RESEX). Protected sites in public land created by demand or in consultation with inhabiting traditional communities, whose
livelihoods depend on extraction of natural resources. The main objective
of REXECs is to protect the ways of life and the cultural habits of traditional communities. Public visiting is allowed when compatible with local
interests and scientific research. The management plan of these sites must
be approved by the deliberative council of the reserve.

National Forests (FLONA). Protected sites created in forested public lands
aiming at the sustainable and multiple use of forest resources and the
development of scientific research, emphasising methods for sustainable
exploitation of native forests. FLONA allows the permanence of traditional
inhabitants, in accordance with its regulations and management plan. Each
FLONA must have a consultative council headed by the environmental authority responsible for its administration, and with representatives of governmental organisations, NGOs and residents.

livelihoods were jeopardised by the seizure of their lands to promote regional development projects. Extractive Reserves were initially conceived to promote an alternative settlement system in the Brazilian Amazon to protect the lifestyles of rubber tappers and Brazil nut and other nut collectors. Nowadays the seventeen existing Extractive Reserves protect the livelihood of over 45,000 inhabitants, who earn their living from renewable extraction with sustainable practices for a wide range of products such as fish and other freshwater and marine products, essential oils, natural resins, tropical fruits and medicinal plants.

The Extractive Reserve model represents a turning point in Brazilian conservationist policy. It introduced a new element into the existing procedures for the creation and management of reserves. For the first time the inception of a protected area was motivated by popular demand rather than by an authoritarian governmental initiative. The co-management model devised for Extractive Reserves is carried out by representatives of governmental organisations, civil society and the local community. Such a model is directed to capacity building, increase of self-esteem and empowerment of local communities, and improvement of health, education and transport facilities so as to promote better living standards of those communities, as well as to advance conservationist practices. The points were fully explored in chapter 4.

The Extractive Reserves remain a vigorous ideal. In its first decade RESEX established 7.9 per cent of the national area under special protection status. Furthermore, the implementation of these reserves has greatly benefited from an international four-year grant ($9.45 million) obtained from the G7 countries under the Pilot Programme for the Protection of Brazilian Tropical Forests (PPG7). The latest assessment of the investments made by that Programme shows a considerable improvement in biodiversity conservation status of all reserves under the auspices of PPG7, as well as better living standards and public participation (Brasil 2000; Abers 2000).

The Private Natural Heritage Reserves (RPPNs) were also legally instituted in 1990 (Decree 98.914/1990). This is the latest of a series of protected area categories, which emphasises private initiatives. It represents a complementary trend in the remodelling of Brazilian conservationist public policies. The ideal is to reduce land taxes of estate owners who legally register 'in perpetuity', so long as it is in the public interest, part or all of their properties under integral protection status for biodiversity enhancement. Since RPPNs are meant to be a gene bank under total and irrevocable protection, extractive activities are not permitted. RPPN is a flourishing initiative in which educational and ecotourism activities have played a major role. However, as the size of RPPNs tends to be smaller than public reserves they still account for a tiny fraction (less than 0.5 per cent) of the federal and state conservation effort (see Table 10.2).

The national network of public protected areas currently embraces about 23.2 million ha of federal and state biodiversity integrated protection reserves and 50.7 million ha under sustainable development protection status. Such figures show that while 8.74 per cent of the national territory is under special protection, only 0.05 per cent is under private conservation.

Indigenous reserves also have a degree of importance for biodiversity protection. By 1998 there were 559 sites requested by different indigenous groups corresponding to 84 million ha (9.85 per cent of the national territory). Brazilian indigenous areas occupy a different status of conservation. A reasonable portion of them may be effectively protected, especially where ethnic groups are territorial and repel illegal colonists, loggers and miners. However, there is also strong evidence that some groups exploit natural resources in such reserves, causing considerable destruction (Redford and Stearman 1993). Over 61 million ha of indigenous reserves have already been defined, ratified and registered in Brazil, accounting for 7.18 per cent of the national territory (Brazil 1999).

Effectiveness of protected areas management in Brazil

Conservationist non-governmental organisations have long set a target to build networks of protected sites covering at least 10 per cent of all natural habitats in the globe. That goal represents a particular economic, social and political burden for highly diverse tropical countries with huge territories. In Brazil the careful design and effective maintenance of a network of protected sites that can ensure representative samples of all biomes and their biological diversity are far from being achieved.

The effort Brazil has made in the last three decades to establish a reliable and comprehensive patchwork of protected areas has been recognised world-wide. However, flaws in the designation of protected sites and poor implementation of protective strategies have proved problematic for the effective maintenance of ecological functions and species safeguard. This is due to an imbalance in resources being invested in each biome, the unevenness of the regional institutional capacity, and the lack of proportion in the number and size of protected sites throughout the country.

A survey of 985 environmental organisations shows that biodiversity conservation ranks as the most frequently cited theme for Brazilian

Table 10.3 *Most frequent issues raised by environmental organisations in different regions of Brazil, regarding biodiversity conservation priorities, 1995–6*

Interest	North-west	North-east	Mid-west	South-east	South	Average %	Total
Fauna and flora (biodiversity)	70.1%	69.4%	74.0%	65.5%	66.4%	67.6%	666
Forests	73.6%	49.3%	47.1%	55.2%	50.0%	53.9%	531
Water resources	42.5%	60.4%	56.7%	53.8%	53.15	53.9%	531
Waste (solid and liquid residues)	34.5%	50.0%	41.3%	51.4%	58.8%	50.4%	496
Urban environments	39.1%	54.2%	44.2%	50.9%	50.0%	49.4%	487
Protected areas	51.7%	46.5%	49.0%	47.4%	48.7%	48.1%	474
Environmental legislation and public policies	37.9%	48.6%	50.0%	50.0%	45.6%	47.7%	470
Sanitation	16.1%	34.7%	21.2%	37.7%	35.4%	33.1%	326
Agriculture and rural development	32.2%	31.3%	33.7%	29.2%	34.5%	31.5%	310
Pesticides	11.5%	29.2%	29.8%	20.0%	38.5%	25.9%	255
Alternative technologies	26.4%	27.1%	26.0%	28.3%	17.7%	25.3%	249
Traditional and extractive populations	36.8%	16.0%	23.1%	17.2%	9.3%	17.6%	173
Marine resources	4.6%	29.6%	8.7%	15.3%	10.6%	14.7%	145
Indigenous peoples	35.6%	11.1%	18.3%	12.7%	8.4%	14.1%	139
Energy	3.4%	6.3%	13.5%	14.2%	12.8%	11.7%	115
Climate change	14.9%	8.3%	11.5%	10.6%	8.0%	10.2%	100
Speleolgy	5.7%	9.0%	16.3%	10.8%	7.1%	9.8%	97
Others	18.9%	11.8%	15.4%	11.1%	6.2%	10.9%	107
Total number of institutions	87	144	104	424	226		985

Source: Crespo and Carneiro 1996.

governmental and non-governmental environmental institutions in all regions of the country (see Table 10.3). The same survey shows that 62 per cent of governmental bodies and 79 per cent of NGOs target local community development (Crespo and Carneiro 1996).

However, the number of institutions and the availability of resources vary considerably in the different biomes. An analysis of biodiversity investments for twenty-seven sources showed that Amazonian and Atlantic forests benefited most from governmental and non-governmental schemes, while Caatinga biome received only 4 per cent. In spite of severe habitat

BOX 10.2 COMPARISON OF BIODIVERSITY CONSERVATION
STATUS IN BRAZILIAN MAJOR BIOMES

The Amazonian Forest is the inner and largest biome in Brazil with over 4 million km^2 which represent 47 per cent of the territory. This last frontier has been mostly threatened by fires and the cutting down of forest for agriculture, cattle-ranching and selective logging. It is the most well-protected biome in Brazil, with about 85 per cent of its extent still forested, and roughly 10 per cent allocated to protected sites. The largest state protected areas are in the Amazonian region; seven of them are over 1 million ha in size, and one, the Island of Marajó, is nearly 6 million ha. Besides that, the reserves of Amanã, Mamirauá, Jaú, Anavilhanas and Rio Negro, together with the Environmental Protection Areas of the Right Bank and Left Bank of Rio Negro make a continuous stretch of protected sites of nearly 8.6 million ha. This is the largest area of protected tropical forest in the globe, an area bigger than Austria. In the Brazilian Amazon there are 188 environmental institutions (69 are governmental and 119 non-governmental) that represent 19 per cent of the environmental institutions regularly working in Brazil (Crespo and Carneiro 1996). According to a study developed by an NGO, 22 per cent of the projects on biodiversity in the country are located in the Brazilian Amazon, not including the scientific projects funded by three major federal research funding agencies (ISPN 1996).

The Atlantic Forest and Coastal Zone represent a small part of the country (4.9 per cent of the territory). The Atlantic Coastal Zone was the first development zone and contains the most populous and industrialised areas. It suffers from pollution, estate speculation and habitat destruction. Currently over 90 per cent of the Atlantic Forest has already been deforested and only about 1 per cent of its original biome has been designated as protected area. In comparison to other parts of the country, the Atlantic Forest and Coastal Zone have the greatest number of small and medium-size reserves. The degree of insulation of the reserves of this biome in respect to the adjacent areas, the uniqueness of the Atlantic Forest and the extremely biologically rich ecosystems of the whole biome have put the Atlantic Coastal Zone at highest conservation priority. Nearly 30 per cent of the biodiversity projects have been developed in this biome, and about 60 per cent of the country's environmental organisations (442 non-governmental and 148 governmental) are established in these two zones (Crespo and Carneiro 1996).

The highly biologically diverse Brazilian savannah (Cerrado) is the second biggest biome with nearly 1.9 million km^2 (22.2 per cent of the country). Its less majestic features and a rate of agricultural and cattle-ranching expansion of 3 per cent per year have caused Cerrado's recent rapid habitat loss and poor protection status. Conversion of the Cerrado ecosystem for economic use involving the total loss of the original vegetation now totals 40 per cent of the area, and more than 50 per cent of the remaining natural ecosystems has been degraded. Only 1.47 per cent (27,700 km^2) and 0.78 per cent (14,700 km^2) of the Cerrado are protected by integral protection sites and sustainable use reserves (Marino 1997). Nevertheless, the Cerrado's integral protection reserves are considered to be the best-managed reserves in the country. Crespo and Carneiro (1996) state that 23.5 per cent of the country's environmental organisations (150 non-governmental and 81 governmental) have concentrated their action on the Cerrado, but they have been granted few funds, so they can only develop 14 per cent of the conservation projects nationwide.

The worst conservation status and weakest financial assistance is for the Caatinga – the third-biggest Brazilian biome with 939,4oo km^2 (11 per cent of the territory). High temperatures and low rainfall account for its thorny scrub and dry deciduous forest vegetation. Extractive activities, subsistence farming, extensive agriculture and cattle-ranching, and agricultural second-rate management techniques have all furthered the destruction of over 50 per cent of the original area of this biome and a widespread desertification process. Less than 5 per cent of Caatinga is under special protection status. But the poor implementation of its reserves gives the biome the worst conservation rank – only 0.02 per cent of Caatinga is effectively protected (WWF 1999). About 11 per cent of environmental organisations are established in the Caatinga region (46 governmental and 65 non-governmental), and help to implement only 4 per cent of the biodiversity projects developed in the country (Crespo and Carneiro 1996).

loss in this biome the amount of financial resources invested in biodiversity protection and the number of environmental institutions in this biome are the lowest in comparison to other parts of the country. Therefore, conservation actions in Caatinga are less developed and protected sites are badly maintained.

This is, in part, a function of federal priorities, which are in part a feature of state capacities and their priorities, but also a function of the vision and commitment of staff on the ground. They are also an outcome of international financing biases and expectations. Without more consistent international support, this awkward variability in Brazilian biodiversity management will become more evident.

International preferences towards Brazilian tropical forests and humid ecosystems have influentially framed the negotiation and the scope of programmes funded by international grants and preferential loans. International resources have been tremendously important to biodiversity protection in Brazil. In the last decade nearly 75 per cent of the resources invested in protected areas came from international funding sources, especially through the National Programme for the Environment (PNMA). Much of the distortion observed in biodiversity protective action derives from lack of information, misconception of priorities, and irregular participation of pressure groups and other political actors in the country and throughout the world.

A second factor that jeopardises the effectiveness of protected areas in Brazil is the lack of political support. This makes it frustratingly difficult to integrate conservationist plans and actions with other policies (Egler 1998). Therefore, the boundaries of a number of National Parks and other strictly protected sites have often been changed during periods of rampant economic growth so as to reduce their size and give preference to development policies and programmes. A conspicuous example is the Chapada dos Veadeiros National Park. This Park was created in October 1960, with 600,000 ha, but since then has been reduced to accommodate regional development needs and infrastructure public programmes covering nearly 10 per cent of its original extent. Biologists argue that the critical reduction of the reserve makes it inappropriate for the conservation of large mammals whose territory size varies from 250 to 300 ha (Fonseca 1992; Terborgh 1975).

Lack of political support has also jeopardised the implementation of a buffer zone 10 km wide around protected areas in which landuse is subject to special rules and regulations (see Table 10.4). The absence of a buffer zone forces the genetic insulation of protected sites which can no longer maintain gene flows with adjacent areas and therefore become prone to genetic erosion. The absence of buffer zones in reserves greatly increases their vulnerability to fire, pollution of water resources and other damaging actions and accidents. This is precisely the circumstance of Emas National Park (see Fig. 10.1), whose boundaries are occupied by very intensive agriculture. Campanilli (1997) showed that over the past thirty years at least 70 per cent or more of the area of this reserve is burnt every three years, and in other years it is also burnt in smaller but significant amounts, typically around 20 per cent.

Table 10.4 *Main sources of vulnerability of protected sites (as a percentage of eighty-six integral protected sites studied)*

	Geographic region				
	South	South-east	North	Mid-west	North-east
Sectoral projects conflicting with the objectives of the protected site	85	78	62	88	67
Insulation[a]	38	61	12	38	57
Risk from economic activities[b]	23	28	12	25	24

[a] When 50 per cent or more of the adjacent area of the reserve is deforested.
[b] When 50 per cent or more of the adjacent area of the reserve is occupied by intensive agriculture, industrial zone, urban centre or mining.
Source: Modified from WWF (1999).

Table 10.5 *Some international grants and loans directed to Brazilian integral protected sites in the 1990s*

Funding institution	Amount	Purpose
KfW and World Bank	US$25.69 million	Implementation of forty-five integral protected areas and five Environmental Protection Areas
Interamerican Development Bank	US$2 million	Implementation for the Serra da Capivara National Park
Interamerican Development Bank	US$2 million	Creation of Conduru National Park
Interamerican Development Bank	US$500,000	Implementation of four Private Natural Heritage Reserves
USAID and Conservation International	US$700,000	Elaboration of management plan for the Serra do Divisor National Park

Source: Brazil 1999.

The third disruptive influence on the effectiveness of biodiversity conservation action is the poor level of reliable management of reserves in Brazil. In spite of the increase in national and state investments in protected areas and a number of international loans and grants (see Table 10.5), there is still plenty to do. Non-official estimates suggest that investments in protected areas in Brazil represent less than 20 per cent of the necessary amount. This situation became even worse after 1999 when the official budget suffered great cuts in order to reduce fiscal debts. At the time, the implementation of the Brazilian first big environmental international programme (PNMA) reached its end, and the implementation of the Project Ecological Corridors, under the Pilot Programme for the Protection of Tropical Forests in Brazil (PPG7), and the second phase of PNMA, were both seriously delayed because of protracted negotiations.

A WWF study on the status of Brazilian integral protection reserves shows that 55 per cent out of eighty-six sites surveyed are in precarious implementation condition, 37 per cent have inadequate management, while only 8.4 per cent are reasonably managed (WWF 1999). The same study indicates that 45 per cent of all protected areas have less than half of the necessary financial resources, 73 per cent have less than half of the necessary staff, 62 per cent have been managed in disagreement with the standards legally set by each category of protected site and 41 per cent

Table 10.6 *Main sources of vulnerability of protected sites (as a percentage of eighty-six integral protected sites studied)*

	Geographic region				
	South	South-east	North	Mid-west	North-east
Exploitation of natural resources affecting 10 per cent or more of the reserve	15	11	8	0	24
Reserves altered in 70 per cent or more	0	6	4	0	5

Source: WWF 1999.

have more than half of the buffer zone deforested and occupied with highly intensive economic activity.

The poor implementation of protected sites in Brazil leaves them vulnerable to poaching, fire erosion and damage, all of which reduce the effective long-term protection of Brazilian landscapes and biodiversity (see Table 10.6). The WWF study concludes that 75 per cent of the Brazilian national parks, amongst the most protected reserves in the country, are at different levels of risk from a combination of inadequate management and high vulnerability of the sites. The poor implementation of protected sites has been well described as a common flaw in many countries (Adams and McShane 1992; Diegues 1996; Kothari *et al.* 1996). The main problem derives from the fundamental misconception that biodiversity protection should largely be separate from the current ways of life of local human populations.

Because of the lack of integration of social and cultural components in protected areas, conservationist programmes have failed to recognise the value and practices that emphasise natural protection through the revival of local traditions. Therefore, most conservationist programmes in Brazil have not made any contribution to stem the cultural erosion that lies at the very root of biodiversity loss in the nation.

Any future improvement in protected areas management will depend on shifts in mindset to favour the co-evolution of natural landscapes and human societies. It is very important to pursue the improvement and dissemination of innovative models such as biosphere and extractive reserves. Case studies on those models have shown that buttressing local communities is effective in gaining their support and sympathy in the struggle for environmental quality and biodiversity management (Furze *et al.* 1996; Pimbert and Pretty 1997).

The politics of biodiversity in Brazil

The return of democracy and international financial assistance have been the major drivers in advancing conservationist politics in Brazil. The high administrative and political costs of trying to maintain top-down procedures encouraged new initiatives based on increasing participatory experiences. Elsewhere (Egler 1998) I have compared the evolution of different institutional arrangements created to negotiate and co-ordinate the implementation of national environmental programmes dealing with conservation of biodiversity. I concluded that an increasing and gradual trend to include private and non-governmental organisations in key deliberative and participatory arrangements can be observed in the National Programme for the Environment (PNMA), set up at the beginning of the 1990s, in the Pilot Programme for the Protection of Brazilian Tropical Forests (PPG7), initiated in 1993, and in the National Programme for Biodiversity (PRONABIO), financed by the Global Environment Facility since 1995.

A recent study of the PPG7 experience shows that the successful accomplishment of the Extractive Reserves Project in comparison with other projects under the same programme was largely due to the more effective participation process for planning, co-ordinating and implementing the project. This welcome participatory effort included traditionally excluded local populations (Abers 2000). The Extractive Reserves Programme has also benefited from the bottom-up process through which the reserves have been created, which brought about a strong communal sense and a better local organisation. Additionally, the numbers of key players and of conflicting interests are relatively smaller in well-focused projects such as RESEX than in more complex projects with a wide range of political actors.

All these experiences have positively affected institutional procedures, elaboration and negotiation of new conservation projects, and the adaptation of Brazilian biodiversity conservation legislation.

The creation in 1998 of four National Parks (Jurubatiba, Virua, Serra da Mocidade and Serra das Confusões) totalling 1 million ha, after six years of no designation, marked the beginning of a new era for IBAMA. The formation of these parks was enhanced by the political activity of key people and institutions supporting and demanding it, by lively public debates, and by a notable degree of local consultation. IBAMA is also improving partnerships with local communities, NGOs and private initiatives for the management of some parks, especially those with attributes that facilitate tourism.

Table 10.7 *Targets of non-governmental environmental organisations in Brazil, 1995–96*

Target public	Number of institutions	%
Local communities	571	78.8
Schools	435	60.0
Children and adolescents	443	61.1
Local authorities	325	44.8
Community leaders	305	42.1
Scientific leaders	242	33.4
State and federal government	219	30.2
Business people	155	21.4
Women	143	19.7
Company staff	79	10.9
Others	101	13.9
TOTAL	725	

Source: Crespo and Carneiro 1996.

The current importance of non-governmental environmental institutions for improvement of inclusionary actions in biodiversity management can be observed by the target group they work with, by the creative themes they have in their institutional agenda, and by their capacity to raise financial resources and implement projects. Crespo and Carneiro (1996) show that from 1995 to 1996 nearly 78.8 per cent of the NGOs surveyed had local communities as the target public, while 44.8 per cent were focused on local authorities and 30.2 per cent at other government levels (see Table 10.7).

The same study shows that a considerable number of NGOs have been involved with the development of projects with local communities and with biodiversity conservation (see Table 10.8).

Data from the National Environment Fund, a state-managed fund run by the Ministry of Environment, show the importance of NGOs in the implementation of projects in biodiversity conservation and management. From 1990 to 1997 NGOs were able to raise 51 per cent of the total amount of US$26 million invested by FNMA (Fig. 10.5), of which 37 per cent is in biodiversity protection and management (Fig. 10.6).

It is anticipated that participation of local communities and NGOs in biodiversity conservation and use in Brazil will pick up over the next five to ten years since local initiatives and participation by NGOs is now required in the planning and management actions of most new conservation projects. This includes financial assistance to protected sites in

Table 10.8 *Preferential themes in the agenda of non-governmental organisations in Brazil*

Activities	Number	%
Environmental education	627	86.5
Projects with local communities	424	58.5
Campaigns to mobilise public opinion	450	62.1
Conservation projects	367	50.6
Environmental inspection	300	41.4
Research and development	250	34.5
Advice and technical consultancies	229	31.6
Environmental monitoring	176	24.3
Ecotourism	168	23.2
Administration of natural resources	85	11.7
Total institutions surveyed	725	

Source: Crespo and Carneiro 1996.

the second phase of the National Programme for Environment (PNMA), the Ecological Corridors project funded by G7 countries, the 10 per cent Conservation Action initiated by WWF and FAO, and the National Biodiversity Project (PROBIO) funded by the Global Environment Facility.

Moreover, the New National System of Protected Areas (SNUC), established by law No. 9.985 of 8 July 2000 as a response to article 8 of the Convention on Biological Diversity states that the creation of all but Ecological Stations and Biological Reserves must be preceded by technical studies and public consultation in which 'people power' is required to furnish adequate information in a manner that can be understood by lay people. This legislation consolidates advances in the participatory creation and management of protected sites, widely debated in public meetings and workshop seminars (WWF 1996), and summarised in chapter 3.

SNUC establishes and harmonises criteria to create protected sites and also sets management principles and procedures for all reserve groups. These set the norms of all management plans for each protected site. Management plans must be prepared and approved by Consultative Councils or Management Committees, depending on the category of the reserve, but in any case involving local communities and representatives of civil society.

The presence of inhabitants inside protected sites was one of the most controversial issues for the SNUC. It took eight years of bargaining to reach common ground amongst different social actors. In reserves of the Sustainable Development Group, occupation and use of natural

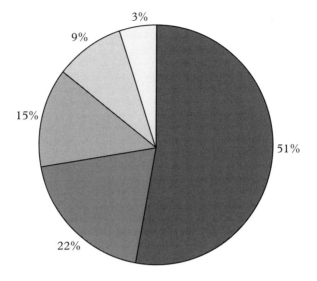

■ NGOs

▨ Municipalities with less than 120,000 inhabitants

▤ Federal

▢ State

☐ Municipalities with more than 120,000 inhabitants

Fig. 10.5 Percentage of resources implemented by different institutions supported by the National Environment Fund (FNMA) between November 1990 and September 1997

resources follow criteria set in management plans for each area, while inhabitants of integral protection reserves must be fairly compensated and resettled. Some articles of SNUC still need further regulation, currently being co-ordinated by the Ministry of Environment. Debates on regulation issues have been promoted in public seminars and suggestions can be made directly to the Ministry.

Recent changes in the legislation and in the characterisation of conservation programmes, as well as the growing importance of NGOs in the development biodiversity management projects in Brazil, indicate a new trend towards the integration of social well-being in conservation projects. However, the achievement of such a comprehensive approach is far from being an easy task. It is revealing that social scientists deem conservation issues as very important but prefer this to be tackled by natural

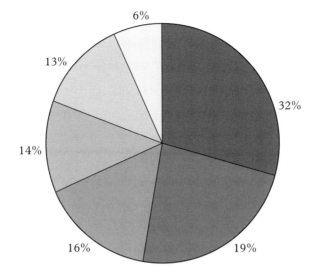

- ■ Environmental education and dissemination

- ■ Research and technological development

- ☐ Extractivism, forest management/conservation of natural resources

- ☐ Environmental control

- ☐ Protected areas

- ☐ Institutional strengthening and development

Fig. 10.6 Percentage of projects (totalling 498) in different areas supported by the National Environment Fund (FNMA) between November 1990 and September 1997

scientists. This new integrative approach is demanding a truly interdisciplinary style of research from communication scientists, environmental managers, civil society and the local community. All of this in turn will require tolerance and solidarity between all partners, the use of adaptive management styles and the establishment of sound technical and financial support.

Private initiatives and biodiversity management

The involvement of the private sector in biodiversity management in Brazil has changed significantly in the last two decades. That change is partly derived from a growing concern of all societal groups with

Table 10.9 *Investments in biodiversity projects during 1985–96*

	No. of projects	Total value (US$)	%
Foreign governmental organisations	37	73,922,269	54.7
National governmental organisations	430	19,034,701	14.1
International organisations	29	18,950,764	14.0
State foundations	1,579	14,270,973	10.6
Non-governmental organisations	418	8,922,948	6.6
TOTAL	**2,493**	**135,101,655**	**100**

Source: ISPN 1996, adapted from Brazil 2000.

environmental issues and partly from marketing (Crespo and Leitão 1993; Ottaman 1994; Passos 2000).

Private action towards biodiversity protection was initiated in Brazil in 1958 with the creation of the first national non-governmental organisation – Fundação Brasileira para Conservação da Natureza (FBCN). From the mid-1980s the country experienced growth in the establishment of national and international environmental non-governmental organisations that focused their initiatives upon the development of research and conservation projects. The Rio Conference (1992) and the dissemination of the sustainable development approach brought about a diversification of themes in the agendas of NGOs, all of which began to integrate conservation and social issues.

The private sector has increased dramatically in its commitment to biodiversity over the last decade. Currently there is a network of over 7,000 institutions addressing social and development issues. A survey on financing mechanisms in forty different funding sources shows that twenty-seven of them regularly support biodiversity projects and that 6.6 per cent of all the money invested between 1985 and 1996 originated from non-governmental organisations and foundations (see Table 10.9).

The creation of a new group of protected sites (Private Reserves of Natural Heritage, RPPN) in 1990 fostered the participation of a wider range of private groups in direct biodiversity protection actions. Nearly 34 per cent of the area legally assigned as reserves (421,445 ha) is managed by profitable enterprises, about 27 per cent is in individuals' or families' hands, while 39 per cent is under environmentalist NGOs or religious groups.

The participation of the private sector in the formation and implementation of public policies has been encouraged more recently with the creation of some institutional arrangements to improve public–private partnerships in biodiversity management. In 1995 the National Programme for Biodiversity (PRONABIO) instituted a non-profit private fund (Fundo Nacional para Biodiversidade, FUNBIO). This fund supports projects in biodiversity conservation, and sustainable use and fair sharing of benefits derived from that use, and is controlled by a board mainly represented by non-governmental groups. The financial source of FUNBIO is a combination of private investment and international grants negotiated by the government on the basis of a 33:67 ratio.

PRONABIO also supports the Biodiversity Information Network (BIN-BR), a database on Brazilian biodiversity information that integrates the clearinghouse mechanism of the Biodiversity Convention. BIN-BR is also developed by a non-profit private group (Fundação Tropical André Tosello) that has been greatly involved with environmental information systems.

The increasing commercial value of biodiversity products, which at the beginning of the 1990s was estimated at US$2–10 billion and by 1998 was worth US$500–800 billion (Kate and Laird 1998), has spurred other sorts of private investment for biodiversity management. A big Brazilian body-care industry entered into a partnership in 2000 with the state government of Acre. Under this arrangement they will buy raw natural products and take the responsibility of improving local capacity to create those products in order to add value at the local level. Similar arrangements have been made by the Dutch Cosmetic Industry (Cognis) and the Brazilian Institute for Natural Renewable Resources (the federal governmental agencies responsible for Extractive and other national Reserves). Pharmaceutical and body-care industries as well as banks have developed different types of biodiversity research and development projects all of which have widened participation of the private sector in biodiversity management (see Table 10.10).

In the wake of all this activity, and aiming to attract private investment to promote the sustainable development of the Amazonian region, the government created the Programme for Biotechnology in the Amazon (PROBEM) in 1997. The objective of PROBEM is the accumulation of value of Amazon products derived from biodiversity by means of biotechnological techniques to be developed in a 12,000 m^2 research centre in the city of Manaus. This bold initiative, conceived by the Ministry of Environment, became one of the forty-nine priority programmes of the federal government.

Table 10.10 *Private investments in biodiversity projects in Brazil*

	Period	No. of projects	Total (US$)
World Wildlife Fund	1986–96	127	3,220,125
Ford Foundation	1986–96	25	2,602,585
Conservation International	1986–96	78	1,948,362
Fundação O Boticário para Conservação da Natureza	1986–96	188	1,151,876
Extracta/Glaxo	2000–01	1	3,200,000
Bioamazônia/Novartis[a]	2000–01	1	4,000,000
UNIP/National Cancer Institute	4 years	1	1,000,000
ER2	3 years	3	4,150,000

[a] The contract, signed in May 2000, was invalidated; the Brazilian Government realised that bioprospection could not be developed before a proper legislation on access to genetic resources had been approved by parliament.
Sources: Brazil 1999; Folha de São Paulo (Os Principais Acordos do Brasil, 19 June 2000).

PROBEM represents an even greater advance in public–private relationships for Brazilian biodiversity, for the whole programme should be implemented by Bioamazônia, a social organisation specially instituted to ensure a favourable balance between private initiative and achievement of social interests. Social organisations are a kind of quasi-nongovernmental organisation, created by law in 1997, in order to facilitate public–private partnerships across state and federal government. They are private institutions that receive public money to develop a certain set of activities, that are regulated by the so-called management contract. Through this special model of contract the governments set the activities that will be developed by private initiatives, the specific goals to be achieved during a certain period, the indicators that will be used to measure the successes and failures of each activity, the resources available and the disbursement plan. Private institutions must receive a special credential from the government to obtain the title social organisation, and hence to be able to develop public interest actions in health, environment and science and technology sectors with public resources. As a private institution it is desirable that social organisations establish fund-raising mechanisms that are difficult for Brazilian public bodies to operate.

Bioamazônia was awarded that credential from the Brazilian president in 1998. This act denoted the great significance of PROBEM for top political authorities. In October of the same year it had its management contract signed by three ministers. The management contract includes twenty-six activities, amongst them building the capacity for local people to work as parataxonomists, and their training to be aware of their rights regarding the principle of fair sharing of benefits derived from the use of biodiversity. Bioamazônia also became responsible for the creation of a special fund to promote research and development with biodiversity products and to safeguard the needs and interests of local communities.

Unexpectedly, PROBEM is facing huge legal and political difficulties. First, the bioprospecting activities of the programme are being delayed by the lack of a clear mechanism to provide access to genetic resources as required by the Convention on Biological Diversity. In accordance with article 15 of the Convention, access to genetic resources shall be given by national governments in accordance with their legislation. Brazilian legislation was initiated in 1995, but no common ground was reached in the Brazilian parliament until 1999. In the absence of appropriate legislation, the government could not hire bioprospecting activities from any private entity, in the case of PROBEM from Bioamazônia. Second, the Ministry of Environment excluded bioprospection activities from the first management contract with Bioamazônia. This was even though Bioamazônia set up a bioprospection contract with the pharmaceutical corporation Novartis Pharma in May 2000, via a social organisation with special credentials from the Brazilian government. The misuse by Bioamazônia of its legitimacy with government to act in a private interest caused mistrust to develop between the directorship of Bioamazônia and the authorities of the Ministry of Environment. Moreover, that particular initiative triggered a huge public outcry, charging that Bioamazônia's private profit-seeking arrangements have prevailed over the public interest in biodiversity. Congressmen/women opposed to the government called public meetings to demand explanations from the Ministry of Environment and from Bioamazônia's director general, to discover any possible illegitimate or illegal partnership between the government and Bioamazônia.

Subsequently, the relationship between the Ministry of Environment and Bioamazônia became tense, arrangements for the management contract were interrupted, initiatives to increase control over social organisations were developed, and the flexible management structures were blocked. Bioamazônia's failure became even worse when different sectors of the government publicly disagreed over the right for Bioamazônia to set bioprospection contracts. The economic ministries argued that Bioamazônia was created precisely to develop bioprospection activities, while the environment ministry claimed that Bioamazônia could not conclude bioprospection contracts without the official regulatory principles set by the Convention on Biological Diversity. This episode publicly exposed the conflict and custodial perspective that the Ministry of Environment confronts on many government initiatives, including strategies and special programmes of the Pluriannual Plan (PPA). In order to accommodate the lack of consensus in respect of bioprospection, the Presidency of the Republic passed a Provisional Law regulating the access to biodiversity. The decision to use an autocratic instrument to regulate a sensitive and complex matter, that did not require urgency, has inflamed public aversion to Bioamazônia. This time, this dislike was aggravated by congressional rage at seemingly being usurped over their legislative rights. The Provisional Measure could only reaffirm that access to genetic resources should be given by a governmental authority. But the procedures and institutional responsibilities attached to the measure are difficult to implement. Meanwhile, the activities of public research institutions, which depend on access to and exchange of genetic resources, have been cancelled because the functioning of these institutions must follow official legal statutes.

Conclusion

A wide number of political actors have been involved with biodiversity management in Brazil, as a consequence of greater concern with environmental issues, the steady democratisation of the political culture, and new market options.

The Brazilian pilot experiences involving local communities in the design of protected sites and with biodiversity management are still recent and not numerous, which makes it difficult to compare different situations, results and conclusions with respect to biodiversity conservation improvement and social betterment. As a matter of fact, a clear evaluation of the outcome of public policies needs at least a decade of implementation, and therefore the only Brazilian experience that can currently be assessed is that of the Extractive Reserve.

The first studies have shown some improvement in biodiversity conservation standards that can be judged either by the recent decrease of deforestation rate in certain areas, or by the aggregation of value on their produce and the empowerment of their communities with respect to the management of the areas they live in. So far the experiment of inclusionary actions towards biodiversity management in Extractive Reserves has not brought about significant improvements in living standards of the local communities concerned. After a decade of public investment in infrastructure development and capacity building, as well as in health and educational services, extractivist communities are still poor and continue to complain of lack of public support.

Because the replication of Extractive Reserves is limited to specific public areas, financial conditions and social groups, other models of biodiversity management must be enforced. Comprehensive approaches, pursuing the integration of conservation goals with rural development practices, must be fostered in Brazil. It is important to pay more attention to the development of buffer zones for all reserves, integrating local and national sectoral actions. In that sense, further development of inclusionary bioregional planning actions is much needed in Brazil.

Economic development of local communities in reserves that have been established by top-down models has been based on their involvement with some services, such as reserves management and tourism guiding. These are only possible in those few reserves that can be easily visited. Economic growth has also been pursued by some sort of value aggregation to local community produce, but this is still at a low level, with weak technological and market support. Private initiatives have a major role to play, but their acceptance and success demand cultural and attitudinal changes that, so far, are not forthcoming.

Most Brazilians retain their misgivings over the participation of private institutions in biodiversity conservation, development and use, especially those that are profitable. Aversion to private initiatives has been demonstrated in civic reaction towards the leasing of management activities of public reserves to private institutions. This antipathy is also evident in cases where the private sector has invested in the development of products derived from biodiversity initiatives. The private investments that so far have mostly been socially accepted are those mediated by public bodies, like the agreements of cosmetic industries with the state of Acre and with IBAMA.

The pharmaceutical arena in Brazil is highly complex since the new industrial code, approved in 1996, permitted patenting in pharmaceutical products. Besides the difficult relationship Bioamazônia established with the Ministry of Environment, it made a serious strategic mistake in choosing to begin bioprospection in the pharmaceuticals sector rather than in other economically viable options, such as cosmetics, alimentary products or even herbal supplements. Moreover, its commercial association with Novartis, although beneficial in many respects, failed to offer the necessary public transparency. This strengthened the collective misgivings towards private entities, blemished an important innovative programme towards biodiversity management, and reinforced bureau-cratic procedures that in many ways limit innovation and flexibility.

A better approach to biodiversity management in Brazil will surely depend on institutional arrangements involving both public and private sectors, incorporating local people, and guaranteeing the sustainable de-velopment of bioproducts. Such initiatives can only be driven by ideals set in the Convention on Biological Diversity, such as a reliable involve-ment of local communities, the right balance between the gains obtained from the access to biodiversity and the access to information, training and technologies, and fair and equitable sharing of benefits. They must also strive to find a trustworthy and legitimate ability openly to negotiate, and whenever possible jointly develop, those projects with all three sectors of modern governance.

Brazilian experience reinforces the themes of this book, outlined in chapter 1 and expanded by Norman Myers in chapter 3. The great tropi-cal and subtropical biomass of Brazil remains in a state of serious biodiver-sity decline, even when public–private partnerships and innovative private reserves are supported and experimental. The crucial missing ingredi-ent is social resilience, namely the socially just and politically legitimate 'payoff' for protection beyond protection. Without this vital coupling of social and ecological resilience, the future for biodiversity in Brazil is bleak indeed.

REFERENCES

Abers, R. (coord.) 2000. *A Participação dos Grupos Tradicionalmente Excluídos no Programa Piloto para Proteção das Florestas Tropicais do Brasil.* Relatório Preliminar. PPG7. Brasília: Ministério do Meio Ambiente.
Adams, J. and McShane, T. 1992. *The Myth of Wild Africa: Conservation without Illusion.* New York: Norton.
Anderson, A.B.W. and Posey, D.A. 1985. Manejo do Cerrado pelos Índios Kayapó. *Boletim do Museu Paraense Emílio Goeldi. Botânica* 2(1), SCT/CNPq/ MPEG.
Barreto Filho, H. 1996. Política de incentivo à Criação de UCs. *Parabólicas* 3(18).
Brasil 1998. *Projeto Corredores Ecológicos.* Programa Piloto para a Proteção das Florestas Tropicais do Brasil (PPG7): Brasília: Ministério do Meio Ambiente, dos Recursos Hídricos e da Amazônia Legal.
2000. *Projeto Reservas Extrativistas.* Relatório Final da 1a Fase 1995–1999. Brasília: IBAMA/Ministério do Meio Ambiente.
2001. *Avança Brasil. Eixos Nacionais de Integração e Desenvolvimento. Eixos da Amazônia, Madeira-Amazonas e Arco Norte e Eixo Oeste.* Concorrência AB/CN-10/2001. Brasília: Ministério do Planejamento, Orçamento e Gestão.
Brazil 1999. *First National Report for the Convention on Biological Diversity.* Brasília: Ministry of Environment.

Bruck, E.C., Freire, A.M.V. and Lima, M.F. 1995. *Unidades de Conservação no Brasil. Cadastramento e Vegetação (1991–1994)*. Brasília: Relatório Síntese. IBAMA. DF.

Campanilli, M. 1997. Governo Propõe Corredores Ecológicos para o País. *Parabólicas* 34(4): 8–9.

Cascudo, L.C. 1972. *Dicionário do Folclore Brasileiro*. São Paulo: Editora Ouro.

Colchester, M. 1997. Salvaging nature: indigenous peoples and protected areas. In K. Gilmire and M. Pimbert (eds.), *Social Change and Conservation: Environmental Politics and Impacts of National Parks and Protected Areas*. London: UNRISD/Earthscan.

Crespo, S. and Carneiro, L.P. 1996. O perfil das entidades ambientalistas do Brasil. In *Mater Natura. Ecolista: Cadastro Nacional de Instituições Ambientalistas*, 2nd edition. Curitiba: WWF.

Crespo, S. and Leitão, P. 1993. *O que o Brasileiro Pensa da Ecologia*. Rio de Janeiro: Brasil América.

Dias, B.F. de S. 1996. A implementação da convenção sobre diversidade biológica no Brasil: desafios e oportunidades. In *Workshop Biodiversidade: Perspectiva e Oportunidades Technológicas, Campinas, 29 April to 1 May 1996*. São Paulo.

Diegues, A.C.S. 1988. Diversidade biológica e culturas tradicionais litorâneas: o caso das comunidades Caiçaras. In A.C.S. Diegues, *Trabalhos e Estudos*. São Paulo: NUPAUB-USP.

1996. *O Mito Moderno da Natureza Intocada*. São Paulo: Hucitec.

Egler, I. 1998. Implementation of the Biodiversity Convention in Brazil. PhD thesis, University of East Anglia.

1999. *Perspectivas Brasileiras de Desenvolvimento Sustentável. Anais do Seminário Desenvolvimento sustentável e Poder Local*. Núcleo de Estudos para América Latina – NEAL. Recife: UNICAP/AUSJAL.

Fonseca, G.A.B. 1992. Fauna nativa. In B.F.S Dias (eds.), *Alternativas de Desenvolvimento dos Cerrados: Manejo e Conservação de Recursos Naturais Renováveis* pp. 57–62. Brasília: FUNATURA e IBAMA.

Furze, B., De Lacy, T. and Birckhead, J. 1996. *Culture, Conservation and Biodiversity: The Social Dimension of Linking Local Level Development and Conservation through Protected Areas*. Chichester: John Wiley.

Instituto Sociedade, População e Natureza (ISPN) 1996. *Levantamento e Caracterização de Projetos de Biodiversidade no Brasil*. Relatório Final de Pesquisa, Fase I e Fase II. Brasília: ISPN.

Kate, K. and Laird, S.A. 1998 *Commercial Use of Biodiversity: Access to Genetic Resources and Benefit-Sharing*. London: Earthscan.

Kothari, A., Sign, N. and Suri, S. 1996. *People and Protected Areas: Towards Participatory Conservation in India*. New Delhi: Sage.

Laurence, W.F., Cochrane, M.A., Bergen, S., Fearnside, P.M., Delamônica, P., Barber, C., D'Angelo, S. and Fernandes, T. 2001. The future of the Brazilian Amazon. *Science* 291: 438–9.

Marino, M. 1997. *Levantamento da Localização e Representatividade das Áreas Naturais Protegidas no Brasil. Brasília*. Brasília: PNMA/Ministério do Meio Ambiente, dos Recursos Hídricos e da Amazônia Legal.

Mittermeier, R.A., Gil, P.R. and Mittermeier, C.G. 1997. *Megadiversity: Earth's Biologically Wealthiest Nations*. Agrupación Sierra Madre, Mexico: CEMEX.

Ottaman, J. A. 1994. *Marketing Verde*. São Paulo: Makron Books.

Passos, D.A. 2000. O poder ambiental. *Qualidade de Vida* 2(19): 1–3.

Pimbert, M. and Pretty, J. 1997. Parks, people and professionals: putting participation into protected area management. In K. Ghimire and M. Pimbert (eds.), *Social Change and Conservation: Environmental Politics and Impacts of National Parks and Protected Areas*. London: Earthscan.

Posey, D.A. 1984a. A preliminary report on diversified management of tropical forest by Kayapó Indians of Brazilian Amazon. In G.T. Prance and J.A. Kallunki (eds.), *Ethnobotany in the Neotropics*. New York: Norton.

1984b. Ethnoecology as applied anthropology in Amazonian development. *Human Organization* 43(21): 95–107.

1985. Native and indigenous guidelines for new Amazonian development strategies: understanding biological diversity through ethnoecology. In J. Hamming (ed.), *Impact on Forests and Rivers: Change in Amazon Basin*. Manchester: Manchester University Press.

1987. Manejo de floresta secundária, Capoeiras, Campos e Cerrados Kayapó. In B. Ribeiro (ed.), *Suma Etnológica Brasileira*, vol. 1. Vozes: Petrópolis.

1998. Os povos tradicionais e a conservação da biodiversidade. In *Manejo Participativo por Populações Tradicionais*. Textos Complementares, vol. 2. Piracicaba.

Posey, D.A. and Balée, W. (eds.) 1989. *Resource Management in Amazonia: Indigenous and Folks Strategies*. New York: New York Botanical Garden.

Raven, P.H. 1988. Our diminishing tropical forests. In E.O. Wilson (ed.), *Biodiversity*. Washington: National Academy Press.

Redford, K.H. and Stearman, A.M. 1993. Forest-dwelling native Amazonians and the conservation of biodiversity: interests in common or in collision? *Conservation Biologist* 7(2): 248–55.

Rocha, C.M. 1986. *Legislação de Conservação da Natureza*. São Paulo: CESP/FBCN.

Schubart, H.O.R. 2000. Biodiversidade e Território na Amazônia. *Logos Tempo e Ciência* 5: 5–18.

Terborgh, J. 1975. Faunal equilibria and the design of wildlife reserves. In F. Golley and E. Medina (eds.), *Tropical Ecological Systems: Trends in Terrestrial and Aquatic Research*. New York: Springer Verlag.

World Wildlife Fund 1996. Presença humana em unidades de conservação. In A. Moreira, A. Ramos, A. Anderson, N. Bensussan and A. Freitas (eds.), *Anais do Seminário Internacional sobre Presença Humana em Unidades de Conservação*, 26 a 29 de novembro. Brasília. R.M. Lemos de Sá and L.V. Ferreira (coords.). Brasília: WWF Brasil.

1999. *Áreas Protegidas ou Espaços Ameaçados: O Grau de Implementação e a Vulnerabilidade das Unidades de Conservação Federais Brasileiras de Uso Indireto*. R.M. Lemos de Sá and L.V. Ferreira (coords). Brasília: WWF Brasil.

11 The mixed experience of private sector involvement in biodiversity management in Costa Rica

Michael Sturm

Biodiversity under threat in Costa Rica

The small Latin American country of Costa Rica is generally known as 'environmentally friendly', and therefore has become a paradise for thousands of ecotourists. The Costa Rican Tourism Institute (ICT, Instituto Costarrecense de Turismo) has initiated an expensive advertising and image promoting campaign with the slogan 'Costa Rica – no artificial ingredients'. The target groups are North American citizens (USA and Canada), between 25 and 54 years of age, who earn $75,000 or more a year, and have a university education (*Tico Times*, 7 Aug. 1998). In 1999, the number of tourists reached 1 million (*Tico Times*, 17 Dec. 1999). A quarter of the country is considered to be protected (see Fig. 11.1). The World Bank and the Global Environmental Facility (GEF) have spent millions of dollars to support official nature conservation measures and the responsible governmental departments. NGOs provide information and environmental education on site.

Nevertheless, the current condition of the biodiversity in Costa Rica is disappointing. Despite regulations, management initiatives and international financial support, Costa Rica, formerly densely forested, has become an agricultural country. Virgin forests have become rare and are found nowadays only in remote or protected areas. Since the arrival of multinational companies, large areas have been transformed into monocultures, resulting in the pollution of both soil and water.

The reasons for the ongoing destruction of biodiversity in Costa Rica lie in the understaffing of protected areas, together with an apparent demotivation and resignation of agency personnel. Funds designated for projects are frequently misappropriated, and there is a tacitly tolerated but un-authorised destruction of woodlands by both farmers and companies, the result of inadequate surveillance and authoritative management (see www.inbio.ac.cr).

Associations of indigenous people and farmers (*indigenas* and *campesinos*) have joined forces to try to involve the largely neglected indigenous

243

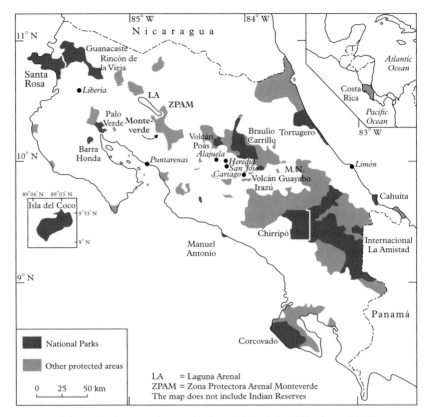

Fig. 11.1 Protected areas in Costa Rica (after Ellenberg 1999)

populations in the active protection of biodiversity. Their proposal for a Campesino–Indigenous Mesoamerican Biological Corridor (CICAFOC) was presented in Paris in 1998 and is supported by, among others, the World Bank (*Tico Times*, 29 Jan. 1998).

Biodiversity is also threatened by invasive species, a problem that has been given too little attention. The Tilapia fish, native to Africa and brought to Costa Rica in 1986, has supplanted numerous native species, for example in the Arenal reservoir (*Tico Times*, 15 June 2001).

Inadequate protection has deep historical roots. Since the establishment of cattle farming in Costa Rica in the seventeenth century (Sturm 1995: 74), some natural resources (such as forests) have been considered a nuisance, others (such as soil) have been abundant, and still others (such as water and air) have simply been taken for granted. In Costa Rica (as well as many other countries) there has never been an exploitation tax on these 'commodities', so they are misused. Rather than being safeguarded, forests and biodiversity were viewed as a nuisance to be eliminated in favour of agriculture.

Agricultural policies such as Volvamos a la Tierra (Return to the Land) under President Monge (1982–6) and its precursor Trato Justo al Agricultor (Justice for the Farmer) under Carazo (1978–82) illustrate this very clearly. They gave uncompromising development of agriculture priority over the protection of natural resources. Their support for large private enterprises, which resulted in extreme inequities in landowner-ship, led to rural exodus and migration.

Occupation of rural lands (*precarismo*) reached its climax in the late 1980s and early 1990s (see Albert and Sturm 1990). Presidents Arias (1986–90), Calderón (1990–4), Figueres (1994–8) and Rodríguez (since 1998) have not been able to alter this unfortunate outcome.

Since the 1950s, large landowners and landless farmers have extended agricultural lands into peripheral areas like Sarapiquí and San Carlos in the northern lowlands, Limón on the Caribbean coast, Golfito and the península Osa in the southern border area of Panamá, as well as into mountainous areas such as the Cordilleras de Talamanca, Central and Tilarán. Myers is right in his claim in chapter 3 that exploitation of biodiversity is often caused by incursion. At the beginning of the 1980s, more than 3 per cent of the primary forest was removed annually – the highest rate anywhere in the world (FAO 1999). In fact, despite Costa Rica's purported image as a model of environmental awareness, this was called into question as early as 1992 when the country was ignominiously granted the 'Eco Devil' award at the International Tourism Fair (ITB) in Berlin (Schliep and Wothe 1994).

In 1999, the Minister of Environment, Elizabeth Odio, produced an update of the state of biodiversity in Costa Rica. The government re-vised its figures downward: rather than 5 per cent, 'only' 4 per cent of all known species world-wide live in Costa Rica, which accounts for a mere 0.01 per cent of the Earth's surface (*Tico Times*, 15 Jan. 1998; Siedenburg 1998). Furthermore, the number of endangered species was increased (Siedenburg 1998; see also http://www.minae.go.cr). These include the golden toad (*Bufo periglenes*), which was last sighted 13 years ago, the green turtle (*Chelonia mydas*), some mammals like colorate monkey (*Ateles geoffroyi*), a tapir (*Tapirus bairdii*) and a jaguar (*Pantera onca*), as well as birds like the harpy eagle (*Harpia harpyja*) and the great green macaw (*Ara ambigua*). Even the survival of the legendary resplendent quetzal (*Pharomachus Mocinno*) is threatened. There are also thirty-six kinds of orchids among the endangered plants (see http://www.minae.go.cr).

The much vaunted reputation of the Costa Rican National Park sys-tem can now be questioned. A quarter of the country's surface has been designated as protected areas, but in practice this status is to a large degree (as elsewhere) a formal one ('paper parks'). More than 40 per cent of the protected areas is in private hands, and owners have not yet been compensated: US$665 million dollars are still owed (*Tico Times*, 14 July 2000). In fact compensation for nineteen of the twenty-six national parks has yet to be paid in total (*ibid.*). For instance, US$10.5 million is owed for 99 per cent of the 14,000 ha Piedras Blancas National Park, $6 million for the Arenal National Park, and $4.2 million for the Tenorio National Park (*ibid.*).

Costa Rica's policy for the protection of forests

The ponderous attitudinal shift towards a sustainable use of resources may best be observed in legislation concerning forests. In the Forest Law (Ley Forestal) No. 4.465 of 1969, ecological considerations regarding forest preservation are barely mentioned, while clear priority is given to economic exploitation of government-owned forests (Schlüter 1990: 98). There was no real incentive to protect the forests, since they were awarded no intrinsic value. Only mild punishment is meted out for excessive exploitation of woodlands.

This deficit was partially addressed in the financial and tax policy stipulations of the Reforestation Law (Ley de Reforestación) No. 184 in 1977. This was meant to encourage reforestation, but its effect proved largely limited because of the resulting high costs (Schlüter 1990). As a consequence, a complete modification of the forest laws was planned.

The Forest Law of 1986 was the product. It redefined the forest as a renewable natural resource whose protection, preservation, use, administration and development were to be controlled by the government (Art. 1: 100). Officials of the General Forest Office (DGF – Dirección General Forestal, founded in 1969) were now supported by the Land Policy Guards (Guardia de Asistencia Rural).

The DGF administers the Forest Fund (Fondo Forestal), a source from which the cultivation, protection and reforestation of existing woodlands, as well as projects for new areas, are to be funded. For example, the DGF can support the foundation of associations and/or co-operatives, and in doing so, influence both migration and cultivation methods. However, despite the increase in official influence over the protection of forests, far-reaching success has proved elusive.

The 1986 Forest Law has been strengthened by further regulatory institutions over the last fifteen years (e.g., the Forest Law of 1990; http://ns.minae.go.cr/estrategia/estudio/cap2-c.html). Other existing laws and institutions have, in principle, gained importance, e.g., the National Park Service (SPN, Servicio de Parques Nacionales), founded in 1977. Similar to the DGF, it is a division of the Agricultural Ministry, and is responsible for the management of the national parks, mainly established in the 1970s.

Other administrative steps have also been taken. In 1987 the Arias administration declared the protection of the forests as a political goal (Richter 2000: 63). In 1992, the General Direction of Wild Life (DGVS, Dirección General de Vida Silvestre) was founded as part of the Ministry for Natural Resources, Energy and Mines (MINEREM, Ministerio de Recursos Naturales, Energía y Minas). In 1995 the National Conservation Areas System was established (SINAC, Sistema Nacional de Areas de Conservación), which was responsible for the co-ordination of the administration and management of the nature reserves.

Perhaps the most important feature of protection has been the attempt to involve all levels of civil society. In 1994, the right to a healthy environment was amended into the Costa Rican constitution (Richter 2000: 64).

These changes in legislation, as well as the foundation and improvement of institutions, were a consequence of the 1992 'Earth Summit' in Rio, and the Convention on Biological Diversity (CBD). To achieve this, Costa Rica launched the Accessory Judicial Commission on Biodiversity (COABIO, Comisión Asesora en Biodiversidad). This agency developed a financial plan that the Ministry for Environment and Energy (MINAE, Ministerio del Ambiente y Energía) presented to the UNDP (United Nations Development Program), who found it acceptable.

In 1989 INBio (Instituto Nacional de Biodiversidad, National Biodiversity Institute) was founded to take an inventory of the national biodiversity (see Table 11.1). In 1991, INBio – and with it Costa Rica – received world-wide media attention because, for the first time, a contract was made with a private company (the US pharmaceutical giant Merck) which set a specific monetary value for biodiversity. It provided Merck with the exclusive use of medicine made of Costa Rican 'raw materials'. In exchange, INBio was to get 1 to 10 per cent of the licence fees (Richter 2000: 69). Meanwhile INBio has made further contracts with companies working in different areas such as pharmatechnology, perfume technology and biotechnology. This is also of advantage for MINAE because 10 per cent of its research budget comes from INBio (Ellenberg 1999: 412).

In the ten years of its existence INBio has been able to earn US$7 million. Its services, as specified in the contracts, include the provision to provide fixed quantities of extracts, micro-organisms and related services. Merck, as well as the University of Strathclyde in Scotland, have received

Table 11.1 *INBio: partners and terms of contracts, 1991–2003*

Serial no.	Partner	goals	1991	1992	1993	1994	1995	1996	1997	1998	1999	2000	2001	2002	2003
1	Merck (USA)	Extractions for industrial pharmaceutical and veterinary use	x[a]	xxxxxx	xxxxxx	xxxxxx	xxxxxx	xxxxxx	xxxxxx	xxxxxx	xxx...[b]				
2	UCR, ICBG, NIH (National Health Institute, USA), University of Cornell, Bristol Myers Squibb.	Studying tropical insects for pharmaceutical use			xxx	xxxxxx	xxxxxx	xxxxxx	xxxxxx	xxxxxx	xxxx				
3	Giraudan Roure	Potential use of scents and fragrances, transfer of technical knowledge					xxx	xxxxxx	xxxxxx	xxx					
4	BTG (UK), ECOS la Pacifica	Search for nematodical extracts in tropical dry forest and their cultivation in greenhouses		xxx	xxxxxx	xxxxxx	xxxxxx	xxxxxx	xxxxxx	xxxxxx	xxxxxx	xxxxxx	xxxxxx	...	
5	Diversa	Search for enzymes from marine or terrestrial micro-organisms					xxxx	xxxxxx	xxxxxx	xxxxxx	xxxxxx	xxxxxx	xxxxxx	...	
6	University of Massachussets, NIH (USA)	Search for insecticides					xx	xxxxxx	xxxxxx	xxxxx					
7	Fund. CR-USA, CIDPA, UME, LEBI, Hosp. de los niños	Studying two plants for extracts for malaria and gastritis			?				?				?		

No.	Institution	Objective						
8	INDENA-SPA	Search for active components for cosmetic use	xx	XXXXXX	XXXXXX	XXXXXX	XXXXXX	...
9	University of Strathclyde (Scotland), private Japanese sector	Search for plant extracts, transfer of technical knowledge		XXX	XXXXXX	XXXXXX	XXX	
10	Phytera Inc.	Production of chemical extracts of plants			XXX	XXXXXX	XXX	
11	EARTH, UNA, NASA, other institutions of Latin America	Search for compounds in plants for *Tripanosomiasis americana*	XXX	XXXXXX	XXXXXX	XXXXXX	XXXXXX	...
12	BID	Support of small enterprises to the use of biodiversity products			XXXXXX	XXXXXX	XXXXXX	...
13	Eli Lilly & Co.	Search for new pharmaceutical compounds			XXX	XXX		
14	Akkadix Corporation (USA)	Search for alternatives of anti-nematodes			XXX	XXXXXX	XXX	
15	University of Guelph (Canada)	Search for new extracts in plants for medical use				XXX	XXXXXX XXXXXXX XXXXXX	

[a] x denotes a period of two months approximately.

[b] ... denotes intended continuation.

Source: croldan@inbio.ac.cr, 24. 07. 2001, author's compilation.

extracts from plants and insects and have also gained access to technologies, equipment and training.

Other contracts have related to the search for new scents and flavours (Givaudan-Rooure 1995–8); the breeding of plants in greenhouses to extract substances against parasites (BTG, Ecos/La Pacífica S.A.; since 1992); the extraction of substances against malaria and gastritis (Fundación CR-USA); the production of new medicines by using biotechnological methods (Phytera Inc. 1998–2000); or the use of plant tissue in the search for new medicines (University of Guelph, Canada; 2000–3).

INBio co-operates with the Universidad de Costa Rica, Universidad Nacional, Museo Nacional, Escuela de Agricultura de la Región Tropical Húmeda (EARTH, School of Wet Tropical Region Agriculture), Instituto Tecnológico de Costa Rica (ITCO) and MINAE (World Resources Institute 1995). The agency is also the author of a study published in 1998 on behalf of MINAE and COABIO. Its title is *National Strategies for the Protection and the Lasting Use of Biodiversity*, and it shows very clearly the seriousness of the threats to biodiversity as well as the possibilities for protection (http://ns.minae.go.cr).

Between 1940 and 1992 forest areas declined from 3.8 million ha to less than 1.3 million. By 1997, there had been a recovery to 2 million ha because of the increase of secondary forest. This is about 40 per cent of the total area of Costa Rica (http://ns.minae.go.cr/estrategia/estudio/cap2-c.html). The improvement is generally attributed to the reduction of lands used for livestock grazing (see website). Another important motivation for the protection of the secondary forests is the intentional use of non-wood forest products (see website), as well as the use of these areas for tourism.

Costa Rica was the first country to undertake trade in climate certificates. In 1994 the Costa Rican Bureau for Joint Implementation (OCIC, Oficina Costarricense de Implementación Conjunta) was founded; to date it has co-ordinated twelve projects. Among these are support for the construction of wind farms at the Arenal reservoir, reforestation programmes and measures for the protection of woodlands (Richter 2000: 68). The World Bank and GEF have provided Costa Rica with a US$41.6 million credit to support the Environmental Service Payments Program intended to compensate farmers for losses due to environmental protection measures (*Tico Times*, 4 August 2000).

The role of private enterprise and NGOs

Costa Rica's inability to make major advances in the protection of natural resources and biodiversity is largely due to the resistance to environmental protection measures among the very populations most directly affected.

NGOs working in nature conservation and environmental education, and private enterprises (mostly from the tourism sector), are beginning to play a significant role in rectifying this situation because they are active at the local level. Their strength lies not only in showing people how to earn a living from biodiversity, but – perhaps more important – how to keep it in their locality.

One of these institutions is a United States NGO, the Organization for Tropical Studies (OET, Organización para Estudios Tropicales). It manages the private nature reserve La Selva in Sarapiquí where it runs an environmental education centre and tourist facilities. Another is the Neotropical Foundation (Fundación Neotrópica), which published a study in 1988 about the connections between socio-economic advantages and protection. One of the most important private NGOs is the Tropical Science Center (CCT, Centro Científico Tropical), which published *Costa Rica Country Environmental Profile – A Field Study* in 1982. With this study CCT presented the first complete analysis of environmental conditions in Costa Rica.

OET and CCT are among fifty organisations that make up the Costa Rican Natural Preserve Net (RCRN, *Red Costarricense Naturales*). This was created at the initiative of the Costa Rican Ministry for Environment and Energy (MINAE), which, in 1995, pointed to the great dangers tourism presents to nature reserves. A general goal of the network is the exchange of information concerning the protection and use of natural resources in conservation areas; a main activity is informing its members about national and international workshops, conventions and seminars.

RCRN also represents and defends the interests of private nature reserves in their interactions with various governmental and international institutions. It is also involved in the development and implementation of plans for the use and protection of the environment, resources and biodiversity. Among its other goals are the preservation of vegetation along the banks of rivers, the use of genetic materials, and the absorption of carbon in carbon sinks (RCRN 1997).

RCRN supports nature reserves for two principal reasons. First, having experienced nature at first hand, people tend to grant it greater esteem and therefore display an increasing willingness to become actively involved (in varying degrees) in its protection. Next, and no less important, the money tourists spend helps to finance the administration of the nature reserves, since part of the income remains in the region for supportive measures such as environmental education, more than would otherwise be the case where official measures are involved.

Yet another Costa Rican institution active in environmental protection endeavours is the National Council for Sustainable Development (CONADES, Consejo Nacional para Desarrollo Sustentable). This was established by Executive Decree in 1994 with the mandate to promote dialogue and build consensus over sustainable development among all sectors of Costa Rican society. CONADES consists of representatives from government, academia, business/co-operatives, and non-governmental and social organisations.

The Reserva Biológica Bosque Nuboso Monteverde as an example of participatory regional development

[B]ased upon our experience here in Monteverde zone, the concept of sustainable land-use is a very complex issue and difficult to analyze. As a matter of practicality, land-use plans are often focussed on either the local, regional, national or global level. The implication of different scales is that there is not one particular land-use that is best, i.e. 'sustainable', at all levels. (Crisp 1990: 2)

The impressive biodiversity in the Reserva Biológica Bosque Nuboso Monteverde in the Cordillera de Tilarán (1,500 m above sea level), is directly related to climatic factors. The mountains overlie part of the Continental Divide, whose north-east side is exposed to the constantly humid Caribbean air. This results in some 6,000 mm of rain annually. In contrast, on the lower south-western slopes of the Pacific side, rainfall is regularly interspersed with dry periods.

The majority of the reserve occupies the cloudforest-covered summits. However, the surrounding countryside, lying protected in the 'Children's Eternal Rainforest' (see below), is home to vegetation and animals that may be termed 'migrants'. This term is given because they have come to the area from the Pacific lowlands through biological corridors, seeking relief in the higher and more humid regions during the dry season. Deforestation of established grazing land, which began in the lower regions, has left only the lofty summits undisturbed.

Members of the US Quaker movement, who refer to themselves as 'Friends of the Earth', established what was to become the Monteverde Reserva in 1950. Their goal was to protect the summit of Cordillera de Tilarán as a freshwater reservoir and to preserve its biological diversity. The official status as a protected area was granted in 1972 (Hartshorn 1982). Today, it covers 10,500 ha and is surrounded by a further 22,000 ha of the Children's Eternal Rainforest (BEN, Bosque Eterno de los Niños).

Since the beginning of the 1990s, the Reserva and the Children's Eternal Rainforest have become part of the Arenal-Monteverde Protected Zone (Zona Protectora Arenal-Monteverde) that covers an area of 45,000 ha (see Fig. 11.2). Tourism is limited in the Reserva, with no more than 100 visitors (a contested number) allowed at a single time.

Table 11.2 *Growth of the Reserva and the Children's Eternal Rainforest (BEN)*

Year	1954	1987	1989	1990	1992	1994	1997	2001
Monteverde Reserva	554	?	10,500	10,500	10,500	10,500	10,500	10,500
BEN	—	1,574	?	5,000	14,600	20,400	22,000	22,000

Source: author's research.

Fig. 11.2 Protected areas in and around Monteverde (Sturm 1997)

The Children's Eternal Rainforest is used exclusively for environmental education. The principal visitors are school classes from all over Costa Rica as well as representatives of international children's forest groups who visit the path established for educational purposes called Senderos

Table 11.3 *Visitors to the nature reserves of Monteverde, 1974–96*

Year	1974	1980	1984	1988	1990	1992	1995	1997	2000
Conservation Area									
Monteverde Cloud Forest Preserve	471	3,172	5,924	15,334	26,657	49,580	50,571	46,917	54,930
Sta Elena College Cloud Forest Preserve	–	–	–	–	–	3,099	13,138	*6,601	?
Sky Walk	–	–	–	–	–	–	–	**6,942	?

* Till September (inclusive).
** March to September (inclusive).
Source: Sky Walk, 1997, 2001, Sta Elena College Cloud Forest Preserve.

Bajo del Tigre and the San Gerardo and Pocosol stations. About 2,000 visitors come to the park annually (see Table 11.3).

The Reserva is administered by the TSC, which was established by 'Friends of the Earth'. The Children's Eternal Rainforest is administered by the Monteverde Conservation League (Asociación Conservacionista de Monteverde), founded in 1986. The League (Spanish: *Liga*) also co-ordinates environmental education programmes for local residents. From the very beginning, they have been involved in all decision making in order to minimise distrust and promote acceptance and participation.

The management aim is to demonstrate to youngsters and adults the connection between their actions and the impact they have on the environment. The theme is the consequences not only for protected areas, but also for their direct surroundings, which form a buffer zone (Zona de Armortiguamiento) containing twenty municipalities with 6,500 inhabitants (Sturm 1995: 138).

The League also offers guided tours through the Reserva and manages contacts with Children's Eternal Rainforest groups from more than forty countries. Donations from these groups play a major financial role in the creation of the Children's Eternal Rainforest. In 1986 the League started the magazine *Huellas de Danta (Tapir Tracks)* in Spanish and English, but was forced to discontinue it in 1995 for lack of funds. In place of *Tapir Tracks* the League publishes a brochure/leaflet with general information, a website and 'Conservation Notes' for donors.

Another important contributor to the environmental protection effort is the Fábrica de Queso, a cheese factory founded in the 1950s.

It purchases milk from regional farmers and has developed programmes for the improvement of pasture vegetation and milk production. Other activities include the planting of more than 500 ha of hedges as wind protection – an activity in which local farmers participated – and the organisation of seminars on livestock care.

The Cheese Factory, with 100 employees and 450 stockholders, is one of the most important employers of the region dealing with local products. To prevent monopolisation and to stimulate participation, no shareholder is allowed to hold more than 5 per cent of the stock.

The farmers have worked in close co-operation with the League since 1980 on a number of environmental education activities. However, since financial contributions from Children's Eternal Rainforest groups around the world have decreased significantly (the groups preferring to buy land instead of paying for park rangers or educational programmes), the hedges-for-wind-protection schemes and environmental education efforts have been cut back.

In 2000 there were still 150 visits involving more than 700 pupils in eight schools in Sta Elena, Monteverde and neighbouring villages. New partners have also been found: these include the Monteverde Institute of Family Life (Vida Familiar del Instituto de Monteverde); the Technical Colleges of Sta Elena and Monteverde (Colegios Técnicos de Sta Elena y Monteverde); the Technical Professional Centre of Sta Elena (Centro Técnico Profesional de Sta Elena); the Integrated Programme of the Youth in Monteverde (Programa de Atención Integraf del Adolescente en Monteverde); Monteverde Committee for Waste Treatment (Comité de Manejo de Desechos de Monteverde); Sta Elena Association of Integrated Development (Asociación de Desarollo Integral de Sta Elena); Sta Elena Cooperative (Coope Sta Elena); Monteverde Producers Stock Corporation (Productores de Monteverde S.A.); the local bureau of the Ministry for Agriculture and Stock Farming (Ministerio de Agricultura y Ganadeia); and the Red Cross (Cruz Roja). The diverse nature of these institutions demonstrates the influence of the League, CCT and Fábrica de Queso. It also emphasises the need for personnel, financing, co-ordination and public relations.

Besides activities related to the improvement of milk production, the Cooperativa de Santa Elena also supports ecological farming (Figure 11.3) in the region. An example of its successes is the fact that high-priced ecologically cultivated coffee from at least ninety small local farmers is sold to tourists and is also exported to the US and Germany under the name of Café Monteverde. Part of the profit from the sales goes directly back to local nature protection programmes. The total amount of coffee produced in 1996 was 18 tons (Siedenburg 1998: 55).

Fig. 11.3 Visit to a finca with ecological cultivation (coffee) on Reforestation Day (Día de la Reforestación) (photo: Michael Sturm, September 1994)

COOPE is supported by Fair Trade, GEPA and Friedrich-Ebert-Foundation. The use of natural fertiliser is quite common and food produced in this region is sold by tourist facilities. High-quality souvenirs made of textiles and wood are produced in the Artisan Centre of Sta Elena and Monteverde, founded 1987 (CASEM, Centro de Artesanía de Santa Elena y Monteverde); 120 local women and some men are employed in CASEM. This is an indication that the arrival of tourists not only creates new jobs, but also supports the emancipation of women by providing sources of income (Sturm 1995: 34).

It should be emphasised that most of this infrastructure has been established or at least initiated by local inhabitants. This has created a high level of local identification with the goal of sustainable, environmentally compatible development. An increasing number of locals now earn a decent living from tourism or agriculture, so the link between tourism and profitable products like coffee, milk and vegetables has become more obvious.

The slogan 'from the region for the region' has been put into practice in exemplary fashion by the people of Monteverde (Siedenburg 1998). An estimated 12 per cent of the total revenues from tourism is invested in nature conservation, and between 16 and 21 per cent of the money spent by tourists provides income for employees.

Siedenburg (1998: 93–3) postulates that only 60 per cent of the income from tourism leaves the region on the following evidence.

Around 60–70 per cent of all expenditures by tourists ($4–4.7 million) flows into local enterprises (excluding the reserves).

Fifty-six per cent of all income from tourism (around $3.7 million annually) is spent on accommodation and restaurants, of which 70 per cent are owned by local residents.

Depending on the season, 25–30 per cent of the employed population find jobs in the tourism sector. Concomitantly, between 16 and 21 per cent of all tourism-related expenditures in Monteverde are passed on to employees as wages (90 per cent of all employees come from the local population).

Around 4.9 per cent of all income from the tourism sector ($325,000 per year) is passed on to the local population because of the links between hotels and restaurants and local agriculture. This represents, when viewed statistically, 5 per cent of all jobs. In comparison, only 3.2 per cent of all income leaves the region.

Roughly 19 per cent of revenue goes to the parks and the excursion sector, of which about 12 per cent is invested in nature conservation.

Besides the examined links between tourist enterprises and agriculture, the region benefits from income from a variety of indirect sources related to ecotourism.

Conclusions

The link between ecology and sustainable rural development is realistic pricing of resources, coupled with vital savings mechanisms at the local level. (Stuckey 1988: 39)

The Quakers' strategy of participation can be viewed as the most important factor for success. Involvement was practised from the beginning and, as Pretty advocates in chapter 4, respected and transmitted existing knowledge led to new insights. The transparency of the goals and the chance to participate in the profits associated with the more sustainable use of natural resources form a solid foundation for the enhancement of biodiversity.

The second success factor is that regulations are neither rigid nor inflexible; in fact, they were specifically drafted to be adaptable to changed or new conditions. Examples include the design of tourist facilities and the limits set on the number of tourists permitted to use nature reserves.

The third factor is the combination of ecological research and the impact tourism has on these regions. This has been accompanied by national and international monitoring of farming practices, environmental education, settlement growth, and all related consequences. Such analyses support the participatory programmes, as suggested might be the case in chapter 5.

The objective has been to provide a knowledge base for concerned groups and thus to develop a pragmatic tourism policy. Participation in the decision making processes by people directly affected or the connection of protected areas via corridors may be more difficult on a national or even international level, but they are possible and are demonstrating positive results. The La Amistad National Park co-operates with Panama and spans the two countries' common border. Especially ambitious is the plan to create corridors between selected representative habitats on a Mesoamerican level to enable the migration of numerous animals and plant species. This practice is being followed in the CAPE project in South Africa (see chapter 8).

REFERENCES

Aguilar, I. and Solis, M. 1988. *La Elite Ganadera en Costa Rica*. San José: Editorial Costa Rica.

Albert, R. and Sturm, M. 1990. Agrarerschliessung im Cantón Sarapiquí, Probleme bei der Einbindung einer Region der nördlichen Peripherie Costa Ricas in regionale und nationale Entwicklungsprogramme. In L. Ellenberg and A. Bergemann (eds.), *Entwicklungsprobleme, Costa Ricas*, pp. 149–70. ASA-Studien 18, Saarbrücken: Breitenbach.

Altenburg, T., Hein, W. and Weller, J. 1990. *El Desafío Económico de Costa Rica: Desarrollo Agroindustrial Autocentrado como Alternativa*. San José: Editorial DEI.

Bendel, P. (ed.) 1993. *Zentralamerika: Frieden – Demokratie – Entwicklung? Politische und wirtschaftliche Perspektiven in den 90er Jahren*. Frankfurt/Main: Vervuert Verlag.

Bourgois, P. 1994. *Banano, Etnia y Lucha Social en Centro America*. San José: Editorial DEI.

Crisp, J. 1990. Commentary. *Tapir Tracks* 1: 2.

Ellenberg, L. 1999. Schutz der Biodiversität in Costa Rica durch ihre Nutzung. *Geographische Rundschau* 51(7–8): 408–13.

FAO (ed.) 1999. *Forest Profile Costa Rica*. Rome: FAO.

Fonseca, E. 1996. *Centroamérica: Su Histórica*. San José: Editorial Universitaria Centroamericana and Facultad Latinoamericana de Ciencias Sociales – Programa Costa Rica.

Gudmundson, L. 1983. *Hacendados, Políticos y Precaristas: La Ganadería y el Latifundismo Guanacasteco 1800–1950*. San José: Editorial Costa Rica.

Hartshorn, G. (ed.) 1982. *Costa Rica Country Environmental Profile: A Field Study*. San José: Tropical Science Center.

Hedström, I. (ed.) 1989. *La Situación Ambiental en Centroamérica y el Caribe.* San José: Editorial DEI.

Porras, A. and Villareal, B. 1986. *Deforestación en Costa Rica: Implicaciones Sociales, Económicas y Legales.* San José: Editorial Costa Rica.

RCRN (Red Costarricense de Reservas Naturales) 1997. Red de Reservas Privadas, los inicios de la Asociación. *Boletín Informativo* 1: 1–8.

Richter, L. 2000. Waldzerstörung in Zentralamerika und die Folgen. In Working Team Costa Rica (ed.), *Costa Rica: Bericht zur Hauptexkursion 2000,* pp. 62–70. Geographisches Institut der Humboldt Universität zu Berlin.

Schliep, R. and Wothe, S. 1994. *Projektbericht Praktikum in Costa Rica: Regionalstudie zu Quepos und Nationalpark Manuel Antonio.* Berlin: Technische Universität Berlin.

Schlüter, H. 1990. Costa Rica: Die Zerstörung des Waldes – eine Herausforderung für Recht und Verwaltung. In L. Ellenberg and A. Bergemann (eds.), *Entwicklungsprobleme Costa Ricas,* pp. 91–109. ASA Studien 18, Saarbrücken: Breitenbach.

Seligson, M.A. 1984. *El Campesino y el Capitalismo Agrario de Costa Rica.* San José: Editorial Costa Rica.

Siedenburg, K. 1998. Regionale Verflechtungen des Ökotourismus in Monteverde/Costa Rica. Wirtschaftlicher Nutzen für die lokale Bevölkerung? Diploma thesis, Geographisches Institut der Philips-Universität Marburg.

Sky Walk 1997. Estadistica aproximada de ingreso de personas a Sky Walk. Monteverde, Puntarenas: unpublished.

Solera, A.R. and Ulloa, T.M. (eds.) 1988. *Desarrollo Socioeconómico y el Ambiente Natural de Costa Rica: Situación Actual y Perspectivas.* Serie Informes sobre el Estado del Ambiente, San José: Fundación Neotrópica.

Stuckey, J.D. 1988. Kicking the Subsidized Habit: Viewing Rural Development as a Function of Local Savings Mobilization: The Santa Elena Case: Modifications for the 1990's. Final Graduation Project, National University San Diego.

Sturm, M. 1995. *Ansätze nachhaltiger Nutzung in Monteverde/Costa Rica.* Marburg: Tectum Verlag.

1997. Monteverde in Costa Rica. In L. Ellenberg, M. Scholz and B. Beier (eds.), *Ökotourismus: Reisen zwischen Ökonomie und Ökologie,* pp. 229–34. Heidelberg, Berlin and Oxford: Spektrum Akademischer Verlag.

Tapir Tracks (Huellas De Danta) 1990. A publication of the Monteverde Conservation League. Monteverde.

The Tico Times. English-language weekly paper in Costa Rica, various editions, www.ticotimes.net: San José, Costa Rica.

World Resources Institute 1995. *National Biodiversity Planning: Guidelines Based on Early Experiences around the World.* Washington, DC: World Resources Institute.

Zuñiga Marin, S. 1997. Editorial. *MINAE/SINAC* 2(1): 2. San José.

12 The uncertain role of biodiversity management in emerging democracies

Martin Welp, Daniela Hamidović, Damayati Buchori and David Ardhian

Editorial introduction

The three case studies that follow all exhibit the subtle links between economies and democracies in transition and protecting beyond the protected. The first case is Estonia, a Baltic state of immense biological richness, but in the zone of economic renaissance. It is possible for that economic pathway to favour biodiversity, so long as governance and democracies swing in tandem. Similarly Croatia is an emerging, post-war democracy with enormous cultural vibrancy and ecological-geological diversity. Harmonising this vibrancy and diversity through the opportunities afforded by a new European integration could create genuine double resilience. Indonesia is also a young nation in terms of democracy, with a legacy of brutal domination of minority cultures and endemic corruption. How far it can shake off this legacy in the name of protecting even the protected remains an open question.

Citizen involvement in biosphere reserve management in Estonia

Martin Welp

Introduction

Estonia is located on the coast of the Baltic Sea. Formerly part of the Soviet Union, Estonia re-established its independence in 1991. It is a young democracy, striving to become a member state in the European Union. With strong economic growth and a determination to base its legislation on EU standards, it is becoming a primary candidate for membership during this decade.

Estonia enjoys enormous biological diversity. If implemented successfully, the Estonian Natura 2000 sites will considerably enrich the

Europe-wide network. Compared to other regions with similar geographies, the diversity of Estonian flora and fauna is one of the richest in the world (Peterson 1994).

Estonia is facing the challenge of preserving species and habitats in a period of land and property reform and other profound economic, social and political changes. Estonians are learning how the new democracy can assist such transformations. Biodiversity protection may pose limitations to newly established freedoms and private ownership. Nature protection professionals are beginning to recognise the benefits of participation and involvement of various stakeholder groups. Estonians generally value nature, so a hierarchical approach in biodiversity management could seriously harm this enthusiasm.

Threats to biodiversity in Estonia

In the European context Estonia stands out for its biodiversity, since many species and habitats (e.g., coastal meadows, wooded meadows) have nearly disappeared elsewhere in Europe. The total number of wild species has been estimated to be over 20,000: 5,400 species of plants, 3,400 fungi, 11,000 invertebrates and 500 vertebrates have been registered in Estonia (UNEP 1998). This richness of flora and fauna is due to favourable climatic conditions, the influence of the sea and many inland waters, diversity of soils, large areas of natural landscapes, and late intensification of agriculture.

During the Soviet era the centralised production system targeted some areas for high-input farming, whereas in other regions landuse was very non-intensive. Estonia has long traditions in nature protection, with a representative set of protected areas (Mathiesen 1937). At present there are four national parks and about 300 other kinds of protected areas (nature reserves, protected landscapes and programme areas). Protected areas cover about 12 per cent of the Estonian territory (Peterson 1994).

In some respects the transition period has been beneficial for the environment: for example, the nutrient and pollution load has decreased considerably owing to the collapse of kolkhoz agriculture and heavy industry. On the other hand, land (including forests) has been given to former owners in the process of land reform. This has intensified forest use. An important challenge for biodiversity management in Estonia results from these changes in landownership, especially the decline of arable and pasture use, since many cultural landscapes are disappearing. Land reform has also given a boost to construction activities, especially on the coast (Welp 2000). Summer cottages and tourism developments, such as marinas and hotels, are increasing.

Biodiversity policies in Estonia

Estonia is committed to fulfil the requirements of the UN Convention on Biological Diversity. The preparation of the Estonian National Biodiversity Strategy and Action Plan was carried out between 1998 and 1999, with participation of around 100 experts (Kull 1999). It sets out specific measures, including legislative reforms and the incorporation of biodiversity in the daily routine of administration, trade and industry. Broad public sector consultation took place in preparing the plan. Conservation in occupied and managed areas is relatively new in biodiversity policy in Estonia. This requires the extension of appropriate legal and management tools. The report further suggested that protection of managed areas may best be achieved by contracts with landowners and other incentive schemes. The integration of biodiversity into sectoral planning and decision making is also of high importance.

Although Estonia is not yet a member of the EU, it is shaping its legislation in preparation for implementing Natura 2000. The European Habitats Directive has thus given momentum to national efforts in biodiversity protection. The Natura 2000 process is supported by a large national programme called Estoniam Natura 2000, which is adopted for the time period 2000–2007, and which is backed by considerable funding. For the transfer of knowledge and exchange of experience, close co-operation with nature protection professionals from Finland, Sweden and Denmark plays an important role (Külvik 2001). Landowners in Estonia are becoming more knowledgeable about the legal possibilities for pursuing their interests. The bigger stakeholder groups, such as farmers and forest owners, are well organised and powerful lobbies. Other users of natural resources, such as hunters, are currently building up their country-wide organisation.

In Estonia the culture of citizen involvement in policy making differs considerably from its western neighbours (Welp 2000). Here people perceive their role as individual citizens in policy making differently from in other countries with longer democratic traditions. According to a survey initiated by the Biosphere Reserve's Hiiumaa Centre conducted in 1994, 70 per cent of Hiiumaa residents were convinced that they could not participate in decision making at the local level (European Heritage Fund 1995; Uljas et al. 1996) The amount of trust in political representatives and public administration was very low. Obviously the historical background plays a significant role here and therefore poses a serious challenge to any effort to increase public participation in planning and decision making. A second survey conducted on Hiiumaa five years later indicated a slight tendency towards more favourable perceptions of the scope to take part in decision making (Uljas 2000).

Designation of the West-Estonian Archipelago Biosphere Reserve

The West-Estonian Archipelago Biosphere Reserve is the only biosphere reserve in Estonia, but amongst the largest in the world (total land and sea area is 1,560,000 ha). It consists of two main islands, Saaremaa and Hiiumaa, plus a number of smaller islands and islets. A zone of 7 nautical miles creates the sea border. In terms of biodiversity they are vulnerable to the intrusion of alien species and the various pressures caused by seasonal and permanent inhabitants and tourists. The main motivation for the establishment of a biosphere reserve in Estonia was to protect Saaremaa and Hiiumaa against intensive agriculture. Further military activities, port development and subsequent clearing of land were also major threats to the islands' environment. The special international status of a biosphere reserve was expected to deliver the sustainable use of resources here.

In the 1980s there were discussions among nature protection professionals about establishing a biosphere reserve in Estonia. The West-Estonian Biosphere Reserve was founded by declaration of the Supreme Soviet of Estonia in December 1989. UNESCO approval to add it to the list of biosphere reserves was confirmed in March 1990. In the same year three biosphere reserve centres were established. In August of the next year Estonia re-established its independence.

The importance of public participation in biosphere reserve management, including the access to information and early involvement of stakeholders, has been stressed in chapters 1 and 5. The West-Estonian Archipelago Biosphere Reserve was established during turbulent times of political and social change. Against this background an analysis of emerging democracy and pioneering public participation in this biosphere reserve is highly interesting. There was no significant local opposition to the establishment of the reserve. On the other hand local people were neither well informed nor consulted. There is little documentation about the process of establishing the biosphere reserve. No public discussion about the reserve took place during the initial phase. Despite the fact that there was no public participation, the biosphere reserve was generally accepted in the beginning. Its legitimacy was never seriously questioned in its early years, in the media or elsewhere. The first time its legitimacy was publicly questioned was during a landuse conflict on Hiiumaa in 1996. An illegally constructed summer cottage was believed to have the status of a principal 'showcase' for future coastal landuse. The biosphere reserve, although not having an official role, was against the construction (Welp 2000).

Biosphere reserve management

After the designation of the biosphere reserve profound changes in the political and administrative arrangements took place. The Estonian biosphere reserve is part of national policy to protect biological diversity, even though its role is still taking shape. The Biosphere Reserves Hiiumaa Centre has played an active role in environment and development issues. The experiences of Hiiumaa highlight and illustrate a number of more general problems and solutions in biodiversity management in Estonia.

The two islands of the biosphere reserve are sparsely populated. For example, Hiiumaa has a land area of 1,000 km^2 and 10,500 inhabitants. The restricted use of the strategically important coastal areas and islands in the Soviet era has resulted in the relatively undisturbed state of the coastal ecosystems (UNEP 1998). This valuable asset is subject to pressures caused by changing agricultural landuse, increasing tourism and seasonal inhabitants (summer cottages). In biosphere reserves, land and water areas are administered and managed by more than one agency or owner. Thus, the Biosphere Reserves Hiiumaa Centre is only one actor among a range of sectoral administrative bodies, in charge of landuse, forestry, navigation, fishing, regional planning, etc.

A challenge for more integrated management is how complex resource use issues can be discussed and decided in a more comprehensive way and simultaneously accord with the desire for transparency and openness of planning and management. In this respect biosphere reserves can adopt different strategies and goals. The Biosphere Reserve's Hiiumaa Centre quickly adopted an adaptive approach to reserve management. The centre was especially interested in promoting community-based planning and management. According to the director, the 'main activities of the centre are connected to promoting nature protection and sustainable development through community-based policies, participatory planning and collaborative management' (Post 1998). After years of the Soviet command-and-control approach the newly established centre wanted to move in a new direction. In a Hiiumaa leaflet (Post 1995) the centre presents itself in the following way.

It is an old-fashioned notion that somewhere wise men make the right decisions and then pour them down on people. On a biosphere reserve it is done in a quite new way – the decisions come from below. Every family, village, community and the county should be entitled to the right and responsibility to take care of the ecological situation on their territory. Why should we consider Hiiumaa people not to be sensible enough to measure twice and then cut? Our responsibility is to help Hiiumaa people acquire the up-to-date knowledge, information and technologies, but they themselves make the decisions.

In the early years following the establishment of the West-Estonian Biosphere Reserve, planning and decision making were far from clear. There were and still are both overlaps and gaps (Peterson et al. 2000). Adequate legislation had to be developed and administrative responsibilities clarified. Such changes can be seen as hindering any prospect for rational planning. Yet it became possible to introduce new and innovative planning arrangements. Young people with fresh ideas entered the administration and the political life on Hiiumaa and elsewhere in Estonia. The old order slowly diminished, but not without a struggle.

In the first half of the 1990s there was also a strong social movement demanding profound change. Although this movement soon dissipated, as many people had to devote themselves to securing their own economic circumstances, the biosphere reserve was expected to be managed as part of an international network. On the other hand, the Biosphere Reserve's Hiiumaa Centre had to cope with scepticism towards this new 'outside intervention' and build trust. The centre was involved in various activities, including conservation, education and development. It was able to create good contacts abroad and was successful in finding partners for various projects. Networks, such as the Eco-Islands Network and the Seven Baltic Islands Network (B7), helped to attract international tourism development. In co-operation with several tourism enterprises and the county government, the centre launched the 'Hiiumaa Green Label' for travel agencies, hotels and restaurants. It also promoted co-operation with businesses (for example, import of wool and export of handmade woollen clothing took place with the German island of Pellworm). The Biosphere Reserve's Hiiumaa Centre also had an active role in initiating the Hiiumaa Development Action Plan 2010. Despite all this active networking, a consultative framework along the lines advocated in the Seville Strategy for biosphere reserves (UNESCO 1996) was never formally established on Hiiumaa. This strategy suggests stakeholders should be represented in biosphere management, including the full range of interests (e.g., agriculture, forestry, hunting and extracting, water and energy supply, fisheries, tourism, recreation and research). The democratic days are still young.

An example of community-based management

One example of an effort to introduce an adaptive approach to natural resources management in the biosphere reserve was the integrated coastal zone management plan for Käina Bay. This brackish coastal lagoon is situated between the south-eastern coast of Hiiumaa and the small island of Kassari. For biodiversity protection the area has special relevance: the Käina Bay Ornithological Reserve, an important breeding ground and resting place for migratory birds, had already been established in 1971. Currently it is protected as a landscape reserve. Since 1989 it has belonged to the list of Important Bird Areas (IBA) (Peterson 1994). The management plan was created by a team from the HELCOM (Helsinki Commission) Working Group on Management Plans for Coastal Lagoons and Wetlands (Kull 1999).

For the first time in Estonia principles of integrated coastal management (ICM) were applied in an adaptive and participatory way. An earlier ICM effort in Matsalu Bay was carried out more or less without public participation (Integrated Coastal . . . 1996). The identification of interests and possible conflicts was carried out in collaboration with local residents. These were personally asked to attend meetings to discuss management issues in the area. The invitation to attend was made by representatives of the local government. This form of engagement was considered more effective than just making a public invitation in the local newspaper. The Kassary Educational Society, one of the newly established local village groups, was also closely involved. In the meetings people were able to express their ideas and interests relating to the management plan. Local residents, mostly farmers, identified three main resource uses: grazing, reed cutting and tourism. The tourism activities included horse-riding and bird-watching. The municipal administration of Käina proposed developing the Orjaku passenger harbour and its facilities, exploiting therapeutic uses of mud deposits, and tourism development in the Kassari-Sääre area close by.

According to the project report: 'Special attention was also paid to the possibilities the project offered for education and interpretation.' For example, local newspapers printed articles on the value of the bay and potential threats to it. The process and principles of integrated coastal management were presented in the biosphere reserve supplement of the local newspaper (Kokovkin 1996). Basic environmental and socio-economic data were gathered, supported by field research. Research was, however, not used 'scientifically' to justify predefined management principles. The main emphasis was to create a partnership between various stakeholders.

The Käina Bay Integrated Management Plan was a comprehensive statement for a relatively small area. It identified a broad list of current and potential uses, threats and opportunities, and was established using collaborative planning methods and the principles of integrated coastal management. Implementation of the plan was supported by WWF

Sweden. For example, the so-called West-Estonian Archipelago Project is involved in ecosystem management by helping farmers to keep pedigree stock and create small-scale tourism. An association 'Keepers of the National Heritage of the Archipelago' was established, incorporating mainly local farmers.

Conclusions

In Estonia the importance of biodiversity protection has been taken seriously in national policy along with interesting examples of community involvement. The requirements of potential EU membership have increased the commitment to strengthen biodiversity protection. Challenging questions for biodiversity policies in Estonia include what degree of regulation and empowerment is still needed to avoid biodiversity loss. Traditional biodiversity management in protected areas alone cannot do the job. A new mode, which includes private lands and managed areas (forests, agricultural land, pastures, mires, etc.) has to be introduced. This requires innovative policy and management instruments (voluntary agreements, compensation programmes) and a fresh approach based on stronger co-operation and partnerships with landowners and other stakeholders.

The Käina Bay management plan on Hiiumaa is an example of a successful partnership set at a local level. Contracts to manage land for biodiversity have encouraged co-operation amongst farmers and foresters with nature protection. The Biosphere Reserve's Hiiumaa Centre has strongly supported community involvement and an active role of NGOs in the management of natural resources. It produced a handbook for NGOs at the local level (Post 2000). To achieve better co-ordination between administrative bodies and simultaneously provide meaningful possibilities for public participation, biosphere reserves centres and other bodies should further develop existing institutional structures and strengthen local groups and NGOs in Estonia. If participatory elements are included only in sectoral management (such as too narrowly defined biodiversity management), the outcome remains fragmented. The culture of political involvement has to be taken into consideration when designing stakeholder dialogues.

The biosphere reserve centres had no regulatory roles. This means that in many issues, such as municipal landuse planning, they could have influence via the media and through stakeholder negotiations. This 'undefined' and flexible status can be regarded as an opportunity, but the danger of having no clearly stated mandate can make biosphere reserve activities vulnerable. The Biosphere Reserve's Hiiumaa Centre was able to adopt the role of a parallel learning organisation, initiating and facilitating efforts towards improved participation and co-operation. This took place not only in protected areas management (Käina Bay), but also in development planning (Hiiumaa Development Action Plan for 2010). At present the nature protection administration is subject to promising organisational changes. The biosphere reserve centres may in future be split into protected areas administrations with much clearer mandates. It remains to be seen what weight the development and logistic roles of biosphere reserves will have in future. Given the impending link to the Habitats Directive, youthful Estonia may well set the pace for the slower-moving, more mature member states, hinted at in chapter 6.

Biodiversity in a post-war zone

Daniela Hamidović

The Republic of Croatia is situated at the crossroads between Central Europe and the Mediterranean. Its total state area is 89,810 km^2 (land territory 56,610 km^2 and non-island coastline 33,200 km^2).

Croatia is a new republic, whose first decade of existence has been marked by war and post-war reconstruction. Between 1990 and 1995, a large part of the country was occupied, devastated and economically destroyed. Its cultural and natural wealth, the bulk of which was located in the war zone, was severely devastated.

The worst military heritage is the minefields. It is estimated that there are 1–1.2 million mines and unexploded ordnance in Croatia. The contaminated area covers some 4,500 km^2, some of which is nature protected area. Mine clearance is a very complex, slow and expensive process. Unmarked minefields pose great problems since wartime mapping of minefields was not always complete or accurate. Unexploded ordnance presents a big problem, too. Priorities for mine clearance actions are being made (family property under the reconstruction programme, basic infrastructure, national parks and other mutual areas). The completion of flora and fauna distribution maps is still very dangerous for fieldworkers.

It is understandable that the national priorities are for economic recovery. Tourism and industry are top of the list, so it is possible to harmonise nature protection with tourism gains and income redistribution. Also the laws of nature protection are continuing to evolve, in order that economic development does not threaten the basis of tourist revenue. Croatia has preserved much of its natural and cultural heritage.

Taxonomic deficits and delayed biodiversity action plans

Croatia is a ten-year-old Republic with an emerging democracy. The Croatian political system is democratic and based on respect for human rights, laws, national equality and justice, and many recognised political parties. The protection of nature lies under the jurisdiction of the Ministry of Environmental Protection and Physical Planning (MEPPP; http://www.mzopu.hr). The responsibilities of this department operate through the implementation of the National Strategy and Action Plan for Biodiversity and Landscape Conservation of the Republic of Croatia. This document designs and determines nature conservation activities throughout the entire country. The primary activity of the department is international co-operation, through fulfilling obligations taken from the international conventions regarding the preservation of biodiversity and landscape diversity, to which Croatia is a party (see Box 12.1).

The Nature Preservation Act passed in 1994 includes the Statute on the Damage Caused by Illegal Actions on Protected Flora and Fauna Species (passed in 1996), thus modifying the existing preservation acts and statutes dating from the period of the Yugoslavian Federation. The list of legally protected species in Croatia is presented in Box 12.2.

BOX 12.1 INTERNATIONAL AGREEMENTS ON BIODIVERSITY TO WHICH CROATIA IS A SIGNATORY

World Heritage Convention (WHC)
Ramsar Convention on Wetlands
Convention on Biological Diversity (CBD)
Cartagena Protocol on Biosafety under CBD: *still proceeding*
Convention on International Trade in Endangered Species (CITES)
Convention on the Conservation of European Wildlife and Natural Habitats
Convention on Migratory Species (CMS)
Agreement on the Conservation of African-Eurasian Migratory Waterbirds (AEWA)
Agreement on the Conservation of Bats in Europe (EUROBATS)
Agreement on the Conservation of Small Cetaceans of the Baltic and North Seas (ASCOBANS)
European Landscape Convention: *still proceeding*
Memorandum of Understanding concerning Conservation Measures for the Slender-billed Curlew
Memorandum of Understanding on the Conservation and Management of the Middle-European Population of the Great Bustard: *still proceeding*

BOX 12.2 LEGALLY PROTECTED SPECIES IN CROATIA

44 Out of 5,347 taxa of vascular plant species and subspecies recorded (although there should be 92);[1]

130 fungi species; the other species can be gathered for personal purposes up to 2 kg per day;

lichens: owing to scarce data, it is not possible to propose legal protection for endangered lichens species; they may have to be safeguarded through the protection of forest, littoral and mountain area habitats;

none of 145 freshwater taxa (33 of them being endemic) is legally protected; protection could be done through habitat protection;[1] 16 out of 412 recorded sea fish species; the protection dictates the smallest size of the specimen under which it cannot be fished or sold; 37 fish species have endangered status;

all of 20 recorded amphibian species;

37 out of 39 recorded reptile species;

304 out of 394 recorded bird species (12 bird species are extinct);

58 out of 101 recorded mammal species; an additional 22 are temporarily protected;

130 out of 17,575 freshwater and terrestrial invertebrate species and the entire underground fauna;[1]

5 out of 5,427 sea invertebrate species.[1]

---

[1] The number of species for the majority of taxonomic groups is not precisely defined because of lack of expert taxonomist profiles, so the stated number of species is a minimum.

The General Action Plan is divided into several overlapping stages:

> making inventories of Croatian flora and fauna (taxa and habitats);
> distribution mapping (taxa and habitats);
> evaluation of endangerment status (taxa and habitats);
> design of conservation action plans;
> implementation of conservation action plans;
> monitoring;
> implementation instruments (institutional and legislative framework, education, information instruments, funding instruments).

None of the nature protected areas yet has a management plan, but the basis for some is now being prepared.

The national strategy on making action plans for protected areas includes general and special action plans for different habitats and species according to set priority lists. Each action plan contains possible sources of funding for plan design and implementation. For example, each action plan connected to areas and species of international value requires supplementary funding from international biodiversity funding organisations.

Nevertheless, the major funding source for the majority of action plans will be the state budget through the Ministry of Environmental Protection and Physical Planning. County budgets will also be partially included as well as business sector sponsorships. Action plans should be executed by numerous governmental and non-governmental institutions.

Unfortunately, everything still exists only on paper because of the adverse economic conditions. Although NGO involvement is allowed by the National Strategy, MEPPP forbids them to submit their proposals as formal partners.

At the moment, new National Red Books are being made, mostly according to general scientific knowledge. Red Books do not offer sufficiently reliable data for the full evaluation of actual endangered status. For certain flora and fauna taxonomic groups there are no expert taxonomists who are able to determine the species, and make the inventory and distribution maps. In the absence of this fundamental science, the endangerment status evaluation and action plan design cannot be created. This highlights the biggest shortcoming for Croatian biodiversity, namely the lack of adequately trained ecologists whose knowledge and access to critical areas are currently missing, or forbidden, or too dangerous. A proposed nature conservation law, due to be passed in late 2001, seeks to reinforce the responsibility of the MEPPP over wildlife and protected site matters, establish training programmes for rangers in national parks, improve co-ordination and co-operation of funding and management with NGOs (see Box 12.3) and work closely with local interests. The proposed legislation looks fine on paper: Croatian political experience does not suggest that this proposed legislation will achieve its full aims in the next decade. Basically, this is a 'catch 22' situation. Without the *mētis* (see chapter 4) there can be no adequate basis to establish, let alone finance, biodiversity protection in Croatia. Yet healthy biodiversity is not just an international obligation: it is the basis for future economic

---

BOX 12.3 PROTECTED LAND AND MARINE AREAS IN CROATIA

8 National Parks, including the Plitvice Lakes National Park under UNESCO
 World Heritage Site protection
10 Nature Parks, 2 of them under Ramsar protection
2 Strict Reserves
69 Special Reserves
72 Nature Monuments
28 Protected Nature Areas
23 Park-forests
114 Monuments of Park Architecture.

BOX 12.4 NGO INVOLVEMENT IN BIODIVERSITY IN CROATIA

Every year the Government Office for NGOs invites all NGOs to apply for funds. Some 200 NGOs are registered in Croatia. In finding financial support NGOs can also approach international funders, the EU, and Croatian companies (such as Zagrebacka Banka Ltd, Lura Ltd Dairy Company). Some of the most active NGOs which are involved in nature conservation and environmental protection are:

Društvo za zaštitu i proucavanje vodozemaca i gmazova Hrvatske 'Hyla' (*Association for Amphibian and Reptile Research and Conservation 'Hyla'*)

HBSD: Hrvatsko biospeleološko društvo (*Croatian Biospeleological Society*)

Društvo za zaštitu prirode Hrvatske 'Natura' (*Association for Nature Conservation in Croatia 'Natura'*)

BIUS Udruga studenata biologije (*Biology Students' Society BIUS*)

Zelena Akcija, Zagreb (*Green Action*)

Ekološko društvo 'Zeleni Osijek', Osijek (Ecological Society 'Green Osijek')

The HBSD has received a state donation to make a biospeleological database on underground-dwelling species. Making an inventory of these species is part of the long-term action plans in National Strategy.

---

well-being. For example, bird-watching, bat-observing, photo safaris, the economic benefits of experienced hunters and bird-watching guides all may prove valuable in long-term species conservation.

Another means of encouraging local community involvement could be the inclusion of local people in the running of the proposed ranger units in nature protected areas. To date, specific inclusion of locally affected stakeholders is all but non-existent in Croatia. An important intermediary position is the financial and management co-operation with NGOs (see Box 12.4).

The Society of Hunters initiated the reintroduction of beaver, *Castor fiber*, which is proving very successful.

Bat ecology and conservation in karstic environments

An issue relevant to both the European Habitats Directive (see chapter 6) and the forthcoming EU Water Framework Directive is the appropriate allocation of high-quality water for biodiversity purposes. Croatia takes all EU directives very seriously as it seeks eventual membership of the European Union, possibly in this decade. The Water Framework Directive is hugely important in this respect for it will require catchment-wide comprehensive land and water management plans, the control of non-point sources of water pollution, and, under its Article 14, full stakeholder involvement in all declared water protection strategies. In this regard, the role of the endangered long-fingered bat (*Myotis cappaccinii*) could be critical.

The management issue, especially in the karstic (calcium carbonate limestone) environments, is the use of freshwaters for water and electricity supplies, especially in the coastal area, and waterflow alteration for agricultural purposes. Although a 'biological minimum' set by the existing law is in place, the applications of this concept do not follow the natural dynamics of river regimes. The biological minimum is the amount of water which should be let out through any dam. It does not refer to the amount of water that should be in the riverbed for the preservation of whole ecosystems. This is particularly evident in the summer months in the coastal area owing to drought and the massive water demands of mass tourism. Instead of the biological minimum, the lowest acceptable flow concept should be established. This safeguards the amount of water in the riverbed necessary for the survival of the river and wetland ecosystems. Some recent studies have been done with respect to such flows, but none has officially been taken into consideration yet.

In order to monitor each habitat for habitat conservation purposes, a list of 'umbrella species' or bio-indicators per habitat should be established, according to the best scientific knowledge and *mētis* (see chapter 4) knowledge, and action plans and strategies should be created. The World Bank has offered funding for karstic habitat conservation that has initiated the creation of action plans, now in process, opening up the possibility for the long-fingered bat (*Myotis capacinii*) to become a bio-indicator for the karstic habitat. The long-fingered bat in Croatia is tied exclusively to natural karstic habitat: it raises its young only in limestone caves and hunts insects above karstic rivers and lakes. It is completely dependent upon cleanliness and natural karstic freshwater dynamics, joining the two fundamental characteristics of this habitat. Astonishingly, the World Bank funding covers only the northern part of Croatia's karstic habitat even though the interconnections of aquifers do not follow such a crude administrative line, and the karstic region can be followed all the way to the far south of Croatia. Croatian karstic ecosystems, owing to a number of underground dinaric karst species, are unique in the world, and most of the rivers belong to a special Adriatic River Basin. The Croatian karstic habitat is home to more than 500 endemic species, and its southern part is the home of the biggest nursery colony of long-fingered bats in Europe.

The long-fingered bat is distributed only in north-west Africa, southern Europe and south-west Asia. Little is known about the basic biology of this species. It does not show any possibility of adapting to co-existence with humans, unlike almost all other European bat species. During the day it roosts only in humid and warm caves and pits near karstic rivers and lakes. It is adapted in its unique wing shape to hunt insects very close to the water surface. Hibernation roosts are recorded in colder caves. Neither its migrations nor the percentage and the frequency of any gene flow between isolated European populations have been studied. In its area of distribution it is characterised by mosaic dispersion and low abundance. According to the IUCN Red List the long-fingered bat is considered vulnerable, amongst the seven most endangered bat species in Europe. The population status in Europe is greatly endangered. It is extinct in Switzerland, and is severely threatened in Spain.

The long-fingered bat population in Croatia is estimated to be 8,000 individuals, grouped in eight probably isolated sub-populations, one of which (in Miljacka II Cave) accounts for at least 6,000 individuals. According to existing evidence, the area of distribution of this bat has decreased in Croatia, and at least three sub-populations have already disappeared. Although this species has been legally protected since 1978 there is no money or political priority in Croatia for research into its feeding habits, its bioindicator value or its guaranteed survival.

The management plan for the wolf, which has been legally protected since 1995, has been created with the participation of the Faculty of Veterinary Medicine and MEPPP. Education of field experts for the evaluation of damage caused by wolves has been completed and the state pays for any domestic animals proved to be killed by wolves. The wolf is still not an accepted animal in local communities, because in some protected areas it does not have any of its natural food and so is forced to kill domestic animals.

BOX 12.5 INITIATIVES INVOLVING BIODIVERSITY ENHANCEMENT IN CROATIA

Jama Baredine is a privately run cave opened for tourist purposes, to raise public awareness on underground habitat beauty and conservation. The owner has a significant annual income from cave visits and promotes ecotourism.

Dr Goran Sušic who has been conducting research and conservation of the highly endangered griffin vulture (*Gyps fulvus*) population on the island of Cres has established Ecocentre NGO 'Caput Insulae' Beli. He has established a rescue network for young griffins involving local fishermen as well. One part of the Ecocentre's activities is marking and making educational footpaths through the cultural and natural heritage of the island. Bird-watching is available and volunteers are welcome.

The 'Lonjsko polje' nature park is promoting bird-watching, ecotourism and breeding of endangered species of domestic animals (Posavina horse and Turopolje pig). It also involves some cultural heritage conservation (to protect vernacular architecture).

The Flora Croatica Database (http://hirc.botanic.hr/croflora/), initiated by Dr Toni Nikolić, is financially supported by the Ministry of Science and Technology. The database analyses the vascular flora of Croatia (Pteridophyta, Spermatophyta). It is derived from systematics, horology, bibliography, etymology and ecology. It is part of a process that must be replicated in many more ways.

Hopefully, in tandem with economic growth, there will be more international, national and private funds available for establishing such professional and amateur networks so that active conservation does not depend only on individuals and NGOs. It is also necessary to synchronise the efforts of all the ministries and institutions involved (Ministry of Environmental Protection and Physical Planning, Ministry of Science and Technology, Ministry of Economy, Ministry of Tourism, Ministry of Interior, Ministry of Education and Sports, Ministry of European Integration, Ministry of Finance, Ministry of Maritime Affairs, Transportation and Communications, Ministry of Public Works, Reconstruction and Construction) to bring about the full recognition and implementation of biodiversity conservation.

Right now, that co-operation simply does not exist, and many imaginative schemes are thwarted by the ignorance and arrogance of officials who remain insular and unhelpful. Perhaps the onset of European directives plus the general drift to the kind of participatory governance outlined in chapter 5 will help create sustainability of biodiversity in Croatia.

I would like to finish with the words of Dr Toni Nikolić (from the 7th Congress of Croatian Biologists, Hvar, Croatia, 2000): 'The most endangered species in Croatia is the biologist/taxonomist.'

Local involvement in emerging democracy: a case study of biodiversity management in Indonesia

Damayati Buchori and David Ardhian

Biodiversity management in Indonesia reveals how the efforts to conserve and rehabilitate natural resources are very weak in comparison with the depletion and erosion of genetic resources. In fact, one of the reasons why biodiversity plays a central role is because of the economic value of the natural resources that are exploited for the economic growth of the country.

For thirty-two years economic growth in Indonesia was based on development supported by a centralistic and authoritarian regime that disregarded the rights of local people in resources management. This highly

BOX 12.6 THE STATE OF INDONESIAN BIODIVERSITY

As one of the centres for megadiversity in the world, Indonesia is home to 10 per cent of the world's flowering plants, 17 per cent of bird species, 7.3 per cent of the world's reptiles and amphibians (WCMC 1992; Mittermeier and Mittermeier, 1997; State Ministry of Population and Environment, 1992). The uniqueness of Indonesia comes also from its geological history and the fact that it is an archipelago with different islands possessing different evolutionary forces that have influenced the genetic diversity of much of its flora and fauna. There are many endemic species of flora and fauna, such as in Irian Jaya with 52 per cent of its avian population, 58 per cent for mammals and 35 per cent for reptiles. Mollucca has 33 per cent endemic birds, 17 per cent mammals and 18 per cent reptiles (State Ministry of Population and Environment, 1992). Based on data from the World Conservation Institute (1991), Indonesia has more than 2,904 mammalian species, thus making it the first-rank holder for mammalian diversity. Indonesia is third in the world for reptile diversity, fourth for Aves and fifth for amphibians.

Table 12.1 *Indonesia's endemic species*

Name of island	Aves	Endemic	Mammalia	Endemic	Reptilia	Endemic
Sumatra	465	2	194	10	217	11
Java	362	7	133	12	173	8
Kalimantan	420	6	201	18	254	24
Sulawesi	289	32	114	60	117	26
Nusa Tenggara	242	30	441	12	77	22
Mollucca	210	33	69	17	98	18
Irian Jaya	602	52	125	58	223	35

Source: McKinnon and McKinnon 1986; BAPPENAS 1991; State Ministry of Population and Environment, 1992.

All of this biodiversity is threatened by the constant loss of habitat due to deforestation and other destruction. Up to now, even though many have claimed that Indonesia holds the world's third-largest forested area, it is still unclear exactly how much land is still forested in the 'pristine' areas. The total forested area is still hotly debated because of unrecorded landuse changes. The government has claimed that the total forested area is 143.8 million ha (Ministry of Forestry and Estate Crops, 1999), while the FAO reported in 1990 only 109 million ha. This covers roughly 57 per cent of the whole terrestrial area of the country. Meanwhile, according to a National Forest Inventory, the total forest area is 140.3 million ha. This includes 30.8 million ha of protected forest, 18.8 million ha of nature reserve and national park, 64.3 million ha of productive forest, and about 6.6 million ha converted to other types of landuse. According to the latest data (Central Bureau of Statistics 2000), the Indonesian forested area is now about 111.5 million ha. This is claimed to consist of 29 million ha of protected forest, 19.06 million ha of nature reserve and national parks, including tourism forest, 29.6 million ha for limited production forest, and 33.23 million ha of productive forest. There are altogether thirty-six national parks in twenty-four different provinces, scattered in different islands such as Java, Bali, Sumatra, Kalimantan, Sulawesi and Irian Jaya. The total area of national park is a mere 14.1 million ha. This covers 72.64 per cent terrestrial areas and 27.36 per cent coastal ecosystem.

exploitative approach destroyed not only ecological functions, but also the social functions of local people. The fall of the authoritarian regime in 1998 enabled the local people to express their interests more freely. In many areas, there were movements by local communities to reinstate their rights in various natural resources.

Indonesian biodiversity: damage behind the richness

Indonesia is one of three countries in the world that possess a particularly rich and diverse biological resource. Indonesian biodiversity is a highly valuable asset, which has been the lifeblood of natural wealth for the welfare of all Indonesians. The richness of its biodiversity lies not only in the vastness of the natural forest but also in the diversity of its marine life and agricultural traditions which encompass hundreds of endemic varieties of rice, sweet potato, beans, and other type of crops.

Damage to forest ecosystems

Damage to forests is mainly due to illegal logging, land conversion and forest fires. The damage is so vast that the exact losses are difficult to estimate. The effects are not only physical but also cultural, for indigenous and traditional local knowledge is slowly eroding away. Areas differ in the amount of their losses, ranging from 7 to 90 per cent. Much of the loss in Java and Bali is due to population pressure on those islands that leads to agricultural activities and the development of residential areas and industries. The losses in Sumatra and Kalimantan are more related to illegal logging, mining and development of oil palm plantations. The deforestation rate in Indonesia is currently 17 million ha per year. Up to 20 million ha of forest has been lost since 1990. In 1998 alone the damaged forest area reached 16.57 million ha. From 1990 to 2020 the deforestation rate could increase from 4.5 million ha to an estimated 19.4 million ha. This damage is mostly attributed to irresponsible logging in the productive forests, estimated to destroy around 2.52 million ha of forest each year. This area has increased dramatically since the country was hit by economic crisis in 1997 (State Ministry of Environment 1999).

The illegal logging in national parks occurs because there is limited law enforcement, and the capacity of the existing bureaucracy to monitor the situation is very weak. The timber industries, which are located near to national parks, also contribute to the high rate of forest degradation (Kartodihardjo, 1999a, b).

The Environment Investigation Agency (EIA), a network of Indonesian NGOs, reports that illegal logging in many national parks in Indonesia is controlled by timber barons, and government officers. This is especially true in Tanjung Puting National Park (in Kalimantan) and Gunung Leuser National Park (in Sumatra) (Anon. 2000, Lisa *et al.* 2000). The situation is made more serious because illegal logging is not simply a recent reaction to a political power vacuum. It is an acceleration of illegal activities, corruption and collusion endemic prior to the present circumstances. Local communities, although taking part in illegal activities, have reacted to the corruption they have experienced all around them for years. They are now being used in ever growing numbers to create anarchy in the forestry sector to the continuing advantage of the local timber barons and the corrupt officials who support them. Illegal logging has been reported in other national parks in Indonesia, including Berbak NP (in Jambi), Bukit Dua Belas NP (Riau), Kerinci Seblat NP (West Sumatra) and Bukit Tigapuluh NP (Riau). Other cases of damage were reported by WWF in Taman Nasional Bukit Tiga Puluh in Riau province, where illegal catching of Sumatran tiger and tropical birds including the cockatoo, kuau (*Argusianus argus*), hornbill and eagle (*Spilornis cheela*), is driving threatened species to extinction. It has been reported that a Sumatran tiger can be sold on the black market for Rp. 25,000,000 (about US$3,000).

Coastal resources also in crisis

The damage to the coastal ecosystem is vast (Table 12.2). This ranges from large-scale illegal fishing operations that contribute to coral reef destruction to the rapidly disappearing mangrove forest; coastal resources have long been highly exploited for immediate profit making. This situation has undermined or destroyed traditional sustainable community management systems and has left Indonesia's fishing communities among the poorest of the poor. One of the primary causes of coral reef destruction is international demand for reef products – like aquarium fish and decorative corals – which supports the unsustainable exploitation of corals. Indonesia supplies 41 per cent of world exports of products from coral reefs, with the United States importing over half.

Several studies have found that coral reefs are being destroyed by fish bombing – the illegal use of explosives to catch fish – as well as by coral

Table 12.2 *Marine facts and figures*

Land area	1.9 million km^2
Sea area	3.1 million km^2
Coastline	81,000 km
Estimated sustainable catch	6.18 million tonnes/yr
Actual Indonesia catch	3.6 million tonnes/yr
Fisheries exports	US$2.2 million/yr
Estimated loss from stolen catch	US$4.5 billion
Coral reefs	60,000 km^2 (12–15% of world total)
in good condition	6%
estimated value	US$70,000/km^2
Mangroves 1982	4.2 million ha
Mangroves 2000	2.7 million ha
Oil and gas deposits	70% under the sea

Sources: Republika 19 and 20 Nov. 1999; Government Research and Technology Agency, BPPT figures; LIPI in Bisnis 5 Nov. 1999; *Banjarmasin* Pos 17 Nov. 1999; *Suara Pembaruan* 15 Feb. 2000; *Indonesian Observer* 25 Feb. 2000; *Kompas* 25 Feb. 2000.

mining and pollution. According to the Oceanology Study and Development Centre of the Indonesian Institute of Sciences (LIPI), only 7 per cent of corals are in good condition and 70 per cent have been badly damaged. This destruction is widespread throughout the archipelago.

Mangroves have suffered a similar fate to coral reefs. According to recent government data, 1.5 million ha have been wiped out since 1980. These valuable breeding grounds for fish and shrimp have been reduced from 4.2 million ha in 1982 to 2.7 million in 2001. Along the eastern coast of Sumatra, as much as 90 per cent of mangrove forest is reported to have disappeared. In Indramayu District, West Java, coastal abrasion due to mangrove loss is threatening to swallow up the homes of 50,000 people in twenty-eight coastal villages and to swamp the coastal road. In Bengkalis district, Riau, villagers have moved inland as the sea encroaches by 5 to 15 m each year.

A further major problem is illegal fishing by trawlers in coastal waters. These operations are known to bypass laws by relying on the collusion of the local authorities.

Damage to agro-ecosystems

Biodiversity losses in the agricultural sector are somewhat different compared to those of the forestry and coastal/marine habitats. Here, the issues apply to land conversion and the 'uniformity' or 'monoculture' school of thought versus 'diversity', or the traditional way of conducting agriculture. Traditional agriculture is usually associated with a high diversity of plants (multiple cropping) and arthropod communities, which include natural predators as well. Modern agricultural technology is decreasing the diversity of cultivation practices as well as of agro-ecosystems. In Indonesia, land conversion is not restricted solely to forested areas. In Java, during a ten-year span, approximately 1 million ha of productive farming land were transformed into industrial land without adequate substitution for agricultural lands in other areas. As a result less and less agricultural land is available to produce food. The situation is made worse as a result of population growth. The most serious case of land conversion was the mega-project of 1 million ha of peat soil in central Kalimantan, unsuccessfully, for rice-paddy farming. This mega-project turned into a disaster and wrecked the whole ecosystem.

Damage in the agricultural sector mainly comes through Green Revolution technology, where pesticides and fertilisers are heavily used, killing off many beneficial organisms and polluting the soil and water at the same time. In addition there are losses of traditional local varieties of crops (such as rice) and the loss of traditional knowledge through the excessive use of high-yielding varieties. Losses of traditional knowledge were forced on people by authoritarian central government instructions. This created an 'idle community' waiting to be told what to do, with the consequential loss of creativity and freedom to manage one's own farm.

Biological diversity in agro-ecosystems seems to be heavily influenced by the trade politics of the big transnational corporations via their interest in expanding their markets to the small farmer. NGOs condemn this practice, and the genetically modified crop debate in Indonesia is caught up with all this.

Disputes over national parks: the illegal logging of protected areas

The investigation of Yayasan Telapak, a local NGO based in Bogor, discovered that owing to illegal logging, the orang utan population in Tanjung Putting National Park in Kalimantan has decreased dramatically from 2,000 in 1994 to just 500 in 2000 (Ruwidrijanto 2000). Illegal logging is very complex but seems very well organised. 'Organised crime' built a logging way for transportation of the illegal logs. The word 'illegal' becomes more difficult to understand, based on the experience of the Tropical Forest and Ecology Laboratory at Gunung Palung. The Laboratory investigated the illegal logging in Gunung Palung National Park. How can one describe these activities as 'illegal' when they are observed by the local military officer, the police, and the local subdistrict officers and district and provincial officers? (Lisa *et al.* 2000).

Some of the recommendations that have been put forward by various stakeholders:

> closing all illegal sawmills in the nearby national parks and implementing external audit to protect the legal sawmill owners;
>
> the investigation of corruption, conducted without any discrimination, irrespective of the involvement of government officers;
>
> policy for forestry management to respect the rights of local people and to increase the participation of local people in forest management;
>
> creating Community Forestry Assemblies – groups that concentrate on running dialogues on forestry management among different stakeholders;
>
> enhancing the role of the Directorate General of Protection and Nature Conservation in the Ministry of Forestry in park management, especially on participatory mapping of the national park borders.

The politics of biodiversity in Indonesia

In general, it is safe to say that the implementation of the Convention on Biological Diversity in Indonesia is still superficial, without real action at the community level.

The National Development Planning Bureau (BAPENAS) and the Ministry of Environment (Kantor Menteri Lingkungan Hidup) have prepared a 'Biodiversity Action Plan in Indonesia'. It is unfortunate that this national strategy has not been widely publicised and that there is no clear budget for biodiversity conservation in the National Budget Plan. This clearly shows the low interest and lack of goodwill of government in biodiversity action programmes in the country.

The responsibility for protecting and managing biodiversity is divided between several government institutions. The Directorate General of Protection and Nature Conservation (PKA), Ministry of Forestry is the agency in charge of managing protected forest area, both terrestrial and aquatic. The Ministry of Agriculture through the National Committee on Germ Plasm Preservation has the responsibility for managing agricultural crop diversity and medicinal plant diversity, as well as animal husbandry. The Ministry of Marine Resources is responsible for the conservation of marine natural resources. The Office of the Ministry of Environmental Affairs is responsible only as a co-ordinating body. Its main responsibility is in co-ordinating policy and biodiversity programmes, while the

National Development Planning Bureau is the institution that has the power to create national programmes throughout the whole country.

The complexity of the situation is made even worse by the fact that landuse management in Indonesia involves many sectors and policies, such as the forestry sector, mining, transmigration, irrigation, environment and industry. Conflicts of interests often arise because there is no clear division of authority between the related agencies over landuse and spatial planning. For example, through provincial spatial planning, the local government (e.g., regency) issues a directive for land allocation such as for forestry, agriculture, mining, industry or tourism. The provincial government, through the National Land Use Bureau (BPN), is responsible for making landuse maps for non-forestry areas. The aim of the maps is to provide legal security for businesses, such as clear land tenure for plantation companies. In practice, because this provincial spatial planning is only one enabler, the plantation site may not be distinguished definitively (State Ministry for Environment and UNDP 1998). This is due to the lack of availability of accurate basic maps at the local government agencies and also to the lack of availability of regional landuse and spatial planning, particularly at the regency level. Overall, it is clear how natural resource management in Indonesia is dominated by the vested interests of different bodies and unclear institutional relationships.

Involvement of the stakeholders

In Indonesia, NGOs have long sought to empower local communities, campaign for people's rights and bring alternative perspectives to environmental awareness. Wahana Lingkungan Hidup, better known as WALHI, is mainly involved in exposing environmental destruction and empowering local people in many land tenure cases. KONPHALINDO, another Jakarta-based NGO, concentrates on advocating the right of the local people to retain local germ plasms and opposes the Green Revolution regarded as one of the main causes of genetic erosion. KONPHALINDO is also building a database on natural resources and specifically is concentrating on biodiversity and justice for local communities. Pesticide Action Network (PAN) is an NGO that monitors pesticide use from an environmental perspective. One of the biggest NGOs in Indonesia, that also funds many organisations working on biodiversity conservation, is the Yayasan Keanekaragaman Hayati Indonesia (also called KEHATI or Indonesian Biodiversity Foundation). KEHATI supports funds for small NGOs who seek to bring awareness of local indigenous knowledge.

For nearly two decades, NGOs have tried to present alternative perspectives that could force policy change. Hopefully, although they have not been heard so far, emerging democracy could bring a new atmosphere for NGOs as intermediaries for local people. The factors that might bring about these changes are the freedom to express one's opinion and the willingness publicly to criticise government policy.

Business plays an ambiguous and contradictory role. For the most part, business is actively involved in biodiversity losses. HPH or Hak Pengusahaan Hutan provides concession rights given to certain companies. Theoretically, the condition of the logged forests and surrounding areas should be safeguarded by a rigorous EIA (environmental and social impact analysis) (Kartodihardjo 1999b). Many companies do not follow the regulations. There are many cases where forest industries can acquire an HPH permit without having to deal with an EIA and, worse, often marginalise the local community even further (Sudiono 2000). Business in forest management could provide biodiversity enhancement and jobs, as much of this book seeks to show. So far, there is no recognition of this relationship in Indonesia. One hopes that the new democracy and regional participation may begin to change this. But one cannot be too optimistic.

Local involvement in biodiversity management: building the new perspective in an emerging democracy

The recent debate on the role of civil society in democracy in Indonesia has been mainly focused on urban political issues. Less attention has been given to how local/rural people are actively participating in policy change in natural resource management. It is widely accepted that the role of local people is often marginalised in many issues of natural resource management.

A remarkable case study in which local communities took action by learning and conducting experiments in the field and thus became leaders in agro-ecosystem biodiversity management is the Farmers' Field School (FFS) in Indonesia. The introduction of pesticides destroyed much of the local ecosystem. Groundwater and soil became contaminated, while pest attacks became even worse. In the 1980s, the government banned fifty-six pesticides and introduced the Farmers' Field School concept. Farmers received training on basic arthropod ecology and taxonomy and ecosystem management, and essentially were trained to think and make decisions based on what they saw and perceived in the field. They were trained to understand that, by having a more diverse group of natural enemies, pest outbreaks could be suppressed. Through these schools, farmers learned about biodiversity (i.e., arthropod biodiversity) and conservation of natural predators. Farmers began to acquire their independence again and thus became managers in their own fields, something that was quite rare during the Green Revolution era. It is thus interesting to see how the movement became even stronger as these graduates of the Farmers' Field School became leaders in pest management, and eventually started to disseminate their knowledge to their friends and neighbours. Thus, the birth of a free society has started. It may be a long and winding road to achieve democracy, but the seed has been planted.

The IPM FFS alumni become the local community organisers who promoted biodiversity management. One of the IPM FFS alumni who is widely respected for his struggle on conserving biodiversity management is Mbah Suko (Grandfather Suko) – a 61-year-old farmer from Magelang, central Java who successfully conserved twenty-seven local rice varieties in his simple seed stock. Mbah Suko collected seed from many villages in central Java, beginning in 1989. With his farmer group Mbah Suko annually regenerates the germ plasm of rice. His experiments in conserving germplasm were done without the knowledge of the Extension Officer. He was concerned that if the Extension worker knew of his activities he would be discriminated against in his village. Mbah Suko is a picture of a man who has lived through the three phases of agricultural revolution. His tireless efforts in conserving local rice varieties and conducting agricultural practices based on local wisdom about environmentally sound agriculture have proved that there are benefits to be gained through utilisation of local biodiversity (2001).

BOX 12.7 THE ROLE OF THE IPM FARMERS' FIELD SCHOOL IN INDONESIA

In the IPM Farmers' Field School, farmers meet weekly during a full cropping season to conduct experiments and to monitor and discuss crop management interventions. The four key principles of FFS on IPM are:
grow a healthy crop;
observe the fields weekly;
conserve natural enemies;
understand ecology and become expert in one's own field.
Usually an IPM FFS is conducted for a full planting season with twenty-five to thirty members.

In an FFS, farmers were taught observation methods. Weekly observations compare IPM plots with plots managed under common (i.e., Green Revolution) practices. Plants are sampled and carefully observed while pest and natural predator population sizes are monitored and recorded. Groups describe the situation in their fields in drawings and present their agro-ecosystem analysis for discussion among farmers. Conservation and utilisation of local natural predator and useful insects and beneficial organisms play an important role in the control of insect pests. Participants also look at the role of soil nutrients and water management.

BOX 12.8 FARMERS' FIELD SCHOOL AND TRAINING OF TRAINERS IN INDONESIA

Beyond the Farmers' Field School for integrated pest management, there are Training of Trainers (TOT) courses to prepare extension staff to conduct FFS training. During TOT they carry out comparative experiments and grow and monitor the target crops to learn about the problems that farmers face throughout a cropping season.

Table 12.3 *FFS achievements: total number of farmers and farmer trainers trained from Fiscal Year (FY) 1993/4 to FY 1999/2000*

FFS	FY 1993/4	FY 1994/5	FY 1995/6	FY 1996/7	FY 1997/8	FY 1998/9	FY 1999/2000[a]	Total
Rice	50,050	109,893	149,087	236,027	109,537	59,475	12,375	726,444
Soybean	3,172	4,313	7,764	30,952	6,511	4,400	2,050	59,162
Vegetables[b]	3,885	1,000	3,800	12,225	4,375	1,675	475	27,435
Others[c]	825	1,525	0	20,025	17,850	17,850	13,125	70,800
Total	57,932	116,731	160,651	299,229	137,873	83,400	28,025	883,841
Farmers trained	1,282	2,050	4,890	6,090	4,860	3,250	4,100	26,522

[a] Estimate.
[b] Chilli, shallot, potato and cabbage.
[c] Includes tungro, rats and follow-up FFS, farmers' studies and farmers' forums based on specific needs of farmer groups.

Source: Data from the country report for Indonesia that was presented to the Programme Advisory Committee Meeting, July 1999, Yogyakarta, central Java, Indonesia.

The national IPM Programme phase 1 (1989–92) was funded by GOI with assistance from USAID in the form of a US$17 million programme grant. The World Bank provided 'bridging' loan assistance amounting to US$5.3 million for 1993 during preparation of a longer-term investment project. The national IPM Programme phase 2 (1993–2000) was funded by GOI (US$14 million), the World Bank (US$32 million loan) and USAID (US$7 million grant). Technical assistance has been provided by FAO, national universities and research institutions, and independent contractors for specialised studies (evaluation and pesticide regulation).

Other organisations are also actively involved in IPM for rice and vegetable crops in several provinces, such as World Education (WE) with its NGO network in North Sumatra, Lampung and central Java and FADO (Flemish Organisation for Assistance in Development) with projects in east Java, Bali and Nusa Tenggara.

Since 1991, 3,500–5,000 farmers per year have been trained in rice and vegetables through FFS activities.

Training achievement

The first phase of the Indonesia National IPM Programme was funded by Indonesia USAID who pioneered the field-based IPM training for extension workers and the IPM Farmers' Field School approach. Since 1989 some 300,000 farmers have graduated from season-long IPM FFS.

Phase 2 of the national IPM Programme aims to provide full-season IPM field training for 800,000 farmers. A large number of farmers during phase 2 have been trained by other farmers via a 'farmer to farmer' programme.

Initially, and perhaps still today, there was a general belief that IPM was too complicated for illiterate farmers and that more research was needed before effective IPM techniques could be introduced. The Farmers' Field School demonstrates that farmers have the ability to understand the ecosystem of their fields and to make management decisions based on their own insight. With the Farmers' Field School, farmers themselves become initiators and implementers, and receive the full benefit of IPM activities based on participatory learning. It enhances their individual and collaborative decision making ability, and their confidence and business development skills, and therefore strengthens local organisation. It empowers rural communities to take better control of their own situation and decrease its dependence on external services. Moreover this process has an impact on rural civil society empowerment through emerging democracy.

Box 12.9 summarises the role of the Katu communities in biodiversity protection. For hundreds of years, Katu communities have lived in relative harmony with their surroundings in the forests of central Sulawesi. Katu life is a model of a local community living in the forest and using local wisdom to manage and conserve natural resources. Several studies have shown that their indigenous way of conducting agriculture is a practice of sustainable agriculture. They also conserve their local plant varieties and view this as an integral part of their life. Their existence was threatened when the government made the land they are living on part of the Lore Lindu National Park. The government then tried to relocate the Katu but with no success. The Katu communities believed that according to their 'adat' law (indigenous law), they should not leave their land. Previously, in 1949, the Katu were relocated to another area; soon afterward seventy people died because of food shortages. This experience was so deeply rooted in their beliefs that it became very difficult for the government to relocate the community.

In 1999, an agreement was reached between the Katu people and the National Park authorities (Laban 2001). Based on this agreement, the Katu communities are seen as an integral part of the Park by the head of

---

BOX 12.9 LEARNING FROM TOI KATU WISDOM

Katu (Toi Katu) are traditional people who have been living in harmony since 1800. There have been many occasions when their existence has been threatened and they have been relocated because their homeland has become a protected area in the name of Lore Lindu National Park. The Toi Katu's struggle to gain the right to live on their own land resulted in the agreement with Lore Lindu National Park. At the beginning of April 1999, Toi Katu became the first community in Indonesia to become part of national park management.

Even though Toi Katu have access to life in Lore Lindu, they have to follow an agreement drawn up with the government. There is management and regulation of landuse allocation for agriculture, animal husbandry and public facilities that they have to follow. According to Aryanto Sangaji, the head of Yayasan Tanah Merdeka, a local NGO specialising in environmental advocacy and tenurial community empowerment, Katu have traditional wisdom in managing their ancestors' land. Toi Katu communities managed their forest on the basis of two categories which they called *pandulu* and *lopo*. *Pandulu* is the primary forest and *lopo* is the forest which has been converted into farming land. As the primary forest, the *pandulu* is believed to be the inheritance for the next generation and thus should not be touched. The *lopo* is divided into two, *lopo ntua* and *lopo lehe*. *Lopo ntua* is the forest with big trees which was used for farm land twenty years ago and the Katu collectively own the land. *Lopo lehe* is the younger forest, and the owner is the one who formerly opened the land. Other people who want to manage it should get permission from the owner. Toi Katu use their land in cycles. After using an area of *lopo lehe* for agriculture, they leave it, and slowly convert it to *lopo ntua*. They then open up a new *lopo lehe*, formerly *lopo ntua*.

Thus there is a hierarchical system within the forest in order to make it sustainable. From this partnership, the National Park has to facilitate the independence and self-reliance of Toi Katu communities.

---

the National Park area and will not be separated from the management of the National Park. The Katu also have the obligation to protect the forest and keep the public facilities.

Conclusion

The involvement of local people in decision making processes and management via the stakeholder approach is the key to building new perspectives of biodiversity management in the emerging democracy in Indonesia. Biodiversity, as the lifeblood of natural resources, is the most important treasure to protect. The meaning of biodiversity, what it encompasses and how it should be managed should not be determined solely by the government, but instead should be based on agreement between stake-holders through participatory processes.

The model of exploitation and authoritarian control has proved to be a failure of the old regime to manage biodiversity. Nor could it reduce the damage caused by illegal practices. In simple logic, it is a mission impossible to keep safe the millions of hectares of protected area from illegal practices under conditions where the income from stealing is more than that from protecting. Involvement of local indigenous people should be seen as a valuable asset in biodiversity management since they have hundreds of years of experience in nature conservation. The best hope is for a steady process of inclusion backed by guarantees for participation linked to long-term supportive funding. Removing corruption will be a steeper hill to climb, but must be faced by a combination of providing funds for wardens, and perhaps privatising some sites. Private operators would have a vested interest in policing against corruption, using local people as wardens. This is one opportunity to link *métis* with local commitment to reliable income generation, and it will surely test the successful evolution of democracy in Indonesia.

REFERENCES

An Overview of the State of the Biological and Landscape Diversity of Croatia 2000. Zagreb: Ministry of Environmental Protection and Physical Planning.

Anonymous. 2000. Investigation report: Illegal logging in Gunung Leuser National Park, Langkat. Paper presented at the Illegal Logging Conference, 22–24 November, Bogor (in Indonesian).

BAPPENAS. 1991. Biodiversity Action Plan for Indonesia. Jakarta: BAPPENAS (in Indonesian).

Central Bureau of Statistics. 2000. *Statistics of Indonesia.* Jakarta: Central Bureau of Statistics.

Direktorat Bina Kawasan Pelestarian Alam. 2001. Taman Nasional di Indonesia. Direktorat Bina Kawasan Pelestarian Alam, Departemen Kehutanan. Jakarta. www.Dephut.org.id./menu perlindungan dan konservasi alam/ html.

Dulcie, J. 2000. Rare fishes in Croatia (I), *Hrvatska vodoprivreda* 9(96): 50–2 (in Croatian).

Environment Investigation Agency. 1999. *NGO Sign-On on Illegal Logging in Indonesia's National Parks.* Jakarta: Environment Investigation Agency.

European Heritage Fund. 1995. Island and mainland views – how to identify and balance the perceived needs of local population and guests. *Eco-island Newsletter* 2: 4–9.

FORDUK (Third World Forum) and SHEPHI (NGO Network for Forest Conservation). 1995. *Profile of Indonesia Biodiversity Threats and Issues.* Papers for delegates and participants of the Second Meeting of Parties to the Convention on Biodiversity, Jakarta.

Guillen, A. 1990. *Myotis capaccinii* (Bonaparte, 1837). In A.J. Mitchell-Jones *et al.* (eds.), *The Atlas of European Mammals*, pp. 106–7. London: Academic Press.

Integrated Coastal Zone Management Plan for the Matsalu Task Area. 1996. *HELCOM PITF MLW*. Estonian Ministry of the Environment, Tallinn.

Kartodihardjo, H. 1999a. *Belenggu IMF dan World Bank: hambatan Struktural pembaharuan Kebijakan Pembangunan Kehutanan di Indonesia.* Jakarta: Pustaka LATIN.

1999b. *Masalah Kebijakan Hutan Alam Produksi.* Bogor: Pustaka LATIN.

Kokovkin, T. 1996. *Integrated Coastal Zone Management: Käina Bay, Estonia.* Kärdla: HELCOM PITF MLW, Käina Bay Area Task Team and Biosphere Reserve Hiiumaa Centre.

Kull, T. (ed.) 1999. *Estonian Biodiversity Strategy and Action Plan.* Tallinn-Tartu: Ministry of the Environment, United Nations Environmental Program and Environmental Protection Institute of the Estonian Agricultural University.

Külvik, M. (ed.) 2001. *Soome ja Eesti Looduskaitsesild 1990-ndatel aastatel.* Tartu: Estonian Ministry of the Environment and Finnish Ministry of the Environment.

Laban, B.Y. 2001. Gagasan Aplikasi Konservasi dalam Otonomi Daerah. Paper presented during the Fifth Regular Meeting of Community Forestry Communication Forum (Forum Komunikasi Kehutanan Masyarakat, FKKM), Bandar Lampung.

LATIN 1998. *Reformasi tanpa Perubahan: Kehutanan Indonesia pasca Soeharto.* Bogor: Pustaka LATIN.

Law on Environmental Protection, Narodne novine, No. 82/94 (in Croatian). (Narodne novine (NN) is the official publication of the Republic of Croatia with published laws, statutes, etc.)

Law on Nature Conservation, Narodne novine, No. 82/94 (in Croatian).

Lisa, H. *et al.* 2000. Penebangan Liar Skala Kecil: Laporan Singkat Analisis Trend, Penyebab dan Konsekwensi dari Wilayah Taman Nasional Gunung palung, Kalimantan Barat. Paper presented to the Illegal Logging Conference, 22–24 November, Bogor.

Lukač, G. 1998. List of Croatian birds. *Naturalist Croatia* 7, Suppl. 3: 1–160.

MacKinnon, J. and MacKinnon, K. 1986. *Managing Protected Areas in the Tropics.* Jakarta: Gadjah Mada University Press.

Mathiesen, A. 1937. On the development of nature protection in Estonia. *Looduskaitse*: 19–20.

Mittermeier, R. and C. G. Mittermeier. 1997. *Megadiversity: Earth's Biologically Wealthiest Nations.* Conservation International, Canada.

Ministry of Environmental Protection and Physical Planning. 2000. *An Overview of the State of the Biological and Landscape Diversity of Croatia with Protection Strategy and Action Plans.* Zagreb: Republic of Croatia.

Ministry of Forestry and Estate Crops. 1999. *Conservation of Natural Resources and Biodiversity for Environmental Management.* Jakarta (in Indonesian).

Nikolić, T. (ed.) 1994. Flora Croatica, index florae Croaticae 1. *Naturalist Croatia* 3, Suppl. 2: 1–116 (in Croatian).

1996a. Flora Croatica, index florae Croaticae 2. *Naturalist Croatia* 6, Suppl. 1: 1–232 (in Croatian).

1996b. Notulae ad indicem florae Croaticae 1. *Naturalist Croatia* 5(1): 95–7 (in Croatian).

2000a. Flora Croatica, index florae Croaticae 3. *Naturalist Croatia* 9, Suppl. 1: 1–324 (in Croatian).

2000b. Notulae ad indicem florae Croaticae 2. *Naturalist Croatia* 9(3): 217–21 (in Croatian).

Peterson, K. 1994. *Nature Conservation in Estonia: General Data and Protected Areas.* Tallinn: Huma.

Peterson, K., Koitjärv, K., Ehrlich, Ü., Haapanen, A. and Helminen, M. 2000. *Eesti kaitsealade juhtimissüsteemi analüüs.* Tallinn: Keskkonnaministerium and Euroopa Liidu Integratsiooniprojekt.

Petts, G.E. and Meddock, I. 1992. Flow allocation for in-river needs. In P. Callow, and G.E. Petts (eds.), *The Rivers Handbook*, pp. 289–307.

Post, R. 1995. Hiiumaa is a part of a Biosphere Reserve. In *Hiiumaa – Getting to know*, pp. 17–23. County Government of Hiiumaa, Kärdla.

1998. Local participation in the West-Estonian Archipelago Biosphere Reserve: the case of Hiiumaa. In M. Hytönen (ed.), *Social Sustainability of Forestry in the Baltic Sea Region*, pp. 309–14. Proceedings of workshop organised by the Nordic Research Programme on Social Sustainability of Forestry. Helsinki: Finnish Forest Research Institute.

2000. *Kassari Käsiraamat: Juhiseid kogukonna edendamiseks.* Kassari Haridusselts.

Read. 2001. Attempt to counter the imperialism in agricultural sector Experiences of Suko, a common farmer in Mangunsari, Sawangan, Magelang. In *The Life Industry: Biodiversity, People and Profit* (Indonesian version). M. Bauman, J. Bell, F. Koechlin and M. Pimbert (eds.), Jakarta: READ Publishing.

Republic of Indonesia. 1994. Law of Republic of Indonesia Number 5 1994. Ratification of United Nations Convention on Biological Diversity, Jakarta.

Ruwidrijanto. 2000. *Penebangan Kayu secara liar.* Procedings of Second Workshop on Illegal Logging. Jakarta: Ministry of Forestry and Estate Crop (in Indonesian).

Shiva, V. 1993. *Monocultures of the Mind: Biodiversity, Biotechnology and the Third World.* Penang: The Third World Network.

State Ministry of Environment. 1997. *Agenda 21: National Strategy for Sustainable Development.* Jakarta: State Ministry of Environment, Republic of Indonesia.

1999. *Policy, Strategy, and Action Plan of Environment Management 2000–2005.* Jakarta: State Ministry of Environment, Republic of Indonesia.

State Ministry for Environment and United Nations Development Programme. 1998. *Forest and Land Fires in Indonesia: Impacts, Factors and Evaluation.* Jakarta: State Ministry of Environment, Republic of Indonesia.

Sudiono, E. 2000. Sistem HPHH (IPHH) = Banjir Cap Model II. Samarinda 7 Agustus, 2000.

Uljas, J. 2000. *Preliminary Results of the Sociological Poll in 1999 and Comparision with the Data of 1994.* Kärdla: Biosphere Reserve Hiiumaa Centre.

Uljas, J., Hellström, K. and Sagara, K. 1996. *Hiiumaa ja hiidlane: sotsioloogiline uurimus.* Kärdla: Biosphere Reserve Hiiumaa Centre.

UNEP 1998. *First National Report on the Convention on Biological Diversity: Estonia.* Tallinn: UNEP.

UNESCO 1996. *Biosphere Reserves: The Seville Strategy and the Statutory Framework of the World Network.* Paris: UNESCO.

Vode Hrvatske, Monografiija o vodama i vodoprivredi Republike Hrvatske, 1991, Izdavači Ministarstvo vodoprivrede RH, ZGB, Javno vodoprivredno poduzeće 'Hrvatska vodoprivreda' Zgb, Proleterskih brigada 220. Zagreb.

Waters of Croatia, Monografiija o vodama I vodoprivredi Republike Hrvatske, 1991. Izdavači Ministarstvo vodoprivrede RH, ZGB, Javno vodoprivredno poduzece 'Hrvatska vodoprivreda' Zgb, Proleterskih brigada 220. Zagreb (in Croatian).

Welp, M. 2000. *Planning Practice on Three Island Biosphere Reserves in Estonia, Finland and Germany: A Comparative Study.* Paris: INSULA (International Scientific Council for Island Development.

Winarno, Yunita T. 1999. Pembangunan: Pemasungan kreativitas Petani dalam. *Jurnal Antropologi Indonesia* 23: 66–79.

World Conservation Monitoring Centre. 1992. *Global Diversity.* London: Chapman and Hall.

Part IV

Perspective

13 Enhancing biodiversity and humanity

Susanne Stoll-Kleemann and Tim O'Riordan

On biodiversity and humanity

This volume has covered aspects of the state of biodiversity, the threats and the possible solutions, many of which give hope and offer much promise. In poverty-stricken and war-torn lands the fabric of people, species and habitats is being repaired, often at the micro-scale. Where there is a real bond between biota, people and economic opportunity, there can be enriched biodiversity. The following list from Jeff McNeeley (1995: 5) shows that there are many good reasons for protecting beyond the protected:

maintaining the essential ecological processes that depend on natural ecosystems, and which provide real economic services;

preserving the diversity of species and the genetic variation between them;

ensuring the productive capacities of ecosystems as a central element of future economies;

preserving historical and cultural features of importance to the traditional lifestyles and well-being of local peoples so that they remain at peace and strengthen their collective esteem;

safeguarding habitats that are critical for the sustainable use of species for a variety of moral, utilitarian and spiritual purposes;

securing landscapes and wildlife that enrich human experience through their beauty;

providing opportunities for community development, scientific research, education, training, recreation, tourism and mitigation of the forces of natural hazards;

serving as sources of national pride and human inspiration;

providing the basis for genetic safeguard and evolution, for pharmaceuticals and for forest evolution.

All of these opportunities and values are well known nowadays. They appear in many text books, consultants reports and national strategies. They dominate international conferences and scientific workshops. They form the basis of technical assistance and development aid. For example, the UK Department for International Development (DfID 2001: 2) is committed to a programme of aid aimed at:

halving the number of poor by 2015;

providing universal primary education in all countries also by 2015;

ensuring girls have the same educational opportunities as boys;

reducing by two-thirds the infants who die before they are five;

cutting by 75 per cent the number of women who die in child-birth;

full access to reproductive services for everyone who wants them by 2015;

assisting all countries to implement sustainable development strategies by 2015.

To do this via biodiversity, DfID proposes to work on the livelihood approach outlined in Box 13.1, to incorporate participatory poverty assessments into planning and programme design, to strengthen civil society along the lines outlined by Pretty in chapter 4, and to unite environmental impact and strategic environmental assessment into sustainable development strategies. The German Office for Technical Co-operation (GTZ) is similarly committed to broadly the same objectives (see Stoll-Kleemann 2001: 40–3). Other countries are following suit.

The DfID initiative is essentially part of a wide range of international commitments to increase the centrality of biodiversity in social and economic development, to pump-prime the Global Environment Facility and its sister funding agencies, to ensure genuine training and implementation capacity at the local level, that is fully incorporated into historical and cultural *mētis* (as introduced by Jules Pretty in chapter 4), and to ensure property rights in indigenous knowledge and communal stewardship. Furthermore, and also working with international organisations, DfID is reaching into the world trade patterns to enable small producers to identify niche markets based on sustainability, distinctiveness and equity. In this call, the role of the retail sector to operate its own agreements and practices for socially responsible sourcing and marketing will be crucial. So far the major retailers are on the path of consideration, but not yet of commitment.

The case studies in this volume offer both hope and unease. There are many good practices and many exciting initiatives. There is also far too much corruption, despair, mismanagement and power broking. At times there is a will but no capacity (South Africa) and at times there is a capacity but no will (Europe, Brazil). So there is still much to be done. We look in particular at three aspects: promoting ecological advocacy; marrying

BOX 13.1 A FRAMEWORK FOR SUSTAINABLE RURAL LIVELIHOODS

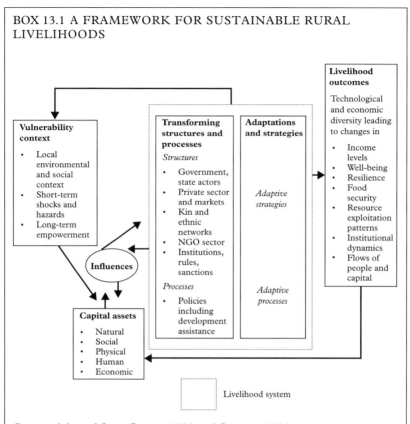

Sources: Adapted from Carney 1998 and Scoones 1998.

Livelihoods combine social and ecological well-being with reliable income. The conditions for reducing vulnerability apply to adaptive strategies and processes, empowerment and shifts in rights and markets, plus partnerships. This is the kind of mix aimed at by DfID and other aid agencies as outlined in the text.

ecological and social resilience; and exploring the exciting opportunities for public–private partnerships.

Ecological advocacy and biodiversity strategy

This perspective has led to a powerful belief amongst ecologists that it is time for humans to nurture the biosphere, rather than for the biosphere to provide services for humans. This is the time for a sustainability science to help society to protect nature rather than to exploit it, through revealing its own synergy with biodiversity. This is why ecologists are moving from the approach of measuring and modelling biological and species tolerances to disruption and to harvesting towards the whole ecosystems viewpoint. A White House Task Force (1995: 1) observed that 'the goal of the ecosystem approach is to restore and maintain the health, sustainability and biological diversity of ecosystems while supporting sustainable economies and ecosystems'. A major review of biodiversity science by Sala and his colleagues (2000: 1,770–4) called for much greater co-operation amongst climatologists, ecologists, social scientists and policy makers to understand, predict and control the driving forces of biodiversity change on both an ecosystem basis and a regional setting. This powerful call echoes that of an equally influential group of scientists (Lubchenko *et al.* 1991) calling for the establishment of a broad framework of ecosystem theory for managing natural resources and the environment.

Two important trends are appearing from this threat-framed ecosystems approach to biodiversity. One is the emergence of ecological advocacy in the design of policy and biodiversity practice. The other is the emphasis on place-based combinations of change, analysis and responsiveness, tailored to cultures and traditions, as well as national and local political capabilities. The switch in emphasis to locality combines globalism and localism. As O'Riordan and Church (2001: 3) outline, 'place-centredness is the amalgam of global change and local identity. Every place reveals itself as a variety of scales. Local perceptions are shaped by global influences, the combination of which process local actions.' Sustainability science aims to look at the combination of influences, both physical and social, that shape locality in a global age. This perspective imbues biodiversity as a global imperative with sympathetic local action.

Bazzaz was the first alphabetical surname of an impressive array of ecologists to make the case for a more socially and politically engaged ecology.

In our view, it is necessary to train students in ecology who will be ready and willing to devote part of their professional lives to stemming the tides of environmental degradation and the associated losses of biodiversity and its ecological services, and to teaching the public about the importance of these losses. We believe that such efforts should be rewarded as part of the process through which ecologists are considered for academic posts, granted tenure in universities, elected to membership in learned societies, and so on. (Bazzaz *et al.* 1998: 879)

This is a controversial arena for sustainability science. Kaiser (1998: 1,183–90) protests that advocacy without responsibility and peer review could devalue science and remove some of its authority and influence over policy matters. Yet conservative-minded peer review may stifle advocacy science just when it is required to persuade new directions in policy, and build confidence in innovation and experimentation. Biodiversity is one of many scientific arenas nowadays where the natural and the social connect and create united perspectives for analysis and management.

Biodiversity with advocacy is most fully appreciated by the ecosystem approach. Yet promoting biodiversity as a redirection of social as well as environmental policy runs the danger of controversy and contradiction as advocates clash to different agendas and funders. Advocacy in ecology involves the incorporation of social purposes and values with which many in society may not be familiar. Ecologists may promote a mission – to safeguard, to monitor, to protect – and in so doing may exhibit political prejudices and social demands which lie outside accepted interpretations of democracy, consultation and inclusiveness. Advocacy for biodiversity has to be sensitive to social circumstances, to political positioning, to cultural norms and to established views of property rights and landuse practices. This interrelationship does not form an arena in which many ecologists are yet trained or comfortable, even though science and politics have long mixed. We shall see from the case studies that advocacy ecology has to become integrated with styles of political and social involvement and co-operation if it is ever likely to achieve its aims. This provides an important training opportunity and a research collaboration role for ecologists which lie beyond the disciplinary innovations advocated by Bazzaz and his concerned colleagues.

In one of the most critical, yet optimistic, appraisals of biodiversity futures, Pimm and his equally distinguished co-authors (2001: 2,207) conclude that much can still be done to shift the tides of destruction.

1 Most biodiversity losses do not advantage people or economies in the long run. Indeed, it is more likely that such losses impoverish and destroy livelihoods. It is now possible to evolve agri-ecosystems that both nurture biodiversity and enhance livelihoods.

2 It is quite possible financially to save the critical 'hotspots'. The core areas could be protected by an annual injection of $300 billion. To this 'minimum 15 per cent' could be added another 2 million km^2 of biodiversity through sensitively, and inclusively, designed 'stewardship agreements'. These would cost some $4 billion annually. Of the remaining threatened 'hotspots', some 1.2 million km^2 could be secured through livelihood covenants, costing some $25 billion annually.

3 Management of protected livelihoods of biodiversity can be achieved in many different ways. Much has to do with addressing the root causes outlined in Box 1.2. An additional mechanism is the training and

empowerment of conservation professionals and community 'monitors' who act as a link between scientific and cultural approaches to management. About $500 million would support twenty-five regional centres for conservation training with strong links to socio-economic advantage for the protected areas concerned.

4 Targeted assaults on all of the perverse policies, price signals and regulations that favour losses of the vital socio-economic values attached to maintaining and enriching biodiversity are now overdue. This must be a prime focus for ecological advocacy, if for no other reason than that this is a life- and economy-enhancing task. This will also mean reshaping loans and other incentives so that lending institutions and socially responsible financial markets collude to redesign aid and trade. Fresh approaches to financing sustainable agri-environmental development through such devices as transferable development rights, mitigation and sequestration audits, and tax shifts, are now possible.

Sustainability science and biodiversity advocacy

Advocacy ecology therefore may become infused into sustainability science. This is a concept that is still evolving, but whose qualities are slowly becoming appreciated. According to a summary from a group of supportive colleagues (Kates *et al.* 2001), sustainability science will need to:

> span the range of spatial scales to encompass cause, effect, cumulative initiating actions and international agreements;
>
> account both for short-term inertia where no discernable change is taking place while ecosystem tolerances are being studied, and for convulsive synergisms whose immediate consequences may be dramatic, but whose longer-scale outcomes may not be foreseeable;
>
> deal with the complexities of discontinuities and unexpected combinations of processes and social responses in an arena of uncertainty;
>
> recognise and appreciate the wide range of ways of knowing and understanding through which societies address nature and cope with dangers and opportunities, including the roles of instinct and intuition.

Sustainability science may not yet be fully defined, or initiated, or even accepted by those now facing the management of global environmental change (see Box 13.2). At its heart, whatever its final destination, is the notion of a creative and open-hearted partnership between government, business, civil society and scientists. Such partnerships will be based on combined approaches to acquiring information on sharing appreciation of

BOX 13.2 SUSTAINABILITY SCIENCE IN ACTION

The diagram below summarises the six principal components of sustainability science. At its heart lies a fresh role for science in public affairs, as well as more innovative approaches to methodology and enquiry. The most notable extensions to existing transformations in scientific activity are:

Improving the scope for interdisciplinarity amongst the natural and social sciences as well as between them. There is a growing need to link chemistry to physics to ecosystem processes to discontinuities to sophisticated modelling and prediction. Exciting developments are already occurring, notably around the theme of interactive and integrated assessments of possible biodiversity futures.

Widening the basis of knowing and feeling, so that reason and judgement are explicitly connected in scientific enquiry, as much as they are in human experience. This means evolving tools for incorporating quantitative and qualitative approaches to analysis and prediction, as well as to expand the role of intuition and instinct as bases for forming personal outlooks and establishing social bonds.

Including all manner of interests, biases, social networks and political power relationships in the interactive and listening mode of science. These sciences become a partnership network that enhances and strengthens scientific advocacy and legitimacy.

Sustainability science

Spanning global to local via many interacting pathways	Managing short-term sacrifice for future planetary safeguard	Analysing many forms of human–nature relationships
Act and think globally and locally	Leadership for sustainable democracy	Interdisciplinary methodologies and participatory monitoring
Accommodating irreconcilable outlooks and expectations	Incorporating knowledge with knowing and feeling	Designing participatory, environmentally sound and socially just futures
Learning through sharing, owning via revealing	Combining understanding with intuition	Creating futures through learning, adapting and forecasting

Source: based on Kates *et al.* 2001: 641–2.

differences in understanding of causes, pathways and consequences, and on joint funding and action. We saw in the case studies that participation in biodiversity management can prove more effective and durable in such partnerships.

Sustainability science through partnership also introduces more demanding requirements for research method and policy evaluation. Inclusion of interested parties to the point where they become active co-managers may result in more attention being given to a mix of quantitative data gathering and forecasting, and qualitative means of exhibiting how various possible future states can be displayed. The act of visualisation, or representation, is likely to be value laden, advocacy driven and subtly coercing. Even if the act of exhibition and portrayal seeks to minimise such biases, there is still the matter that choices will reveal values, expectations, trust and views on fairness and equity, for the well-being of others and of ecosystems. Sustainability science for biodiversity management, therefore, is likely to be even more firmly placed in the participatory realms of advocacy, in socio-political zones where, heretofore, science has not properly positioned itself.

Sustainability science extends interdisciplinarity into the arena of knowledge and feeling, of measurement and judgement, of information and ethics, and of explanation and participation (O'Riordan 2000: 16). Interdisciplinarity is built on the premise that there is no distinction between a natural system and human interpretation of that system. To quote the American philosopher Richard Tarnas (1993: 430–4) the 'truth' of nature lies in the unfolding of human understanding, responsiveness and empathy both to the natural world, as revealed, and to the social world, as proclaimed by action through adaptive management or protest.

This quality of local empathy to the natural world is an intrinsic component of sustainability science. It places special emphasis on social memory, that is, the collective history of management of an area, the underlying expectations of future benefits for natural resources exploitation, and how various groups share a common identity with biodiversity.

On social resilience and vulnerability

Vulnerability remains a theme for unresolved analysis, even at the end of this volume. The notion of vulnerability relates to a household, or larger grouping, that is exposed to danger, decreasingly capable of avoiding or absorbing that threat, and usually unable to exert any political demand to improve conditions. The causes of vulnerability are widely argued (see especially Hewitt 1997: 141–63; Battenbury and Forsyth 1999; Locke *et al.* 2000). Hewitt (1997: 141) is in no doubt that 'society, rather than nature, decides who is more likely to be exposed to dangerous geophysical agents and to have weakened or no defences against them'. For Hewitt (p. 143) vulnerability assessment is essentially the human ecology of endangerment. He characterises vulnerability in forms of powerlessness or defencelessness, frailty or ignorance of danger. He locates vulnerability in various social and natural spaces, again pointing out the lack of capacity to cope as a defining variable.

Built into vulnerability analysis is the potential for adaptation or resilience. This may be achieved by migration (Locke *et al.* 2000), or by support, training and subsidy (as we have seen in the case studies), or by extending livelihood practices into biodiversity protection so as to link ecology to economic opportunity. Or it may be approached through various sincere means of inclusive partnerships through participation. The theme of adaptation is one of learning and socio-political reform. The first may incorporate an external agency of support (a training programme, funds for agreed management that are tied to involvement and supportive community action), or some change in technology, or in civic or property rights. At times, well-meaning efforts to widen adaptation simply fail (Berkes and Folke 1998: 17–22). One cause of this is inadequate reform of social traditions and political cultures. There are huge inertias in such processes. Even sincere attempts to create adaptive change run into a host of barriers, as is evident in the examples from Brazil, Costa Rica, the emerging democracies (chapter 12) and even the USA (chapter 7). This is why the hopeful evidence of small-scale initiatives summarised by Pretty in Table 4.3 (pp. 78–9) is so heartening.

Any adaptive switch to more fair, just and equitable management of biodiversity will require an approach that encourages creative learning towards gaining income and social respect from maintaining and repairing healthy ecosystems. This is a linkage that is notable for its rarity. There are many good reasons for this. As noted in chapter 5, democracy is not a perfect art. Democracies are often frail and may be plagued by micro-level disputes, power plays and blatant opportunism. Commons property may be managed by patterns of sharing and reciprocity, but not universal responsibility. Vulnerability is often institutionalised in a culture of adaptation, so that the process of its attempted removal is often dysfunctional. Much as social and ecological resilience is a dreamed-of goal, its manifestation is rarely observable or even imaginable in day-to-day reality.

What this complicated and inconclusive literature shows is that adaptation is both in-built and assisted. Adaptive strategies are influenced by patterns of power and vulnerability. These patterns control what individuals know, what rights they have, and how much room for manoeuvre they are granted. Many 'traditional' regimes inculcate vulnerability. So any scheme for participatory partnerships becomes embroiled in local power politics and manipulation. This appears to be the case in Brazil, Costa Rica and Indonesia, judging from the evidence presented in this book.

Participatory approaches to biodiversity management may best prove successful through responsive governance and appropriate property rights. The examples from Namibia and Costa Rica appear to bear this out. Responsive governance means sharing power, opening up responsibility, building capacity for learning, and overcoming prejudice against groups of interests. Appropriate property rights mean capturing the responsibilities of ownership to ecosystems and the interests of descendants, not just to the narrow confines of property management. Such arrangements are not easy to achieve in the absence of an ecological advocacy that is sensitive to enhancing livelihoods, yet cognisant of precautionary adaptive management for the maintenance of ecosystem processes.

Redesigning agro-ecosystems for biodiversity resilience

So far, food production has more or less kept up with population growth. The fact that 1.7 billion people are hungry is due less to shortage or scarcity than to inappropriate property rights, inadequate food entitlements and endemic poverty. Agro-ecosystems are areas where cropping and grazing predominate yet people still essentially rely on ecosystem resources for their sustenance. The World Resources Institute study (World Resources Institute 2000: 56–67) suggests that between 30 and 55 per cent of the global land surface lies in agro-ecosystem management, with over 800 million people employed in food production in urban areas. Some 44 per cent of global population relies directly on such systems for their livelihood and survival. Yet soil degradation affects 65 per cent of this land overall, with 24 per cent moderately degraded and 40 per cent strongly degraded. Combined with severe stresses on water availability, this degradation would lead to 25 per cent yield reduction over the next twenty years, with a consequent loss to local economies of over one third of effective production. Yet some 40–45 per cent of temperate broadleaf and boreal forest, as well as a similar amount of tropical deciduous forest, has already been lost to agriculture.

There is a huge opportunity to enhance biodiversity through fresh approaches to sustainable agro-ecosystem management. In chapter 4, Jules Pretty assessed the options. Multiple cropping that is sensitive to soils, drainage and hazard, on-farm tree planting for carbon storage and

BOX 13.3 AGRODIVERSITY AS A BASIS FOR SUSTAINING
BIODIVERSITY

Brookfield and Stocking (1999: 77–80) distinguish between agro-biodiversity
and agrodiversity. The former applies to biodiversity on lands also used for
agriculture. Agrodiversity applies to the many ways in which farmers use the
natural diversity of their environment for production, for the use of water and
biota, and for marketing in order to design for the unexpected and ensure
some food production even in climatically hazardous conditions. The upshot
of this approach is the mutual reinforcement of biodiversity in agriculture, so
that the one maintains the other. The fundamentals of agrodiversity can be
summarised:

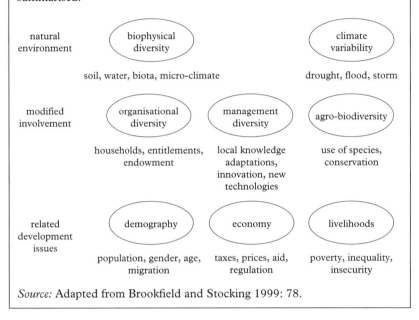

Source: Adapted from Brookfield and Stocking 1999: 78.

biofuels, widening the basis of wild crop genetic resources, more integrated use of chemicals, and the scope for urban agricultural communities are all evolving in ways that genuinely can link biodiversity to human
well-being.

Box 13.3 outlines the scope for integrating various 'scales' of biodiversity into an evolving agrodiversity. Of interest here is the unresolved debate over the increasing dependency on pesticides and fertilisers,
the possible widespread use of genetically modified plants and animals
in the developing world, and the difficult relationships between established agricultural practices and imported technologies and management
approaches.

The diagram suggests that agriculture can sustain biodiversity, and in turn be improved by biodiversity. Insects are both pests and sources of food: crop genes permit adaptation to climate change or natural hazard. Non-food use of biodiversity improves health and offers markets. Tourism and agrodiversity can and do mix to enable cultures to share experiences and understanding. The cultural landscape thus induces the ecological conditions for ecosystem resilience. In so doing, food can be produced so that it is more widely available, more nutritious and more wealth creating. People are empowered and encouraged to innovate and adapt. Much of the extension to global biodiversity will come through creative and inclusive agrodiversity.

Public–private partnerships in biodiversity and the ecosystem approach

The timeliness of the entry of the private sector into biodiversity management, as introduced in Brazil, Costa Rica and South Africa, suggests that it is possible to foresee a world that is sustaining its ecosystems yet creating and sharing wealth.

The privately managed reserve has plenty of incentive to market biodiversity for fee-paying customers. Game trophies, rich assemblages of plants and birds, emblematic species to photograph or to marvel at, and the care of paying clients through friendly and welcoming service can combine to manage habitats and protect species in perpetuity. Private reserves have to follow basic principles of strategic planning and budget management. Fees can go to wardening, scientific appraisals, liaison with all manner of local and national organisations. Private reserves have a vested interest in making peace with local societies and economies. This is beginning to be the case in Namibia, and to some extent in Costa Rica. In the US, however, private landownership rights do not always fit well with conservation objectives, which often are seen as governmental meddling. But even in the US, as noted by Toddi Steelman in chapter 7, efforts to include economic and social interests in private–public partnerships are beginning to bear fruit.

Yet public–private partnerships are beneficial where there is insufficient state capital, or management capacity, as in South Africa or Costa Rica. Such partnerships often enable long-term supportive investment that would otherwise be missing. Private reserves can be very helpful in conserving genes or managing for particularly endangered species. The role of the Clean Development Mechanism under the Kyoto Protocol on climate change, and carbon trading generally, also offers scope for profitable investments in biodiversity (Beltran and Essler 1999).

For private reserves to become more effective in future biodiversity management, more work needs to be focused on their legal status, their scope for public partnerships, how profits can be used, and how sustainability science can be promoted.

But we should also beware. The experience of Costa Rica and Brazil is not encouraging when global pharmaceutical corporations become involved. Rarely are the property rights in local knowledge fully and faithfully compensated. In South Africa, a deal between the National Botanical Institute and a US company over the medicinal properties of fynbos genes appears massively to favour the wealthy corporation and provide too little income for local economies and societies. Such arrangements require particularly careful scrutiny.

Controversy surrounds the role of the NBI in signing an arrangement for the transfer of the property rights of fynbos genetic material to an Australian company called Ball Horticultural Company (Glazewski 2001). The original agreement was signed on 4 October 1999. Under the Convention on Biological Diversity, bioprospecting should safeguard the fair and equitable benefits between the reporting country and the importing organisation. In this case, the US has not ratified the Convention and Ball is a private corporation. This means that the 1999 Agreement was not strictly legal, and required political approval. For a variety of reasons, NBI did not specifically obtain approval from the South African Minister of Environment and Tourism. Following revelations in the *Cape Times*, the NBI agreed to investigate the matter through a taskforce headed by Jan Glazewski, a lawyer for the University of Cape Town.

The central argument of the Glazewski inquiry was that the 1999 Agreement did not take into account the non-monetary benefits of bioprospecting as required by Article 1 of the Convention. The 1999 Agreement provided for an initial fee from Ball of $125,000 to NBI, plus an annual research service fee of $50,000, together with royalties of differing percentages (10 per cent, 4 per cent, 2 per cent) depending on whether the marketable product is NBI material or NBI–Ball material. The nature of the arrangement was that Ball had effective access 'to all South African species as well as the knowledge built up by NBI and SA botanists over centuries' (Glazewski 2001: 5). Moreover, the down payments were tied to the costs to NBI in servicing the arrangement; they could not be used for improving scientific knowledge.

On the non-monetary aspects, Ball were not committed to any particular investment to improve the transfer of resources or technology to assist South African economies, or social or environmental well-being. Henne and Fakir (1999: 21) conclude: 'perhaps one of the weakest aspects of the contract is that the agreement does not strongly commit Ball to invest directly in technology transfer and product development within South Africa'. In essence, this agreement was signed without the NBI staff being freely consulted, with no ministerial endorsement, with vague and non-binding wording, and with open-ended scope for Ball to profit from any material advantages with little cost or commitment to non-monetary transfer of resources, skills or scientific expertise. Indeed, South Africa may have been impoverished by the arrangement, the Ball money essentially being diverted specifically to finance the bioprospecting. Any royalty fees would have arrived far into the future.

The NBI–Ball Agreement is currently being renegotiated. It will seek to meet the provisions of the Convention, and biodiversity for sustainability. What will emerge from the discussions will be a fascinating test case. This story suggests that governmental agencies cannot always be guaranteed to protect beyond the protected. There has to be constant vigilance, fresh legal safeguards, a courageous press, and a broadly based civic constituency of watchfulness and support.

There is still much to be done. The science of ecosystem functioning requires continual investment in national research centres and local monitoring effort. Surprisingly small amounts of money, given the huge planetary gains involved, could ensure this effort, and it must be the first priority. Local knowledge, combined with fresh ways of learning and communicating, could do wonders to improve our knowledge of the role and social values of ecosystem services. As these life sustaining activities become better understood, no more to incorporate them into wealth production will be rewarded and transferred as a new form of folk knowledge. Nurturing these innovations in management will require careful redesign of property rights, incentives and audits. All these are possible with local mobilisation and global support.

The learning of such innovation means people involvement and empowerment, listening, learning, sharing and creating. With the internet, with local outreach, and with many successful pilot schemes that are locally transferable, so much can be achieved. Here is where incentives through public–private partnerships can prove so catalytic. The overriding message of this book is that many interpretations of biodiversity, inclusion, sustainability and resilience can be channelled into fresh partnerships for reliable and enduring mosaics of management opportunities, linking local action to global survival. This approach is beginning to be endorsed by WWF (Maginnis *et al.* 2001) in their guidance on landscape appraisal. What is missing is a collective sense of the urgency to change the present course, to be honest in response to the signals from the ground, and progressively to shift a culture of complacency and denial into one of engagement and belief.

What is also certain is that changes in biological diversity will inevitably increase, irrespective of how we manage for biodiversity. Climate change, pathogens, alien invasions and all manner of landuse disruption will see to that. So the more we do to conserve both ecological and social resilience now, the better the planet will be equipped for the convulsions to come. Species may prove more resilient. Habitats may prove more adaptable. Science and monitoring may enable new biodiversity assemblages to be created. And the best current practices of people and ecological care may be copied. Our best legacy is to enable the world to be better prepared, and better adapted for circumstances that lie beyond imagination, so that biodiversity and humanity can co-exist in peace and prosperity.

Frankly, the omens are not good. Despite the many hopeful sustainable experiences and experiments, the patterns of non-sustainable economics, and politics, and the displacement of vulnerable and impoverished peoples combine to diminish and destabilise biodiversity. Only a fundamental culture change in the hearts and minds of people throughout the globe will alter this. Resilience of ecosystems and societies is a vital objective. Yet we are far from understanding just how that coupled resilience can be attained and ensured. This is why we do need ecological advocacy, participatory democracy, economic valuation of ecosystem processes as part of the currency of sustainable development, and a business–government recognition that this unique genetic heritage is a true guide for our sense of humanity. Biodiversity has to be placed at the centre of all of our lives, lived through and respected, altered and enhanced. We may dispute just what mix of species and habitats this totality of 'biodiversity' will become. Some will be historic and some futuristic. Placing biodiversity in our centre of knowing and acting is what counts. For the evolving consequence will surely enhance biodiversity and humanity for generations to come.

REFERENCES

Battenbury, S. and Forsyth, T. 1999. Fighting back: human adaptations to marginal environments. *Environment* 47: 6–11, 25–30.
Bazzaz, F. *et al.* 1998. Ecological science and humsan predicament. *Science* 282: 879.
Beltran, J. and Essler, T. 1999. *Analysis of the Contribution of the Non-politic Sector to In-site Nature Conservation in Costa Rica, Honduras and Nicaragua.* Cambridge and Eschborn: World Conservation Monitoring Centre and GTZ.
Berkes, F. and Folke, C. (eds.) 1998. *Linking Social and Ecological Systems: Management Practices and Social Mechanisms for Building Resilience.* Cambridge: Cambridge University Press.

Brookfield, H. and Stocking, M. 1999. Agrodiversity: definition; description and design. *Global Environment Change* 9(2): 79–80.

Carney, D. (ed.) 1998. *Sustainable Rural Livelihoods: What Contribution Can We Make?* London: DfID.

Department for International Development. 2000. *Biodiversity and Development.* London: DfID.

Gaston, K.J. 1996. *Rarity.* London: Chapman and Hall.

Glazewski, J. 2001. *The NBI/Ball Agreement: A Critical Assessment.* Cape Town: Department of Law, University of Cape Town.

Henne, G. and Fakir, S. 1999. NBI–Ball Agreement: a new phase in bioprospecting? *Biotechnology and Development Monitor* 39: 18–21.

Hewitt, K. 1997. *Regions at Risk: A Geographical Introduction to Disasters.* Harlow: Longman.

Kaiser, J. 2000. Ecologists on a mission to save the world. *Science* 287: 1,118.

Kates, R.W. *et al.* 2001. Sustainability science. *Science* 292: 641–2.

Locke, C., Adger, N. and Kelly, M. 2000. Changing places: migrations and their social and environmental consequences. *Environment* 42: 24–35.

Lubchenko, J. *et al.* 1991. The sustainable biosphere initiative: an ecological research agenda. *Ecology* 72: 371–412.

McNeeley, J.A. 1995. *Expanding Partnerships in Conservation.* Washington, DC: Island Press.

Maginnis, S., Jackson, W. and Dudley, N. 2001. *Guidelines to Landscape Appraisal for Forest Conservation.* Geneva: WWF/IUCN.

O'Riordan, T. 2000. Environmental science on the move. In T. O'Riordan (ed.), *Environmental Science for Environmental Management*, 2nd edition, pp. 1–28. Harlow: Prentice Hall.

O'Riordan, T. and Church, C. 2001. Synthesis and context. In T. O'Riordan (ed.), *Globalism, Localism and Identity: Fresh Perspective on the Transition to Sustainability*, pp. 3–24. London: Earthscan.

Pimm, S.C. *et al.* 2001. Can we defy nature's end? *Science* 293: 2,207–10.

Sala, O. *et al.* 2000. Global biodiversity scenarios for the year 2100. *Science* 287: 1,770–4.

Scoones, I. 1998. *Sustainable Rural Livelihoods: A Framework for Analysis.* IDS Working Paper 72. Brighton: University of Sussex.

Stoll-Kleemann, S. 2001. Reconciling opposition to protected area management in Europe: the German experience. *Environment* 43(5): 32–44.

Takacs, D. 1996. *The Idea of Biodiversity: Philosophies of Paradise.* Baltimore: Johns Hopkins University Press.

Tarnas, R. 1993. *The Passion of the Western Mind.* London: Pimlico Press.

White House Interagency Ecosystem Management Task Force 1995. *The Ecosystem Approach: Healthy Ecosystems and Sustainable Economics.* Washington, DC: The White House.

World Resources Institute 2000. *People and Ecosystems: The Fraying Web of Life.* Washington, DC: World Resources Institute.

Epilogue

Walter V. Reid

Maintaining the planet's biodiversity is an important societal goal. Meeting the needs and aspirations of a growing world population is also an important societal goal. If the steps needed to achieve these goals always coincided, and if society's goals dictated public and private actions, then there would be little need for this book. But neither of these conditions holds true. Development needs are often best met through actions that simplify biodiversity – agriculture being a case in point. And all too often societal goals are undermined by actions taken by the wealthy or powerful within government or the private sector to accrue more wealth or power.

As a result, we have less biodiversity today than we did in 1900 and we will have far less biodiversity in 2100 than we do today. Is this a catastrophe? From a utilitarian standpoint, probably not. The extinction of most species over the coming decades will have few practical consequences for human livelihoods. This is not to say that extinctions do not sometimes have serious ramifications. Chapter 1 shows that the ecosystem values of biodiversity can be considerable and could have major effects on future economies if lost to future generations. In general, the economic and social impacts of the hundreds of species that have gone extinct over the past century or thousands facing extinction today are still on the small side. From an ethical and cultural standpoint, on the other hand, it is a tragic loss, as Norman Myers points out in chapter 3. The diversity of life is part of humanity just as humanity is part of that diversity. Future generations will lead spiritually diminished lives because of what is being lost today.

In the face of accelerating biodiversity loss, a battle to safeguard the remaining diversity has been underway for decades. The first phase of this battle involved efforts to 'protect' biodiversity from people through the widespread establishment of protected areas. The second phase, represented by some of the case studies in this book, involved a tactical shift whereby the same goal of protection was pursued but now at a larger scale (both within and surrounding protected areas) through efforts to create conservation incentives for the communities involved.

311

The chapters in this book paint a revealing picture of the challenges that these efforts face as they seek to slow the loss of biodiversity. But the outlines of a new phase of this battle for biodiversity conservation can also be seen in the picture that emerges. Rather than adopting yet another tactical approach to achieve the goal of 'stopping the loss of biodiversity' it is apparent that we have been pursuing the wrong goal. A lesson from this book is that a more appropriate goal should be to reintegrate humanity and biodiversity. Should that goal be achieved we will retain far more biodiversity for future generations while also doing far more to meet human needs.

If we persist with the narrow goal of halting the loss of biodiversity, then the outlook is bleak. If instead we seek to maintain a biologically diverse world supporting human cultural, environmental, and livelihood security, then this book provides considerable grounds for hope. Make no mistake. It is inconceivable, with humans occupying as much space and using or co-opting as much of the world's water and nutrients as we do, that the world can avoid a significant continuing loss of biodiversity. But more diversity will remain if we pursue strategies that link biodiversity with human cultural, ethical and utilitarian needs.

The grounds for hope can be seen at the micro-scale, where for example community-based fisheries management efforts may result in the protection of spawning areas in order to increase fish harvests, as well as at the macro-scale. Human demands for ecosystem 'goods and services' such as food, fuel and clean water are growing, just as the supply of these services is being diminished. More effective management of ecosystems and changes to ecosystems could significantly aid human well-being in the coming decades. This can be done both directly through the supply of goods and services, and indirectly, through increased resilience of communities in the face of environmental, social, and economic perturbations. At the same time, more effective management of these systems will almost certainly aid biodiversity conservation. It is clear that we have not fully accounted for the trade-offs inherent in such activities as the spread of intensive agriculture, destruction of coastal habitats or the modification of rivers. As we begin to look in a more integrated way at the goods and services ecosystems provide, more and more opportunities emerge to meet human needs through actions that will lessen pressure on biodiversity. For example, one of the most cost-effective means of ensuring supplies of fresh water for consumption or power production or minimising the risk of flooding is to maintain the structural land cover in the watershed. An effective way of increasing the cost effectiveness of agriculture, restoring downstream fisheries, and restoring freshwater biodiversity is to increase the efficiency of fertiliser applications. Rural communities often increase their resilience to both environmental and economic shocks by planting a mixture of high-yielding varieties and drought resistant local cultivars rather than discarding the traditional varieties.

It is not surprising that attempts to pursue these synergies between biodiversity, ecosystem management, and human well-being are fraught with difficulty. At both the local scale and the global scale, these strategies are inherently multisectoral, multistakeholder, and multidisciplinary. And they are being pursued in a world with highly sectoral institutions, inequitable distribution of wealth, little experience with participatory processes, and little reward for multidisciplinary research. But these strategies do often succeed and the lessons from success and failure are guiding new initiatives today.

In 2100, will people be living in a biodiverse world or peering through fences at the last remaining parks and zoos? A future with biodiversity integrated with human society is achievable. But this will not be without major progress on challenging issues. First, more effective mechanisms are needed to bring science to bear on decision makers' needs. This is not to say that better science necessarily leads to better decisions, but decisions made in the absence of the best information are unlikely to be sound. At all scales, from global to local, both ecological and economic information concerning the consequences of ecosystem change for human well-being need to reach decision-makers in a form they can use and through a process that has sufficient credibility that they will use it. That information also needs to reach the public so that they can hold decision makers accountable for their actions. As a corollary, more effective mechanisms are needed to bridge the epistemological gulf between traditional knowledge and formal 'science'. Nowhere are the contributions – and shortcomings – of each way of knowing the world more apparent than in considering the role of biodiversity in human cultural, economic and social systems. At the global level, the Intergovernmental Panel on Climate Change provides a useful model for linking science with policy that is now being emulated for issues related to ecosystems and biodiversity. But most decisions concerning biodiversity are taken at the national or sub-national level and far more needs to be done to strengthen the voice of policy-relevant science in most countries. This is touched upon in chapter 13, around the theme of 'sustainability science'.

Second, more effective mechanisms for governance and stakeholder participation in resource management decisions are needed. Most challenging is the question of how best to reflect the interests of stakeholders at all scales – ranging from the individual in the local community deciding whether to convert a forest to a cash crop, to people living far away who create the market for that crop or who are concerned about the loss of biodiversity. Clearly, national governments at best can represent only national interests and do not speak on behalf of a particular community or on behalf of the good of the world's people. Increasingly, new institutional and governance arrangements are being developed that seek to give voice to the interests of the 'local' and the 'global' and that seek to involve all stakeholders from civil society, private sector and government. This perspective is introduced in chapter 5. This book documents the significant challenges confronting new participatory mechanisms. But the alternative to new governance arrangements and more effective stakeholder participation in decision making has clearly failed and the task now is to build and strengthen new institutions that enable effective participation.

Third, despite the seemingly overwhelming challenge, there are many 'low-hanging fruit' that should not be ignored. For example, in many cases ecosystems are being converted even when the long-term economic benefits of conservation outweigh the benefits of conversion, because short-term economic benefits can be captured by a small number of people. These cases need to be identified and groups working for the protection of these ecosystems empowered. Low-hanging fruit also exist in the form of perverse policies that harm both development and biodiversity, such as subsidies for agriculture and fertilizers. And perhaps the most highly leveraged investment in biodiversity continues to be protected areas themselves. Certain regions harbour so much threatened biodiversity that could be protected at relatively little cost that it would be foolish not to invest in their conservation. A goal of integrating people and biodiversity does not mean that protected areas should be abandoned anymore than a goal of an educated society should mean that schools should be abandoned – each is an instrumental tool needed to achieve the goal.

It will take more than redoubled efforts to protect biodiversity if humans are to continue to live in a biodiverse world. As *Protecting Beyond the Protected* demonstrates, it will require that our goal is changed from 'protecting nature from people' to 're-integrating humanity and biodiversity'. If we fail to achieve this integration, then the amount of biodiversity remaining and the quality of human life will both be diminished. Whether it is through new watershed protection efforts, community-based conservation projects, *in situ* conservation of crop landraces, efforts to manage the 'matrix' of lands between protected areas to support biodiversity, or efforts to promote the 'gardenification' of nature, we can see today a vast array of efforts to re-establish the links between humanity and biodiversity. If these efforts succeed, protecting beyond the protected should come to be seen as 'living with and because of biodiversity'.

Index